LANDING A FEDERAL LEGAL JOB

Finding Success in the U.S. Government Job Market

Richard L. Hermann

AMERICAN BAR ASSOCIATION
Defending Liberty
Pursuing Justice

Cover design by Andrew O. Alcala

The materials contained in this book represent the opinions and views of the authors and/or the editors, and should not be construed to be the views or opinions of the law firms or companies with whom such persons are in partnership with, associated with, or employed by, nor of the American Bar Association unless adopted pursuant to the bylaws of the Association.

Nothing contained in this book is to be considered as the rendering of legal advice, either generally or in connection with any specific issue or case. Readers are responsible for obtaining advice from their own lawyers or other professionals. This book and any forms and agreements in this book are intended for educational and informational purposes only.

Printed in the United States of America

15 14 13 12   5 4 3 2

Library of Congress Cataloging-in-Publication Data
Includes index.
ISBN: 978-1-61632-835-1
Landing a federal legal job / by Richard L. Hermann.
    p. cm.
    1. Government attorneys—United States. 2. United States—Officials and employees—Selection and appointment. 3. Law—Vocational guidance—United States. I. Title.

KF299.G6H473 2011
340.023'73—dc22   2011000115

Discounts are available for books ordered in bulk. Special consideration is given to state bars, CLE programs, and other bar-related organizations.

Inquire at Book Publishing, ABA Publishing, American Bar Association, 321 N. Clark Street, Chicago, Illinois 60654-7598.

www.ShopABA.org

Also by the Author

Managing Your Legal Career: Best Practices for Creating the Career You Want

The Lawyer's Guide to Job Security

The Lawyer's Guide to Finding Success in Any Job Market

JD Preferred! 600+ Things You Can Do with a Law Degree (Other Than Practice Law)

The ALJ Handbook: An Insider's Guide to Becoming a Federal Administrative Law Judge

Dedication

To Ken Bossong, my great friend and sounding board for much of what appears in this book, and a dedicated public servant who embodies what successful government law practice infused with a high standard of ethics should be all about.

Contents

Part VIII
Where to Work

Acknowledgments

Anne Marie Canali Hermann is always there for me. Her creative and editorial contributions to my books allow me to write quickly and make mistakes because I know that she is going to save me from embarrassing myself.

Erin Nevius, my editor at ABA Publishing, is always encouraging, positive, efficient, enthusiastic, and coherent. Her sharp editing eye contributes mightily to making my books readable, and her "hyperbole-alert" keeps me from going off the reservation.

Introduction

This book is designed to strip away the mysteries surrounding the federal legal establishment—what it consists of, where it does its work, how it recruits and hires attorneys, how to get hired, what to watch out for, what the future holds, and where the best opportunities reside. Upon finishing *Landing a Federal Legal Job*, it is my hope that you will have a solid understanding of the U.S. government's legal employment opportunities and hiring processes, and that what looks at first glance to be a confounding rat's maze will become clarified for you, enough so that you can make an intelligent decision about whether you want to work for the largest legal system in the world. The other primary objective of this book is to give you a decided edge over your competitors in pursuing a U.S. government attorney or law-related position.

It is not my intention to act as a promoter of government legal employment. Rather, in the course of explaining what the federal legal system is all about, I aim to bring to light both its attractive features and its warts, both of which are abundant.

I have spent a large portion of my career studying the federal legal system and its countless nuances, and performing the detective work necessary to find answers and solutions to the often daunting and perplexing adventures of applying for and securing a federal legal job and crafting a rewarding and satisfying federal legal career.

This book is my attempt to share the results of my studies and experiences—as well as those of my legal career counseling clients —with you, as well as the solutions that I devised to help them obtain a federal legal job. To do this most effectively and efficiently, I have divided the book into eight parts:

- **Part One: Federal Legal Demographics** examines the size of the federal attorney population, the number of attorney and law-related jobs, who makes up the U.S. government attorney workforce (its diversity), and how this compares to the civilian workforce.
- **Part Two: The Pros and Cons of a Federal Legal Career** is an in-depth look at the pluses and minuses associated

with working for the federal government and provides you with the opportunity to balance the good against the bad of federal employment, as well as suggestions on mitigating the downsides.

- **Part Three: Where the Federal Lawyers Are** reviews the geographic scope of the federal legal establishment, the federal legal structure, and the many practice areas and law-related arenas in which federal attorneys do their work.
- **Part Four: How the U.S. Government Hires Lawyers** explores the federal legal hiring process in general (as well as specifically for mainstream attorney positions, law-related positions, top-level and lower-level political appointments, and special hiring programs) and discusses some of the ways in which candidates can gain a competitive edge.
- **Part Five: Frequently Asked Questions about Landing a Federal Legal Job** poses the most common questions that outside candidates have about federal employment and provides the answers.
- **Part Six: Getting Hired** describes the strategies and techniques that differentiate successful candidates for federal legal jobs from the competition.
- **Part Seven: Long-Term Trends** predicts the factors that are likely to impact federal legal jobs and careers in the first part of the twenty-first century.
- **Part Eight: Where to Work** offers the author's assessments of the best and most interesting functional areas where attorneys work, law-related positions, and federal legal offices.
- **Appendices** include the following:
  - *Appendix A,* "U.S. Government Job Listings," directs you to more than 20 websites that provide the best information about current federal job opportunities.
  - *Appendix B,* "U.S. Government Information Resources," contains 30 resources where you can go for both general and specific government information useful for a federal job campaign.

- *Appendix C,* "Useful Networking Organizations for Federal Legal and Law-Related Jobs," lists almost 60 organizations that are relevant to federal job campaigns from the standpoint of providing you with knowledge, inside information, and potential contacts.
- *Appendix D*, "Credential Enhancers for Federal Legal and Law-Related Jobs," is a selected list of 77 certificate and related educational programs in 26 subject-matters areas that can bolster your law degree and arm you with added credentials suitable for a federal job campaign.
- *Appendix E,* "An Application Ordeal," presents a verbatim federal law-related job vacancy announcement that is representative of some of the more exasperating aspects of federal job-hunting.
- *Appendix F,* "Presidential Memorandum on Improving the Federal Recruitment and Hiring Process, May 11, 2010," is included because it may have a significant, positive impact on the federal legal and law-related hiring processes.

Glossary

Before diving into the substance of this book, some consideration of government terminology is in order. When I first arrived in Washington to work at the Pentagon, I was overwhelmed by the massive number of acronyms that seemed to pepper every sentence. It was like learning a new language.

I do not want to overwhelm you with the almost infinite array of government terms, abbreviations, and acronyms in use today. That might make you believe you have picked up a nineteenth-century Russian novel laden with patronymics and would be a major deterrent to continuing on in this book. Rather, I am providing a rather streamlined glossary of terms that should give you a leg up with respect to both understanding this book and applying for—and hitting the ground running in—your first U.S. government job.

Agency. The literal definition is one of the 150-plus federal organizations in the executive branch that is not a cabinet department. I use the term generically in this book to encompass any federal organization, including cabinet departments and legislative and judicial branch agencies.

Career Appointment. A permanent appointment to a U.S. government competitive service position. With respect to attorneys, career appointments apply only to those serving in law-related positions (see below).

Career-Conditional Appointment. A probationary appointment to a U.S. government Competitive Service position. Career-conditional appointments may automatically convert to career appointments after a certain amount of time has passed, provided that the employee has performed adequately. This status, too, is applicable only to attorneys serving in law-related positions.

Competitive Service. The federal civil service component in which virtually all law-related positions are located, and to which the full array of civil service hiring, promotion, and firing rules applies.

Czar. A presidential advisor on a specific issue or governmental function whose appointment is not required to be approved by the U.S. Senate. The federal government now sports more czars than the Romanov Dynasty did in its 300-year history.

Department. One of the 15 cabinet departments.

Excepted Service. The federal civil service component in which attorneys are located, and with respect to which federal offices have almost 100 percent plenary authority with respect to hiring, promotion, and firing.

General Schedule. The federal pay system under which the large majority of attorneys (my estimate is approximately 80 percent) are compensated. Attorney grade levels range from General Schedule (GS-9) to GS-15. Each pay grade consists of 10 steps, each step equating to a dollar amount. For example, in 2010, a GS-9, Step 1 employee earned $41,563 in annual base pay while a GS-9, Step 10 worker earned $54,028. The highest-paid GS employees, at GS-15, Step 10, earned $129,517. In addition, federal employees can earn more depending on where in the country they work (locality pay).

GS-905. The government job classification series for attorneys. This designation accompanies all "mainstream" attorney federal job vacancy announcements and customarily appears immediately after the job title.

Honors Program. A recruitment program through which a federal agency hires entry-level attorneys. There are currently 19 such agency programs.

KSAs. KSA is shorthand for "Knowledges, Skills and Abilities." Federal job vacancy announcements frequently ask candidates to respond with essays to KSA questions. As of November 1, 2010, vacancy announcements were no longer supposed to require KSAs.

Law-Related Job. A position where a J.D. degree is preferred but not necessarily required, and where legal education or a legal background is an advantage in hiring and in performing the job.

Mainstream Attorney Job. An attorney position in either the chief legal office of an agency, another agency law office, or a non-law office (i.e., a program, operational, or administrative office) where the attorney is actually practicing law.

Merit Promotion. This concept applies to competitive service employees who may be considered for promotional opportunities through merit competition.

Office of Personnel Management (OPM). The OPM is the federal government's personnel office, responsible government-wide for establishing and administering certain hiring rules as well as regulations governing promotions, background investigations prefatory to employment, employee discipline, pay and benefits, terminations, retirement systems, and other personnel matters. Agencies sometimes ignore OPM pronouncements and go their own ways with respect to certain employment and personnel matters.

Reduction-in-Force (RIF). Downsizing of a department or agency. Such personnel actions are governed by an extensive set of regulations that may or may not apply to attorneys in the excepted service. RIFs may also be governed by the provisions of a collective bargaining agreement between an agency and a federal employee union. Many federal attorneys are union members.

Senior Executive Service (SES). The top-level management positions in the U.S. government attainable by career federal employees. The original theory was that the SES would be a trained managerial corps able to move seamlessly around the government in any management role. It did not turn out that way. Instead, SES employees almost always are promoted from within the ranks of their own agency and stay there.

Part I

Federal Legal Demographics

The U.S. government is by far the largest employer of attorneys in the entire world. The attorneys work in more than 3,000 federal law offices, in every state and in many foreign countries. They range in age from recent law graduates to seasoned veterans and are a very diverse group, generally much more so than is found in most areas of the private sector. They also tend to stay on the job longer than most of their private-sector counterparts. Part I looks at the federal legal workforce from a demographic perspective.

Chapter 1

The Numbers

In 2009, U.S. government employment grew by more than 82,000 employees, a huge increase. That growth trend appears to be continuing in 2010.

No organization can provide a precise number for the attorney population of the U.S. government—neither the U.S. Office of Personnel Management (OPM) nor the Bureau of Labor Statistics have an exact figure. This information gap is largely due to the fact that attorneys occupy numerous federal law-related positions that do not carry the title "attorney." The best estimate is that there are more than 40,000 attorneys currently working for the federal establishment in "mainstream" legal positions with the job title "attorney." They work primarily in offices of general counsel, offices of chief counsel, other predominantly legal offices, and in operational, program, and administrative support offices.

Approximately 11,000—or just over 25 percent—of the federal attorney workforce is in the Department of Justice. The Justice Department is far and away the largest legal employer in the U.S. government. Other federal organizations with a high concentration of attorneys include the following:

Agency	Approximate # Attorneys
Department of Treasury	2,000+
Securities and Exchange Commission	1,000+
Department of Commerce	690
Federal Communications Commission	400+
Department of Labor	380
Environmental Protection Agency	350
Department of State	325
Department of Transportation	325
Federal Trade Commission	315
Department of Veterans Affairs	290
Department of Defense	280*

*These are civilian positions. The number does not include 6,000-plus military lawyers who work in the Judge Advocate Generals' Corps of the Armed Services.

In addition to the 40,000-plus mainstream government lawyers, there are a very large number of attorneys who work in one of the more than 150 law-related jobs in the government. Again, no one has undertaken a census of law-related government professionals. The following are some educated guesses as to the federal law-related job titles that employ the largest number of attorneys.

Job Title(s)	# Employees	Estimated # Attorneys
Contract administrator	37,000	7,500
Compliance specialist	14,500	4,500
Employee/labor relations specialist	4,000	800
Claims administrator	4,000	400
Environmental protection specialist	3,715	550
Hearings/appeals officer	2,200	2,000
Patent examiner	2,000	1,300
Administrative law judge	1,500	1,500
Regulatory analyst	1,500	750
Legal researcher	1,500	1,450
Legislative affairs specialist/analyst	1,000	600

The number of federal law-related jobs is growing steadily and attorneys are increasingly sought after by federal employers for a number of different positions. The reasons for this are the utility of legal training and legal analysis for these positions, which give lawyers a huge advantage over non-lawyers. Moreover, the track record of attorneys holding such positions is very impressive. Federal employers know that they will be getting hard workers who can move up the learning curve very quickly and are both alert and analytical, with strong organizational skills and good judgment.

In addition to the law-related job titles listed above, some of the other more interesting law-related positions include:

- analyst in social legislation
- asylum officer
- bankruptcy analyst
- civil rights investigator
- competition advocate
- ethics program specialist
- export control specialist
- FBI special agent
- foreign commercial service officer
- foreign law specialist
- foreign service officer
- futures trading investigator
- GAO evaluator (tax)
- intelligence research specialist
- land law examiner
- licensing specialist
- mediator
- pension law specialist
- privacy officer
- realty specialist
- scientific attorney investigator
- securities transaction analyst
- tax law specialist
- technical publications writer/editor (legal)
- technology transfer officer

Many of these positions are discussed in Part VIII.

Chapter 2

Diversity

Workforce diversity has increased in importance on many levels. Most telling for the legal community, perhaps, is the emphasis corporate clients have placed on diversity when deciding among competing outside law firms. That development probably has done more for diversity in the legal marketplace than anything else, but still, while the private sector has been rather slow on the diversity uptake, the U.S. government has, for years, been in the forefront. Whether the target group is women, minorities, individuals with disabilities, veterans, Native Americans, or lesbian, gay, bisexual, and transgender people (LGBTs), the U.S. government has been something of a pioneer in recruiting and hiring a diverse workforce.

Yet government employers still have a long way to go in terms of diversity. All agencies are required by law to develop outreach programs to identify qualified candidates to meet agency workforce diversity goals. However, over the years there has been little follow-up with respect to these programs and even less enforcement. This is typical of personnel-related decrees from presidents and agency heads—a lot of fine words ". . . full of sound and fury, signifying nothing," to borrow from *Macbeth*. Good intentions need to be followed by execution, but, often, they are not.

One way that this lack of follow-up manifests itself is the sporadic and uneven nature of the government's own workplace diversity data. In fact, the Bush administration directed federal agencies *not* to collect demographic data from applicants for federal employment, a policy that was subsequently reversed by the Obama administration. Diversity numbers are almost totally absent with respect to attorneys.

Here is what we can glean from the figures the government does collect:

- The U.S. government workforce is 66.5 percent Caucasian.
- The proportion of minorities in the total federal workforce rose to 33.5 in fiscal year (FY) 2009. Minority employment rolls increased by more than 30,000 in FY 2009. Comparable civilian minority employment statistics reveal that 29.4 percent of the civilian workforce is made up of minorities.
- African-Americans constituted 17.8 percent of the federal workforce in FY 2009.
- Asian/Pacific Islanders constituted 5.5 percent of FY 2009 government employment, while Native American employment was at 1.8 percent.
- Women represent approximately the same percentage of the federal workforce (44.2 percent) as they do of the civilian workforce (45.9 percent). Certain groups of women in government—African-American, Asian/Pacific Islander, and Native American—exceeded their representation in the civilian labor force in 2009.
- Hispanic employment statistics are not collected government-wide, but rather selectively. The *Ninth Annual Report to the President on Hispanic Employment in the Federal Government* (2010) reveals that, despite a trend of increasing Hispanic representation in the government, Hispanics remain underrepresented compared to the civilian workforce. Hispanics represent 8 percent of the federal workforce compared to 13.2 percent of the civilian labor force.

The large agencies that hire the most Hispanic employees are the Department of Homeland Security, the Equal Employment Opportunity Commission, the Social Security Administration, the Department of Justice, and the Department of Treasury. The large agencies with the lowest percentage of Hispanic employees are the Department of Health and Human Services, the Department of Commerce, and the Department of Education, the Office of Personnel Management, and the State Department. Government data on Hispanic attorney hiring shows a modest increase in FY 2009, when 2.9 percent of the 2,165 attorneys hired by the largest agencies for mainstream legal positions were Hispanics.

As of this writing, the U.S. Office of Personnel Management (OPM) is leading an interagency task force on diversity that will develop recommendations for improving the government's Hispanic hiring efforts.

• Some progress has also been made with respect to the representation of women and minorities at higher level government positions. The number of women in grades GS-13 through GS-15 was 125,208 in 2009 (30.4 percent of higher-level employees), compared to 121,124 in 2008.

  The representation of minorities at the same grade levels rose to 86,119 in 2009, from 82,511 in 2008 (4.4 percent increase). Minorities now constitute 7.2 percent of higher-level employees.

• Representation of women and minorities in professional and administrative positions has also increased. Employment of minorities in these positions rose by 25,297 to 332,934 in 2009, from 307,637 in 2008. The number of women represented in professional and administrative positions increased by 32,321 to 505,111 in 2009, from 472,790 in 2008. The number of minorities and women in clerical jobs is steadily declining.

The Obama administration has created three new offices within the OPM that are focused on increasing government diversity: the Office of Diversity and Inclusion, the Senior Executive Service Office, and the Student Programs Office. These offices are principally advocacy offices designed to encourage government agencies to achieve greater diversity. They do not have a direct role in the application and recruitment process. For information on how to apply for federal jobs, see Parts IV and VI.

Chapter 3

Ageism

The term "ageism" is usually used to describe age discrimination. While the federal government is (1) marked by an older workforce than the private sector and (2) is prohibited by a variety of laws, regulations, and executive orders from discriminating in employment on the basis of age, that does not mean that ageism has been completely expunged from government. If you walk through the halls of certain agencies—the Department of Justice, the Federal Trade Commission, and the Securities and Exchange Commission, for example—you will encounter what may strike you as a very young workforce. I think that is no accident.

I single out these three agencies only as examples of a certain amount of tacit age discrimination in federal employment. Moreover, because government is not a monolith, and it is unfair to generalize (even about any of the multiple law and other offices in any one agency where attorneys work), it cannot be said that it is uniform agency policy to tilt toward youth. Much depends upon the inclinations of the office chief of the moment and his or her deputies.

My point is that, shocking as it may seem, age discrimination in employment does occur in the U.S. government, albeit subtly in most instances. Extensive empirical experience indicates that it occurs much less frequently in the federal government than anywhere else, and, in an imperfect world, "seasoned" attorneys have a better shot at securing U.S. government positions than they do in the private sector.

There are even places in the U.S. government where seasoning has some value over youth. The average age of the almost 1,600-strong federal administrative law judge (ALJ) corps is indicative. Even after officials were privately urged to hire with a view to making the corps "younger," the average age of more than 100 new ALJs appointed in 2007 after a 10-year hiring pause (during which the corps' average age obviously increased) was 56.7!

One final point about ageism in government. Federal hiring officials have almost unfettered leeway when it comes to hiring attorneys (see Chapter 23, "Hiring for Attorney Jobs"), thus making it easier to intentionally and even inadvertently discriminate on the basis of age. There are precious few rules or even guidelines that apply to the recruitment or hiring of attorneys, in great contrast to the hundreds of civil service laws and regulations that govern the employment of attorneys in "law-related" positions that do not carry the designation "attorney." The result is that there are probably fewer instances of ageism in the federal law-related realm than in government hiring for its law offices.

While this same statement holds true about the subject of the next chapter—individuals with disabilities—it has to be tempered with a nod to Albert Einstein: It's all relative.

Chapter 4

Disability

On July 26, 2010, the 20th anniversary of the signing of the Americans with Disabilities Act, Pub. L. 101-336, the U.S. Bureau of the Census reported that 54 million Americans were disabled, amounting to 19 percent of the civilian, non-institutionalized population. The Census Bureau went on to state that 54 percent of disabled adults were unemployed, and that the unemployment rate among the severely disabled was 69 percent. Other organizations estimate that the real unemployment rate among the severely disabled is considerably higher.

The federal government, on paper at least, has tried and is still trying to do something about this. The federal program designed to encourage—even mandate—federal disabled hiring looks great on paper but tends to pale in its execution. Chapter 35, "Disability Hiring—The Selective Placement Program," goes into detail about the special federal hiring program for individuals with disabilities, including how to invoke and negotiate it.

Almost 210,000 individuals with disabilities, or 7 percent of the federal civilian workforce, are employed by the U.S. government, according to the U.S. Office of Personnel Management. They work in hundreds of occupations and in every federal department and agency. Some have risen to very high positions in government.

That looks, on its face, like a pretty impressive number and accomplishment. However, if you delve a little further into the numbers, the picture looks quite different. Although total federal employment of disabled individuals has remained constant at 7 percent for the past 30 years, in that time period the U.S. population grew from 227 million to an estimated almost 310 million—an increase of 83 million people or 36.5 percent. Given that the overall number of federal employees has remained pretty constant over this time period, the only way employment of individuals with disabilities could have increased would be through a conscious effort on the part of the government to establish goals and move toward them. This turns what looked like a promising and encouraging picture into a disappointing one. This stasis in government disability employment then is actually a decline. This is despite the fact that one of the only remaining affirmative action hiring programs in the U.S. government is directed specifically at individuals with disabilities. Moreover, nothing much seems to get accomplished, despite a spate of executive orders emanating from the Oval Office, as well as the efforts of White House staff members whose sole job is to promote disabled employment, and the placement of a designated disability employment coordinator in each federal agency. Disabled Americans are still struggling to get through the door into the U.S. government.

Adding to the frustration and irony is the fact that, almost to a person, federal hiring managers extol the virtue and value of their disabled employees. Nevertheless, I need to conclude this chapter with the same observation that I put forth at the end of the last chapter on ageism. Disappointing as the situation is in the world in general, there is no better place for a disabled attorney to seek employment and to be treated well once on the job than in the federal government.

Part II

The Pros and Cons of a Federal Legal Career

Like any other employer, the U.S. government has its good points and bad points. The ones that I talk about in this Part are gleaned from the totality of my legal career transition counseling experience assisting several thousand attorneys move into and out of the federal sector. How you factor these into your own equation is going to be different for each one of you. Some will merit greater weight in your personal assessment of whether going into federal legal work is the right move for you.

Chapter 5

The Pros

Imminent Massive Retirements

The U.S. government has an aging workforce. The average federal employee is pushing age 50. Moreover, 50-plus is the average age of employees in many departments and agencies. Since federal employees with the requisite number of years of service can retire in their mid-50s, the government anticipates a sudden spike in demand for new hires in the next several years. Some of the attorney-heavy organizations likely to be immersed in the recruitment and hiring market include:

- Department of Education
- Department of Energy
- Department of Health and Human Services
- Department of Labor
- Department of Treasury
- Department of Veterans Affairs
- Agency for International Development
- Commodity Futures Trading Commission
- Environmental Protection Agency
- Equal Employment Opportunity Commission
- Federal Mediation and Conciliation Service
- Federal Communications Commission

- Federal Labor Relations Authority
- Federal Maritime Commission
- Merit Systems Protection Board
- Nuclear Regulatory Commission
- Small Business Administration
- Smithsonian Institution
- Social Security Administration

It is possible to "filter" this list through another variable that makes it even more highly targeted to where the demand for new legal hires is likely to be the most intense. The variable is "mission creep," but in the best sense of the term—increased demand for services and/or expanded duties and responsibilities imposed on a department or agency due to a change in administration policy priorities or congressional requirements. If you run this list through the mission creep filter, some of the agencies that come out on top are:

- Department of Energy—added responsibilities include nuclear facility security, paying former Soviet nuclear scientists to refrain from working for Iran and other U.S. "enemies," and joint federal/private-sector research ventures.
- Department of Health and Human Services—added responsibilities include overseeing the digitizing of patient medical records by physicians and the insurance coverage components of the Patient Protection and Affordable Care Act.
- Department of Treasury—added responsibilities include financial crimes enforcement, foreign assets control, and assisting emerging democracies and economies.
- Commodity Futures Trading Commission—added responsibilities include regulating certain over-the-counter derivatives trading.
- Environmental Protection Agency—added responsibilities include a panoply of climate change regulatory initiatives.
- Nuclear Regulatory Commission—added responsibilities include assisting foreign countries with nuclear reactor safety and health effects.

Student Loan Repayment

The federal Student Loan Repayment Program permits federal agencies to repay federally insured student loans as a recruitment or retention incentive for job candidates or current employees of the agency. The program implements 5 U.S.C. 5379, which authorizes agencies to set up their own student loan repayment programs to attract or retain highly qualified employees.

Virtually any employee is eligible, except certain political appointees. For attorneys, loans eligible for payment are those made, insured, or guaranteed under parts B (The Federal Family Education Loan Program), D (The Ford Federal Direct Loan Program), or E (Federal Perkins Loans) of Title IV of the Higher Education Act of 1965, Pub. L. 89-329.

While the loan is not forgiven, agencies may make payments to the loan holder of up to a maximum of $10,000 for an employee in a calendar year and a total of not more than $60,000 for any one employee.

An employee receiving this benefit must sign a service agreement to remain in the service of the paying agency for a period of at least three years. An employee must reimburse the paying agency for all benefits received if he or she leaves voluntarily, or is separated involuntarily for misconduct, unacceptable performance, or a negative suitability determination. In addition, an employee must maintain an acceptable level of performance in order to continue to receive repayment benefits. This is a discretionary incentive program, so loan repayment is not automatic.

This is a pretty good deal for any law student. According to *Forbes* magazine, the average amount of law school debt at graduation is just over $100,000. Getting someone else to pay off 60 percent of this should be enticing.

Job Security

Job security has become a disappearing phenomenon throughout most sectors in the U.S. economy. As jobs become more volatile—subject to sudden technology advances, globalization pressures such as legal services outsourcing to India and other countries, and other external influences that seem to loom much larger in the twenty-first century—job security is suffering and lawyers are not protected from this trend. One national legal organization predicts that the typical 21st century law graduate will hold an average of eight jobs between law school graduation and retirement.

Fifteen years ago, if a client came to me for legal career counseling with a resumé that showed that he or she had held three jobs in 10 years, I silently classified him or her as a "job hopper" who was likely to be perceived as unstable by prospective employers. Now, the world has changed so dramatically that I consider such a resumé to be a sign of a stable work history. In many cases, I become suspicious of legal resumés that do not show at least some job movement because that could be a signal that the candidate lacks ambition.

The U.S. government, however, has so far been an exception to job instability. The federal government is probably the most secure employment proposition extant in today's increasingly precarious work environment.

For attorneys, this is even more the case. Despite the fact that the federal personnel rules that apply to lawyers working in mainstream attorney jobs make it much easier both to hire and fire them than almost any other civil service employees, federal attorneys have incredible staying power. It is almost unheard of that a government lawyer is ever let go for cause. Instances of downsizing of attorneys for other reasons are also extremely rare. My former company was the "go-to" outside contracting organization for government mass terminations of attorneys and, in three decades, we handled only six such actions, only one of which did not involve (1) the "sunsetting" of a temporary agency or legal department formed to deal with a crisis (such as the creation of the Resolution Trust Corporation to deal with the collapse of the savings and loan industry in 1989-1990 and its statutorily mandated shutdown in 1995); (2) the termination of an entire federal agency upon Congress's concluding that it had completed its mission (such as the demise of the tiny Pennsylvania Avenue Development Corporation); or (3) the transfer of an agency from one location to another (such as the move of the Bureau of Public Debt from Washington, D.C. to Parkersburg, West Virginia). If job security is a priority for you, you likely cannot do better than go to work for the U.S. government.

Work/Life Balance

The vast majority of U.S. government attorneys enjoy a 35–40 hour work week. The exceptions are Department of Justice litigators who serve in either the department's seven litigating divisions (Antitrust, Civil, Civil Rights, Criminal, Environmental and Natural Resources, National Security, and Tax) and assistant U.S. attorneys who work in one of the 93 U.S. attorney offices around the country. Even for them, work schedules are inconsistent. They tend to work long hours when preparing for trial, interspersed with a more "humane" work schedule at other times.

Vacation policy is quite generous. Entry-level federal attorneys accrue 13 days of annual leave each year for their first three years of service, approximately 20 days (four weeks) of annual leave between years three and 15, and 26 days (five-plus weeks) thereafter. In addition, they are paid for 10 federal holidays each year. When federal holidays fall on a Thursday or Tuesday, employees are often also given Friday or Monday off.

Sick leave, retirement, health insurance, and other benefits match up quite well with large private-sector employers. Federal health insurance premiums paid by employees, as well as health insurance benefits, exceed most private employer plans

Flexible Work Schedules

The U.S. government embraced flexible work schedules more than 30 years ago and today they are omnipresent throughout the government. In this respect, the government was light years ahead of the private sector. Many federal employees work a slightly longer workday four days per week in order to earn one day off. For many, this means frequent three-day weekends.

Flex-time is also very popular in the government. When I was an attorney at the Pentagon, many of my colleagues were able to craft flexible hours for themselves, typically arriving at 7 A.M. and leaving at 3 P.M. As rush-hour traffic congestion has become more of a problem in the Washington, D.C. area, many more federal departments and agencies have become amenable to the flexible work hour concept.

Detailed information on federal flexible work schedules can be obtained at http://www.opm.gov/oca/aws/index.asp#Introduction.

Telecommuting Possibilities

Similarly, the idea of working from home or from a telework center near one's home but far from the office has taken hold in the government. The Trademark Office at the U.S. Patent and Trademark Office (PTO) pioneered telecommuting in 1997 through its Trademark Work at Home Program. The program started as a small pilot project, with 18 trademark examining attorneys working from home three days per week and sharing office space with other program participants two days a week. The hope was that current technology could be leveraged to allow employees to enjoy the benefits of working remotely, while still meeting the same qualitative and quantitative goals as their colleagues who worked in the office five days a week. PTO found that the trademark attorneys who were able to work from home became more productive.

After the Trademark Work at Home pilot program proved to be successful, the PTO ultimately expanded its telework initiative to include patent examiners and employees in other business units throughout the agency. The ability to telework is very popular among PTO employees; 85 percent of trademark examining attorneys who are eligible choose to telework. In the patents organization, PTO has a goal that 3,000 patent examiners will be teleworking by 2011.

When PTO moved its offices from Arlington, Virginia, to Alexandria, Virginia, several years ago, officials found that the office needed less space. Thus successful telecommuting policies allowed the office to save a considerable amount of money. Trademark attorneys who telework may now live anywhere they like in the United States since they only have to report in person to the office two days each month. As a result, some reside hundreds of miles away.

The legal duties and responsibilities of trademark attorneys—working fairly autonomously, processing applications, not requiring much interaction with either colleagues or the public—are replicated in a variety of federal department and agency law offices, and some have adopted or are experimenting with their own telecommuting policies. Advances in telecommunications technology—Smartphones, Web conferencing, powerful and affordable personal computers, easy access to high-speed Internet—make telecommuting more viable every year.

Today, the government maintains 14 telework centers in the Washington, D.C. outer suburbs, exurbs, and beyond. Eligible employees who reside near them may commute to a center each day and do their work from there, thus avoiding heavy traffic and enabling them to live in more affordable housing.

Both presidents George W. Bush and Barack Obama endorsed telecommuting and have given the concept some support. Each department and agency now has a telework coordinator to serve as a telecommuting information resource for his or her organization.

Telework offers many benefits to federal agencies, their employees and the environment, including:

- *Employee quality of life.* Allowing employees to telework gives them more time with their loved ones and less time on the road. Employees report that the ability to telework helps them have a better balance between their professional and personal lives.
- *Employee retention.* PTO has seen that offering employees the ability to telework helps with employee retention, allowing the agency to keep highly qualified employees, saving hiring and training costs, and contributing to a high quality of work.
- *Maximizing office space.* As more employees choose to telework, more office space becomes available. This, in turn, gives the agency more flexibility to hire more staff without having to acquire and pay for additional space.
- *Reducing emissions.* Telework can mean a significant reduction in auto emissions. For example, the nearly 950 trademark examining attorneys and patent examiners who work remotely rather than driving to an office four days a week reduce auto emissions by up to 5,000 tons per year.

The Work Itself

A lot of the work that federal attorneys do has national and sometimes global importance. Often, it is "top-of-the-fold" work that makes the national news. Much of it is cutting-edge. Cases of first impression are common legal fodder for federal lawyers.

While this is true of many federal law offices, it is not true of all. There are also a lot of places in the U.S. government where lawyer duties and responsibilities are mundane and repetitive. It takes a certain personality to write claims decisions for the signature of the Comptroller General of the United States at the Government Accountability Office (GAO), a repetitive function with little exposure to cases of first impression and virtually no leeway for creative legal research, analysis, and writing.

In contrast, if you investigate and prosecute Medicare fraud at the Department of Health and Human Services' Office of Counsel to the Inspector General, you are going to run up against some of the most creative scams ever conceived by the mind of amoral man. Moreover, when you bring a scammer to justice, your sense of accomplishment and public service will be at its zenith.

While these two examples tend to remain consistent and timeless—there will always be claims against the government that must be weighed and decided by the GAO, and there will be Medicare fraud as long as Medicare exists—the legal work of other agencies can change quite dramatically, depending on policy shifts and the dynamism and proactivity (or lack thereof) of agency and office heads. If you happen to work today at the Nuclear Regulatory Commission (NRC), for example, you are likely to find what you do to be quite exciting, given the current policy emphasis on reviving the 30-year dormant nuclear reactor industry and the multiple complexities that such a major policy reversal entails. However, if you had been at the NRC 10 years ago, with no end to the reactor moratorium in sight, your daily assignments would probably not have provided the same level of excitement.

Every attorney's legal pulse does not race at the same speed given the same assignments. Before you decide on a suitable agency and federal law office for yourself, make sure that you take your own legal pulse and understand what triggers or curbs your enthusiasm.

The Policy Component

One of the best ways to realize the ambition of doing something involving public policy is by working for the U.S. government. Inevitably, a very large number of federal government attorneys become deeply involved in policy matters in the course of their work. This is a very interesting and exhilarating facet of federal legal practice. The underlying principle of exempting attorneys from the strictures of the competitive civil service was established because of the need for federal lawyers to be part of the policy-determining process. Intense, sometimes daily, interaction with policy-makers is part of the job description for many U.S. government lawyers.

Several anecdotes from my government practice and those of my clients exemplify the opportunity for policy involvement:

- I was able to prevent what I believed would be a military recruiting policy disruptive of families from going into effect by virtue of my legal contribution to the policy process.
- My first assignment at the Department of Energy was developing a set of regulations to govern the geothermal steam industry in the event geothermal energy became economically viable (true, they are still gathering dust on a shelf because geothermal is still too expensive to be a suitable fossil fuel substitute, but the legal considerations that went into the regulations drove the policy).
- One of my clients who worked in the Federal Deposit Insurance Corporation's (FDIC) legal division was charged with putting together a series of nationwide environmental rules that would be applied to bank real estate assets whenever the FDIC took over the operations of a failed bank. The regulations she crafted determined how billions of dollars of real estate assets were managed and when they would be sold.
- Another client's involvement in drafting evidentiary procedures for handling domestic terrorism investigations led to policy adjustments that became standard operating procedure in such cases.

Early Responsibility

In contrast to private practitioners, U.S. government lawyers often arrive on the job and are given major responsibility for cases from day one. For many, this is a trial by fire. For entry-level attorneys, it can be daunting and fraught with tension. This is especially the case for attorneys emerging into the workforce from the vast majority of law schools where the realities of actual practice are sacrificed to the theoretical constructs of law.

Numerous newly barred attorneys come into federal law offices and are handed 20 to 30 cases that require immediate attention. Very few federal law offices have strong mentoring or training systems, and it is almost impossible to predict which ones do and do not at any given time, because they can change on a dime depending on the philosophy and priorities of the office head.

In some ways and for some attorneys, this is a positive because it (1) demands a total immersion approach, (2) forces them to come up the learning curve at light speed, and (3) quickly builds confidence. For others, it can be a very difficult and sometimes painful transition. On balance, the majority of federal attorneys that I handled as a legal career transition counselor found this to be a positive experience.

Incentive Awards and Bonuses

The opportunity to earn an incentive award exists in every federal department and agency. If you are able to streamline a process, innovate, propose a way to save taxpayer money, or something comparable, your boss can nominate you for an incentive award. The monetary component of such an award can be substantial, depending upon what you have proposed or implemented. Moreover, receipt of an incentive award makes for a nice enhancement to a resumé.

Bonuses are fairly common at senior governmental levels. In some years, more than 30 percent of federal employees serving in the Senior Executive Service have received a bonus. At lower governmental levels, bonuses are not as freely awarded. However, in a few instances, especially where lawyer productivity can be measured, it is possible to earn a bonus for exceeding a production quota. Perhaps the best example of this is the Trademark Office. Trademark examining attorneys who exceed a pre-established production quota of trademark filings disposed of are eligible to receive an annual bonus, which may amount to $10,000 or more.

Intra-governmental Fungibility

Getting your foot-in-the-door as a government attorney puts you in a strong position to move laterally, both within your immediate office and within your agency, as well as within the entire government legal establishment. Other federal employers tend to favor current federal employees for a variety of reasons. They know the "system" and are thus able to hit the ground running or come up the learning curve quickly in a new agency. They understand the relationship between law and regulation. They are more likely to have experience with both the regulatory development, compliance, and enforcement processes and also with the federal administrative regime.

Moreover, savvy federal legal managers understand that an attorney who has become an expert in one of the many complex regulatory arenas has a big advantage in moving to an entirely new regulatory arena, notwithstanding that the substantive law and matters that he or she will be required to understand and handle might be quite different. Caveat: Not all federal managers are savvy, so you should assume that you will need to explain how your technical, regulatory knowledge and processing skills can transfer from one federal employer to another.

Being the world's largest employer of lawyers means that there are always opportunities for advancement in another agency or in another office within your current agency. Once you do get your foot in the door, it is to your great advantage to monitor routinely what is going on in your immediate office and subordinate unit, your agency, and government-wide so that, when the time comes to make a strategic move to advance your federal career, you will be prepared.

Chapter 6

The Cons

This chapter is written with the idea in mind that some of the apparent downsides of government legal practice are not absolutes. In other words, they may not be universally applicable to every single federal agency or office and, in certain circumstances, they may be mitigated.

Bureaucracy

The first thought that pops into most people's minds when they hear the word "government" is bureaucracy. And while that is a legitimate response and a valid concern if you contemplate going to work for government, it should not necessarily be determinative for three reasons:

- First, bureaucracies—with all of their negative connotations—are all around us. They exist in government agencies, corporations, law firms, universities, hospitals, and other nonprofit organizations. Bureaucracies are nothing more than a function of size; the larger the organization, the more likely it is to be bureaucratic.

    In any large organization, there often is a considerable amount of "red tape," many levels of review, numerous management layers, and a great deal of frustration if you hap-

26

pen to be goal-oriented. Several of the worst manifestations of bureaucracy I witnessed were in the private sector in *Fortune* 500 corporations.

- Second, government is not a monolith. You will encounter this precept often in this book because it is so important. In this context, it means that federal departments and agencies differ from one another. It is dangerous and very often self-defeating to assume that an organization can be categorized without very careful analysis—without performing adequate due diligence before you reject or accept it as a target employer. Generalizing without analysis is one way to guarantee that you will make poor career decisions.

  This is one of the most important factors that should guide your consideration about (1) going to work for the government and (2) where in government to focus your job campaign.

  By far the largest organization I ever worked in or consulted for was the Department of Defense, probably the poster boy for the most common concept of bureaucracy. However, I worked in a unit of the department that was relatively small and not at all bureaucratic. I had tremendous autonomy, something I did not appreciate until I got older and gained much more work experience in a variety of venues. It's important to analyze the culture of the precise government unit in which you'll be working.

- Third, not every federal organization is big enough to be labeled a bureaucracy. Certain agencies and offices are much too small to be deemed bureaucracies in the negative sense of the term.

  The tiny Administrative Conference of the United States (ACUS), the agency with perhaps the most bizarre history in our two-plus centuries of existence as a country, is not even remotely large enough to merit labeling as a bureaucracy. The agency's mission is to study and recommend improvements to federal administrative and regulatory processes and practices. It has only a handful of employees. For approximately 27 years, the agency developed recommendations for improving procedures by which federal agencies administer various programs. Over the course of its existence, the conference served as a private/public think-tank doing basic research on how to improve the regulatory and legal process. Among its accomplishments was the launching and proliferation of alternative dispute resolution throughout the federal government. During its initial incarnation, it saved taxpayers tens of billions of dollars in return for a modest annual (seven-figure) expenditure that probably would not pay for a rivet on an F-35 Joint Strike Fighter airplane.

ACUS lasted from 1968 to 1995, when it fell victim to Speaker of the House Newt Gingrich's need to demonstrate something in the nature of a federal downsizing as promised in his "Contract with America." He looked around and unearthed ACUS, the tiniest, most obscure federal agency in the entire U.S. government. Unfortunately, ACUS was probably also the most effective agency in history in terms of bang it provided for the taxpayer buck. Nevertheless, Gingrich and his majority colleagues voted ACUS out of existence. In 2004, Congress reauthorized ACUS, but no funding was provided until 2009, after heavy lobbying by the American Bar Association, academics, Supreme Court Justice Steven Breyer, and many other influential individuals and organizations, and giving it new life, a phenomenon unique in the annals of government.

ACUS is proof positive that small can be effective and that government does not have to drown in bureaucracy. With never more than 20 employees, it developed 200 recommendations, most of which were adopted by Congress and federal agencies to the great benefit of government and the public.

The other very important point to be recognized from this is that virtually every agency is really a collection of many—often hundreds—of component parts, some of which are quite small and operate without much oversight. It is these components that are worth a closer look. This is where your "employer due diligence" efforts can really pay off.

Less Compensation

The federal government pays attorneys much less than they are likely to be able to earn in large and medium-size law firms and corporate in-house counsel offices. The compensation schemes for most U.S. government departments and agencies are governed by the general schedule. The general schedule (GS) is divided into 15 pay grades, and each grade is further subdivided into 10 steps.

Entry-level attorneys typically start their federal careers at either GS-9, Step 1 ($41,563 in 2010) or GS-11, Step 1 ($50,287 in 2010). The ten steps within each pay grade are significant because they could mean (1) a higher starting salary and (2) an ability to earn more in succeeding years through step increases and promotions. A GS-9 attorney, for example, who begins at a pay rate of Step 10, would earn $54,028 in 2010, while a GS-11 attorney at Step 10 would earn $65,371. See Chapter 41, "Job Offer and Acceptance Questions," for suggestions on how to negotiate a higher step once a federal job offer is presented to you.

Promotions to higher grades occur rapidly for most attorneys who work for federal "mainstream" law offices, a department or agency general counsel or chief counsel office. Attorneys who work in other federal law offices or nonlegal offices generally do not get promoted as quickly or as often. This is also true of attorneys who work outside of the Washington, D.C. area.

Locality pay is a very important federal compensation concept. It is based on the reality that costs-of-living vary from one geographic area to another. Consequently, the government adds a locality pay adjustment to every federal employee's salary, the amount varying with the location. The following list identifies the different areas subject to locality pay adjustments:

- Atlanta-Sandy Springs-Gainesville, GA-AL
- Boston-Worcester-Manchester, MA-NH-RI-ME
- Buffalo-Niagara-Cattaraugus, NY
- Chicago-Naperville-Michigan City, IL-IN-WI
- Cincinnati-Middletown-Wilmington, OH-KY-IN
- Cleveland-Akron-Elyria, OH
- Columbus-Marion-Chillicothe, OH

- Dallas-Fort Worth, TX
- Dayton-Springfield-Greenville, OH
- Denver-Aurora-Boulder, CO
- Detroit-Warren-Flint, MI
- Hartford-West Hartford-Willimantic, CT-MA
- Houston-Baytown-Huntsville, TX
- Huntsville-Decatur, AL
- Indianapolis-Anderson-Columbus, IN
- Los Angeles-Long Beach-Riverside, CA
- Miami-Fort Lauderdale-Pompano Beach, FL
- Milwaukee-Racine-Waukesha, WI
- Minneapolis-St. Paul-St. Cloud, MN-WI
- New York-Newark-Bridgeport, NY-NJ-CT-PA
- Philadelphia-Camden-Vineland, PA-NJ-DE-MD
- Phoenix-Mesa-Scottsdale, AZ
- Pittsburgh-New Castle, PA
- Portland-Vancouver-Beaverton, OR-WA
- Raleigh-Durham-Cary, NC
- Richmond, VA
- Sacramento—Arden-Arcade—Yuba City, CA-NV
- San Diego-Carlsbad-San Marcos, CA
- San Jose-San Francisco-Oakland, CA
- Seattle-Tacoma-Olympia, WA
- Washington-Baltimore-Northern Virginia, DC-MD-VA-WV-PA
- Rest of the United States
- Alaska
- Hawaii
- Other Non-foreign Areas

A number of federal agencies employ compensation schemes other than the GS system. These schemes usually provide more pay flexibility and the potential for higher pay. Most federal financial regulators employ—and enjoy—such a system, and their attorneys earn considerably more than their GS counterparts. In fact, senior attorneys who work for the Federal Deposit Insurance Corporation, Federal Reserve Board, Office of the Comptroller of the Currency, and Office of Thrift Supervision (soon to be merged in the comptroller's office) can earn over $100,000 more per year than they can under the GS system. What makes this possible is that these four agencies are "self funding"—they assess an annual fee upon the financial services institutions that they regulate, which means that they do not have to rely on congressional appropriations of taxpayer dollars.

While the GS system covers the vast majority of federal attorneys, there are a number of other pay systems under which certain federal attorneys are compensated.

Senior executive service (SES) managers are the highest paid career government employees. The SES pay range has a minimum rate of basic pay equal to 120 percent of the rate for GS-15, step 1 ($119,554 in 2010), and the maximum rate of basic pay is equal to the rate for Level III of the Executive Schedule ($165,300 in 2010), with an exception carved out for certain agencies that base pay partially on performance. Those agencies have a maximum rate equal to Level II of the Executive Schedule ($179,700 in 2010). The Executive Schedule is the pay system under which top political appointees (numbering around 3,000) are compensated.

The almost 1,600 federal administrative law judges (ALJs) operate under a separate pay system. The eight ALJ pay grades range from $103,900 (grade AL-3/A) to $155,500 (grade AL-1). It is rare that an outside candidate begins his or her ALJ service at a grade higher than AL-3/A. However, locality pay adjustments to compensate for higher cost-of-living regions boosted 2010 ALJ compensation from a minimum of $108,804 to a maximum of $165,300.

Federal administrative appeals judges (AAJs) pay in 2010 ranges from $103,900 to $143,700. AAJs work in a variety of federal agencies, where they review ALJ decisions and render final administrative decisions. Locality pay adjustments raise the minimum salary to $108,804 and the maximum salary to $165,300.

Members of federal boards of contract appeals earned $146,170 in 2010. Vice chairs earned $150,855, while chairs earned $155,000. Locality pay adjustments increased basic pay to a minimum of $162,840 and a maximum of $165,300.

There is a strong impetus at work at present in the federal government to allow federal agencies much more wiggle room when it comes to compensating their employees. If this comes to pass, it will be good news for the vast majority of federal attorneys.

Attorneys in the federal judicial branch are compensated under a system that closely resembles the General Schedule. Legislative branch compensation is also similar for those attorneys who work for congressional agencies (see Chapter 17). For those lawyers who work in member offices, on congressional committee and subcommittee staffs, and for congressional support offices and congressional caucuses, organized compensation schemes do not exist and, consequently, pay is all over the map.

"Shock and Awe" on Day One

One of my clients was offered a position with one of the Drug Enforcement Administration's (DEA) law offices. When he reported for duty, he was asked to complete a questionnaire. One of the (predictable) questions concerned past instances of drug use. In response to a question about cocaine use, he provided a lengthy narrative about a time many years before when he attended a party and snorted a line of cocaine. The job offer was (predictably) immediately withdrawn. He rushed to my office, hysterical. There was nothing that we could do to salvage the situation.

Many federal agencies and law offices do something similar to this on the day that you report for duty. You are asked to fill out a form that may pose some uncomfortable questions. Clearly, if you are applying to an agency charged with drug enforcement, you could safely predict that questions about drug use might arise.

I won't get into the moral quandary that most people feel when facing such a question other than to say that you have to (1) be cognizant that questions like this are likely to be asked and (2) consider how you are going to respond before being confronted with them.

Another day-one surprise that you have to be aware of is the possibility that your new job will not exactly match the description in either the vacancy announcement or what you took away from your interview. The usual ways in which this manifests itself in the federal government arena are:

(1) *The job is "less than meets the eye."* Federal job vacancy announcements tend to be written in a language that deviates somewhat—sometimes a lot—from plain English. Seasoned federal employees call this "Fedspeak." Job announcements also tend to throw in the kitchen sink. Examples of both are encompassed in the sample job announcement that is reprinted in Appendix E, "An Application Ordeal."

One of my counseling clients got a position with a large federal law office that supported a critical government function involving the purchase of billions of dollars of essential energy supplies for the armed services. The vacancy announcement contained, as one of the duties of the position, "advising, counseling and briefing senior civilian and military officials at the highest levels on the legal ramifications of proposed agency actions." This was very intriguing and exciting to my client and he was eager to find himself in such an important position. For his first two years in the office, he accompanied the general counsel or deputy general counsel to briefings of the most senior agency officials, generals, and admirals where it was his job to turn the oversized pages of flip charts (this predated PowerPoint). He never opened his mouth at these briefings. He left the job in frustration and joined a private-sector organization, taking a reduction in pay.

The way to protect yourself is to ask your interviewer questions designed to clarify in detail what it says in the vacancy announcement. If the announcement says that you will be testifying frequently before Senate and House committees, ask how frequently and whether you will be doing the actual speaking at the hearing or, as is often the case, you will be sitting behind a superior as a "horse holder," at best only whispering into his or her ear when called upon to provide him or her with a response to a committee question to which he or she does not know the answer. I leave it up to you to word your question to the interviewer in a more sanitized way.

(2) The job is different from what you were given to understand.
This could be both good and bad. A review of the anecdotal
evidence would come down on the bad side. A job announcement that touts heavy involvement in litigation should be a
red flag and prompt you to delve deeper into just exactly
what "involvement in litigation" means. In my formative
years, I assumed that litigation meant that, at least occasionally, a litigator had to stand up and say something in
court or in an administrative hearing. However, once I became involved in legal career advising, I discovered that
my definition was much narrower than the rest of the legal
community's idea of litigation. Hundreds of my litigator clients never set foot in a court room or hearing chamber.

I also discovered that the folks who prepare federal attorney job vacancy announcements shared the prevailing
view dominant in the greater legal community, namely that
even the most remote involvement with litigation in any way,
shape, or form made one a litigator. So, if you have your
heart set on litigating in *my* sense of the term, probe very
carefully if the vacancy announcement promises that you
will be a litigator.

You need to apply the same kind of employer due diligence whenever you believe that there might be more than
one possible meaning to a description in a vacancy announcement or with respect to something that an interviewer
tells you.

*(3) The things the employer did not tell you about prove to be
"job killers."* What might constitute a "job killer" is going
to be different for each individual. I once applied for and
accepted a position with a federal agency general counsel
office, only to discover on my first day at work that the
draft decisions I was required to write for the agency head's
signature had to be dictated. I had never dictated a legal
document—or anything else—in my life and found the process to be extremely difficult and monumentally discouraging. I doubted that I would ever be able to do it successfully.
This unexpected component of the position, about which
both the vacancy announcement and the interviewers were

completely silent, upset me so much that it (along with some more minor irritations) prompted me leave the job very soon.

Of all the potential Day One shocks, this is the one that is the most difficult to anticipate before you arrive at the job. My best advice is to try to determine from your interviewer or from other current or former office employees exactly what a typical day is like on the job, and ask a lot of questions. Your goal should be to try to break down your prospective position into its component parts to as great an extent as possible.

(4) *Filling out a Federal Employment Application Form (SF-171 or OF-612).* The requirement that virtually all U.S. government job applicants had to fill out an SF-171 form was eliminated in 1995 and no more SF-171 forms were printed by OPM thereafter. However, certain agencies or their law offices still use the form, arguing that they are using it for a different purpose. They claim that they want the form for data collection purposes for their personnel records, and have new hires fill it out when they process into the organization on their first day of work.

The SF-171 was replaced by two forms that did very little to streamline the application process: the OF-612 (Optional Application for Federal Employment) and the OF-306 (Declaration for Federal Employment), which together largely replicated the information requirements of the SF-171. There was only one catch—they were *optional* forms. The predictable result was total confusion. Federal job applicants could, theoretically, submit anything they wished and it would be deemed an application for employment. Agencies for the most part paid lip service to this new scenario, even asserting it in boilerplate on federal job vacancy announcements, then proceeded to direct applicants to submit very specific information, often on an SF-171 or OF-612, and used the OF-306 inconsistently, if at all.

I always recommended that my clients contact the agency directly and ask which form, if any, they *really* wanted submitted rather than take what they read on a vacancy announcement at face value. That is still good advice today for those positions that require that candidates submit a paper application directly via postal mail or e-mail.

Two other conundrums sometimes trip up a number of newly hired federal attorneys, causing some of them to lose their new jobs before they begin. The problems arise when a new hire first shows up for work and is asked to complete an SF-171, OF-612, and/or OF-306 as part of the routine check-in process.

The first problem that this can create is when seemingly harmless responses given during the application process do not square with information provided on one of the forms. Inconsistent answers to questions on the forms, such as your salary at a former job, can lead to the new hire being shown the door.

A second problem can arise because both the SF-171 and OF-306 ask what are called "suitability" questions, inquiries that probe character. In addition to a series of questions about citizenship and criminal history or pending charges, these forms pose a question that has been the downfall of many an attorney candidate: *"During the last 10 years, were you fired from any job for any reason, did you quit after being told that you would be fired, or did you leave by mutual agreement because of specific problems?"* It is the last clause of this question that vexes many attorneys. If you answer "yes," then you must provide an explanation of the circumstances of your departure from a prior job. If you answer "no," then you are home free until you get to the bottom of the form where you are informed that:

A false statement on any part of your application may be grounds for not hiring you, or for firing you after you begin work. Also you may be punished by fine or imprisonment (U.S. Code, title 18, section 1001).

If you are a male born after December 31, 1959, you must be registered with the Selective Service System or have a valid exemption in order to be eligible for federal employment. You will be required to certify as to your status at the time of appointment.

I understand that any information I give may be investigated as allowed by law or Presidential order.

I consent to the release of information about my ability and fitness for Federal employment by employers, schools, law enforcement agencies and other individuals and organizations, to investigators, personnel staffing specialists, and other authorized employees of the Federal government.

I certify that, to the best of my knowledge and belief, all of my statements are true, correct, complete, and made in good faith.

18 U.S.C. 1001 is probably the broadest federal perjury statute extant and its expansive use by federal prosecutors has consistently been upheld by the courts. While the number of attorney applicants for federal positions who have actually been prosecuted for false statements on one of these forms is very small, the number denied federal employment is much larger—and that, for most of us, would be punishment enough.

It is very important to know that the SF-171 of OF-306 might be in your future as you begin your federal legal job campaign, and to act accordingly, making sure that you tell the truth and that your "story" is consistent with that of your former employers, schools, etc.

With any forms, it is essential that you make and keep a copy for your own reference.

Drug Testing

Drug testing of new employees has, in recent years, become quite common in certain federal agencies and law offices. Government drug testing, while nowhere nearly as sophisticated as it is rapidly becoming in the professional athletic world, is improving steadily as the technology advances. Since you cannot afford the top-of-the-line chemists that pro athletes can, do not attempt to beat the system.

That is all that need be said on the subject.

Background Investigations

Because of federal attorneys' heavy policy involvement (see Chapter 5, "The Pros"), virtually all prospective appointees must undergo a background investigation before being appointed to their jobs. For most individuals, this will be a routine, pro forma investigation that does not uncover much that would cause hesitation or outright withdrawal of a contingent job offer on the part of the prospective employer.

The scrutiny of your background associated with such investigations depends on the type of security clearance attached to the position, which can range from confidential to secret, top secret, and beyond. Lower-level clearances usually merit rather casual background investigations, ones that are often conducted by outside contractors engaged by the Office of Personnel Management (OPM). Frequently, these are conducted at "long distance" via e-mail and mail communications without any personal, face-to-face contact with references and others.

Top secret and higher level clearances usually mean that the FBI conducts the investigations and that the investigators will question references and others who know you professionally or personally in their homes or offices.

Background investigations, especially for higher-level clearances, can take a very long time, six months or more. In addition, they can mean withdrawal of the job offer if adverse information about past or present behavior is uncovered.

Promotion Ceilings

Like governments everywhere, seniority rules for the most part in the federal government. While considerable lip service is paid to the concept of getting ahead on merit, the reality is that it is seniority that governs virtually all promotions, pay increases, and the like. It is extremely rare that merit alone ever leapfrogs anyone—attorneys included—over someone who has been with the agency or served in government longer than someone else. If you are consumed with ambition, the federal government may leave you somewhat frustrated.

One of the most important pieces of information in a U.S. government job vacancy announcement is the reference, if any, to "promotion potential." This is a euphemism for how high you can go if you accept the particular position being advertised in the vacancy announcement. If it says something like "promotion potential to GS-12," then it is telling you that GS-12 is the top of the line for this position. In order to advance beyond that grade level, you will need to find another job in your agency or elsewhere in the federal government.

This is very important to know if you go to work for a small agency or an agency with relatively few lawyers. It is much less important if you plan to work for a very large agency, such as the Department of Labor, with its thousands of employees including numerous law offices, or an agency like the Justice Department—essentially a gigantic law office with almost 11,000 attorneys—or the Securities and Exchange Commission, which has a disproportionate number of attorneys (1,000-plus). In places such as these, the number of attorneys and law offices affords much more opportunity to advance and much more flexibility in so doing.

One additional caveat to consider is the impact of your geographic location on your promotion possibilities. The best place to work if you're contemplating a federal legal career is at the seat of government—Washington, D.C. and its environs. Here you find by far the highest concentration of federal law offices and the largest number of attorneys. That means more fungibility when it comes to changing jobs. The second-best geographic location is in one of the 10 federal regional centers (see Chapter 8), all of which contain multiple law offices. If all of these 11 possible locations are out of the question, then another large city with several federal law offices would be best if flexibility and promotions are high on your list of requirements.

Less Perceived Prestige

This downside of government employment is going to be much more important to some attorneys than to others. Lawyers are indoctrinated from day one in law school with the peculiar notions that (1) you only have status and even value if you go to work for a large law firm and (2) your overall societal worth is demarcated by the size of your paycheck. Those are difficult notions to set aside given the barrage of such information assaulting you from all sides during law school and beyond. Many (actually most) attorneys come very quickly to believe it. Consequently, working for the government can make them feel demeaned.

If you attend cocktail parties or go bar-hopping in the Washington, D.C. area, saying that you work for the government is no big deal because Washington is the "company town." You are likely never to find yourself in a situation where you are the only person in the room who works for the government or the only one who is not earning the big bucks at a large law firm. In any other city, all bets are off.

If you are one of the indoctrinated, perhaps the government is not the place for you.

Production Quotas in Certain Offices

Certain types of federal legal work lend themselves to easy performance measurement. In the absence of the dreaded billable hour, a few government law offices have instituted the idea of the production quota. What this means in practice is a stated objective that each government lawyer that works in these offices "should" achieve. Law firms whose attorneys do not meet their billable hour requirements sometimes (increasingly, it appears) suffer the most draconian of all workplace sanctions—termination of employment. That is rarely the case in the federal government. However, what failure to meet the production quota often does mean is slower promotions and pay step increases, or the absence of a bonus.

When speaking of production quotas, two government law offices stand out:

- The Trademark Office within the U.S. Patent and Trademark Office. The 400 trademark examining attorneys in the office are expected to process a certain number of trademark applications each year (1,500 is the stated goal). If they exceed the goal by a certain amount, they are eligible for a bonus. They also tend to become management's fair-haired boys and girls, receiving more favorable treatment than their colleagues.
- The Department of Veterans Affairs' Board of Veterans Appeals (BVA) expects its staff attorneys to draft five deci-

sions per week after a "break-in" period when they are first hired.

While the many trademark examining attorneys I have interviewed do not seem to be particularly intimidated by what appears on its face to be a monumental mountain to climb each year (many, in fact, exceed the quota and qualify for the bonus), the same cannot be said for their BVA peers. I advised and assisted a number of both short-term and long-time BVA lawyers seeking to escape from the pressure of their production quota, all of whom exhibited considerable stress.

In analyzing the work of both offices, I concluded that trademark filings are not particularly complicated and tend to share common characteristics and thus, can be examined and processed quickly and efficiently. In contrast, veterans claims denied at lower levels are often characterized by fairly complex issues at the nexus of law, regulation, and medicine, and require considerable analysis and thought before a decision can be drafted. While some claims can be decided and decisions drafted quickly, that is not the case with respect to others. In other words, a production quota applied to trademarks seems much more reasonable and fair than one applied to veterans' claims.

Other federal law offices that believe that their work resembles that of either of these two offices have instituted their own production quotas or are considering doing so. Foremost among these are certain divisions within the Office of General Counsel of the Government Accountability Office, a legislative branch agency that, among other responsibilities, decides certain claims against the government and drafts decisions regarding them.

Marketability Outside Government

Your appeal as a government employee to the private sector might pose more of a problem than admitting to a cocktail party acquaintance that you work for the U.S. government. Again, the precept that the government is not a monolith bears repeating. Your marketability is by no means the same if you work for the Securities and Exchange Commission's Division of Enforcement or the Federal

Election Commission (FEC). Attorneys in the former organization
are likely to be in great demand by both law firms and corporate in-
house counsel offices should they wish to transition to the private
sector. Securities investigations are complicated, highly charged,
and can involve huge amounts of money put at risk. The very sur-
vival of a company may be at stake. Consequently, lawyers who
have had an immersion in securities law and enforcement are enormously attractive to the private sector.

Attorneys at the FEC have much more difficulty moving to the
private sector. There is little demand for lawyers with knowledge of
campaign finance law and regulation, a very narrow practice area
even during presidential election years. Law firms and corporations
have very little interest in these attorneys' backgrounds and areas
of expertise.

Again, this goes back to the kind of sophisticated due diligence
required of you *before* you accept a federal job offer. It is very
important to assess the future marketability of the position you contemplate. In a volatile job market, you always need to think several
moves ahead.

Additionally, you need to be aware that marketability outside
of the government is not likely to be the same as marketability within
the government. It is a great deal easier to move from one federal
job to another than to move from the public sector to the private
sector, even if you happen to have worked in a rather narrow, esoteric area of law such as campaign finance. The reason for this was
stated above in the discussion of intra-governmental fungibility—
federal employers value the technical knowledge of regulation and
the administrative process that you gained in your FEC job and
realize that it is transferable to an entirely different regulatory subject-matter area.

Buck Slipping

One of my assignments as a senior legal consultant to a federal
national security organization was to head a task force that reviewed
all of the standby emergency legislation, executive orders, and regulations that were available to the federal government in the event of
a national emergency or in wartime. These documents had been

drafted in the late 1940s and had not been reviewed for almost 40 years. After many months of review, analysis, and discussions with federal legal and program officials, my task force made numerous recommendations with respect to which authorities were obsolete or needed updating, as well as what new standby authorities should be added to the mix.

All but a handful of our recommendations were endorsed, so the next step was for the task force to draft the necessary updates and new legal documents. Once they were completed, we needed the agency head to sign off on their inclusion in the standby package, but he kept delaying and finding excuses to avoid the matter until our task force was about to terminate. At that point, one of his political aides came to see me and directed me to sign off on the inclusion document. I asked if that was valid, given that I was an outside consultant, and was told not to worry about it. I signed.

I discovered as the years rolled by that my experience was not unique. Federal bureaucrats tend to fear being "exposed" if they become involved in something that might be perceived to be controversial. The standard government methodology for dealing with sensitive matters is to attach what is quaintly known as a "buck slip" to the potentially offending document and "buck" it up to the next higher authority. The term, of course, derives from the famous quotation that President Truman kept prominent on his Oval Office desk: "The buck stops here." Often in the federal government, the buck never stops. It just keeps on going round and round.

I could cite numerous other examples of buck slipping, many of them quite fascinating, but you get the point. If you are seeking bold decision-making, the federal government may not be the place for you.

Occasional Hiring Constraints

When President Reagan was inaugurated on January 20, 1981, his inaugural address contained the statement that he was going to impose an open-ended hiring freeze on the executive branch. When the speech ended, he immediately signed an executive order implementing the hiring freeze. This caused a great deal of hand-wringing among existing and potential applicants for federal jobs, attorneys among them. Thousands of words were expended in print and in law schools nationwide about the shutdown of federal legal hiring.

While hiring was initially halted, the freeze proved to have a great many hot spots where the ice had melted. Agency heads that felt that they needed attorneys requested waivers from the freeze and invariably received them. In short order, the freeze melted completely of its own weight. There was never even an executive order or other issuance that formally rescinded it.

Hiring freezes are not uniform. The Reagan freeze was—at least for public perception political purposes—across-the-board, blanket, and absolute. Others have been agency-specific or had other permutations, such as a requirement that two employees must leave before one new one may be hired.

It is inevitable that, from time-to-time, presidents and agency heads are either going to freeze hiring or put other hiring constraints in place. Usually, this happens when the government finds itself in budgetary extremis. Or, rather, when politicians decide that a hiring constraint is necessary to make it appear to the public that they are actually doing something about the federal deficit and national debt. Like so many other areas of human conduct, perception counts much more than reality when politics are involved.

This kind of uncertainty is a fact of life in the federal government. The only bittersweet solace is that it has also become a fact of life in every other employment sector as well.

The point about hiring freezes, whatever their formulation, is that you should not assume too much from the pronouncements that you hear from politicians, if any, and you should not be deterred by them. Most of the time, the loopholes and exceptions are such that a freeze quickly becomes a bump in the road rather than a firewall.

Part III

Where the Federal Lawyers Are

Locating the federal attorney workforce is not a simple task. Location in this context means much more than just geography. It also encompasses the entire federal government's legal structure—where attorneys are located in terms of branch of government and type of organization, and where particular practice areas tend to congregate. This part examines all three locational categories.

Chapter 7

"Mainstream" Attorney and "Law-Related" Jobs

Federal government legal employment can be categorized in two ways:

1. "Mainstream" jobs
2. "Law-related" jobs

Mainstream Jobs

Federal mainstream jobs are those in which the attorneys are actually practicing law. These positions are usually found in an agency's chief legal office (such as the Department of Defense Office of General Counsel) or subordinate legal office (such as the Defense Intelligence Agency's Office of General Counsel). Of the approximately 40,000 mainstream legal positions in the U.S. government, probably 90 to 95 percent are found in these general counsel and chief counsel offices.

Within each of these offices, there are usually both legal specialists who focus on one or a few practice areas and generalists who handle a variety of issues. A good example of this structure is the Office of General Counsel of the Department of Health and Human Services, which is organized by separate specialized divisions for:

- Medicare and Medicaid services;
- children, families, and aging;
- civil rights;
- ethics;
- food and drugs;
- legislation; and
- public health.

In addition, a separate General Law Division handles a wide range of nondepartment-specific matters, such as appropriations; copyright law; Federal Tort Claims Act, Pub. L. 79-601 (including medical malpractice); the Freedom of Information Act, Pub. L. 89-554; Privacy Act, Pub. L. 93-579; federal contract law; personnel law; equal employment opportunity; and labor relations.

It is very important, however, to be always cognizant that different agencies organize their mainstream legal functions in different ways. If, for example, you were to examine the legal structure at the Department of Education, you would see right away that civil rights enforcement and compliance is completely separate from the Office of General Counsel because, in the federal education context, civil rights is of major importance compared to its role and corresponding visibility in the Department of Health and Human Services. In fact, the Education Department's Office for Civil Rights has a very large legal staff amounting to more than 30 percent of the attorneys in the entire department. This is not the case with the large majority of civil rights offices in other agencies, many of which do not have any attorneys on staff.

Smaller agency law offices are typically staffed with generalists only, who handle virtually all of the legal issues that affect their agency or subordinate unit. Examples of such offices include the Offices of General Counsel of the Access Board, the Advisory Council on Historic Preservation, and the Appalachian Regional Commission. Their work essentially mirrors the work of a corporate in-house counsel office (with the possible exception of a securities law practice).

Mainstream law is also practiced in program, operational, and administrative offices in the federal government. Scattered throughout the federal establishment are program offices that have attorneys hired to practice law assigned directly to them. Examples include:

- Department of Agriculture
  - Animal and Plant Health Inspection Service
  - Foreign Agricultural Service
  - Forest Service
  - Agricultural Research Service
  - Food Safety and Inspection Service
  - Office of Technology Transfer, Agricultural Research Service
  - Farm Service Agency
- Department of Interior
  - Office of Congressional and Legislative Affairs
  - Office of the Deputy Director, Trust Services, Bureau of Indian Affairs
  - U. S. Fish and Wildlife Service
  - National Invasive Species Council
  - Department of the Interior Ethics Office
  - Bureau of Land Management
  - Bureau of Ocean Energy Management, Regulation, and Enforcement (formerly the Minerals Management Service)
  - National Park Service

In addition, attorneys with the job title "attorney" can also be found practicing mainstream law in agency offices of hearings and appeals, inspector general offices, administrative law judge offices, boards of contract appeals, and alternative dispute resolution offices (there are more than 80 such offices in the executive branch alone).

As you can see, mainstream attorney positions are everywhere in the U.S. government. What this means for you as an aspiring federal lawyer is that it is very much to your advantage to expand your horizons to the limit when seeking federal employment. You will be surprised at how many law offices exist and how many non-law offices actually employ attorneys.

Law-Related Positions

In addition to the approximately 40,000 federal mainstream attorney positions, more than 100,000 U.S. government jobs qualify as law-related—positions where a law degree is often directly related to the work involved and/or where a law degree may be preferred or desired, but not necessarily required. These jobs are harder for applicants to identify as those of interest to lawyers because they do not have a job title that contains the word "attorney" or "counsel" or anything comparable.

Unlike traditional attorney positions, almost all of these law-related positions are in what is called the "competitive service." Agencies must comply with all of the voluminous laws and regulations that govern civil service hiring, unlike the leeway they have with respect to filling attorney positions. Competitive civil service jobs, for example, must be advertised. See Chapter 33, "Hiring for Federal Law-Related Jobs," for a more detailed discussion of the classification and hiring procedures that apply to law-related positions.

However, while this means more uniformity in hiring procedures from one agency and office to another than you will ever find for mainstream attorney jobs, it does not change the hiring process appreciably from the standpoint of the candidate. The documents that you submit will not look much different from those you would use to apply for a federal attorney position. The hiring process is also quite similar; the most significant exception being that the leeway accorded federal law offices is not present. Rather, the entire panoply of civil service hiring and selection rules applies.

Law-related positions are found in every federal agency and throughout the United States and abroad. And, as new federal agencies and functions emerge as a result of the Great Recession, advances in technology, changes in policy directions, and other external influences on government functions, keep an eye out for new positions that qualify as law-related.

The list that follows is a sampling of some of the more popular federal law-related job titles that employ attorneys:

- asylum officer
- bankruptcy analyst

- competition advocate
- contract administrator
- copyright examiner
- environmental protection specialist
- equal employment opportunity specialist
- equal opportunity compliance specialist
- general claims examiner
- intellectual property administrator
- labor relations specialist
- land law examiner
- legal instruments examiner
- legislative analyst
- mediator/alternative dispute resolution specialist
- pension law specialist
- regulatory impact analyst
- tax law specialist
- technology licensing specialist
- trade specialist/analyst

The list of law-related positions and the number of job opportunities under each job title are constantly evolving. For example, technology licensing has expanded as the number of federal government laboratories with technology transfer departments grows and as agencies increasingly engage in public/private partnerships and see their counterparts actually earn revenue from technology transfers and licensing. There are currently 11 federal agencies with significant federal laboratory operations. Federal laboratories now number more than 700, and more than 300 have active technology transfer offices. In addition, you can find similar offices in a number of institutes at the National Institutes of Health and in other federal agencies. Many of these offices employ attorneys.

Another example of enormous growth in federal law-related job opportunities is the contracting and procurement function. The rapid growth in defense and homeland security spending and the thousands of projects funded by the American Recovery and Reinvestment Act of 2009, Pub. L. 111-5 stimulated a major increase in the hiring of contract personnel. Of the 37,000 contract and procurement professionals working in the U.S. government, more than one-fifth are attorneys.

The lesson to be taken from this is the same as the lesson to be learned from the ubiquity of mainstream practices and practitioners found throughout the government, including in some very unlikely places that are easy to overlook: You need to expand your horizons when seeking federal legal employment and look beyond positions that include the word "attorney."

Chapter 8

Federal Legal Geography

Domestic Presence

U.S. government attorneys can be found in every state and territory of the United States and in many foreign countries. There are currently more than 3,000 federal law offices in the United States. Domestically, there has been a vast expansion of the federal legal presence in the twenty-first century, fostered by an increasingly complex world, a reversal of a generation of deregulation and *laissez-faire* ideology, and much closer governmental scrutiny of systems that do not appear to operate effectively anymore, such as financial services, health care, and energy.

The Seat of Government

The Office of Personnel Management (OPM) reports that only about 13 percent of the federal civilian workforce is employed in the Washington, D.C. area. The remainder are scattered around the country and abroad (3.3 percent). However, the proportion of federal attorneys who work in the Washington, D.C. area is considerably higher. With only a handful of exceptions, the headquarters offices of all of the U.S. government's many agencies are located in Washington, D.C. or its Maryland or Virginia suburbs. That means that the principal agency law office—usually the office of general counsel, solicitor, or chief counsel—is also located here. These offices harbor many more attorneys than any agency field offices.

While there are no readily available statistics on the number or percentage of federal attorneys located in the Washington, D.C. area, my best estimate would be 30–35 percent.

Federal Regional Centers

Federal law offices are concentrated, in the first instance, in the Washington, D.C. metropolitan area, and secondarily in and around the 10 "Federal Regional Centers": Boston (35 law offices), New York (51 law offices), Philadelphia (36 law offices), Atlanta (48 law offices), Chicago (43 law offices), Kansas City (33 law offices), Dallas/Fort Worth (48 law offices), Denver (41 law offices), San Francisco (48 law offices), and Seattle (36 law offices).

Some federal regional center law offices are heavily staffed, such as the U.S. Attorney Offices in these 10 cities, or the Securities and Exchange Commission's Enforcement Division office in New York. Most, however, are rather small.

Other U.S. Locations

Beyond these concentrations, the next largest number of federal law offices can be found in other major U.S. cities, including: Baltimore, Miami, Orlando, St. Louis, New Orleans, Detroit, Milwaukee, Minneapolis/St. Paul, Houston, San Antonio, Los Angeles, San Diego, and San Jose. Smaller municipalities also are home to some federal law offices, such as:

- Office of Counsel, Naval Air Systems Command, China Lake, California
- Office of Chief Counsel, Golden Field Office, U.S. Department of Energy, Golden, Colorado
- Office of the Federal Public Defender, Ocala, Florida
- Office of the Legal Counsel, Federal Law Enforcement Training Center, Glynco, Georgia
- Office of the Chief Counsel, Federal Aviation Administration, Des Plaines, Illinois

- Regional Counsel Office, U.S. Department of Veterans Affairs, Bedford, Massachusetts
- Enforcement Bureau Regional Office, Federal Communications Commission, Lee's Summit, Missouri
- United States Trustee's Office, Central Islip, New York
- Chief Counsel Field Office, U.S. Army Corps of Engineers, Galveston, Texas
- Office of Chief Counsel, Bureau of the Public Debt, Parkersburg, West Virginia

Hundreds of military bases around the country have law offices that consist of both military judge advocates and civilian attorneys.

A handful of federal agencies are headquartered outside of the Washington, D.C. area, including the Railroad Retirement Board (Chicago), Tennessee Valley Authority (Knoxville, Tennessee), Bureau of Public Debt (Parkersburg, West Virginia), and the International Boundary and Water Commission (El Paso, Texas).

Foreign Offices

There are also a growing number of federal law offices, and other federal offices with attorneys, abroad. While there are no hard and fast figures on either the number of U.S. government lawyers or the number of federal law offices and other offices with legal staffs outside the United States, my most recent compilation of related data counted 90 countries where U.S. government civilian attorneys are currently stationed.

The geography of government law practice is steadily expanding with globalization. In fact, despite the gradual pull-back of our military forces from Germany and Japan now that World War II has been over for more than 65 years, federal lawyers now find themselves in more countries than at the peak of the Cold War.

Recently, for example, the Food and Drug Administration opened three offices in China (Beijing, Shanghai, and Guangzhou) and also opened offices in India (New Delhi and Mumbai), Europe (Brussels), and Latin America (San Jose, Costa Rica, and Santiago, Chile), with plans to expand to the Middle East, in order to provide greater protections to American consumers and globalize agency efforts to enhance the safety of imported food and medical products.

The Federal Bureau of Investigation maintains Legal Attaché offices and smaller sub-offices in 75 cities around the world.

A number of U.S. embassies around the world are assigning at least one official to serve as an intellectual property rights coordinator. Expect this trend to accelerate.

Twenty years ago, few U.S. government agencies had international affairs units. Today, most agencies have established such units, and an increasing number of them have established footholds beyond our borders. This is a trend that is sure to continue.

Chapter 9

Overview of the Federal Legal Structure

The word "structure" is used loosely here, only in order to visualize how federal government legal duties and responsibilities are apportioned and allocated. Structure implies some kind of overarching and rational organizing principle, and that is only partly the case.

The United States Constitution is the bedrock upon which the U.S. government's legal structure rests, but only because it is possible to divide legal offices among the three branches of government that the Constitution establishes—executive, legislative, and judicial. After that, all bets are off.

However, even the Constitution cannot suffice to encompass the entirety of federal agencies and law offices. For example, where would you fit the Government-Sponsored Enterprises, the financial services corporations created by Congress to encourage home ownership—i.e., the Federal National Mortgage Association (Fannie Mae), Federal Home Loan Mortgage Corporation (Freddie Mac), and the 12 Federal Home Loan Banks; agricultural mortgages and loans—i.e., the Farm Credit Banks and the Federal Agricultural Mortgage Corporation (Farmer Mac); and until 2004, when Congress withdrew its charter, the Student Loan Marketing Association (Sallie Mae)? These quasi-public entities don't really fit neatly into the constitutionally created federal framework.

As mentioned, perhaps the most important point that you need to take away from this book is the following:

The "Government as Monolith" Myth

The U.S. government is NOT a monolith. This is going to be an often-recurring theme of this book. Understanding this and incorporating it into your federal job campaign will greatly expand your federal legal job opportunities and help you avoid unnecessarily limiting yourself when negotiating the federal legal hiring process.

Debunking the monolith myth is essential when considering the federal legal structure, which often differs dramatically from agency to agency. It also applies to practice areas (see Chapter 21, "Federal Practice Areas") in the sense that certain law offices practice in areas of the law that are surprising to many job applicants. It applies as well to how you go about applying for different federal legal positions and to whether you are seeking a mainstream attorney position or one that is law-related.

What you have to keep foremost in mind is that there is no uniformity among federal departments and agencies when it comes to legal structure or much of anything else.

Agency Creation and Destruction

In the past two decades, only five federal agencies have "sunsetted"; (1) one predictably because it was intended to be temporary (the Resolution Trust Corporation, which went out of business after victory was declared in the savings and loan crisis of 1989 to 1995); (2) one due to deregulation of a significant portion of its regulatory mandate (the Interstate Commerce Commission), the remainder of its duties transferred to a new unit in the Transportation Department; (3) one that was just recently revived after 15 years (the Administrative Conference of the United States); (4) one very small agency that is, alas, gone forever (the Office of Technology Assessment, which did some of the finest work in all of government); and (5) one that completed its mission (the Pennsylvania Avenue Development Corporation).

In contrast, a whole slew of new departments, agencies, and offices with legal staffs have been created in this century, some bringing with them multiple law offices. These include:

- Office of the Director of National Intelligence
- National Nuclear Security Administration (unit of the Department of Energy)
- Election Assistance Commission
- Federal Housing Finance Agency
- Millennium Challenge Corporation
- Department of Homeland Security (DHS)
- Transportation Security Administration (unit of DHS)
- Homeland Security Council (unit of Executive Office of the President [EOP])
- Office of Energy and Climate Change Policy (unit of EOP)
- Office of Health Reform (unit of EOP)
- Office of Faith-Based and Neighborhood Partnerships (unit of EOP)
- Office of Medicare Hearings and Appeals (unit of Department of Health and Human Services [HHS])
- Office of the National Coordinator for Health Information Technology (unit of HHS)
- Office of Consumer Information and Insurance Oversight (unit of HHS)
- Office of the Federal Detention Trustee (unit of Department of Justice [DOJ])
- National Security Division (unit of DOJ)
- Office of Privacy and Civil Liberties (unit of DOJ)
- Office of Sex Offender, Monitoring, Apprehending, Registering and Tracking (SMART) (unit of DOJ)
- Defense Privacy Office (unit of Department of Defense)
- Office of the Ombudsman for the Energy Employees Occupational Illness Compensation Program (unit of Department of Labor)
- Office of Chief Counsel, Pipeline and Hazardous Materials Safety Administration (unit of Department of Transportation)

- Office of Chief Counsel, Alcohol and Tobacco Tax and Trade Bureau (unit of Department of Treasury)
- Office of Chief Counsel, Insurance Division (unit of Pension Benefit Guaranty Corporation)
- Office of the Intellectual Property Enforcement Coordinator (unit of EOP)
- Bureau of Consumer Financial Protection (independent agency within the Federal Reserve Board)
- Financial Stability Oversight Council
- Office of Financial Research
- Federal Insurance Office (unit of the Department of Treasury)
- Office of the Investor Advocate (unit of the Securities and Exchange Commission [SEC])
- Whistleblower Office (SEC)
- Office of Market Intelligence
- Asset Management Unit (SEC)
- Market Abuse Unit (SEC)
- Structured and New Products Unit (SEC)
- Foreign Corrupt Practices Unit (SEC)
- Municipal Securities and Public Pensions Unit (SEC)
- Office of Credit Rating Agencies (unit of SEC)
- Office of the Associate Director for Compliance and Training (unit of the National Security Agency)

This is not a complete list of new twenty-first-century agencies with law offices. But it is very representative of what happens regularly in the federal government. New offices are constantly being created; old ones rarely die and, to quote General MacArthur, never even "fade away." This means that new and interesting federal job and career opportunities for lawyers are constantly appearing on the scene.

Chapter 10

Executive Branch—Overview and the Executive Office of the President

Overview

The federal executive branch consists of the Executive Office of the President, 15 cabinet departments, and more than 150 "independent" and other agencies (depending on who is counting). Each department and agency has a chief legal officer and primary legal office, usually—but not always—called the Office of General Counsel. In addition, many departments and agencies also have other law offices, plus attorneys who serve in non-legal offices, i.e., program offices, administrative offices, and other offices. Many of these non-law-office attorneys are placed there to practice law—usually taking the form of providing legal advice to the office managers and staff about day-to-day issues that arise and require more immediate attention than they might receive from consulting the agency's chief legal office.

Executive Office of the President

The Executive Office of the President (EOP) consists of the White House and its multiple advisory and support organizations, including "czars." President Abraham Lincoln ran the White House with a staff of two personal secretaries and still successfully fought a major war. No one knows exactly how many people work within and in support of today's White House, but experts believe that the number is in the thousands. While all of the top EOP jobs and many others are political appointments, a large number are merit-based positions. One of my legal career counseling candidates was hired by the White House Office of Administration's Office of General Counsel (not the same as the White House Counsel's Office—see below) purely on the basis of her qualifications—i.e., without any political connections.

The major EOP offices and their legal components are described below.

Office of Counsel to the President

The Office of Counsel to the President advises the President on all legal issues concerning the President and the White House, including the legal aspects of policy questions, legal issues arising in connection with the President's decision to sign or veto legislation, ethical questions, financial disclosures, and conflicts of interest during employment and post-employment, and defines lines between official and political activities. The Counsel's Office also oversees executive appointments and judicial selection, handles presidential pardons, reviews legislation and presidential statements, and handles lawsuits against the President in his role as President, as well as serving as the White House contact for the Department of Justice.

This office is highly political, and its attorneys almost always come from a political background.

Office of the General Counsel, Office of Administration

The Office of Administration provides comprehensive administrative support and business services to all EOP components. Services encompass human resource management; design and communication services; employee learning and development support; financial, accounting, travel, and procurement services; information technology, IT security, and records management; operational activities that maintain and run the physical and logistical aspects of the EOP complex; safety, security, and emergency preparedness; legal support; and promoting equal employment opportunity and diversity.

The Office of the General Counsel (OGC) provides legal advice and counsel on a wide variety of issues affecting the White House Office of Administration and EOP officials, including procurement and contracting law, acquisitions, appropriations and fiscal law, personnel and equal employment opportunity law, information disclosure, records management, ethics, and litigation. OGC also identifies policy issues and problems requiring attention and develops legislative proposals.

In other words, OGC is much more of an apolitical, purely legal office than the Office of Counsel to the President, and handles the more routine legal matters that affect EOP. Non-political candidates have a shot at positions in this office.

Office of General Counsel, Office of Management and Budget

The Office of Management and Budget (OMB) assists the President in overseeing the preparation of the annual federal budget and in supervising its administration in executive branch agencies. OMB evaluates the effectiveness of agency programs, policies, and procedures; assesses competing agency funding demands; and sets funding priorities. OMB also ensures that agency reports, rules, testimony, and proposed legislation are consistent with the President's budget and with Administration policies and its legislative program.

OMB also oversees and coordinates the Administration's procurement, financial management, information, and regulatory policies.

OMB's Office of General Counsel (OGC) works intensively with other agencies' counsels, the Government Accountability Office, and congressional staff. OGC aids negotiations between agency authorities in drafting executive orders, serving as the executive branch expert on appropriations law and interpreting OMB's own statutes, such as the Privacy Act, Pub. L. 93-579, and the Paperwork Reduction Act, Pub. L. 96-511.

OGC hiring is merit-based.

Office of Federal Procurement Policy, Office of Management and Budget

The Office of Federal Procurement Policy (OFPP) is primarily a policy office that shapes the policies and practices federal agencies use to acquire the goods and services they need to carry out their responsibilities. Its congressionally mandated mission is to provide overall direction for government-wide procurement policies, regulations, and procedures and to promote economy, efficiency, and effectiveness in acquisition processes. OFPP is headed by an administrator who is appointed by the President and confirmed by the Senate, and usually employs a number of attorneys who are hired on the basis of their qualifications, not their politics.

Office of the Intellectual Property Enforcement Coordinator, Office of Management and Budget

This office was created by the Prioritizing Resources and Organization for Intellectual Property Act of 2008 (PRO-IP Act), Pub. L. 110-403. Its mission is to coordinate the work of the federal agencies that are involved with stopping piracy, counterfeiting, and reducing the number of infringing goods in the United States and abroad, such as counterfeit car parts, illegal software, pirated video games, knockoff consumer goods, dangerous counterfeit medicines, and many other types of products—including very sophisticated technology.

Sounds like a great place to work for an attorney, doesn't it? However, don't get too excited, at least not yet. As this is written, the office has two full-time employees.

Legislative Reference Division, Office of Management and Budget

The legislative analysts and attorneys who constitute the professional staff of this division are responsible for managing OMB's central legislative clearance process. The basic purpose of the clearance process is to ensure that presidential policies are reflected correctly on legislative matters before the Congress.

The analyst's basic responsibilities include:

- assisting in preparing the President's annual legislative program—that is, the major bills to be proposed to Congress by the Administration each year;
- coordinating the development and interagency review of executive branch agency legislative proposals;
- coordinating the interagency review of agency testimony and letters to Congress expressing views on bills it is considering;
- staying abreast of legislative developments in Congress and ensuring that the Administration's positions or concerns about bills are made known to Congress in a timely manner; and
- preparing memoranda to the President, including signing statements and veto messages as appropriate, on legislation presented to him by Congress for approval or disapproval.

Each analyst performs these duties in particular subject matter areas, such as environment, health, education, drug abuse, etc.

Office of Information and Regulatory Affairs, Office of Management and Budget

The Office of Information and Regulatory Affairs (OIRA) carries out several important functions, including reviewing federal regulations, reducing paperwork burdens, and overseeing policies relating to privacy, information quality, and statistical programs.

OIRA policy analysts (a significant number of which are attorneys) oversee the federal regulatory system so that agencies' regulatory actions are consistent with economic principles, sound public policy, and the goals of the President. They also review requests by agencies for approval of collections of information (including surveys, program evaluations, and applications for benefits) under the Paperwork Reduction Act of 1995, Pub. L. 104-13. In addition, they review and analyze other Administration and congressional policy initiatives.

Policy analysts in OIRA work directly with high-level policy officials and have a great deal of responsibility in a wide array of policy areas. Major topic areas include virtually every domestic policy area, including environment, natural resources, agriculture, rural development, energy, labor, education, immigration, health, welfare, housing, finance, criminal justice, information technology, and other related domestic policy issues.

Specifically, an OIRA policy analyst:

- oversees and evaluates the regulatory, information, and other policy initiatives of one or more government agencies by applying economics, statistics, and risk assessment;
- analyzes agency regulations prior to publication to ensure that the regulations adhere to sound analytical principles and that agencies evaluate the need for, societal costs and benefits of, and alternatives to new regulations;
- reviews and approves agency collections of information in accordance with the Paperwork Reduction Act of 1995, Pub. L. 104-13;
- ensures that agency collections reduce, minimize, and control paperwork burdens and maximize the practical utility and public benefit of the information created, collected, disclosed, maintained, used, shared, and disseminated by or for the federal government;
- coordinates the review of regulations and collections of information within OMB and the Executive Office of the President, as well as among other relevant federal agencies;
- monitors and analyzes legislative and policy proposals and testimony for conformance with the policies and priorities of the President; and
- performs special analyses and advises senior policy officials on specific issues.

Office of General Counsel, Council on Environmental Quality

The Council on Environmental Quality (CEQ) coordinates federal environmental efforts and works with agencies and other White House offices to develop environmental policies and initiatives. The Council chair, who is appointed by the President with the advice and consent of the Senate, serves as the President's principal environmental policy adviser. In addition, CEQ reports annually to the President on the state of the environment; oversees federal agency implementation of the environmental impact assessment process; and acts as a referee when agencies disagree over the adequacy of such assessments.

CEQ dates from the National Environmental Policy Act of 1969 (NEPA), Pub. L. 91-190. Additional CEQ responsibilities were contained in the Environmental Quality Improvement Act of 1970, Pub. L. 91-224.

CEQ's Office of General Counsel handles a variety of matters concerning oversight of NEPA and other legal matters pertinent to CEQ's functions.

Office of Legal Counsel, Office of National Drug Control Policy

The Office of National Drug Control Policy (ONDCP) establishes policies, priorities, and objectives for the nation's drug control program. The goals of the program are to reduce illicit drug use, manufacturing, and trafficking; drug-related crime and violence; and drug-related health consequences. ONDCP also evaluates, coordinates, and oversees both the international and domestic anti-drug efforts of executive branch agencies and ensures that such efforts sustain and complement state and local anti-drug activities.

ONDCP's Office of Legal Counsel (OLC) advises on all legal questions confronting the agency. OLC's primary function is to advise the director and agency personnel on the scope and effect of their legal authority. It also is responsible for monitoring and commenting on drug control measures, proposed legislation that impacts drug control policy, overseeing compliance with federal ethics laws and regulations by ONDCP, and ensuring agency compliance with federal records laws and Freedom of Information Act requests. OLC is also responsible for advising the director and senior staff on issues of administrative, contract, copyright, fiscal, procurement, personnel, security, and appropriations law.

Office of General Counsel, Office of the United States Trade Representative

The Office of the U.S. Trade Representative (USTR) develops and coordinates U.S. international trade, commodity, and direct investment policy, and leads or directs negotiations with other countries on such matters. Through an interagency structure, USTR coordinates trade policy, resolves disagreements, and frames issues for presidential decision. The agency provides trade policy leadership and negotiating expertise in its major areas of responsibility, including:

- all matters within the World Trade Organization (WTO);
- trade, commodity, and direct investment matters managed by international institutions, such as the Organization for Economic Cooperation and Development (OECD) and the United Nations Conference on Trade and Development (UNCTAD);
- expansion of market access for American goods and services;
- industrial and services trade policy;
- international commodity agreements and policy;
- bilateral and multilateral trade and investment issues;
- trade-related intellectual property (TRIPS) protection issues; and
- negotiations affecting U.S. import policies.

USTR also has administrative responsibility for the Generalized System of Preferences (GSP) and complaints against foreign unfair trade practices, as well as noncompliance with Section 1377 of the Omnibus Trade and Competitiveness Act of 1988 (covering telecommunications access), Section 337 of the Tariff Act of 1930 (authorizing domestic industries to prove that imported articles have infringed their U.S. intellectual property rights), and import relief cases under Section 201 of the Trade Act of 1974.

USTR has offices in Washington, D.C. and in Geneva, Switzerland. USTR's Geneva Office covers general WTO affairs, Non-tariff Agreements, Agricultural Policy, Commodity Policy, and the Harmonized Code System.

The Office of the General Counsel (OGC) advises the U.S. Trade Representative and the agency's staff on all areas of international trade law and agency responsibilities. OGC is responsible for:

- ensuring that all actions of the United States related to trade are analyzed for conformity with U.S. rights and obligations under international agreements affecting trade;
- developing Administration positions on trade legislation;
- carrying out dispute settlement proceedings under the General Agreement on Tariffs and Trade (GATT);
- developing and carrying out U.S. antidumping and subsidy/countervailing duty policy;
- investigating/prosecuting certain cases;
- reviewing certain unfair import trade cases; and
- providing advice on questions involving government ethics, conflicts of interest, financial disclosure, and Freedom of Information Act/Privacy Act issues.

Other Units of the Office of the United States Trade Representative

Because the USTR is so deeply immersed in treaties, executive agreements, and U.S. and foreign law, attorneys can be found throughout the agency. The principal offices where attorneys are on staff include the following: Environment and Natural Resources; Intellectual Property and Innovation; Labor Affairs; Small Business, Market Access and Industrial Competitiveness; Policy Coordination and Information; Trade and Development; Services and Investment; and WTO and Multilateral Affairs. In addition, lawyers are also found in the USTR's Bilateral Negotiation Offices: Western Hemisphere; Europe and the Middle East; Central and South Asian

Affairs; Southeast Asia and the Pacific; Japan, Korea, and APEC Affairs; China Affairs; and African Affairs.

Czars

Presidents since the 1930s have appointed a variety of White House advisors to coordinate disparate federal activities that often compete and conflict concerning specific issues. These individuals are not subject to the constitutional requirement of Senate advice and consent and operate independently of cabinet departments and executive branch agencies. They often have very small budgets and staffs and wind up having very little clout as a consequence. Most are quickly put on the back burner and have little influence on policy or on the direction of government.

President Obama has appointed more czars (35) than served during the 300-year Russian Romanov dynasty. These individuals are never officially labeled "czar." Here is a partial list of the current bunch:

- Special Representative for Afghanistan and Pakistan
- Director of the Office of National AIDS Policy
- Senior Advisor President's Automotive Task Force
- Director of Recovery for Auto Communities and Workers
- Special Representative for Border Affairs
- Special Envoy for Climate Change
- Director of the White House Office of Cybersecurity
- Director of the White House Office of Health Reform

The important point about czars is that they have staffs, albeit small in number, and that their staffs often include attorneys. However, these positions are rarely filled on a merit basis.

Chapter 11

Executive Branch— Cabinet Departments

Thirteen of the 15 cabinet departments employ the term "Office of General Counsel" for their chief legal office. Two departments— Interior and Labor—call their primary legal office the "Office of the Solicitor." Most (but not all) cabinet departments also have Regional Counsel offices that are the local expression of the chief legal office and report directly to it.

Regional Counsel offices are generally located in each of the 10 Federal Regional Centers (Boston, New York, Philadelphia, Atlanta, Chicago, Kansas City, Dallas, Denver, San Francisco, and Seattle). When they are located elsewhere, it is because the nature of the department's responsibilities requires a different location. For example, the U.S. Department of Agriculture has only four Regional Counsel offices (Atlanta, Kansas City, Denver, and San Francisco), but also has 13 Branch Counsel offices, some of which are in small cities in areas of important agricultural production (Columbus, Ohio; Harrisburg, Pennsylvania; Milwaukee; Montgomery, Alabama; Chicago; Little Rock; St. Paul, Minnesota; Temple, Texas; Albuquerque; Missoula, Montana; Ogden, Utah; Juneau, Alaska; and Portland, Oregon).

Every cabinet department also has law offices in addition to its General Counsel and Regional Counsel offices. Certain departments have many such offices, some with their own regional structure.

For example, the Department of Transportation (DOT) carries out most of its functions through its nine "modal" administrations ("modal" referring to transportation modes), all but one of which has its own Office of Chief Counsel. DOT's Federal Aviation Administration (FAA) Office of Chief Counsel exemplifies this. FAA has nine Regional Counsel offices and two Center Counsel offices around the country.

Each cabinet department (as well as 58 federal agencies) has an Office of Inspector General (IG) with its own Counsel's office completely independent of the departmental legal structure and reporting relationships. Federal IGs are tasked with ferreting out "waste, fraud, abuse and mismanagement," and their attorneys play a central role in this mission. While most IG Counsel offices are quite small in number of attorneys, the one at the Department of Health and Human Services is a significant exception, numbering over 80 attorneys (and growing).

That is not the end of the story. Many cabinet departments have additional law offices that do not fit into any of these paradigms. Going back to the DOT example, its Surface Transportation Board—the partial successor agency to the now defunct Interstate Commerce Commission—resolves railroad rate and service disputes and reviews proposed railroad mergers, both functions heavily permeated with legal considerations. Consequently, the board has two legal offices—the Office of General Counsel and the Office of Proceedings—and another office with both legal and other responsibilities, the Office of Public Assistance, Governmental Affairs, and Compliance. DOT also harbors the St. Lawrence Seaway Development Corporation, which maintains its own Office of the Chief Counsel in Massena, New York. In addition, DOT has an Office of Hearings comprised of administrative law judges and staff attorneys. This office holds hearings under the Administrative Procedure Act (5 U.S.C. §§ 551 et seq.) and decides cases arising from decisions rendered by each of DOT's modal administrations. Drilling down below the departmental level unearths additional law offices, such as the Federal Motor Carrier Safety Administration's Regulatory Ombudsman Office, and 10 Federal Transit Administration Regional Legal Counsel offices.

DOT is not unique among its cabinet brethren. Virtually every department has a similar collection of law offices scattered throughout its headquarters and regional structure. Two cabinet departments, however, require a separate discussion because they are unique in certain respects:

The Department of Justice (DOJ) is the government's law firm. Consequently, virtually all of its functions, divisions, sections, branches, etc., are in fact law offices. DOJ has 59 separate law offices at its Washington, D.C. headquarters and several hundred additional law offices around the country, including the 93 U.S. Attorney offices, 96 U.S. Trustee offices, 59 immigration courts, 56 FBI Field offices (many of which have counsel offices), six Federal Bureau of Prisons Regional Counsel offices, and nine litigating division field offices.

The Department of Defense is also unique, but in another way. In addition to its civilian attorneys, it also has several thousand military lawyers who often work side-by-side with their civilian counterparts in the same locations and on the same legal matters.

As of this writing, the 15 cabinet departments have no fewer than 1,324 law offices, broken down as follows (the number of offices for each department appears in parentheses following the name of the department):

- Agriculture (27)
- Commerce (38)
- Defense (418)
- Education (16)
- Energy (35)
- Health and Human Services (27)
- Homeland Security (103)
- Housing and Urban Development (53)
- Interior (27)
- Justice (378)
- Labor (35)
- State (3)
- Treasury (81)
- Transportation (48)
- Veterans Affairs (35)

By the time you read this, the federal government will have added quite a few additional law offices, thanks to the rollout of health-care reform legislation and especially the Dodd-Frank Wall Street Reform and Consumer Protection Act, Pub. L. 111-203.

Certain cabinet departments comprise a collection of what appears to be (and in some instances is) a gaggle of unrelated agencies. The Department of Commerce, for example, is so broad-based that it encompasses the U.S. Patent and Trademark Office, the National Weather Service, the National Marine Fisheries Service, the Census Bureau, the National Institute of Standards and Technology, and the National Telecommunications and Information Administration, among other subordinate units.

When contemplating a U.S. government legal career, or when hunting for a federal job, do not limit your search only to federal *law* offices. Thousands of federal attorneys perform legal functions in executive branch program, operational, and administrative offices, such as:

- Animal and Plant Health Inspection Service (Department of Agriculture)
- Directorate of Real Estate, U.S. Army Corps of Engineers (Department of Defense)
- Technology Transfer Department, Lawrence Berkeley National Laboratory (Department of Energy)
- Agency for Health Care Research and Quality (Department of Health and Human Services)
- U.S. Coast Guard National Vessel Documentation Center (Department of Homeland Security)
- Bureau of Ocean Energy Management Regulation and Enforcement (Department of Interior)
- Employment and Training Administration (Department of Labor)
- Bureau of International Organization Affairs (Department of State)
- Office of Technical Assistance (Department of Treasury)
- Office of Employment Discrimination and Complaints Adjudication (Department of Veterans Affairs)

Chapter 12

Executive Branch— The Agencies

Note: Whether a federal agency is legally part of the executive branch or independent is completely irrelevant to this discussion. Suffice it to say that, for federal legal employment purposes, there is no meaningful distinction (despite former Vice President Cheney's occasional claim that he was part of the legislative branch because he presided over the Senate!). Also, do not get hung up on whether an agency is a regulatory agency or something else. Many agencies have both regulatory and non-regulatory missions. So does every cabinet department. "Agency" in this context is really only a term that differentiates a federal organization from a cabinet department.

The 150+ federal agencies are similar to the cabinet departments in that they all have a chief legal office that goes under the name of either the Office of General Counsel or something comparable. Most agencies also have more than one law office; some, in fact, rival the cabinet departments in their multiplicity of law offices. The Social Security Administration, a very large agency, has 172 law offices as of this writing. The Securities and Exchange Commission, a middle-size independent agency, has 28 law offices (with more coming as a result of financial regulatory reform legislation). Even a very small agency like the Commission on Civil Rights has no fewer than eight law offices.

As indicated in the cabinet discussion above, 73 agencies (15 are in cabinet departments) have Inspector General offices, but only about half of these have their own legal counsel office.

Another trait that the agencies share with the cabinet departments is their "embedding" of attorneys in non-law, line operations, program, and administrative offices where they practice law, but where law is not the primary function of the office. Examples include:

- Division of Clearing and Intermediary Oversight (Commodity Futures Trading Commission)
- Office of Solid Waste and Emergency Response (Environmental Protection Agency)
- Office of Federal Operations (Equal Employment Opportunity Commission)
- Wireless Telecommunications Bureau (Federal Communications Commission)
- Division of Bank Supervision (Federal Deposit Insurance Corporation)
- Office of Markets, Tariffs and Rates (Federal Energy Regulatory Commission)
- Office of Governmentwide Policy (General Services Administration)
- Office of the Chief Accountant (Securities and Exchange Commission)
- Europe and Eurasia Bureau (U.S. Agency for International Development)
- Office of Tariff Affairs and Trade Agreements (U.S. International Trade Commission)
- Division of Consumer and Community Affairs (Federal Reserve Board)
- Office of Product Development and Licensing (Smithsonian Institution)
- Office of International Programs (Nuclear Regulatory Commission)

Federal agency law practice differs not at all from practice in a cabinet department. The issues that arise and must be managed are largely the same. Both departments and agencies have internal clients that must be accommodated and external constituencies that require advice, counsel, scrutiny, and the occasional slap on the wrist.

Some agencies have very narrow missions, such as the Federal Election Commission or the U.S. Chemical Safety and Hazard Investigation Board; others have missions that are very broad in scope, such as the Federal Reserve Board, which may be the most important economic regulator, or the Federal Trade Commission, which has two very broad and somewhat unrelated functions: (1) serving as a watchdog over competition and antitrust matters, and (2) overseeing a vast spectrum of consumer protection matters encompassing advertising practices with an emphasis on claims for food, over-the-counter drugs, dietary supplements, alcohol, and tobacco and on conduct related to high-tech products and the Internet, such as the dissemination of spyware; consumer and business education; consumer protection enforcement litigation, including with respect to a variety of consumer protection rules covering industries such as nurseries, automobile parts, jewelry, leather and imitation leather products, funeral homes, private vocational and distance education schools, wool products, fur products, hobbies, appliances, used cars, eyeglasses, home insulation, and many, many more; certain financial practices; marketing practices such as Internet, telecommunications, direct-mail fraud, and the Do Not Call provisions of the Telemarketing Sales Rule; and privacy and identity theft.

While agencies are often regulatory in nature, like the Federal Trade Commission, Securities and Exchange Commission, and Federal Communications Commission, others are not, such as the African Development Foundation, the Commission on Civil Rights, or the Corporation for National and Community Service. Some agencies have regulatory functions that they share (or that duplicate or overlap) with other agencies and/or cabinet departments. For example, the Federal Trade Commission's regulatory jurisdiction over for-profit educational institutions is, to a degree, replicated at the Department of Education. You will find this kind of confusing blurring of jurisdiction and mission lines throughout the federal structure, especially the legal structure.

Chapter 13

Executive Branch— Article I Courts

While the vast majority of federal courts are in the judicial branch (established under Article III of the U.S. Constitution), there are a number of courts in the executive branch (established under Article I). These adjudicative bodies hire a large number of lawyers.

Like Article III courts, Article I court judges hire judicial law clerks, who are usually recent law school graduates. In addition, most Article I courts employ staff attorneys in both permanent and temporary positions. Staff attorneys are found in either the court clerk's office or a separate staff attorney office.

The Article I courts include:

- **U.S. Court of Appeals for the Armed Forces**. This 60-year-old court was established by Congress at the same time that it enacted the Uniform Code of Military Justice. The court has worldwide jurisdiction and is the military court of last resort for trials by court-martial in the military services. The five judges are all civilians.
- **U.S. Court of Appeals for Veterans' Claims**. This court dates to 1988. It reviews decisions adverse to claimants by the Board of Veterans' Appeals, an administrative body within the U.S. Department of Veterans' Affairs. Most cases are about disability or survivor benefits, or the amount of

those benefits. A few deal with education benefits, life insurance, home loan foreclosure, or waiver of indebtedness.

- **U.S. Court of Federal Claims.** This court was created in 1982 but is really the continuation of the more than a century-old Court of Claims, with some new jurisdiction added (bid protests, vaccine compensation, civil liberties, product liability, oil spills, etc.). The court hears primarily money claims founded upon the Constitution, federal statutes, executive regulations, or contracts, express or implied-in-fact, with the United States. Approximately 60 percent of the cases involve tax refund suits or government contracts. The court also hears a large number of cases involving eminent domain and environmental and natural resource issues. Another large category of cases involves intellectual property, Indian tribe, and various statutory claims against the United States by individuals, domestic and foreign corporations, states and localities, Indian tribes and Nations, and foreign nationals and governments. Some of the litigation is highly technical.

- **U.S. Tax Court.** The Tax Court is a judicial forum where affected persons can dispute tax deficiencies determined by the Commissioner of Internal Revenue prior to paying the disputed amounts.

- **Territorial Courts.** These courts—in Guam, the U.S. Virgin Islands, and the Northern Mariana Islands—are the equivalent of U.S. District Courts. They serve a dual purpose in also functioning like state and local courts for their respective jurisdictions.

Chapter 14

Legislative Branch— Overview, Politics v. Merit Hiring, and Members' Offices

Overview

Attorneys seeking federal employment often overlook Capitol Hill. That is a mistake. Several thousand lawyers work for Congress in its members' personal offices, its committees and subcommittees, and its agencies and support offices. Yes, Congress has agencies just like the executive branch. Not as many, certainly, but their number has grown steadily over time.

In addition to lawyers with the job title "attorney," there are more than 1,500 legislative analysts and legislative directors serving on members' personal staffs, many of whom have law degrees. These positions are often great stepping-stones to attorney jobs elsewhere on and off the Hill.

Politics v. Merit Hiring

Naturally, since we are talking about the branch of government where most of the professional politicians reside, politics can play a huge role in the hiring of attorneys (or anyone else). That means that "knowing" someone can give your candidacy a big boost. "Knowing" someone does not mean having shaken a senator's hand in a receiving line. However, it also does not mean that you play golf with the senator once a week, either. Many legislative branch employees got their jobs through indirect contacts, such as members of a senator's or representative's personal or committee staff, a lower-level politician from the member's home state or district, or even a law school or college professor who served as an advisor to the member.

Not all legislative branch hiring is politically based. The farther away from the member's personal office you get, the more merit enters into the equation. A larger number of committee and subcommittee lawyers are merit hires. An even larger number of attorneys hired purely on their qualifications and credentials work for congressional support organizations, and virtually every attorney who works for a legislative branch agency is hired on merit alone.

Members' Offices

The 541 members of Congress all have both personal staffs based in Washington, D.C. and state (senators) and district (representatives, et al.) offices "back home." There are 100 senators, 435 voting representatives, five non-voting delegates—Washington, D.C., Guam, American Samoa, U.S. Virgin Islands, Northern Mariana Islands—and one resident commissioner (Puerto Rico). Some of these personal staffs are quite large. This is especially true of senators from the larger states, who may have as many as 90–100 personal staff employees.

Representatives may employ up to 18 permanent employees, plus four additional employees (interns, part-time employees, shared employees, temporary employees, and employees on leave without pay). The House and Senate appropriate an amount each year to each member for staffing purposes. Then, it is up to the congressperson to decide how this money should be allocated among his or her staff, up to a limit established by the Speaker for House members and by the full Senate for senators.. Each member is the employing authority; the member determines the terms and conditions of employment and service for his or her staff.

Two caveats:

1. Congressional staff salaries are generally quite low. Members tend to think that the privilege of working for them on matters of national importance is compensation enough. Do not buy into this completely. How good your staff experience will look on your resume depends on factors beyond merely having worked in a member's office. What you did, and for whom, is just as important. Some members are simply more important than others.

2. Be careful to scope out what your responsibilities will be before accepting a member personal staff job offer. Occasionally, new employees, including some with rather exalted job titles, find themselves performing a disproportionate number of clerical tasks. While this is fairly rare, it is not completely unusual. One of my legal career transition counseling clients gave up a position as a bank general counsel to come to Washington, D.C. at the behest of his senator to serve in a very senior position in the senator's office, only to find himself spending months writing Christmas cards to constituents for his senator's signature. Following the holiday season, he spent the bulk of his workday answering constituent phone calls and letters. He resigned after six months and returned to his home state.

The vast majority of attorneys who work in member offices in Washington or in the member's home state or congressional district do not possess the job title "attorney." Rather, they principally serve in positions labeled Chief of Staff, Legislative Director, Legislative Analyst, or Legislative Correspondent if in Washington, or State or District Director, Constituent Services Representative, Field Representative, Caseworker, or something else if they are back in the home state or district. It is up to the member to assign job titles.

Chapter 15

The Legislative Branch— Congressional Committees and Subcommittees

Congress divides its tasks among around 200 committees and subcommittees. The Senate and House have similar committee systems, but each has its own guidelines, within which each committee adopts its own rules, including how it goes about hiring staff. This creates considerable variation among the panels.

Most committees and subcommittees employ attorneys, and in the aggregate, committees and subcommittees employ numerous attorneys. Certain committees, such as the Senate and House Judiciary Committees and the House Ways and Means Committee, are heavily staffed with attorneys.

Standing committees generally have legislative jurisdiction. Subcommittees handle specific areas of the committee's work. Select and joint committees generally handle oversight or housekeeping responsibilities.

The chair of each committee and a majority of its members represent the majority party. The chair largely controls committee business. Each party assigns its own members to committees, and each committee distributes its members among its subcommittees.

83

Committees receive their operating funds from congressional appropriations, and the funds vary from committee to committee. Staffing levels are also not uniform. Each committee hires its own staff, with the majority party controlling most committee staff and resources, but sharing a portion of the funding with the minority.

Standing committees are permanent committees established under the standing rules of the House or Senate and specialize in particular subject areas.

Joint committees include membership from both houses. Joint committees are usually established with narrow jurisdictions and normally lack authority to report legislation. The chairmanship of joint committees usually alternates between the House and Senate with each new Congress.

Special or select committees are established by the Senate or House for a limited time period to perform a particular study or investigation. Like so many purportedly temporary federal organizations, many such committees continue in existence much longer than initially contemplated. These committees might be given or denied authority to report legislation to the Senate.

Subcommittees are sub-units of a larger committee that specialize in specific areas and help to divide a committee's workload. Subcommittee recommendations must be approved by the entire committee before being reported to the Senate.

The work of committee and subcommittee staffs is much more substantive than what goes on in members' personal offices, where constituent casework can take up a lot of staff time. Committee work is largely concerned with developing, considering, and marking up legislation; undertaking investigations; and holding legislative, confirmation, investigatory, and oversight hearings.

Committee and subcommittee staffers are usually hired because of political connections, but often merit plays a role, too. Sometimes, merit is the paramount consideration due to the importance of the work and closer scrutiny by the media, as compared to member offices. The Judiciary and Armed Services Committees of both Houses, the House Ways and Means Committee, and the Senate Foreign Relations Committee have hired one or more of my counseling clients purely on merit.

Senate Committees

Standing Committees

- Agriculture, Nutrition, and Forestry
- Appropriations
- Armed Services
- Banking, Housing, and Urban Affairs
- Budget
- Commerce, Science, and Transportation
- Energy and Natural Resources
- Environment and Public Works
- Finance
- Foreign Relations
- Health, Education, Labor, and Pensions
- Homeland Security and Governmental Affairs
- Judiciary
- Rules and Administration
- Small Business and Entrepreneurship
- Veterans' Affairs

Special, Select, and Other Committees

- Impeachment Trial Committee (Porteous)
- Indian Affairs
- Select Committee on Ethics
- Select Committee on Intelligence
- Special Committee on Aging

Joint Senate-House Committees

- Joint Committee on Printing
- Joint Committee on Taxation
- Joint Committee on the Library
- Joint Economic Committee

House Committees

- Committee on Agriculture
- Committee on Appropriations

- Committee on Armed Services
- Committee on the Budget
- Committee on Education and Labor
- Committee on Energy and Commerce
- Committee on Financial Services
- Committee on Foreign Affairs
- Committee on Homeland Security
- Committee on House Administration
- Committee on the Judiciary
- Committee on Natural Resources
- Committee on Oversight and Government Reform
- Committee on Rules
- Committee on Science and Technology
- Committee on Small Business
- Committee on Standards of Official Conduct
- Committee on Transportation and Infrastructure
- Committee on Veterans' Affairs
- Committee on Ways and Means
- House Permanent Select Committee on Intelligence
- House Select Committee on Energy Independence and Global Warming

Chapter 16

The Legislative Branch— Congressional Support Offices and Member Organizations

Congressional Support Offices

Congressional support offices are also worth mining for legal and law-related job opportunities. These offices support the activities of Congress in much the same manner that corporate support offices support a corporation.

The following is a review of congressional support organizations that have attorneys on staff.

Senate Office of Legislative Counsel—established by law in 1919 to assist "in drafting public bills and resolutions or amendments thereto" upon the request of any senator, committee, or office of the Senate. The office is strictly nonpartisan and provides legislative drafting services for Senate committees and both majority and minority members. The Legislative Counsel is appointed by the president pro tempore of the Senate "solely on the basis of his or her qualifications to perform the duties of the position" (take this and other similar statements applying to support offices with at least a grain of salt). The Legislative Counsel appoints senior counsels, assistant counsels, support staff, and other employees. All appointments are made without regard to political affiliation and are subject to the approval of the president pro tempore.

In 2010, the office had 36 attorneys with annual salaries ranging between $72,500 and $172,500.

Office of Senate Legal Counsel—established in 1979 by the Ethics in Government Act, Pub. L. 95-521, the office handles legal matters and litigation on behalf of the Senate. It is basically the in-house law firm that represents and defends the Senate's constitutional powers and the separation of powers. The Counsel and Deputy Counsel are appointed by the president pro tempore of the Senate, "without regard to political affiliation and solely on the basis of fitness to perform the duties of the position," from among recommendations submitted by the majority and minority leaders. The Counsel appoints assistant Senate legal counsels. As this book goes to press, the office has four attorneys earning between $149,500 and $172,500.

Office of the Secretary of the Senate—dates from 1789 and supervises the many offices and services that manage the day-to-day operations of the U.S. Senate, including clerks, curators, computers, payrolls, certain acquisitions, the education of the Senate pages, and the maintenance of public records. Office responsibilities include legislative, financial, and administrative functions.

Legal and law-related functions include:

- The *Executive Office* employs two attorneys earning $169,400 and $85,000, respectively (as this book goes to press).
- The *Chief Counsel for Employment* provides legal advice to, and represents, Senate offices in employment law matters and lawsuits under the Congressional Accountability Act, Pub. L. 104-1, which brings the Senate under 11 federal laws regulating the employer-employee relationship. In 2010, this office employed 10 attorneys earning between $124,400 and $169,400.

- The *Parliamentarian* advises the presiding officer, senators and their staffs, committee staffs, representatives and their staffs, administration officials, the media, and members of the general public on all matters requiring an interpretation of the Senate's Standing Rules, precedents, unanimous consent agreements, and provisions of public law affecting Senate proceedings. In the name of the presiding officer, the parliamentarian refers to the appropriate Senate committees all legislation, messages, communications, reports from the executive branch, and petitions and memorials from state legislatures and private citizens. This office employs four professionals earning between $123,500 and $171,300.

- *House Office of the Administrative Counsel*—advises the Chief Administrative Officer and the office staff on whether the actions of the organization conform to applicable laws regarding the proper use of government funds, procurement guidelines, and Congressional Accountability Act issues, and reviews member district office and vehicle leases to ensure compliance with Committee on House Administration regulations. In 2010, this office employed three attorneys earning between $128,000 and $168,400.

- *Office of House Employment Counsel*—provides advice about employment practices and acts as legal representative for all employing authorities in the House. The office is available to provide advice and guidance on employment matters generally, and on establishing office policies consistent with the specific employment laws that apply to House employing offices under the Congressional Accountability Act, Pub. L. 104-1 (Fair Labor Standards Act, Pub. L. 81-393; Title VII of the Civil Rights Act of 1964, Pub. L. 88-352; Americans with Disabilities Act, Pub. L. 101-336; Age Discrimination in Employment Act, Pub. L. 90-202; Family and Medical Leave Act, Pub. L. 103-3; Employee Polygraph Protection Act, Pub. L. 100-347; Worker Adjustment and Retraining Notification Act, Pub. L. 100-379; Rehabilitation Act of 1973, Pub. L. 93-112; Uniformed Services Employment and Reemployment Rights Act, Pub. L. 103-353; Federal Labor-Management Relations Act, Pub. L. 80-

101; public service and accommodations provisions of the Americans with Disabilities Act; and the Occupational Safety and Health Act of 1970, Pub. L. 91-596). In 2010, this office employs seven attorneys earning between $135,500 and $168,400.

- *House Office of the Law Revision Counsel* prepares and publishes the *United States Code*, the consolidation and codification by subject matter of the general and permanent laws of the United States.

- *House Office of Legislative Counsel* assists committees and members of the House of Representatives in the drafting of proposed legislation on an impartial and confidential basis and by request. The office consists of approximately 40 attorneys and is headed by the Legislative Counsel of the House, who is appointed by the Speaker of the House and, subject to the approval of the Speaker, appoints and fixes the compensation of the office's personnel.

  The operation of the office is in many ways unique among governmental offices. There are no formal committees or departments. Attorneys in the office naturally develop special expertise in certain areas of the law.

  While a new Legislative Counsel may be appointed whenever control of the House changes, the attorney staff usually does not turn over. Most of the attorneys are hired on a merit basis and develop strong legislative drafting expertise that makes them extremely valuable employees.

Other congressional support offices with attorneys on staff include:

- Congressional Executive Commission on China
- Commission on Security and Cooperation in Europe (Helsinki Commission)
- House Democracy Partnership Commission

Please note that the above list includes only offices with positions labeled "attorney" or "counsel" (with the exception of the four Parliamentarian positions, which have been—off and on—filled by attorneys). There are, in addition, numerous other attorneys serving in congressional support offices under other job titles, such as Contract Administrator, Policy Advisor, Legislative Clerk, Consultant, etc.

Although merit-based hiring is more prevalent among congressional support offices than in either member offices or committee and subcommittee staffs, this does not mean that political connections do not boost a candidate's chances. They do. However, some of these offices require a fairly high level of technical legal expertise. The House Office of Law Revision Counsel, for example, requires individuals who understand, on a very sophisticated level, the legislative process and how public laws, statutes at large, and codification into the United States Code all relate. Both the Senate and the House Offices of Legislative Counsel employ attorneys in drafting legislation. The Office of the Senate Legal Counsel needs litigators. Consequently, these offices are somewhat more focused on merit hiring.

Congressional Member Organizations ("Caucuses")

Caucuses are informal congressional groups and organizations of members with shared interests in specific issues or philosophies. These groups typically organize without official recognition by the chamber and are not funded through the appropriation process.

Caucuses exist to discuss issues of mutual concern and possibly to perform legislative research and policy planning for their members. There are regional, political or ideological, ethnic, and economic-based caucuses.

As of this writing, there are 288 Congressional Member Organizations, more commonly known as congressional caucuses. The reason I cite the number is because these are the most ephemeral of federal organizations that employ attorneys in both legal and law-related positions. Some do not even last through the entire two years of a Congress.

Selected examples of 111th Congress Member Organizations include:

- Algae Energy Caucus
- Bipartisan Coalition for Combating Anti-Semitism

- Children's Environmental Health Caucus
- House Long-Term Care Coalition
- Unexploded Ordnance Caucus

In the Senate there is one officially recognized caucus—the Senate Caucus on International Narcotics Control, established by law in 1985.

You can see from just this very short list that the common thread that runs through these organizations is their single-issue orientation. This explains their transitory nature. If an issue wanes in significance or if members lose interest, then the caucus tends to disappear.

There is no uniformity among caucuses with respect to where they get their funding or how they recruit and hire staff. The House Committee on House Administration makes the rules by which caucuses are formed and governed. Caucuses cross chamber lines and may consist of both representatives and senators. Caucuses get their funding from either members' allowances or their personal funds. Political connections can loom quite large in caucus hiring.

Chapter 17

The Legislative Branch— Legislative Branch Agencies

This brings us to the last employer category in the federal legislative branch, the legislative branch agencies. These organizations bear the closest resemblance of any legislative branch entities to executive branch departments and agencies, and their hiring practices do not differ very much from what you encounter in the executive branch. The overwhelming majority of legal positions in these agencies are filled on a purely merit basis.

Library of Congress

The Library of Congress has many more offices that employ attorneys than any other legislative branch agency. They include:

Office of Counsel to the Inspector General

The Office of Inspector General (IG) is the internal "watchdog" for the Library of Congress, focusing on identifying and recommending means of rectifying waste, fraud, mismanagement, and abuse. The very small Office of Counsel to the IG serves as the IG's independent legal advisor.

U.S. Copyright Office

Office of the General Counsel

The Office of the General Counsel has primary responsibility for coordinating legal matters between the Copyright Office and Congress, the Department of Justice and other government agencies, the courts, the legal community, and a wide range of interests affected by copyright law.

Office of the Register of Copyrights

The Register of Copyrights administers the copyright law, advises Congress, drafts legislation, and prepares technical studies. The Associate Register for Policy and International Affairs provides legal advice and counsel to the Register. The Register's office also oversees the administration of the Copyright Arbitration Royalty Panel (CARP) process.

Congressional Research Service

Congressional Research Service (CRS) experts assist at every stage of the legislative process—from the early considerations that precede bill drafting through committee hearings, mark-ups, and floor debate, to the oversight of enacted laws and various agency activities. CRS's analytic capabilities integrate multiple disciplines and research methodologies. Its work incorporates program and legislative expertise, quantitative methodologies, and legal and economic analysis.

CRS services come in many forms:

- tailored confidential memoranda, briefings, and consultations
- expert congressional testimony
- reports on current legislative issues available 24/7 via a website
- the Legislative Information System (LIS)
- seminars and workshops, including the twice yearly Federal Law Update

- training for congressional staff in legislative and budget procedures
- a premier work in constitutional law, *Constitution of the United States of America, Analysis and Interpretation*

CRS has nearly 700 employees, including more than 450 policy analysts, attorneys, information professionals, and experts in a variety of disciplines—from law, economics, and foreign affairs to defense and homeland security, public administration, education, health care, immigration, energy, environmental protection, and science and technology.

CRS is divided into five interdisciplinary research divisions. However, the one that is home to almost all of the CRS attorneys is the American Law Division.

American Law Division

The American Law Division's work addresses the many legal questions that arise in a legislative context or are otherwise of interest to Congress. The vast majority of CRS attorneys work for this division.

Some issues relate to the institutional prerogatives of Congress under the Constitution. Other questions involve constitutional and legal principles of statutory analysis that cross legislative policy areas, such as federalism, commerce powers, and individual rights. The division also focuses on the intricacies of legal precedent and statutory construction as they relate to business, crime, the environment, civil rights, international law, and other issues. Its reports and memoranda are used by members and committees of Congress in their legislative deliberations and decision making.

The division comprises five research sections:

- Administrative Law
- Business
- Congress
- Courts and International
- Natural Resources

Other CRS Divisions

CRS has four other interdisciplinary divisions parallel to the American Law Division:

- Domestic Social Policy
- Foreign Affairs, Defense and Trade
- Government and Finance
- Resources, Science and Industry

A handful of attorneys can be found in these divisions.

Office of Congressional Affairs and Counselor to the Director

The Office of Congressional Affairs and Counselor to the Director plans, develops, and coordinates matters relating to internal CRS policies, particularly as they affect the Service's relationships with congressional clients and other legislative support agencies. The office staff includes a handful of attorneys.

Law Library of Congress

The Library of Congress began its existence in 1801 essentially as a collection of law books donated by Thomas Jefferson. In 1832, Congress ordered the 2,011 law books of the Library of Congress (639 of which had been part of Jefferson's private library) separated from its general collection, and the Law Library of Congress was thereby established. Its mission is to provide research and legal information to the U.S. Congress as well as to the federal courts and executive branch agencies, and to offer reference services to the public.

The Law Library's collection of legal materials is the largest and most comprehensive in the world, covering all of the approximately 260 existing nations and dependencies as well as many former nations and colonies. In addition to U.S. federal and state materials, the Law Library houses an unparalleled collection of foreign codes, constitutions, official gazettes, law reports, treatises, serials, and international and comparative legal items, and laws from all historical periods—from ancient law to space law.

The Law Library's foreign law specialists serve primarily as the foreign law research arm of Congress, but its reference and legal specialist staff also provide American law reference and foreign law research and reference to other branches of government and to the public. Although there are attorneys working in the Law Library who are reference librarians specializing in American law, most have professional legal training and experience in the foreign jurisdiction for which they have research responsibility. These foreign law specialists provide information and analysis on a wide range of complex issues of law in response to congressional requests which affect national and international interests; provide legal opinions for governmental agencies and the courts on issues of foreign law; author legal and related reports, studies, and articles for publication; and must be able to translate legal material into English and from English into foreign languages as required.

Dispute Resolution Center

The Library of Congress's Dispute Resolution Center (DRC) was established in 1991 and is staffed by a number of attorneys. It was one of the first alternative dispute resolution (ADR) organizations in the federal government. The Library of Congress has established ADR agreements with both its union and its non-bargaining unit (non-union) employees. Each agreement recommends the use of mediation to resolve workplace disputes whether they are equal employment opportunity complaints, grievances, or a category designated as "other."

The Library encourages its employees to resolve their issues directly through informal discussions or through mediation facilitated by DRC conveners. Over its two-decade existence, the DRC has been quite successful in defusing and resolving workplace disputes and has served as a model for the rest of the government and beyond.

Government Accountability Office

The U.S. Government Accountability Office (GAO) is a legislative branch agency that takes its direction from Congress. Congress asks GAO to study federal programs and expenditures, investigate programs, and report back to it about them, usually with recommendations for improvement. GAO is independent and nonpartisan.

The agency's principal mission is to study how the federal government spends taxpayer dollars. GAO advises Congress and the heads of executive agencies about ways to make government more effective and responsive. GAO evaluates federal programs, audits federal expenditures, issues legal opinions, and decides certain claims against the government. GAO's work often leads to laws that improve government operations and save taxpayer dollars.

The majority of GAO's program and agency audits and evaluations are conducted in response to specific congressional requests. It is required to perform work requested by committee chairs and, as a matter of policy, assigns equal status to requests from both the majority and minority. Other assignments are initiated pursuant to standing commitments to congressional committees, and some GAO reviews are specifically required by law. Finally, some assignments are independently undertaken in accordance with GAO's basic legislative responsibilities.

The broad scope of GAO's mission requires a multidisciplinary staff able to conduct assignments wherever needed. Consequently, the agency consists of attorneys, accountants, public and business administration professionals, economists, and social and physical scientists, among other experts.

GAO staff members concentrate on specific subject areas, enabling them to develop a detailed level of knowledge and expertise. Staff members go wherever necessary on assignments, working onsite to gather data and observe in person how government programs and activities are carried out.

Legal Services

GAO's Office of General Counsel (OGC) reviews legislative proposals before the Congress, reports to the Congress on proposed rescissions and deferrals of government funds, and assists in drafting legislation. In connection with congressional reviews of federal rulemaking, OGC prepares reports on all major rules for congressional committees and maintains a database of all rules received for review. OGC also resolves bid protests that challenge government contract awards because, by statute, the Comptroller General (the head of GAO) is required to decide disputes concerning the award of federal contracts. OGC's 130 attorneys advise GAO evaluators in reviews of federal programs, provide legal opinions to Congress and federal agencies, testify before congressional committees, brief members of Congress and congressional staff, draft legislation, render bid protest decisions, and advise GAO senior management.

Personnel Appeals Board

GAO's other legal office is the Personnel Appeals Board (PAB), an independent agency created to afford GAO employees essentially the same rights that employees in the executive branch enjoy. The Personnel Appeals Board and its Office of General Counsel combine the adjudicatory functions of the executive branch's Merit Systems Protection Board (MSPB), the Federal Labor Relations Authority (FLRA), and the Equal Employment Opportunity Commission (EEOC), as well as the investigatory and prosecutorial functions of the Office of Special Counsel and the FLRA General Counsel. The board adjudicates disputes concerning personnel actions or alleging discrimination; the PAB's Office of General Counsel investigates and prosecutes alleged violations in those areas. The board also has the authority to adjudicate unfair labor practices, but, in the absence of a union, does not do so. In addition, the board has oversight authority for equal employment opportunity in GAO's practices and programs.

GAO's professional investigators conduct special investigations and assist auditors and evaluators when they encounter possible criminal or civil misconduct.

GAO Reports, Comptroller General Decisions, and GAO special publications may be obtained on the Internet at www.gao.gov.

Government Printing Office

Created primarily to satisfy the printing needs of Congress, the Government Printing Office (GPO) today is the focal point for printing, binding, and information dissemination for the entire federal government. Congressional documents, census forms, federal regulations and reports, IRS tax forms, and U.S. passports are all produced by or through GPO in a wide range of formats, including printing, microfiche, CD-ROM, and online technology through GPO Access (www.gpo.gov/gpoaccess).

GPO operates like a business. It is reimbursed by its government customers for the cost of work performed. However, GPO also receives two modest appropriations, one to pay for the cost of congressional printing and the other to fund the distribution of government documents as required by law.

Office of the General Counsel

The Office of the General Counsel (OGC) serves as legal advisor to the Public Printer (the head of GPO) and provides legal services to support GPO operations and activities. GPO attorneys represent the agency before the EEOC, the MSPB, and other administrative tribunals; they also assist the U.S. Department of Justice in court cases involving GPO and/or its officials. They review selected procurement contracts, represent the agency in contract and claims disputes, and represent GPO on procurement matters before GAO and the various federal boards of contract appeals. They also review all laws and proposed legislation affecting GPO; review and make recommendations on equal employment opportunity complaints; review the legality and impact of various labor-management proposals; and review for legal sufficiency all agreements and memorandums of understanding to which GPO is a party.

Office of Administration and Counsel—Office of Inspector General

The Office of Administration and Counsel in the GPO Office of Inspector General provides independent legal advice and services to the Inspector General and staff, and serves as liaison to the GPO Office of General Counsel, GPO management, and other federal agencies.

Architect of the Capitol

The Architect of the Capitol is the builder, caretaker, and curator of all of the buildings that constitute the congressional presence on Capitol Hill. These include the Capitol, the new Capitol Visitor Center, Senate Office Buildings, House Office Buildings, Supreme Court,

Library of Congress, Law Library of Congress, U.S. Botanic Garden, and Capitol Campus grounds.

The Architect of the Capitol is a surprisingly large agency, with 2,600 employees.

Office of the General Counsel

The Office of the General Counsel (OGC) is a small legal office that provides advice and services in three broad areas: internal administrative functions, activities for which the Architect has legal responsibility, and litigation. In the first category, OGC advises on procurement, fiscal, budgetary, and personnel matters. In the second category, OGC prepares draft legislation affecting the office; provides advice on issues arising from the Architect's statutory responsibility for superintendence of the buildings and grounds of the Legislative Complex, including claims arising under the Federal Tort Claims Act, Pub. L. 79-601; and provides legal review of contracts for the procurement of materials, supplies, and services. In the third area, OGC provides advice and support with respect to litigation brought or defended by the Architect of the Capitol, particularly with respect to litigation arising out of construction contracts in which the Architect of the Capitol serves as contracting officer.

OGC also represents the Architect in congressional and administrative hearings and, when necessary, arranges for representation of the agency in judicial proceedings by retained counsel or by Justice Department attorneys.

Office of the Employment Counsel for the United States Capitol Police Board

The Office of the Employment Counsel for the United States Capitol Police Board is a relatively self-explanatory, separate legal office within the Architect of the Capitol that deals with employment issues arising within the federal police force charged with protecting Congress while in D.C. Recent legislation authorizes the appointment of a General Counsel to the Chief of Police and the U.S. Capitol Police.

Congressional Budget Office

The Congressional Budget Office's mandate is to provide Congress with objective, nonpartisan, and timely analyses to aid in economic and budgetary decisions on the wide array of programs covered by the federal budget and the information and estimates required for the congressional budget process. CBO currently employs about 250 people, consisting primarily of economists and public policy analysts. CBO's Office of General Counsel currently has three attorneys.

Chapter 18

The Judicial Branch—
Overview and Career Paths

Overview

The judicial branch is becoming as much of an intricate bureaucracy as the executive and legislative branches. It surprises many federal legal employment candidates to discover that the judicial branch has more than 100 law offices scattered throughout the country and found both within federal courts and outside of them. Several thousand attorneys work for the judicial branch in a variety of different capacities. These include working directly for judges as judicial law clerks, "elbow law clerks," or something similar; in court staff attorney offices, court support offices, federal public defender or community defender offices, or in one of the central offices that serve the judicial branch, such as the Administrative Office of the U.S. Courts, Federal Judicial Center, Judicial Conference of the United States, Judicial Panel on Multidistrict Litigation, or the U.S. Sentencing Commission.

Brief descriptions of these legal functions and offices follow.

Justices and Judges

The Constitution sets forth no specific qualification requirements for federal judges. Appointments to the federal bench are highly political, although it is rare that merit considerations do not enter into the equation. These are presidential appointments requiring the advice and consent of the U.S. Senate. The names of potential nominees are often recommended by senators and sometimes by members of the House of Representatives from the President's political party. Federal judgeships are life appointments.

There are currently approximately 866 federal judges serving on the U.S. Supreme Court, the circuit courts of appeal, the U.S. district courts, and the Court of International Trade. The number is very fluid, however, due to retirements, deaths, and vacancies.

Court of appeals and district court judgeships are created by act of Congress. The Judicial Conference assesses judgeship needs of each court every other year and presents its recommendations to Congress. Its most recent recommendations (2009) were for an additional nine court of appeals judges and 38 district court judges.

Judicial pay in 2010 is as follows:

- District Court Judge—$174,000
- Court of Appeals Judge—$184,500
- Supreme Court Associate Justice—$213,900
- Chief Justice of the United States—$223,500

Bankruptcy Judges

U.S. bankruptcy judges are judicial officers of the U.S. district courts. They are appointed by the majority of judges of the U.S. court of appeals of their judicial circuit to exercise jurisdiction over bankruptcy matters. Bankruptcy judges are appointed for 14-year terms. The number of bankruptcy judges is determined by Congress. The Judicial Conference of the United States is required to submit recommendations from time to time regarding the number of bankruptcy judges needed.

There are currently 352 bankruptcy judges authorized and funded by Congress. In 2010, a bankruptcy judge earns $160,000.

U.S. Magistrate Judges

U.S. magistrate judges are judicial officers of the U.S. district courts, appointed by majority vote of the active district judges of the court to exercise jurisdiction over matters assigned by statute as well as those delegated by the district judges. Duties assigned to magistrate judges by district court judges may vary considerably from court to court. A full-time magistrate judge serves a term of eight years. The number of magistrate judge positions is determined by the Judicial Conference of the United States, based on recommendations of the respective district courts, the judicial councils of the circuits, and the director of the Administrative Office of the U.S. Courts.

There are currently 521 full-time magistrate judges. In 2010, a magistrate judge earns $160,000.

Judicial Clerkships

There are approximately 2,000 law clerks assisting the judges of both the U.S. circuit and district courts. Federal judicial law clerks are usually recruited from among law students who then typically begin their one- or two-year clerkships with federal court judges in the fall after graduating from law school. Some judges hire one new law clerk for a two-year term every year, so that there is always one person who has had the job at least for one year, and the senior law clerk can help to train the junior one. Whether law clerks are given term or career appointments is a matter of the individual judge's style; some judges prefer a long-term working relationship.

In recent years, the traditional law clerk system has undergone some changes. For example, a number of judges now hire young lawyers with one or more years of practice experience rather than new law school graduates, preferring a more mature clerk with some practical experience.

These are highly competitive positions and are among the most sought-after in the legal profession. Federal judicial clerkships can lead to Supreme Court clerkships, teaching positions in top law schools, and associate positions with top law firms.

Federal judges have come to rely heavily on their clerks. A law clerk's responsibilities typically include reviewing the submissions of the parties; legal research and cite-checking; coordinating with the lawyers on case-scheduling and related matters; and drafting memoranda for the judge summarizing the facts of the case, the litigants' arguments, and a suggested holding. Some judges ask their clerks to write a first draft of the judicial opinion; others ask their clerks to review, edit, and comment on the judge's draft. Many judges discuss pending cases with their clerks and debate possible rulings. District and bankruptcy court clerks generally have much more diverse responsibilities than appellate court clerks, whose primary duties are legal research and writing, though duties can vary significantly from one judge to another.

Currently, Supreme Court justices are entitled to hire four law clerks each (though some hire only three); court of appeals judges have three clerks, district court judges two, and bankruptcy and magistrate judges are allotted one law clerk position. However, each judge is also permitted to hire a secretary or administrative assistant for chambers, and some judges choose instead to use these funds for an additional law clerk, with the clerks assuming administrative tasks (such as answering the phone and scheduling conferences) in addition to legal work. Appointments are for up to two-year terms. Senior judges (judges who are nominally retired) usually have one law clerk, and terms are generally indefinite.

Judicial law clerk compensation depends upon legal work experience after law school, bar membership, and applicable locality pay adjustments. The federal judiciary uses the same locality pay schedules as the executive branch. The hiring judge sets the clerk's base salary at the time of appointment.

Most recent law school graduates with academic excellence qualify for an appointment at least at grade JSP-11, step 1 (annual base salary of $50,287 in 2010). One year of post-graduate legal experience and bar membership qualifies the appointee for a grade JSP-12, step 1 appointment with an annual base salary of $60,274 in 2010. An appointee with two years of post-graduate work experience, plus bar membership, qualifies for appointment at JSP-13, step 1, with an annual base salary of $71,674 in 2010. Three years of post-graduate work experience (with at least two years as a judicial law clerk, staff attorney, pro se law clerk, death penalty law clerk, or bankruptcy appellate panel law clerk, in the federal judiciary, plus bar membership), qualifies for appointment at JSP-14, step 1, with an annual base salary of $84,697 in 2010.

Career Law Clerks

Career law clerks, who are hired with the expectation that they will serve for an extended period, are much less common than judicial law clerks. They are appointed for four or more years. Their duties depend on what their judge assigns them, and their compensation depends on their experience and is set by the judge.

Temporary Law Clerk Appointments

Occasionally, emergency situations require a judge to obtain additional law clerk assistance for a limited period of time and with a specific termination date. Clerks appointed for one year or less are not eligible for health, dental, vision, and life insurance coverage; retirement; participation in the judiciary's flexible spending accounts; or the thrift savings account. A temporary law clerk appointed for more than one year is eligible for all such benefits except participation in the retirement system or the thrift savings plan.

Death Penalty Law Clerks

These U.S. district court positions assist federal district and magistrate judges in the post-conviction habeas corpus review of state death penalty cases. Responsibilities of the position include, but are not necessarily limited to, conducting research, performing substantive screening, and drafting appropriate recommendations and orders. Maximum starting salary is generally around $66,000.

"Elbow" Law Clerks

Elbow law clerk is a term sometimes used to refer to the law clerks who work in judges' chambers. It suggests the closeness of the working relationship between judge and law clerk; the law clerk is, figuratively and sometimes literally, "at the judge's elbow," unlike other clerks and lawyers who work for the court in other capacities.

Elbow clerk positions are usually term-limited, with the possibility of numerous extensions. Duties usually include legal research and drafting memoranda, jury instructions, and initial drafts of opinions.

Staff Attorneys

Staff attorneys work for the court, not a particular judge, under the supervision of a senior attorney, and are available to all of the judges. Central staff attorneys play an integral role in the federal courts of appeal, with this practice developing in an effort to cope with extremely burdensome caseloads.

Staff attorneys are used by the various courts of appeals in a number of different ways. Some courts use staff attorneys to screen and make preliminary determinations, including on *pro se* (self-represented) submissions, prisoner petitions, and sentencing appeals. Staff attorneys are often asked to review cases for jurisdictional issues or to assess which cases are appropriate for oral argument and full decision on the merits, versus those that can be disposed of on the papers that have been submitted to the court. Some staff attorneys also assist with the preparation of written opinions.

Clerks of Court

The responsibilities of clerks of court have expanded greatly as the business of the U.S. courts has evolved. These responsibilities include case processing, management (of court records, budget, equipment, and personnel), automation, statistics (collecting and reporting court statistical information), and courtroom services. Clerks of court also oversee the court's interaction with the community, including ensuring that court services are delivered in a courteous and efficient manner and providing public education about the courts to schools and citizens. Clerks also supply information to the news media, keeping reporters informed about the business of the courts and providing access to public records and information.

As the responsibilities of the clerk's office have become more demanding, there has been increased diversification and professionalization of court staff in both the district and appellate courts. Clerks of court are now assisted by deputy clerks, docket clerks, case managers, automation specialists, and others (the precise number of which is based on a calculation made by the Administrative Office that takes into consideration the number of judges and court caseload).

The clerk of court remains the primary administrative liaison between the judges and a court's administrative infrastructure. While a law or management degree is not a professional prerequisite for this position, a growing number of clerks of court are attorneys and/or have advanced degrees in business or court management.

Federal Defender Organization Positions

For 40 years, federal judicial districts have been authorized to establish federal defender organizations as counterparts to federal prosecutors in U.S. Attorneys Offices, and as an institutional resource for providing defense counsel in those districts (or combinations of adjacent districts) where at least 200 persons annually require appointment of counsel. Today, there are 79 authorized federal defender organizations. They employ more than 3,300 lawyers, investigators, paralegals, and support personnel and serve 90 of the 94 federal judicial districts. There are two types of federal defender organizations: Federal Public Defender organizations and Community Defender organizations.

Federal Public Defender Organizations

Federal Public Defender organizations are federal entities, and their staffs are federal employees. The chief Federal Public Defender is appointed to a four-year term by the court of appeals of the circuit in which the organization is located.

Community Defender Organizations

Community Defender organizations are nonprofit defense counsel organizations incorporated under state laws. When designated in the Criminal Justice Act (Pub. L. 98-473) plan for the federal judicial district in which they operate, Community Defender organizations receive initial and sustaining grants from the federal judiciary to fund their operations. Community Defender organizations operate under the supervision of a board of directors and may be a branch or division of a parent nonprofit legal services corporation that provides representation to the poor in state, county, and municipal courts.

Federal Defender Job Descriptions

Federal Public Defender. The Federal Public Defender is the head of the office. Requirements generally include a minimum of five years of criminal practice experience, preferably with significant federal criminal trial experience, and supervisory ability.

Executive Director, Community Defender Organization. The Executive Director is responsible for the organization and staffing of the office, manages the program, and often also carries a substantial caseload.

Assistant Federal Public Defender. This is the most prevalent attorney position in the Federal Public Defender system. Duties include representing indigent criminal defendants at both the trial and appellate levels. Salaries are typically based on experience and are commensurate with that of similarly qualified and experienced Assistant U.S. Attorneys in the judicial district.

Assistant Federal Defender—Capital Habeas Unit. Habeas Unit Assistant Federal Defenders provide evidentiary hearing and appellate representation of prisoners on death row who are challenging their convictions and/or sentences in federal post-conviction proceedings. They may also contribute to the organization's training and support programs for private attorneys involved in representation of indigent federal defendants.

Federal Defender Sentencing Counsel. This is an Assistant Federal Defender position that provides consultation and advice to support the Defender Guidelines Committee in carrying out the statutory responsibility of the Federal Defenders—to submit comments to the U.S. Sentencing Commission on the operation of the Federal Sentencing Guidelines and the work of the Commission. Sentencing Counsel formulate and fashion sentencing policy with the Defender Guidelines Committee and the defender community, interact with the Sentencing Commission and other agencies, facilitate communication between the Defender Guidelines Committee and Federal Defenders, and participate in training.

Sentencing Counsel generally have extensive experience with federal sentencing and federal criminal procedure law and practice and a thorough familiarity with federal sentencing policy, preferably through trial and appellate litigation.

Special Litigation Attorney. Duties might include class-action suits to force government agencies to comply with statutory constitutional mandates. Special litigation units anticipate and identify important legal issues affecting Federal Public Defender clients to ensure that those issues are litigated in a comprehensive and strategic manner, consistent with the stated interest of the individual client. Special Litigation Attorneys handle civil and criminal litigation. The attorney works on systemic criminal justice projects in areas such as the reliability of eyewitness testimony, the suppression of exculpatory evidence, and the composition of local jury pools.

Appellate Attorney. Appellate Attorneys provide written and oral advocacy, primarily in criminal appeals and in collateral proceedings ancillary to appellate representation. They also participate as amicus curiae. Other responsibilities include representing clients in post-conviction proceedings, participating in moot courts for colleagues, and advising and training Public Defender and Criminal Justice Act attorneys on legal issues and appellate practice.

Research and Writing Attorney/Specialist. These attorneys provide research and writing assistance to other defender office attorneys, prepare appellate briefs, may participate as second chair in court proceedings, help coordinate office intern programs, and provide reference support to all staff. He or she may also contribute to the organization's training and support programs for private attorneys involved in representation of indigent federal defendants.

Qualifications for this position include excellent research, writing, and advocacy skills; trial and/or appellate experience; computer skills; ability to communicate and work well with others; demonstrated interest in criminal defense issues; and commitment to obtaining justice for indigent persons.

Chapter 19

Judicial Branch—Judicial Branch Agencies

The judicial branch, like its counterparts the executive and legislative branches, also has agencies that handle various non-adjudicative functions necessary for the efficient operation of the federal courts. They are discussed below.

Administrative Office of the U.S. Courts

The Administrative Office is the administrative arm of the federal judiciary. It provides services to the federal courts in three areas: administrative support, program management, and policy development. It implements the policies of the Judicial Conference of the United States and is the focal point for judiciary communication, information, program leadership, and administrative reform.

The Office of the General Counsel provides legal counsel and services to the director and Administrative Office staff, the Judicial Conference of the United States and its committees, federal judges, and court officials. It renders legal opinions on judicial administration issues such as personnel law, judicial benefits, appropriation issues, procurement law, and sentencing and correctional supervision.

The Office of Legislative Affairs is the judiciary's point-of-contact with Congress, other government entities, and private-sector organizations on legislative issues. The office provides legislative counsel and services to the Administrative Office director and staff and the Judicial Conference of the United States and its committees.

Federal Judicial Center

The Federal Judicial Center is the research and education agency of the federal judicial system. Its duties include:

- conducting and promoting orientation and continuing education and training for federal judges, court employees, and others;
- developing recommendations about the operation and study of the federal courts; and
- conducting and promoting research on federal judicial procedures, court operations, and history.

Approximately 25 lawyers work for the Federal Judicial Center.

Judicial Panel on Multidistrict Litigation

The U.S. Judicial Panel on Multidistrict Litigation (1) determines whether, based on one or more common questions of fact, civil actions pending in different federal districts should be transferred to one federal district for coordinated or consolidated pretrial proceedings; and (2) selects the judge or judges and court assigned to conduct such proceedings.

This transfer or "centralization" process is designed to avoid duplication of discovery, prevent inconsistent pretrial rulings, and conserve the resources of the parties, their counsel, and the judiciary.

Since its inception, the Panel has considered motions for centralization in over 2,000 dockets involving more than 300,000 cases and millions of claims. These dockets encompass litigation categories as diverse as airplane crashes and train wrecks; hotel fires; mass torts, such as those involving asbestos, drugs, and other product liability cases; patent validity and infringement; antitrust price-fixing; securities fraud; employment practices; and most recently, actions emanating from the British Petroleum oil blowout in the Gulf of Mexico.

The Multidistrict Litigation Panel consists of seven sitting federal judges appointed by the Chief Justice of the United States. The multidistrict litigation statute provides that no two panel members may be from the same federal judicial circuit.

The permanent staff of the Panel includes a number of attorneys.

U.S. Sentencing Commission

The U.S. Sentencing Commission is an independent agency in the judicial branch. Its principal purposes are:

(1) to establish sentencing policies and practices for the federal courts, including guidelines to be consulted regarding the appropriate form and severity of punishment for offenders convicted of federal crimes;

(2) to advise and assist Congress and the executive branch in the development of effective and efficient crime policy; and

(3) to collect, analyze, research, and distribute a broad array of information on federal crime and sentencing issues, serving as an information resource for Congress, the executive branch, the courts, criminal justice practitioners, the academic community, and the public.

The U.S. Sentencing Commission was created by the Sentencing Reform Act provisions of the Comprehensive Crime Control Act of 1984 (Pub. L. 98-473). The sentencing guidelines established by the Commission are:

- designed to incorporate the purposes of sentencing (i.e., just punishment, deterrence, incapacitation, and rehabilitation);
- provide certainty and fairness in meeting the purposes of sentencing by avoiding unwarranted disparity among offenders with similar characteristics convicted of similar criminal conduct, while permitting sufficient judicial flexibility to take into account relevant aggravating and mitigating factors; and

- reflect, to the extent practicable, advancement in the knowledge of human behavior as it relates to the criminal justice process.

The Commission is charged with the ongoing responsibilities of evaluating the effects of the Sentencing Guidelines on the criminal justice system, recommending to Congress appropriate modifications of substantive criminal law and sentencing procedures, and establishing a research and development program on sentencing issues.

There are two sets of guidelines: Individual Sentencing Guidelines and Organizational Sentencing Guidelines.

Commission attorneys work in the following offices:

- *Office of General Counsel*, providing support to the Commission on a variety of legal issues, including the development and application of the Sentencing Guidelines and guideline amendments, legislative proposals, and statutory interpretation; monitoring district and circuit court application and interpretation of the guidelines and advising commissioners about statutes affecting the Commission's work; and providing training support.
- *Office of Education and Sentencing Practice*, teaching Sentencing Guideline application to judges, probation officers, prosecuting and defense attorneys, and other criminal justice professionals; developing training materials; participating in the Sentencing Guideline segments of training programs sponsored by other agencies; informing the Commission of current guideline application practices; and operating a "HelpLine" to respond to guideline application questions from members of the court community.
- *Office of Policy Analysis*, providing guideline and sentencing-related research and analyses; studying a variety of research topics, including sentencing disparity, projections of the effect of proposed guideline amendments on the federal prison population, sentencing practices related to organizational (corporate) defendants, and appeals; and providing

data and analyses on specific criminal justice issues at the request of Congress, the courts, and others.

- *Office of Special Counsel*, performing all drafting services for the Commission; preparing the *Guidelines Manual* for printing; managing and maintaining all papers and exhibits received by the Commission that constitute requests for Commission action on sentencing policy development; and tracking the Commission's policy initiatives.
- *Office of Monitoring*, maintaining a comprehensive, automated data collection system to report on federal sentencing practices and to track application of the guidelines for individual cases; producing periodic reports about guideline application; providing information for Commission review as it monitors use of the guidelines or considers amending them; and collecting data on appeals, indictments, and Organizational Guideline sentences.

Chapter 20

The Quasi-Federal Sector

While the following organizations are not technically part of the U.S. government, they all share certain commonalities that make them, for want of a better term, public-sector/private-sector "hybrids." These entities are difficult to categorize; one way to view them is as elements of what I call the "hidden" legal job market. To a large extent, their structure and legal work more closely resemble a private-sector corporation than a government agency.

Government-Sponsored Enterprises

For budgetary treatment purposes, Congress has defined the term "government-sponsored enterprise" (GSE) in the Omnibus Reconciliation Act of 1990, Pub. L. 101-508, as follows:

> a corporate entity created by a law of the United States that—
> (A) (i) has a Federal charter authorized by law;
> (ii) is privately owned, as evidenced by capital stock owned by private entities or individuals;
> (iii) is under the direction of a board of directors, a majority of which is elected by private owners;
> (iv) is a financial institution with power to—
> (I) make loans or loan guarantees for limited purposes such

as to provide credit for specific borrowers or one sector; and

(II) raise funds by borrowing (which does not carry the full faith and credit of the Federal Government) or to guarantee the debt of others in unlimited amounts; and

(B) (i) does not exercise powers that are reserved to the Government as sovereign (such as the power to tax or to regulate interstate commerce);

(ii) does not have the power to commit the Government financially (but it may be a recipient of a loan guarantee commitment made by the Government); and

(iii) has employees whose salaries and expenses are paid by the enterprise and are not Federal employees subject to title 5.

What this omits is perhaps the most important feature of a GSE—the huge advantage inherent in the implicit federal guarantee against loss that enhances its borrowing ability by securing lower loan interest rates. At present, there are three GSEs: the investor-owned Federal Agricultural Mortgage Corporation (Farmer Mac), the Federal Home Loan Bank System, and the Farm Credit System, the latter two owned cooperatively by their borrowers.

Fannie, Freddie, and Sallie

Until 2008, there were also three others: the Federal National Mortgage Association (Fannie Mae), the Federal Home Loan Mortgage Corporation (Freddie Mac), and the Student Loan Marketing Association (Sallie Mae). The housing market collapse and subsequent financial meltdown caused the government to take over Fannie and Freddie and put them into receivership. We can debate—and both politicians and economists actually waste a lot of time doing so—whether Fannie and Freddie are still GSEs or something else, but until Congress gets around to the unpleasant task of figuring out what to do with them, they are in a sort of limbo status.

Nevertheless, both former or present GSEs (depending on your take) still have General Counsel Offices as well as a large number of attorneys working in other offices, and are still in a hiring mode.

The eventual status of Fannie Mae and Freddie Mac is still to be determined as this book goes to press. The politically unpleasant prospect of what to do about these institutions that contributed so famously to the "Great Recession" has been tabled for the time being. Consequently, you are well advised to be very careful before accepting a position with either organization until their status is sorted out and stabilized.

Sallie is now a completely private-sector company and is in some trouble now that the government is eliminating student loan middle-men in favor of direct loans to college students. The company recently cut its 8,000-strong staff by 2,500 employees.

Farmer Mac

Farmer Mac (located in Washington, D.C.) has an Office of General Counsel, as does each of the 12 Federal Home Loan Banks (located in Atlanta, Boston, Chicago, Cincinnati, Dallas, Des Moines, Indianapolis, New York, Pittsburgh, San Francisco, Seattle, and Topeka) and the four Farm Credit Banks (Austin, Texas; Columbia, South Carolina; St. Paul, Minnesota; and Wichita, Kansas). In addition, each institution also has compliance officers and other law-related positions.

Federal Home Loan Banks

The Federal Home Loan Banks are 12 regional cooperative banks that U.S. lending institutions use to finance housing and economic development in their communities. Created by Congress, they have been the largest source of funding for community lending for 80 years. The banks provide a stable source of funds to their member institutions through all market cycles. During the current credit crisis, they have actually increased their advances while other funding sources have dried up.

More than 8,000 lenders are members of the Federal Home Loan Bank System, representing approximately 80 percent of the insured U.S. lending institutions. The membership includes community banks, thrifts, commercial banks, credit unions, community development financial institutions, insurance companies, and state housing finance agencies.

To become a member, a financial institution must purchase stock in the Federal Home Loan Bank System. The stock is held at par value and not traded. The banks are entirely privately owned by the members. Consequently, they do not have the pressure of earning high rates of return that publicly traded companies do. As cooperatives, they are able to pass their GSE benefits to their members in the form of lower borrowing costs, which are then passed on to consumers, businesses, and communities.

Each bank has an Office of General Counsel. Staff attorneys are usually recruited from among candidates with several years of experience in such areas as secured transactions, creditors' rights, contracts, derivative transactions, bank regulatory matters, insurance matters, and/or bankruptcy.

The banks are regulated by the Federal Housing Finance Agency in Washington, D.C.

Self-Regulatory Organizations

Self-Regulatory Organizations (SROs) are entities supervised by the Securities and Exchange Commission (SEC) that are authorized to regulate their member organizations and individuals. SROs are authorized by section 6 of the Securities Exchange Act of 1934 (15 U.S.C. § 78f).

The current lineup of SROs is as follows:

- American Stock Exchange
- Board of Trade of the City of Chicago, Inc.
- Boston Stock Exchange
- CBOE Futures Exchange, LLC
- Chicago Board Options Exchange
- Chicago Mercantile Exchange
- Chicago Stock Exchange
- International Securities Exchange
- Financial Industry Regulatory Authority (FINRA)
- Municipal Securities Rulemaking Board
- The Nasdaq Stock Market, Inc.
- National Futures Association
- National Stock Exchange

- New York Stock Exchange
- NYSE Arca
- OneChicago LLC
- Philadelphia Stock Exchange

The clearing agencies are:

- The Depository Trust and Clearing Corporation (parent of DTC, NSCC, and FICC)
- The Depository Trust Company
- Fixed Income Clearing Corporation
- National Securities Clearing Corporation
- The Options Clearing Corporation
- Stock Clearing Corporation of Philadelphia

Section 6 makes the securities industry the principal regulator of itself under the SEC's supervision. The SEC establishes the goals and targets of regulation by prescribing the content of SRO rules and ensures that the SROs fulfill their statutory duties to enforce the rules and monitor their members. However, actual rulemaking and enforcement against members is left up to the SROs.

Like the GSEs, each SRO has a chief legal office.

This is, without a doubt, the best time in history to be thinking about an attorney or law-related position with one of the SROs. A significant portion of the new and expanded authorities contained in the financial regulatory reform legislation (Dodd-Frank Wall Street Reform and Consumer Protection Act, Pub. L. 111-205) enacted in mid-2010 will be implemented by the SROs.

A description of the two SROs employing the most attorneys follows.

Financial Industry Regulatory Authority (FINRA)

FINRA, a combination of the former National Association of Securities Dealers and the member regulation component of the NYSE, is tasked with the following basic mission:

- Writing rules, examining securities firms to ensure that they adhere to those rules, and taking action against brokers or firms that don't comply;
- Registering securities firms, brokers, and mutual fund corporations;
- Informing and educating the investing public;
- Providing real-time transaction and price data for corporate bond trades—thus bringing transparency to the market; and
- Administering the largest forum specifically designed to resolve securities-related disputes.

FINRA also performs market regulation under contract for the major U.S. stock markets, including the New York Stock Exchange, NYSE Arca, NYSE Amex, The NASDAQ Stock Market, and the International Securities Exchange.

FINRA, the largest of the SROs in terms of number of attorneys, has multiple offices throughout the country and multiple legal offices as well. In addition, because of its heavy involvement in broker/dealer compliance and enforcement (it monitors 4,900 brokerage and other firms, about 167,000 branch offices, and approximately 660,000 registered securities representatives), FINRA has a large number of law-related positions in each of its offices. The same is true—but to a somewhat lesser extent—of some of the other SROs, such as the NYSE (New York Stock Exchange) Arca, which is the largest of all of the SROs.

FINRA has almost 3,000 employees nationwide, many of them attorneys. It is headquartered in Washington, D.C., Rockville, Maryland, and New York and has 15 district offices nationwide (Atlanta; Boca Raton, Florida; Boston; Chicago; Dallas; Denver; Jericho, New York; Kansas City, Missouri; Los Angeles; New Orleans; New York; Philadelphia; San Francisco; Seattle; and Woodbridge, New Jersey. Lawyers may work in the following FINRA offices: Legal, Compliance, Enforcement, Regulation, Public Policy, Ombudsman, the National Adjudicatory Council, Office of the Whistleblower, Office of Fraud Detection and Market Intelligence, and also as hearing officers. The Offices of the Whistleblower and Fraud Detection and Market Intelligence were added in 2009 in response to the financial crisis.

Attorneys with undergraduate degrees in finance, accounting, business, or a related discipline will find that these afford an advantage in applying for a position with FINRA.

As I write this, FINRA has 78 positions available. Seven are attorney jobs in various departments, while an additional seven are law-related positions.

FINRA has a reputation for always going after the little guy while ignoring what the big Wall Street firms are doing. In failing to detect the Madoff and Stanford Ponzi schemes and bringing fewer enforcement actions in the twenty-first century than it did in the 1990s, its performance has been criticized as less than vigilant. Moreover, FINRA has a predisposition to secrecy and has not historically deemed transparency to be very important. There is very little in the Dodd-Frank Wall Street Reform and Consumer Protection Act, Pub. L. 111-203, about FINRA, and even less about making its activities more transparent.

NYSE Regulation—New York Stock Exchange (NYSE)

NYSE Regulation, Inc. is a nonprofit corporation charged with strengthening market integrity and investor protection. NYSE Regulation also ensures that companies listed on the NYSE meet financial and corporate-governance listing standards. In addition to its regulatory responsibilities to enforce marketplace rules and federal securities laws of the NYSE, NYSE Regulation oversees NYSE Arca Regulation and NYSE Amex Regulation through regulatory services agreements.

NYSE Regulation's board of directors is composed of a majority of directors unaffiliated with any other NYSE board. As a result, NYSE Regulation is independent in its decision making. It consists of three divisions: Market Surveillance, Enforcement, and Listed Company Compliance.

The Market Surveillance Division monitors trading of NYSE-listed securities by member firms away from and on the floor of the Exchange. Attorneys in this division investigate trading abuses, recommend formal or informal disciplinary actions, and refer matters to NYSE Regulation's Enforcement Division or the SEC for matters outside NYSE Regulation's jurisdiction. Additional areas of focus include market manipulation, breaches of fiduciary duties, violation of agency responsibility and investor protection rules, failure by specialists to maintain fair and orderly markets in listed securities and products, and violation of rules governing members' on-floor trading and auction market procedures. Market Surveillance also has responsibility for floor member education and floor official training, specialist performance evaluation, intermarket cooperation, development of regulatory rules, and implementing the Exchange's allocation policy.

Under a September 2008 agreement with 10 U.S. equity exchanges, the division is also responsible for detecting and investigating possible insider trading of NYSE-, NYSE Arca-, and NYSE Alternext US-securities no matter where they trade in the United States.

Attorneys in the Enforcement Division investigate and prosecute violations of NYSE rules and applicable federal laws or regulations that occur on or through NYSE systems and facilities. Enforcement cases stem from internal referrals (principally from the Market Surveillance Division), investor complaints, examinations of member organizations, and referrals from the SEC. Cases may include:

- failure to cooperate
- financial/operations
- insider trading
- market manipulation
- misconduct on the trading floor
- registration/qualification
- short-sale violations
- supervisory violations
- books and records deficiencies
- other abusive trading practices.

Sanctions range from a censure or fine to a suspension, expulsion, or bar. Disciplinary actions take effect after a decision by the Office of the Hearing Board, an independent division of NYSE Regulation that adjudicates all disciplinary actions. Appeals of Hearing Board decisions may be made to the NYSE Regulation Board of Directors and, thereafter, the SEC, U.S. Courts of Appeal, and the U.S. Supreme Court. Cases outside of the NYSE's jurisdiction are referred to the SEC or other regulatory agencies.

The Listing Companies Compliance Division consists of two components:

- Financial Compliance—reviews a company's reported financial results to ensure that it meets original-listing and continued-listing requirements;
- Corporate Compliance—ensures that listed companies adhere to the highest standards of accountability and transparency, including enhanced governance requirements for configuration of corporate boards, director independence, and financial competency on audit committees.

Other Quasi-Governmental Organizations

GSEs and SROs are not the entire quasi-governmental story. There are several other quasi-governmental organizations that do not fit neatly into either of those two categories.

Federal Reserve Banks (FRBs) are part of the Federal Reserve System, which is governed by the Federal Reserve Board in Washington, D.C., a government agency. FRBs are located in Boston; New York; Philadelphia; Cleveland; Richmond, Virginia; Atlanta; Chicago; St. Louis; Minneapolis; Kansas City, Missouri; Dallas; and San Francisco, and each one has a general counsel's office.

The Public Company Accounting Oversight Board (PCAOB) was created by the Sarbanes-Oxley Act of 2002, Pub. L. 107-204, to "oversee the auditors of public companies in order to protect the interests of investors and further the public interest in the preparation of informative, fair and independent audit reports." The SEC has oversight authority over the PCAOB, including the approval of the board's rules, standards, and budget. PCAOB is headquartered in Washington, D.C., with regional and branch offices in New York; Boston; Atlanta; Charlotte, North Carolina: Tampa, Florida; Chicago; Detroit; Dallas; Irving, Texas; Houston; Denver; Orange County, California; San Francisco; and San Mateo, California. PCAOB has an Office of General Counsel, an Office of the Chief

Hearing Officer, and a Division of Enforcement and Investigations, all staffed by attorneys.

The Legal Services Corporation (LSC) is an independent 501(c)(3) nonprofit corporation headed by a bipartisan board of directors whose 11 members are appointed by the President and confirmed by the Senate. It is the single largest provider of civil legal aid for the poor in the nation, promoting equal access to justice and providing grants for civil legal assistance to low-income Americans. LSC distributes more than 95 percent of its total funding, which comes from the annual federal budget (almost $400 million in fiscal year 2010), to 136 independent nonprofit legal aid programs with more than 900 offices that provide legal assistance to low-income individuals and families throughout the nation.

LSC awards grants to legal services providers through a competitive grants process; conducts compliance reviews and program visits to oversee program quality and compliance with statutory and regulatory requirements, as well as restrictions that accompany LSC funding; and provides training and technical assistance to programs.

LSC employs approximately 40 attorneys in legal positions and other attorneys in law-related jobs.

The United States Institute of Peace (USIP) is an independent, nonpartisan, national institution established and funded by Congress. Its goals are to help prevent and resolve violent international conflicts; promote post-conflict stability and development; and increase conflict management capacity, tools, and intellectual capital worldwide. USIP's programs and activities include:

- Operating on the ground in zones of conflict, most recently in Afghanistan, the Balkans, Colombia, Iraq, Kashmir, Liberia, the Korean Peninsula, Nepal, Pakistan, the Palestinian Territories, Nigeria, Sudan, and Uganda. Specific projects involve:
  - o Mediating and facilitating dialogue among parties in conflict.
  - o Building conflict management skills and capacity.
  - o Identifying and disseminating best practices in conflict management.
  - o Promoting the rule of law.

o   Reforming/strengthening education systems.

o   Strengthening civil society and state-building.

o   Educating the public through events, films, radio programs, and an array of other outreach activities.

- Performing cutting-edge research resulting in publications for practitioners, policymakers, and academia (over 400 to date).

- Identifying best practices and developing innovative peacebuilding tools, including a seminal set of books on international mediation, a portfolio of resources on religious peacemaking, a toolkit for promoting the rule of law in fragile states, guidelines for civilian and military interaction in hostile environments, a preeminent series on cultural negotiating behavior, and field-defining textbooks on conflict management.

- Training on conflict management—including mediation and negotiation skills—to government and military personnel, civil society leaders, and the staff of non-governmental and international organizations.

- Educating high school and college students about conflict, strengthening related curricula, and increasing the peacebuilding capabilities of future leaders.

- Supporting policymakers by providing analyses, policy options, and advice, as well as by sponsoring a wide range of country-oriented working groups.

The Institute employs more than 70 specialists (including attorneys) with both geographic and subject-matter expertise. Through its grant-making program, the Institute has invested $58 million in more than 1,700 peace-building projects in 76 countries around the world.

Quasi-governmental organizations recruit and hire their attorneys more like private-sector companies than government employers. Compensation varies widely but is more akin to corporate attorney compensation than government pay.

Chapter 21

Federal Practice Areas

Practice Area Diversity

U.S. government lawyers operate in what is probably the most diverse practice area environment in the world. The incredible diversity of federal legal practice includes but is not limited to:

- adjudication
- administrative law
- admiralty law
- advertising law
- agricultural law
- alternative dispute resolution
- antitrust and trade regulation law
- appointments/nominations
- appropriations and fiscal law
- art and humanities law
- asset forfeiture
- aviation law
- banking and finance law
- bankruptcy law
- business/commercial law
- campaign finance law
- children's/juvenile law

- civil enforcement
- civil rights/EEO
- claims (torts, etc.)
- commodities law
- communications law
- compliance
- computer law
- constitutional law
- construction law
- consumer protection law
- corporate governance
- corrections law/sentencing
- criminal law
- criminal law/white-collar crime
- death penalty law
- debt collection
- disability law
- disaster relief
- domestic violence law
- drug control/narcotics
- economic development law
- education law
- elder law
- election law
- e-commerce/Internet law
- eminent domain/condemnation
- employee benefits law
- employment law
- endangered species
- energy law
- environmental law
- ethics and professional responsibility law
- export control law
- false claims/qui tam
- family law
- food and drug law
- foreign law
- gaming law

- government contract law
- grant law
- health law
- historic preservation law
- homeland security law
- housing law
- immigration law
- information disclosure/FOIA/privacy law
- insurance law
- intellectual property law—unspecified
- intellectual property law—copyright
- intellectual property law—patent
- intellectual property law—trademark
- intellectual property law—technology transfer/licensing
- intellectual property law—litigation
- intelligence and national security law
- international law—general
- international law—criminal justice
- international law—development
- international law—human rights
- international law—international organizations
- international law—treaties/agreements
- international law—trade and investment
- international law—unfair trade practices
- investigations
- judicial administration
- labor law
- landlord-tenant law
- law of the sea
- legal research and writing
- teaching/training
- legislation and regulations
- litigation—administrative
- litigation—appellate
- litigation—trial
- litigation management
- litigation support
- maritime law

- medical malpractice
- mergers and acquisitions
- military law
- municipal law
- Native American law
- natural resources law
- nonproliferation/arms control
- occupational safety and health law
- pardons
- product liability law
- public benefits law
- real estate and land use law
- records management
- risk management
- science and technology law
- securities law
- securitization
- social welfare law
- space law
- tax law
- transactional law
- transportation law
- trusts and estates law
- utilities law
- veterans law
- water law
- workers' compensation

The Monolith Myth, Redux

Here it is again: a debunking of the myth that the U.S. government is a great monolith reminiscent of the one in *2001: A Space Odyssey*. When it comes to practice areas, obeisance to this myth can be self-defeating.

If you are considering an environmental law practice, for example, your natural inclination would be to zero in on the Environmental Protection Agency (EPA). Most people, attorneys included, assume that EPA is not only the epicenter of federal environmental practice, but the *only* place where environmental law is practiced in the government. If you assume this, you are not only dead wrong, but are also limiting your opportunities in the worst possible way.

Here is a list of the federal agencies and the number of law offices and other offices within each agency that has an environmental practice. As you can see, there are *hundreds* of environmental practices in the federal government.

- Environmental Protection Agency (16 law offices and 6 other offices with attorneys)
- Chemical Safety and Hazard Investigation Board—Office of General Counsel
- Corporation for National and Community Service—Office of General Counsel
- Defense Nuclear Facilities Safety Board—Office of General Counsel
- Executive Office of the President—Council on Environmental Quality—Office of General Counsel
- Federal Energy Regulatory Commission (2 non-legal offices with attorneys)
- Federal Trade Commission—Bureau of Consumer Protection—Division of Enforcement
- General Services Administration—Office of General Counsel and Regional Counsel Offices
- International Boundary and Water Commission—Office of the Legal Advisor
- Library of Congress—Congressional Research Service—American Law Division
- National Aeronautics and Space Administration (5 law offices)
- National Science Foundation—Office of General Counsel
- Nuclear Regulatory Commission (5 law offices)
- Occupational Safety and Health Review Commission (2 law offices and 1 other office with attorneys)
- Small Business Administration—Office of Interagency Affairs—Office of Advocacy
- Smithsonian Institution—Office of General Counsel

- Tennessee Valley Authority—Office of Executive Vice President and General Counsel
- U.S. Agency for International Development—Office of General Counsel
- U.S. Court of Federal Claims
- U.S. Department of Agriculture (18 law offices and 3 other offices with attorneys)
- U.S. Department of Commerce (8 law offices)
- U.S. Department of Defense (220 law offices)
- U.S. Department of Energy (18 law offices)
- U.S. Department of Health and Human Services—Office of General Counsel
- U.S. Department of Homeland Security (16 law offices)
- U.S. Department of Housing and Urban Development—Office of General Counsel
- U.S. Department of Justice (105 law offices)
- U.S. Department of State (1 law office and 2 other offices with attorneys)
- U.S. Department of Transportation (22 law offices)
- U.S. Department of Treasury (2 law offices)
- U.S. Department of the Interior (12 law offices and 4 other offices with attorneys)
- U.S. Postal Service (7 law offices)
- United States Congress (35 committees and subcommittees)

The huge number of separate federal environmental practices is not unique to environmental law. It is replicated by many federal practice areas, including most of the major ones that predominate throughout the public and private legal communities. It is very important that, when considering federal legal employment, you think expansively.

The only resource to which you can turn for this information is one that my company developed years ago, last updated in 2005 and subsequently acquired by Thomson-Reuters. It is called *Federal Careers for Attorneys* and is accessible through www.attorneyjobs.com, a subscription website. The information has, unfortunately, not been updated since the acquisition, but at least it gives you a good starting point for your federal practice area research.

Take Nothing for Granted

Coming into a federal job search absent preconceived notions is critically important, as the list of 515 government environmental law practices above illustrates. Just because a federal agency happens to have the same name as a practice area does not mean that it is the only agency with that practice. The Department of Energy has a great many law offices—32 in 26 cities—where energy law is a principal practice area. These 32 offices are hardly the only federal law offices with an energy law practice. Thirty-three additional federal law offices in 11 agencies also practice energy law.

Even very narrow, esoteric practice areas almost always can be found in more than one government law office. Endangered species law, for example, is practiced in 20 law offices in nine separate agencies.

Federal legal practice as a whole is about as diversified a law practice as you could imagine, and the vast and ever-increasing federal regulation of individual and organizational behavior means that the number of possible federal employers of someone with your particular background or interests is constantly growing to keep pace.

I cannot overemphasize the importance of a holistic approach to federal practice opportunities. Anything less will shortchange your possibilities and could have a negative long-term effect on your career.

Part IV

How the U.S. Government Hires Lawyers

135

How lawyers are hired is probably the most mystifying element of the entire federal legal employment puzzle. Over the years of advising thousands of attorneys on job-hunting in the government, I fielded more complaints and soothed more anguished feelings concerning the federal legal hiring process than any other issue by far. To say that my clients often became frustrated by the process is a monumental understatement.

This part is designed to demystify the federal attorney hiring process and make you feel more confident about electing to pursue federal legal jobs and careers.

Chapter 22

Hiring Process Overview

The Most Confusing Information in This Book

U.S. government recruitment and hiring is both perplexing and constantly in flux. It is, therefore, difficult to pin down. It has been criticized as being too slow, too cumbersome, too confusing, too resistant to change, and too antiquated, which is why it is continuously being examined and "tweaked." This does not mean, however, that every modification is an improvement; unfortunately, it often means the opposite.

Two major hiring process reforms of the past 15 years merit more in-depth discussion to shed light on some of the problems with the process and to set the scene for the discussion in Part Six on how to overcome the obstacles to getting hired.

National Performance Review

In 1995, President Clinton assigned Vice President Gore the task of reviewing and reforming the federal personnel system. Gore's National Performance Review came up with some useful tweaks and some that proved to be somewhat less than positive, thanks in part to the Law of Unintended Consequences.

The principal hiring process reform that emerged from the effort was the elimination of the dreaded standard application form

(Standard Form—or SF-171) that had been in use for decades among most of the agencies for most of their positions. The Administration decreed that the SF-171 would no longer be required, that the government would stop printing and distributing blank SF-171 forms, and that henceforth federal job applicants could apply using any document they desired.

The SF-171 was a four-page nightmare. It was fraught with ambiguity and often resulted in candidates being summarily rejected for jobs because of how they filled out the form (or omitted information, including information of no job-related significance whatsoever) rather than what they reported about themselves. It was a classic case of form over substance and played right into the hands of federal human resources (HR) office personnel specialists who did not want to slog through hundreds of applications from top to bottom. If they found a completion error or omission, sometimes no matter how minor, that was frequently enough to reject a candidate. Horror stories of federal job applicants being eliminated for such minor errors as exceeding the space allowed to fill in a response were legion. It was the stuff of Talmudic scholars and bureaucrats' dreams and provided a lot of fodder for bloviating politicians who resorted to the time-honored and effective strategy of attacking Washington for all of society's ills.

Unfortunately, two immutable laws came into play almost immediately and sabotaged the worthy goal of the reformers. First, the Law of Bureaucratic Resistance to Change, coupled with the usual failure of so many government reform efforts to accompany reforms with compliance and enforcement mechanisms, combined to defeat the purpose. Federal HR offices had become accustomed to the SF-171 over the years and were comfortable with it, so many continued to (1) print and distribute the form, (2) mandate that candidates use it to apply, and (3) reject candidates who opted to use something else. *Plus ça change, plus c'est la même chose*—everything changes and nothing changes. Other HR offices told candidates that they *preferred* the SF-171, which candidates naturally took to mean that they had better use it. To this day, you will see federal positions advertised that *require* you to use the impossible-to-kill SF-171.

Further confusing the issue was the institution of two new application forms designed to replace—or not replace—the SF-171. I discussed the replacement OF-612 and OF-306 forms in Chapter 6, "The Cons." Suffice it to say that henceforth neither hiring agencies nor federal job candidates had a clear idea of what they could and could not submit when applying for a U.S. government job.

Second, the Law of Unintended Consequences had a field day. Agencies became confused as to what they could and could not accept. They frequently opted for hiring processes that would not have passed muster under the new rules—assuming there had been any compliance oversight or enforcement. Attorney hiring had always been "different," often following its own rules because lawyers were not part of the competitive civil service. Thus, federal law offices did not know if they were covered by the new rules or not. Many continued to do what they had always done. Most Justice Department offices, for example, had always preferred a traditional resumé, one that almost every private-sector law firm or in-house counsel office would accept. That did not change following the reform. Other law offices had been devising and using their own forms instead of the SF-171 and continued to do so. Moreover, many federal law offices avoided HR offices completely and had their attorney job applicants apply directly to them.

On the candidate side, chaos quickly took over. My office was besieged by confused and frustrated attorneys wanting to know what document to use, what information to include, and where to go with a completed application. The answers were not always clear, even after we contacted both law and HR offices and discussed the specifics with them. One hiring attorney told us that the way he interpreted the reform was that a candidate could use whatever piece of paper he or she wished, provided that all of the requisite information was on it. He said that even a piece of toilet tissue with the candidate's name on it would be acceptable (we did not recommend that approach).

Federal job vacancy announcements were all over the map with respect to application documents and thus became more complicated than ever. We spent hours with our clients attempting to understand the requirements cited in them, and made hundreds of calls to law and HR offices to discern their real intent. Some offices were very specific about including information that seemed unnecessary—such as the candidate's high school and its ZIP code—while others said nothing at all in their vacancy announcements about what to include, but when contacted would list an array of required information. Decisions about accepting and rejecting applications became even more inconsistent than before, and the "system" soon became so muddled that many highly qualified attorneys interested in public service were deterred or gave up halfway through the ordeal.

The Office of Personnel Management (OPM) attempted to assert some authority over the agency legal hiring process but was often rebuffed by the agencies, if not ignored. Legal hiring officials almost never listened to OPM simply because they did not have to; even offices that did pay attention because their positions were in the competitive civil service successfully resisted many of OPM's pronouncements despite being legally bound to follow them.

It took many years and the advent of the Internet and e-mail to bring a modicum of order to the chaos. Eventually, as younger employees who were both new to the government and comfortable with technology moved into HR and law offices, the idea of the resumé as the preferred application document took hold. While this did not completely eliminate the confusion—the federal format resumé, with all of its additional and often irrelevant information requirements still prevails in some places—it went a long way toward calming both employers and candidates.

The Internet

The Internet was both the best and the worst thing that ever happened to the federal hiring process. It was the best thing for OPM because its efficiencies and ease of use made for its rapid adoption by agencies for their hiring processes. It was so convenient to attach a resumé to an e-mail that this quickly became the application procedure of choice. However, it was probably the worst thing that could happen to federal job candidates.

Both hiring agencies and OPM saw opportunities in the new technologies to gain turf-battle advantages. Internally within agencies, HR offices requested and received funds from Congress to build resumé databases into which applicant resumés would be automatically entered upon receipt and extracted when needed, using search engines. What this meant was that candidates had to be very careful to predict what key words would be used as the agency's search criteria to extract their resumés. If the attorney hiring official told the personnel specialist to bring him or her all of the "antitrust" resumés, then the term "antitrust" had better be somewhere in that resumé if the candidate hoped to be considered. After some horror-story feedback from both attorney candidates and agencies, my office began to recommend that attorney aspirants include a key word index at the top or bottom of their resumés. The index would laundry-list every conceivable key word they could think of in order for their resumés to make it out of the database and into the hands of a human being.

OPM also viewed the technology revolution as an opportunity to achieve predominance over agency HR and law offices when it came to recruitment and hiring. It hired an outside contractor to build an online application system that it hoped it could foist upon its agency "clients." The first iteration of this multimillion-dollar system was a disaster. Sometimes it would freeze while a candidate was entering his or her information; other times the information would disappear after the candidate had spent hours completing the application form. In addition, there was no guarantee that once the form was submitted, it would actually arrive at OPM.

OPM is now into the third iteration of its government-wide online job application system. Some of the same problems that afflicted the first two efforts are still present. However, agency HR offices have gravitated to the system because it makes their jobs easier in many respects. It can be almost a paperless process, and that is now a very attractive enticement throughout government.

Taking their lead from the OPM online template application form, some law offices have designed their own electronic template form and require candidates to use it in lieu of the OPM version. However, many federal legal hiring managers say they dislike both systems because they strip away the individuality of job candidates, making them all appear to be the same. As we all know, one person's resumé can look very different from another's, and those differences can be determinative. The order in which information is presented often tells a reader a great deal about the candidate's thought processes and organizational skills. Moreover, the opportunity for a candidate to append a "highlights" addendum to the resumé in which he or she can elaborate on a particular achievement is lost. No longer can the hiring official learn from such an appendix how the candidate tackles a problem and solves it.

What this all adds up to is a system that is still badly flawed. It is also one that requires great care on the part of candidates if they want to negotiate it successfully and have a shot at being interviewed and hired. Part Six goes into detail about how to overcome the obstacles presented by this hiring process. Before getting there, however, we must examine how the government goes about evaluating attorney candidates for both mainstream and law-related positions. These are the topics that will be addressed in the following chapters.

Chapter 23

Hiring for Attorney Jobs

The "Excepted" Service

U.S. government attorney positions are exempt from normal civil service rules. The government classifies its professional positions as being in either the competitive service or the excepted service. The competitive service is the traditional civil service, replete with thousands of rules governing recruitment, hiring, promotion, pay, benefits, termination, and every other personnel category and function imaginable. The excepted service is defined in the negative by one very brief sentence in the law. Title 5, U.S. Code section 2103 states;

> . . . the "excepted service" consists of those civil service positions which are not in the competitive service or the Senior Executive Service.

Most federal government civilian positions are part of the competitive service. To obtain a competitive service federal job, you must compete with other applicants in open competition. In addition to attorneys, certain entire agencies are exempt from competitive service hiring rules. This means that these agencies have their own hiring system applicable to all employees that they hire, attorneys or others. This also includes law-related positions that would

143

otherwise be subject to competitive service hiring requirements. Following are the excepted service agencies, where attorneys can be found in both mainstream legal as well as law-related positions.

- U.S. Department of Agriculture—Animal and Plant Health Inspection Service
- U.S. Department of Commerce—International Trade Administration and U.S. Patent and Trademark Office
- U.S. Department of Energy—National Nuclear Security Administration
- Nuclear Regulatory Commission
- Tennessee Valley Authority
- Office of Government Ethics
- General Services Administration
- Postal Rate Commission
- Federal Reserve System
- U.S. Agency for International Development
- U.S. Department of State—Foreign Service and U.S. Mission to the United Nations
- International Broadcasting Bureau
- Peace Corps
- Election Assistance Commission
- Library of Congress
- U.S. Department of Homeland Security—Federal Emergency Management Agency, Transportation Security Administration, and U.S. Secret Service
- Central Intelligence Agency
- U.S. Department of Defense—Defense Intelligence Agency
- National Security Agency
- U.S. Department of Justice—Federal Bureau of Investigation
- U.S. Department of Transportation—Federal Aviation Administration
- AMTRAK (National Railroad Passenger Corporation)
- U.S. Postal Service
- Supreme Court of the United States
- Judicial Panel on Multidistrict Litigation
- U.S. Bankruptcy Courts

- U.S. Court of Appeals for the Federal Circuit
- U.S. Court of International Trade
- U.S. Courts of Appeals
- U.S. District Courts
- U.S. Court of Appeals for the Armed Forces
- U.S. Court of Appeals for Veterans' Claims
- U.S. Court of Federal Claims
- U.S. Tax Court
- Administrative Office of the United States Courts
- Federal Judicial Center
- U.S. Sentencing Commission
- U.S. House of Representatives
- U.S. Senate

Attorneys constitute, by far, the largest number of federal employees outside the competitive service. That does not mean, however, that every single attorney who works for the federal government is in the excepted service.

If this is getting complicated, here is a simple, immediate way to determine if a legal position is in the excepted service. If, when advertised in a federal job vacancy announcement, the job title is accompanied by the designation "0905," that tells you that the job in question is in the excepted service. Every 0905 position is for an attorney in the excepted service, regardless of the job title—though virtually every 0905 position has a job title that includes the word "attorney." The most common titles employed are "attorney," "attorney-advisor," "general attorney," "staff attorney," or some variation of these titles. On occasion, you may see the word "counsel" in lieu of attorney. If you see anything else—"chief bottle washer," "wild burro specialist," "aircraft mechanic"—with a 0905 designation, you can still be confident that this is an attorney position. The job title is secondary in importance to the 0905 designation. Such numerical designations, by the way, are called a "Job Classification Series."

There are some federal attorneys in the competitive service, which could be indicated by a different Job Classification Series ("0301," which is kind of a residuary series into which a great many government positions are lumped, is probably the second most likely one in which to find attorney jobs). These positions are discussed in Chapter 33, "Hiring for Federal Law-Related Jobs."

What makes the excepted service distinct is the lack of hard and fast recruitment and hiring rules. That means that federal departments and agencies, and their 3,000-plus legal offices, have a great deal of discretion when hiring lawyers. Unlike almost every other government profession, there is no uniformity among federal legal hiring organizations in how they recruit and hire attorneys (here comes that Monolith Myth again). The hiring procedures that apply to the Office of the Chief Counsel of the Federal Transit Administration, for example, may be very different from those that apply to the Office of Professional Responsibility at the Justice Department. Even more significant, they may also be very different from how the Office of Chief Counsel at the Federal Highway Administration, a parallel "modal" organization in the very same Department of Transportation, goes about the business of hiring attorneys.

Unadvertised Jobs

Unlike regular civil service positions, there is no statutory or regulatory requirement that U.S. government attorney jobs be publicly advertised. While most federal legal positions are, in fact, advertised, many are not. Most federal jobs that never see the light of publication are attorney positions.

Moreover, policies regarding advertising legal job announcements are rather inconsistent, even within the same legal office. An office may advertise a legal position one time, then not advertise a position—even the very same position—the next time it is open. Instead, the office may rely on resumés that they have recently received, either in response to a prior vacancy announcement or unsolicited. Or, it may resort to what some of the Justice Department litigation divisions (Antitrust, Civil, Civil Rights, Criminal, Environment and Natural Resources, National Security, and Tax) have done quite successfully: relying on resumés that their existing attorney-employees bring to the hiring officials.

What this all means is that a federal legal job applicant has to be both *reactive* and *proactive*. The reactive approach means keeping your eyes open for job opportunities that are advertised on www.usajobs.gov or on agency websites. Your proactive strategy means taking affirmative steps to alert a prospective federal employer to your credentials, even without benefit of a vacancy announcement. See Part Six, "Getting Hired," for strategies that you can implement in order to accomplish this.

Candidate Evaluation

The many variations in how one applies and what happens to an application once received also continue on throughout the remainder of the federal attorney hiring process. However, there are some common, time-tested methods of evaluating federal lawyer applications that are still widely used today. A very rough rule of thumb governing the evaluation process for the vast majority of federal attorney jobs is a three-step procedure.

Step One

Federal job vacancy announcements usually (you will see that word a lot) include the name of a contact person for the job being advertised. That individual is, more often than not, an HR personnel specialist who is not an attorney. The personnel specialist is typically someone who handles more than one recruitment at the same time, often for a variety of professions and occupations. He or she usually knows very little about attorneys or the law.

Once the closing date specified in the vacancy announcement for the receipt of applications has passed, the personnel specialist reviews the application documents against a checklist that is either provided by the hiring office or developed by the personnel specialist. This first-level review is very important because only those applications that survive it make it to the next level.

Personnel specialists tend to look for reasons to reject applicants in order to winnow the number of applications down to a manageable few. Thus, they are often rather "nit-picky" when it comes to even minor failures to follow application instructions. You need to make sure that you respond to all of the questions on the online template or paper application form, omitting nothing, even if it does not seem to you to be very important.

Step Two

The surviving application documents are usually then forwarded by the personnel specialist to a rating panel (for want of an official term) comprising a number of attorneys. Attorney hiring panels usually consist of three to five attorneys from the hiring office. In some law offices—not all—the attorneys have to be at the same grade level specified in the job vacancy announcement or at a higher grade level.

The hiring panel attorneys convene at a mutually agreed-upon date and time and begin their application review. The first step is usually the development of a "scoring" system for grading the applications. Most hiring panels adopt a 100-point scoring system and decide how many points to award to an applicant for work experience, education, honors and awards, and other information items they are likely to see in the applications. Someone who attended Yale Law School is likely to be awarded more points, for example, than would a graduate of the Hoboken Night School of Law.

Then, each panel member reads each application and scores it. Depending on the number of applications that survived the Step One review, this process could take as long as a week.

The next phase is much like a college admissions office review process. The panel arranges the scores hierarchically, the highest to lowest. Then they discuss the applications individually, focusing on distinctions and nuances that might merit a scoring change, either up or down. For example, if a candidate presents an unusually outstanding accomplishment in his or her application, he or she might be awarded additional points or even bonus points, which could alter his or her position on the final list.

The final phase is to present the list to the hiring official.

Step Three

The last step in the application evaluation process is the review of the list by the individual who will do the interviewing and hiring, or by the person to whom this function is delegated by the hiring official, in which case the designee will perform the review, recommend whom to interview, perhaps participate in the interviews, and make recommendations to the hiring official. Both the hiring official and any designee may hold very different positions depending on the hiring office and the grade level of the vacant position. If this is an entry-level legal job, the designee may be a lower-level attorney. If it's a lateral position at a senior level, then the decision makers may be very high up in the office and agency.

The hiring process described above applies to the vast majority of mainstream attorneys hired by the U.S. government. There are, however, other hiring systems and procedures that attorneys must traverse in order to compete for certain specific types of federal jobs. The major exceptions are described in other chapters.

More about the Excepted Service (Sorry)

Before leaving the topic of the excepted service, a few additional points about it are necessary. By law, the Office of Personnel Management cannot develop qualification standards, or examinations for attorney jobs. Consequently, agencies can hire attorneys non-competitively using any hiring process they choose. And they do.

Hiring flexibility is the upside of the excepted service. The downside is that it is much easier to fire an excepted service employee than one who is in the competitive service. However, this is not something that should concern you very much. Federal government lawyers rarely get fired for cause. In fact, my experience has been that non-attorney competitive service federal employees are let go for various transgressions much more frequently than attorneys, despite the far more arduous termination process.

Chapter 24

Mainstream Attorney Hiring—New Grads

The U.S. government recruits and hires recent law school graduates in two ways: honors programs and intermittently, as the need arises.

Honors Programs

As this book goes to press, 19 federal agencies run honors programs in order to recruit recent law school graduates. These are the government equivalent of fall recruiting by law firms.

Most honors programs recruit multiple attorneys for temporary/term positions that last either one or two years. Honors program attorneys in most agencies rotate from one legal office to another or from one practice area to another. Most, but not all, agencies offer permanent employment to honors program lawyers who have performed well at the end of the term.

These programs are highly competitive, especially those run by the Department of Justice, the Securities and Exchange Commission, and the Internal Revenue Service. The Justice Department program is the largest and typically numbers around 150 attorneys each year. Some of the smaller programs hire fewer than 10 attorneys.

Honors programs are not always consistent from year to year. While the larger programs hire attorneys every year, some of the smaller ones may skip a year or two now and then.

While agency honors programs are supposed to consider candidates purely on merit, the Justice Department fell down completely on this during the Bush administration, when it politicized the process by putting candidates through an ideological litmus test. This reprehensible and allegedly illegal conduct even extended to the department's summer intern program. Once brought to light by rejected job candidates and congressional committees, this practice was abandoned, and now the department once again administers its honors program based on credentials and qualifications, not politics.

The agencies that currently have honors programs are as follows:

- U.S. Department of Homeland Security General Counsel's Honor Program
- U.S. Department of Housing and Urban Development Legal Honors Program
- U.S. Department of Justice Attorney General's Honors Program
- U.S. Department of Labor Office of the Solicitor Honors Program
- U.S. Department of Transportation Office of the Secretary Honors Attorney Program
- Central Intelligence Agency Office of the General Counsel Honors Attorney Program
- Comptroller of the Currency Chief Counsel's Employment Program for Law Graduates
- Environmental Protection Agency Office of General Counsel Honors Fellowship Program
- Equal Employment Opportunity Commission Attorney Honor Program
- Federal Bureau of Investigation Honors Internship Program
- Federal Communications Commission Attorney Honors Program
- Federal Deposit Insurance Corporation Legal Division Honors Attorney Program
- Federal Trade Commission Entry-Level Attorney Program
- Internal Revenue Service Chief Counsel Honors Program
- National Labor Relations Board Attorney Honors Program

- Nuclear Regulatory Commission Honor Law Graduate Program
- Securities and Exchange Commission Advanced Commitment Program
- U.S. Army Corps of Engineers Chief Counsel's Civilian Honors Program
- U.S. Postal Service Honor Attorney Program

Your law school career services office should be able to provide you with the requisite honors program information and application materials for each agency. Alternatively, you will find information about programs on agency websites and, for some programs, at www.usajobs.gov and/or www.lawschool.westlaw.com.

Direct Hiring of Entry-Level Attorneys

Honors programs are not the only entrée into the U.S. government for newly admitted attorneys. At most in any given year, only around 20 federal agencies even offer honors programs. The remainder get their fresh legal talent through year-round direct hiring, as the need arises. Moreover, even the agencies with honors programs do not always fill their entry-level attorney needs through those programs. They also hire directly, year-round, depending upon need.

The best ways to find these direct-hire entry-level opportunities are:

1. Visit www.usajobs.gov, the government-wide jobs database, often.
2. Check frequently the websites of the agencies in which you have an interest, especially the pages devoted to their legal offices, several of which allow you to sign up for job alerts to be e-mailed to you when opportunities arise.
3. Employ the "advance notice" strategies detailed in Part Six, "Getting Hired."
4. Ask your contacts—friends, social acquaintances, fellow alumni—in relevant agencies and their law offices to alert you to hiring intentions.

Chapter 25

Mainstream Attorney Hiring—Experienced Lawyers

Like virtually every corporate legal employer in the country, U.S. government mainstream law offices value experience. Consequently, the federal government hires many more experienced attorneys than new law school graduates.

The government does not have any organized recruitment programs for experienced attorneys similar to honors programs—they're hired directly, as the need arises. Everything that applies to direct hiring of new lawyers also applies to direct hiring of seasoned attorneys. Chapter 23, "Hiring for Attorney Jobs," details exactly how this hiring process works.

Experienced attorneys are hired and paid at General Schedule grades GS-11, 12, 13, 14, or 15 (with the exception of attorneys serving in the Senior Executive Service, discussed in the next chapter). The General Schedule's promotion ceiling is GS-15. However, some positions top out at a lower grade, which is usually specified in the job vacancy announcement. This does not mean, however, that this is the end of the line with respect to promotion or pay. Once you are inside the government, you will likely have the inside track for other positions in your office and agency, and in other government offices and agencies. It is extremely rare that an attorney remains in one position performing one function for an entire government career. There is a great deal of moving around within government. Here are two examples of candidates whose federal legal careers typify this movement.

- FT began his legal career in the private sector working for the litigation department of a major law firm. After three years with the firm during which he never got near a courtroom, he sought to realize his dream of getting into court and being a prosecutor by switching from the firm to the Department of Justice.

    He accepted an offer from Criminal Division's Narcotics Section, where his first assignments involved prosecuting misdemeanors and felonies in U.S. Magistrate's Court. Gradually, he earned the opportunity to litigate more complex felony cases.

    After four years, he left Main Justice to become an assistant U.S. attorney and began prosecuting increasingly complex cases, principally drug prosecutions. He remained there for over a decade, but then sought a more balanced lifestyle and left the U.S. Attorney's Office to go back to the Criminal Division in a non-litigation, policy-oriented position that permitted him more time with his young family. He rose to become the Principal Associate Director for Policy, where he coordinated Justice Department enforcement policies with other federal investigative agencies and the intelligence community, focusing on reviewing wiretapping requests and examining and recommending criminal surveillance and other telecommunications issues. Once his children were grown and off to college, he returned to the courtroom, this time with another U.S. Attorney's Office.
- WD worked for a Defense Department agency's Chief Counsel Office concentrating on government contract and procurement matters. He began his career participating in and preparing the documentation for defense supply contracts.

After several years, he was able to change jobs within the office to a position where he litigated contract disputes and contractor debarment actions before the Armed Services Board of Contract Appeals. He earned promotions all the way to GS-15 and, after seven years, applied and was accepted for a one-year detail to the Office of Management and Budget's Office of Federal Procurement Policy, an "intellectual" office traditionally headed by an academic that ponders government-wide procurement issues and recommends changes and improvements.

Toward the end of his detail, he was offered the opportunity to spend three years with a multilateral development agency based in Europe advising former Soviet satellite countries on crafting procurement statutory and regulatory regimes. That assignment proved to be a door-opener, as he found himself dealing directly and daily with senior government ministers in the countries he was advising. When he returned to the United States and his old job with the Defense Department, he received a number of offers from various major international law firms and management consulting firms interested in doing business in Eastern Europe at a substantial increase in salary. However, he turned them down in favor of a Senior Executive Service position with another federal agency as its new Director of Competition Policy.

While both of these individuals are exceptional, ambitious, hardworking attorneys, their federal career paths are not unique. These types of new opportunities and job moves are relatively standard for government lawyers.

Chapter 26

Mainstream Attorney Hiring—Senior Executive Service

The Senior Executive Service (SES) was created by the Civil Service Reform Act of 1978, Pub. L. 95-454. It was designed to be a corps of executives selected for their leadership qualifications who could serve in virtually any senior management position in any government agency. The intent was that SES members would be moved around at the discretion of agency heads. This intent has rarely, if ever, been realized.

Attorneys comprise a significant minority of the approximately 6,700 SES positions. Most legal office managers and their deputies are SES members. Members of the SES serve in key positions just below the top presidential appointees. They are the major link between presidential appointees and the rest of the federal workforce, both the "glue" and the institutional memory that keeps government functioning despite turnover at the top. OPM manages the SES program, including establishing hiring procedures and evaluation criteria to be applied to SES job applications and evaluating an applicant's leadership qualifications.

SES pay is determined by each agency within the following limits: Minimum pay is set at 120 percent of the basic pay for GS-15 Step 1 employees ($119,554 for 2010). Maximum pay levels depend on whether or not the employing agency has a "certified" SES performance appraisal system. An agency with a certified system may pay SES members a maximum of $179,700 in 2010, while an agency without a certified system may pay a maximum of $165,300 in 2010.

SES members do not receive locality pay adjustments but are eligible for performance bonuses, which can be considerable. One of the problems with the SES system is the large number of employees who are awarded annual bonuses (more than 20 percent in some years).

SES demographics indicate that the corps is overwhelmingly Caucasian (85 percent), male (72 percent), older (average age 55), and concentrated in Washington, D.C. (76 percent). These statistics date from 2007, the last year for which such data is available.

The SES consists of two classes of employees:

- *Career appointments*: Initial career appointments to the SES are based on merit competition. The Civil Service Reform Act requires each federal agency to establish an Executive Resources Board (ERB) to oversee the SES selection process. A published vacancy announcement launches the selection process. The next steps in the application evaluation process are similar to those used to hire attorneys. Step one is a preliminary review by an HR specialist, followed by rating and ranking of applicants by a panel with in-depth knowledge of the job's requirements. Evaluation procedures then diverge from the attorney hiring process. The next step is an evaluation of each candidate's qualifications by the agency ERB, followed by a final recommendation to the appointing authority. The appointing authority makes a selection and certifies that the candidate meets both the technical and executive core qualifications for the position. The agency then submits the candidate's application package to an OPM-administered Qualifications Review Board (QRB) for certification of the executive core qualifications. If those are certified, the agency appoints the candidate to the SES position.

Some agencies conduct SES Candidate Development Programs (CDPs), which can be another way to qualify for an initial career appointment in the SES. These typically last 18 months, during which the candidate receives extensive management training, at the end of which he or she is appointed to an SES position if one is available and funded.

The authority to conduct CDPs has been seriously underutilized by federal agencies, which is one of the biggest flaws in the rollout of the entire SES concept. Compounding the underutilization has been the occasional restriction of CDPs to current agency employees, which, in my opinion, is contrary to the legislative intent. The end result is a corps consisting of something less than what was contemplated by Congress when it enacted the Civil Service Reform Act: a less-than-adequately-trained, not-quite-so-high-quality group of government managers.

• *Non-career and limited appointments*: Competitive procedures are not required to make non-career and limited appointments. The agency head or his/her designee approves the candidate's qualifications. This means that politics often enters into the selection process. At least 70 percent of SES positions government-wide must be filled by individuals with five years or more of current, continuous government service immediately before initial SES appointment to ensure experience and continuity. Consequently, at any given moment, at least 30 percent of SES positions may be non-career and/or limited appointments ("at least" because career SES appointees who meet the experience requirements may also be appointed to non-career and limited appointments).

Chapter 27

Mainstream Attorney Hiring—Administrative Law Judges

It is worth spending some time discussing this job opportunity for two reasons: first, the large number of federal administrative law judges (ALJs); and second, the number of ALJ positions likely to become available in the next decade.

Background

The ALJ examination is like nothing else in government hiring. It is as close to a merit-based system for selecting judges as you will ever encounter. For all that, it is still an imperfect process that critics say requires considerable "tweaking."

There are now approximately 1,600 federal ALJs (all attorneys) working in 32 federal agencies. Almost 75 percent work for the Social Security Administration adjudicating primarily Social Security Disability Income (SSDI) claims that have been denied at lower administrative levels.

The original concept of developing a corps of apolitical, impartial, merit-selected judges who could hear any case on any subject involving any federal department or agency subject to the Administrative Procedure Act, 5 U.S.C. 551 et seq., was a high aspiration and parallels the original intent behind the creation of the SES. Moving from conception to reality has not been easy for the government in either case. Despite almost 40 years of tinkering, the ALJ hiring process has a considerable way to go.

The biggest vexations for the tinkerers have been:

- establishing reasoned selection criteria related to "real-world" ALJ duties and responsibilities;
- administering a fair and unbiased selection process;
- ensuring a rational and transparent exam scoring system;
- creating an ALJ corps with the flexibility to hear any case; and
- excising politics (both "macro" and "micro") from the ALJ corps.

Ideal v. Reality

If I were scoring the success of the ALJ concept on a scale of 1 to 10, I would give these vexations the following scores:

1. Selection criteria—7
2. Selection process—5
3. Scoring system—3
4. Flexibility—2
5. Politics—zero

Here's my reasoning: *Selection criteria* have to be divided into two somewhat related components: (a) qualifications to serve as an ALJ, and (b) examining for those qualifications.

The ALJ minders examine quite well. After years of fits and starts, they have a pretty good handle on the "right stuff." The selection criteria have been studied, surveyed, dissected, adjusted, and overhauled several times over four decades, and I think that they are very close to accurate.

The ALJ examination process moved the ALJ exam further away from its ideal. Despite being administered by a minuscule bureaucracy—at its peak personnel level, only six people ran the ALJ exam—it was fraught with delay, disorganization, dysfunction, miscommunication and non-communication, and less than consistent treatment of applicants. Inevitably, it became perceived as highly unfair and uneven. After a barrage of criticism and accompanying recommendations for improvement from OPM's Inspector General, and less focused, intermittent diatribes from OPM's customarily inattentive overseers on Capitol Hill, there has been improvement, but there is still some way to go.

ALJ candidate qualifications themselves are not quite up to the right level—in fact, there has been something of a regression from higher to lower standards in the past 15 years.

The ALJ Examination Scoring System

The scoring system has been the biggest issue for both the examiners and ALJ candidates. It has been severely criticized as biased toward military veterans, who, depending upon when and how long they served in the armed forces, can have "Veterans' Preference" bonus points added to their exam scores.

By the mid-1990s, this legal bias was compounded by a 100-point scoring scale that actually posited a floor of 70 points, which meant that Veterans Preference was magnified many times beyond its legislative intent. A 5-point preference added within a 30-point range really meant that the intended 5 percent advantage translated to a 16.67 percent advantage, double that for disabled veterans. A look at the roster of eligible candidates at that time showed that it was top-heavy with veterans.

Consequently, a large group of non-veterans whose names were on the ALJ Register launched a class action challenging the scoring system. The case went on for years, during which the ALJ exam was suspended and no new ALJs were added to the Register of Eligibles. The challengers consistently prevailed through the entire administrative judicial process until the case came before the U.S. Court of Appeals for the Federal Circuit, which held that OPM had discretion to craft such a scoring system.

Six years later (2003), the case was finally put to rest when the U.S. Supreme Court denied certiorari. However, there were enough dicta in the federal circuit's opinion that OPM decided it had license to continue the suspension of the exam, presumably in order to revise it to make it fairer. Meanwhile, the aging Register became quite stale and not very viable as a selection tool.

OPM did nothing, allegedly because the Bush Administration objected to what it perceived to be a predilection by Social Security Administration ALJs to decide benefits cases in favor of disability claimants. When the backlog of Social Security Disability Income hearings reached sufficiently intolerable levels that Congress noticed (almost 800,000 cases), the House Ways and Means Committee called in the OPM director and blasted her delaying tactics to such an extent that the ALJ exam suddenly was reopened in May 2007 and left open for only three days, then abruptly closed with no notice (in the 1990s, the exam was open continuously for years at a time).

Other Problematic Issues

On a micro level, politics also appeared to play a role in the ALJ examination process. Certain candidates in addition to veterans appeared to be favored for a variety of reasons, including women— mainly because the ALJ corps was overwhelmingly male—and staff attorneys working for the Social Security Administration's Office of Disability Adjudication and Review, notwithstanding that their litigation experience was usually limited to drafting preliminary decisions for ALJs. Both are still alleged biases of the ALJ evaluators.

ALJ corps flexibility also has a poor history. The original intent—that ALJs would move around the federal government hearing any case that arises—has never been realized. With few exceptions, agencies quickly "captured" new ALJs and used them for their own cases, period. They became, in effect, de facto agency employees, in direct contradiction to the intent of the ALJ corps creators. The exception is the occasional, informal, and very temporary "borrowing" of an ALJ from agency A by agency B to hear a single case.

Basic ALJ Qualifications

Serving as an ALJ is, despite all of the system's problems, still a very good gig. ALJs are reasonably well-paid, have wonderful benefits, almost unparalleled job security, and the ability to exercise good judgment in the cause of positive outcomes for individuals and the public.

While only experienced attorneys can qualify to become federal ALJs, this is a career that law students and recent grads can be thinking about and planning for, too, because the opportunity can arise quite early in your legal career. You must meet three separate qualification requirements to become eligible for appointment as a federal ALJ:

- *Licensure*. Applicants must be licensed and authorized to practice law in a state or comparable U.S. jurisdiction.
- *Experience*. Applicants must have a full seven years of experience as a licensed attorney preparing for, participating in, and/or reviewing formal hearings or trials involving litigation and/or administrative law at the federal, state, or local level. This does not mean that you have had courtroom or administrative hearing room experience, where you actually had to stand up and say something. Not true. All you need to have done is have some *involvement* with the types of courtroom and administrative litigation outlined in the qualification standard, no matter how distant from the actual courtroom or hearing chamber it happened to be.

  This represents a major liberalization of the standard from what it had been for the half-century following inception of the ALJ concept. Until the ALJ examination was reopened for business in 2007 after its decade-long dormancy, you had to have actually litigated—in the traditional sense of the word—in order to qualify to become an ALJ. While the ALJ handlers will deny this vigorously, the standard was likely liberalized to make it easier for existing federal attorneys at the Social Security Administration's Office of Disability Adjudication and Review to qualify. Most such attorneys, while *involved* with litigation, do not actually appear before judges and litigate.

- *Examination.* Applicants must pass the ALJ examination, the purpose of which is to evaluate the competencies essential to performing the work of an ALJ. Applicants who complete the exam have their names placed on the ALJ Register, which is then used as the source of names to make referrals to agencies for employment consideration when they have vacancies to fill. Names are referred in numerical score order, modified by the duty location of the position(s) to be filled and the geographical preferences of applicants.

Unlike the plenary authority granted mainstream attorney hiring officials, ALJs must be selected from among the highest three available names on the referral list, taking into consideration veterans' preference rules regarding order of selection. *Note: The "high three" selection requirement may be eliminated by the time* Landing a Federal Legal Job *is published. See Appendix F.*

The ALJ Examination

The ALJ examination consists of three components: submission of an Accomplishment Record, sitting for a Written Demonstration, and appearing at a Structured Interview.

- *Accomplishment Record.* This initial exam component requires the applicant to respond succinctly and in narrative form to six "Competencies": Decision Making, Interpersonal Skills, Oral Communication, Writing, Judicial Analysis, and Judicial Management.
- *Written Demonstration.* This exam element is a written essay test. The applicant is presented with a hypothetical fact situation as well as the applicable law and uses both to draft a decision. The Written Demonstration is, in essence, an expanded bar examination essay question. The applicant takes the test in an on-site group setting.
- *Structured Interview.* The final phase of the ALJ exam consists of a 45-minute to one-hour interview by three individuals—usually one current federal ALJ, a member of the OPM ALJ office, and another attorney. Each applicant is

asked the same questions by the interviewers and is then scored on his or her interview performance.

Each exam component is separately scored. At the end of the exam process, the scores are added up and the names of the applicants are added to the ALJ Register of Eligibles, ready for referral to any federal agency seeking an ALJ.

The Selection Interview

The last step in the hiring process is the agency selection interview. A hiring agency requests a referral list and then interviews the highest-scoring candidates. These interviews are also highly structured, although there is a little more wiggle room here for candidates to ask questions. Following the interviews, new ALJs are selected from among the applicants.

Anticipating and Preparing for the Exam

The ALJ exam opens infrequently and only stays open for applications for a few days. The history of the revised ALJ exam dates back only three years but indicates that this very narrow window of opportunity is unpredictable on two counts: (1) when it will open, and (2) how long it will stay open.

The best way to monitor the opening of the ALJ exam is to visit the OPM jobs website, www.usajobs.gov, frequently and search for "Administrative Law Judge." In October 2009, OPM provided an advance notice on its website that the ALJ exam would open soon (they do not always do this). You might also e-mail the ALJ Program Office at OPM at aljapplication@opm.gov and request that you receive notice when the exam reopens. Whether this will actually get you notice is not guaranteed.

It is very difficult to suddenly discover that the exam has opened, drop everything you are doing in order to become comfortable with the online application process, complete the online application, and submit it before the exam abruptly closes. You will be much better off if you have all of your ducks in a row in advance.

You need to worry about two items in your pre-preparation: the Assessment Questionnaire and the Accomplishment Record.

Assessment Questionnaire. The only purpose of the Assessment Questionnaire is to determine if you meet the seven-year experience requirement for becoming an ALJ. The online application provides two text boxes with limited space in which you are asked to respond. The first one is to describe your *litigation* experience; the second is for your *administrative law* experience.

The important points here are (1) to make sure that it is crystal-clear to the examiners that you have seven full years of such experience, and (2) to remember that all you need to show is *involvement* with litigation. Assuming that you meet this qualification requirement, you are asked to list all jurisdictions in which you are currently licensed, the date(s) of admission in each jurisdiction, and your bar license number(s).

The Assessment Questionnaire does not contribute a single point to your overall ALJ exam score. It is not scored at all.

Accomplishment Record. This is the "Big Kahuna." It is scored, and it sets the tone for the remainder of the ALJ exam. You have a limited amount of space on the on-line form in which to demonstrate the six competencies indicated above, first by addressing the competency generally, then by stating exactly how you demonstrated it.

It is not enough merely to state that you possess these competencies. It is critically important to provide detailed, objective information drawn from your experience, ideally with a specific example(s) that speaks directly and unambiguously to each competency. This is where many candidates fall short.

If you score high on the Accomplishment Record, you are well on your way to achieving a good score on the overall exam. While the current version of the ALJ exam, unlike its predecessors, does not indicate how much each exam component is worth, history says that the Accomplishment Record is worth more than the other two exam components. In all prior exam versions, this component was worth 50 percent of the overall score.

Many applicants run into technical problems with the on-line application, principally that (1) the application "freezes" during the completion process, or (2) it was not properly submitted and is never received by the examiners. The short windows during which you can apply immediately turn problems like these into major crises. There are two things you can do about them: First, prepare your responses to both the Assessment Questionnaire and Accomplishment Record beforehand, so that they will be ready to go when the exam opens. Second, follow up with the OPM ALJ Office (www.opm.gov) once you have submitted your application to make sure it arrived.

If you successfully complete the Assessment Questionnaire and Accomplishment Record, you will be invited to travel to a location where you will sit for the three- to four-hour Written Demonstration. This is the downfall of many ALJ applicants who, because they are provided both the facts and the law, believe that there is no meaningful preparation that they can do.

Assuming that some time has passed since you last sat for the essay portion of a bar examination, you can and do need to prepare for the Written Demo. One of the most effective ways to do that is to go to a state bar examiners' website and practice by attempting to answer the sample or past bar exam essay questions provided there. Not all states do this, but enough do that you will easily find questions that will help you retrain yourself in taking such an exam. Some states also provide model answers to past bar exam essay questions. These are also valuable tools for preparing for the Written Demo.

Another candidate downfall is failure to finish the Written Demo. Regardless of where you happen to be in your response, when time is almost up, make sure to include a conclusion. In most instances, that will be a mock decision by you in the role of judge or hearing officer. Points are deducted by the examiners for failure to reach a decision.

The final exam component is the Structured Interview. Each applicant is asked the same questions in the same order and has no opportunity to pose questions to the interviewers.

The examiners may throw in a "trick" question or two. For example: "You are an ALJ conducting a hearing and attempting to cope with a highly unruly counsel. What can you do?" Many applicants answer, "Cite the counsel for contempt," unaware that federal ALJs do not possess contempt power.

In addition to preparing as you would for any job interview, you can supplement your preparation by studying Professor Morell Mullins's *Manual for Administrative Law Judges*, http://ualr.edu/malj, which provides an excellent overview of what federal ALJs do and how they do it.

Make sure you are prepared in advance for the call to the Structured Interview. Sometimes you will receive very short notice of your interview time and place.

If you are dissatisfied with your score, you may appeal to the ALJ Program Office at OPM. However, appealing is much more difficult now than in the past, when you knew your score on each individual exam component and could appeal selective component scores. Moreover, appeals take a long time and generally do not make much difference in your score.

ALJ Compensation

Entry-level ALJs earned $103,900 per year in 2010. Experienced ALJs could earn up to $155,500.

The Opportunity

After reading this, you might conclude that becoming an ALJ is a futile waste of time. Not so. Federal ALJs are an aging population, averaging in the late 50s (until the ALJ exam was reopened in 2007 after its 10-year hiatus, the average age was 63). Almost 50 percent of today's ALJ corps is currently eligible to retire. By 2013, it is estimated that 70 percent of all ALJs will be eligible to retire. You can expect hundreds of openings.

Chapter 28

Mainstream Attorney Hiring—Immigration Judges

The U.S. government currently has around 200 immigration judges. They work for the Executive Office of Immigration Review in the Department of Justice and hear deportation, asylum, exclusion, remission, removal, bond, and other administrative immigration cases. Unlike ALJs, immigration judges are not part of an independent corps, but rather are agency employees without much in the way of distinguishing characteristics that differentiate them from any other agency employees. Immigration judges in 2010 earned $135,845–$165,300.

The immigration court system is fraught with problems, and morale among immigration judges is at rock-bottom. In recent years, the supposedly merit-based selection process was allegedly infused with politics, the accusation being that the Bush Administration used an ideological litmus test in hiring. Given that such a test was unambiguously shown to have been used by Justice Department political appointees to hire even entry-level Attorney General Honors Program attorneys as well as summer law clerks, you may want to excise the term "allegedly." (The Justice Department's own Inspector General blew the whistle on the politicization of these hiring programs.)

Moreover, the immigration courts are trying and failing to cope with surging caseloads and limited resources. There are immigration courts based in more than 50 cities nationwide. Some courts, however, are much busier than others. Most asylum cases, for example, are handled in only four courts. The immigration courts in New York City and Miami decide more than 40 percent of all asylum matters. Add in Los Angeles and San Francisco and these four courts account for approximately 60 percent of asylum decisions.

Every study of immigration judge decisions reveals huge disparities from one judge to another with respect to asylum and other decisions. "Judge shopping" in immigration cases is probably more important to practitioners and their clients than in any other judicial milieu, a situation that speaks volumes about how badly broken are immigration proceedings.

A 2009 *Georgetown University Law Journal* survey of 96 judges found that they were suffering stress and exhaustion similar to prison wardens. The anonymous comments of a majority of respondents repeatedly cited overwhelming caseloads, little time to review cases, antiquated technology that frequently breaks down, and an insufficient number of law clerks and language interpreters.

Unlike ALJs, new immigration judges receive little if any training before being thrown into the fray, and are under severe pressure from administrators to do more and do it faster.

The Justice Department hires immigration judges as needed pursuant to a single vacancy announcement (published on www.usajobs.gov) for single or multiple vacancies at a time, and, surprisingly, does not even require that candidates know anything about immigration law!

Given the centrality of the immigration debate at this time, the system is only likely to improve.

Chapter 29

Mainstream Attorney Hiring—The Military Judge Advocate Generals Corps

The armed services—Army, Navy, Air Force, and Marine Corps— employ almost 6,000 attorneys in their respective Judge Advocate Generals' Corps. Positions can be found throughout the United States and in many locations overseas. These are highly competitive positions with acceptance rates currently on a par with Ivy League universities.

Each year hundreds of 3Ls and recent law school graduates are accepted into the JAG Corps, where they first go through extensive training in military law and litigation and gain excellent experience very early in their careers, experience that has proven to be eminently transferable to civilian practice. The other huge advantage of JAG Corps service is possibly the world's finest alumni network outside of membership in Yale's preeminent secret society, Skull and Bones. No other organizations go the extra mile when it comes to assisting fellow alumni like the military JAG corps. Given that thousands of JAG alums are, at any given time, working in prominent legal positions, they can be immensely important to a young JAG officer's future legal career.

Military JAGs work all over the world, and their practice encompasses much more than court-martial litigation, where JAGs often begin their careers as defense counsel and, once they gain criminal litigation experience, may be assigned as prosecutors. Other JAG practice areas include:

- Administrative Law
- Admiralty and Maritime Law
- Civil Litigation
- Claims
- Environmental Law
- Government Contract Law
- Humanitarian Assistance and Refugee Law
- International Law
- Labor Law
- Legal Assistance
- Medical Malpractice
- Real Property Law
- Space Law
- Teaching

For recruitment and hiring information, see:

- Army JAG Corps—www.goarmy.com/jag/index.jsp
- Navy and Marine Corps JAG Corps—www.jag.navy.mil
- Air Force JAG Corps—www.jagusaf.hq.af.mil/

Chapter 30

Mainstream Attorney Hiring—Foreign Affairs

The Foreign Service

Foreign Service Officers (FSOs) constitute the bulk of the U.S. diplomatic corps. They work in the United States at the Department of State and in 265 embassies, consulates, and missions to international organizations in 180 countries worldwide. Several thousand attorneys serve as Foreign Service Officers (the entire corps numbers over 12,000).

FSOs select one of five career paths upon registering for the Foreign Service Examination:

- *Consular.* Consular Officers protect Americans abroad and strengthen U.S. border security.
- *Economic.* Economic Officers work on economic partnerships and development, support U.S. businesses abroad, and cover environmental, science, technology, and health issues.
- *Management.* Management Officers run embassies and make American diplomacy work.

- *Political.* Political Officers analyze political events.
- *Public Diplomacy.* Public Diplomacy Officers explain American values and policies.

You must be from 20 to 59 years of age on the day you submit your registration for the Foreign Service Examination (see below) and at least 21 years old and not yet 60 on the day you are appointed as an FSO. Foreign language proficiency will enhance your chances of selection.

The hiring process is rigorous and consists of the Foreign Service Examination, a personal narrative, an oral assessment, a medical examination, a security check (background investigation), and a final review panel.

You can get detailed information about FSOs and the hiring process at http://careers.state.gov/officer/employment.html.

Note: A law degree and legal experience will earn you higher compensation both when you enter the Foreign Service and as you proceed through your career.

The U.S. and Foreign Commercial Service (Commercial Service)

The U.S. Commercial Service is responsible for commercial affairs. FSOs in the Commercial Service are assigned to 78 countries and more than 100 domestic field offices, as well as Washington, D.C., to promote the export of U.S. goods and services and defend U.S. commercial interests abroad. Many Commercial Service FSOs have a law degree.

Commercial Service FSO duties include:

- Gathering market intelligence to help U.S. exporters target the right markets for their products and services;
- Trade counseling to provide exporters with the information they need to navigate the export process from beginning to end;
- Business matchmaking services to connect exporters with the right partners and prospects; and

- Trade advocacy for U.S companies to level the international playing field for international procurement.

The U.S. Commercial Service Assessment is a competitive oral and written examination used to recruit new, tenure-track FSOs into the U.S. Commercial Service. Successful applicants who pass the initial online application screening process receive an invitation for the one-day oral assessment. Top candidates who pass the oral assessment exam are placed on a list called the Rank Order Register, valid for two years. The Career Development and Assignments staff uses this Register to tender conditional offers of employment to candidates as vacancies become available, pending the successful completion of a Top Secret security clearance, a medical clearance, and drug testing.

For additional information, see http://trade.gov/cs/employment.asp.

Chapter 31

Mainstream Attorney Hiring—FBI Special Agents

I have included FBI Special Agents under Mainstream Attorney Hiring because (1) so many of them are attorneys, and (2) the FBI actively recruits lawyers.

To become an FBI Special Agent, you must be a U.S. citizen or a citizen of the Northern Mariana Islands, at least 23 years of age but younger than 37 upon appointment. Age waivers may be granted to preference eligible veterans who have passed their 37th birthday. You must have a four-year degree from an accredited college or university and have at least three years of professional work experience.

All applicants for the Special Agent position must first qualify under one of five Special Agent Entry Programs:

- accounting
- computer science/information technology
- language
- law
- diversified

After qualifying for one of the entry programs, applicants will be prioritized in the hiring process based upon certain critical skills for which the FBI is recruiting. The FBI is currently recruiting for one or more of the following critical skills:

- accounting
- finance
- computer science/information technology expertise
- engineering expertise
- foreign language(s) proficiency
- intelligence experience
- law experience
- law enforcement/investigative experience
- military experience
- physical sciences (e.g., physics, chemistry, biology, etc.) expertise
- diversified experience

Because of the demanding nature of the position, candidates must also meet a number of physical requirements, as well as a background investigation, drug testing, and other requirements.

For more information, see www.fbijobs.gov/11.asp.

Chapter 32

Mainstream Attorney Hiring—Fellowship Programs

The U.S. government offers a variety of fellowship programs for which attorneys may qualify and compete. While these are term-limited, they can serve as a great foot-in-the-door for attorneys seeking a full-time, permanent federal legal position, and they look very good on any resume.

A selection of fellowship programs for which attorneys may compete, with brief descriptions, is listed below.

Presidential Management Fellowship (https://www.pmf. opm.gov/). These are two-year, policy-related fellowships wherein fellows are assigned to work with any one of the many agencies of government. Law students in particular are urged to apply. Applications are accepted from 3Ls and LL.M. candidates.

White House Fellowship (www.whitehouse.gov/about/fellows/). This most prestigious and competitive of all government fellowship programs enables fellows to spend one year as a paid assistant to senior White House or top-ranking government officials. Applicants must have a record of remarkable professional achievement early in their careers.

Congressional Black Caucus Foundation Fellowships (http://cbcfinc.org/programs/leadership-development/172.html). These one-year fellowships are designed to increase the number of African-Americans working as professional staff in the U.S. Congress. Fellows work in congressional member and committee offices, attend leadership development seminars, complete a community service project, and produce policy papers. You must have completed a graduate or professional degree prior to commencing the fellowship.

Women's Research and Education Institute Congressional Fellowships on Women and Public Policy (www.wrei.org/Fellows.htm). WREI awards annual fellowships to a select number of graduate students with a proven commitment to equity for women. Fellows work from January to August as congressional legislative aides in Washington, D.C. Only students who are currently in, or have recently completed, a graduate or professional degree program at an accredited institution in the United States are eligible.

EPA's National Network for Environmental Management Studies Fellowship Program (www.epa.gov/ocepa111/NNEMS/students. html). EPA offers more than 40 fellowships each year in EPA headquarters and regional offices and laboratories around the country. Fellows undertake research projects, including ones in environmental law and policy. Law students may apply.

Fellowship Opportunities in Technology Transfer—Negotiator (http://ttc.nci.nih.gov/employment/crtafe.php). The National Cancer Institute (NCI) Technology Transfer Center (TTC) has fellowship opportunities available to qualified candidates. Candidates must possess an advanced degree in the sciences and/or a law degree with a background in the sciences. The TTC is responsible for negotiating agreements and promoting research partnerships between NCI scientists and outside parties, such as universities and biotechnology/ pharmaceutical companies, that allow for federally funded research findings to be further developed and commercialized. Fellows draft and negotiate Cooperative Research and Development Agreements (CRADAs) for NCI scientists and their industrial/academic research partners; plan and negotiate Material Transfer Agreements, Clinical Trial Agreements, and other technology-transfer agreements; development technology-transfer educational programs for scientists; and oversee patent-related issues for NCI scientists. The starting stipend for a J.D. with no experience is $48,300; it is higher if the candidate has relevant work experience and/or additional applicable degrees.

Chapter 33

Hiring for Federal "Law-Related" Jobs

Unlike attorney positions, law-related jobs fall under the competitive civil service with its hundreds of rules and regulations governing recruitment, hiring, promotion, termination, etc. That means that federal employers have far less discretion as to whom they can hire and how they can go about hiring them than they do for "excepted" attorney jobs.

Every law-related position must be publicly advertised; there will always be a published job vacancy announcement of the position. Vacancy announcements can be found at www.usajobs.gov and often on agency websites as well.

The law-related job hiring process also differs from how mainstream attorneys are hired. Because it is so constrained by competitive service rules and regulations, the process is largely uniform from one agency to the next, as well as from one office to the next within each agency. There is very little wiggle room for creative or idiosyncratic hiring approaches. It also means that agency human resources (HR) offices play a much greater role in the hiring process. Whereas attorneys are often hired without any reference to the HR office—certain Justice Department litigating divisions for many years consistently avoided sending their job announcements to the department's attorney-recruiting office, preferring a do-it-yourself approach—law-related positions almost always go through HR.

It is not uncommon for HR to perform the entire initial and follow-up evaluations and then send a list of qualified candidates in ranked order directly to the hiring official.

The hiring official must then select the winning candidate from the top three on the hierarchical list after Veterans Preference points have been added. I once sat on an attorney rating panel that sent a list of 10 qualified candidates to our boss, who ultimately selected the attorney we rated at the very bottom of the list. That could never happen with a law-related position.

Chapter 34

Political Appointments

Top-Level Appointments

Approximately 1,455 top-level political appointments exist in the executive branch. They include agency heads and their immediate subordinates, policy executives and advisors, senior aides who report to these officials, and senior Foreign Service officers, including ambassadors. The duties of many such positions may involve advocacy of Administration policies and programs, and the appointees usually have a close and confidential working relationship with the agency head or other key officials.

These positions are almost all vacant when a new President and Administration takes office and are generally filled within the next 12–18 months. After that, turnover is low until there is another change of Administration.

Following are the major categories of positions:

- 1,141 positions to which candidates are appointed by the President with Senate confirmation; and
- 314 appointments made by the President that do not require Senate confirmation.

In addition, 3,723 Senior Executive Service (SES) "General" positions are available for noncompetitive appointment (read: political). These need to be distinguished from SES "Career" positions that are not subject to political appointment. (See Chapter 26 for a detailed discussion of SES Career positions.)

Lower-Level (Schedule C) Political Appointments

In addition to the continuous hiring that goes on for regular federal attorney and law-related positions, there are also almost 1,700 lower-level political appointments that can be filled by attorneys. The number varies from time to time and has been as high as 2,000. These types of jobs are called Schedule C positions because the appointing authority falls under Schedule C of the General Schedule.

The turnover rate in Schedule C positions is higher than in non-political federal attorney jobs, so there are always quite a few positions available at any given time. In addition, agency and divisional heads frequently "create" new Schedule C positions.

Schedule C positions differ from regular attorney and competitive service jobs because of their confidential or policy-determining character. Agencies may fill Schedule C positions noncompetitively. Because of the nature of Schedule C positions, their incumbents serve at the pleasure of the appointing authority (usually the agency head) and may be removed at any time. The immediate supervisor of a Schedule C position must also be a political appointee. Most such positions are at grade 15 of the federal General Schedule or lower (see the U.S. Government Salary Charts at www.usajobs.gov). A significant number are entry-level professional positions (grades 9 and 11).

Since they are political appointments, Schedule C positions are usually filled on an other-than-merit basis. This means that you have to "know" somebody. However, the people that you have to know are not necessarily the President, his close advisors, or a member of Congress. Your intermediaries/promoters can be almost anyone who knows someone in the Administration or on Capitol Hill, including law professors, many of whom advise politicians and policymakers in Washington or have other connections with these influential people.

The decision whether to place a position in Schedule C is made by the OPM Director upon agency request. Such requests are very easy for an agency to make (a brief letter will usually suffice), are considered by OPM on a case-by-case basis, and are almost never refused.

Schedule C positions authorized by OPM are automatically revoked when the incumbent leaves the position (i.e., there is no such thing as a "vacant" Schedule C position).

While these positions are not advertised, there is actually a published list of new Schedule C positions authorized by OPM to be filled by requesting agencies. This list is published in the *Federal Register* (www.gpoaccess.gov/fr/index.html), usually (but not always) on the fourth Tuesday of each month. A recent monthly list contained 56 Schedule C positions at 24 departments and agencies.

Chapter 35

Disability Hiring—The Selective Placement Program

The Selective Placement Program (SPP) is one of the last remaining expressly affirmative action hiring programs in the U.S. government. It was established by Section 501(b) of the Rehabilitation Act of 1973, Pub. L. 93-112, and reads as follows:

> Each department, agency, and instrumentality (including the United States Postal Service and the Postal Rate Commission) in the Executive Branch shall, within one hundred and eighty days after the date of enactment of this ACT, submit to the Civil Service Commission and to the Committee an affirmative action program plan for the hiring, placement, and advancement of handicapped individuals in such department, agency, or instrumentality. Such plan shall include a description of the extent to which and methods whereby the special needs of handicapped employees are being met. Such plan shall be updated annually, and shall be reviewed annually and approved by the Commission, if the Commission determines, after consul-

tation with the Committee, that such plan provides sufficient assurances, procedures and commitments to provide adequate hiring, placement, and advancement opportunities for handicapped individuals.

This provision is still good law today. Unfortunately, very few government officials know that.

The Civil Service Commission and its successor, the U.S. Office of Personnel Management (OPM), developed and promulgated a series of implementing regulations and guidelines (labeled in the aggregate the SPP and placed in the *Federal Personnel Manual*) that remained on the books until the end of 1995. They required each executive branch entity to appoint someone as its Selective Placement coordinator to be a conduit and advocate for disabled applicants for federal jobs. The regulations specified that a candidate could submit his or her application to the coordinator rather than applying through the customary competitive service process, and that the coordinator would then hand-carry the application to the appropriate hiring official. The hiring official would then have to consider the candidate if he or she were found minimally qualified.

The SPP did not require that the candidate be hired, only that he or she have some affirmative action advantages in the consideration process. Having one's resumé or federal application form delivered to the hiring official in this manner, having to meet only threshold qualifications, and having one's application considered by a hiring official in relative isolation from other candidates are, in fact, huge advantages, if not necessarily perfectly consistent with the legislative intent behind affirmative action.

In addition, the *Federal Personnel Manual* laid out the documentation that an SPP candidate would need in order to be eligible to apply under the program, principally a physician's statement that the candidate had one of the targeted disabilities and was able to work in his or her occupation or profession, and a certificate of eligibility from either a state Vocational Rehabilitation Office or the Department of Veterans' Affairs. Armed with those two documents, the candidate could then apply using the SPP process.

The Manual also specified a number of other SPP principles, the most important of which were (1) the level of confidentiality that was to be maintained by the coordinator and hiring officials, (2) the fact that an SPP hire would initially be in a probationary status, and (3) the fact that an SPP candidate would not be bound by the job application deadlines specified in federal vacancy announcements if he or she applied before a selection was made. The latter was a huge advantage, especially since some positions close for the receipt of applications after being open for only a few days.

In 1995, everything changed . . . and nothing changed. First, the National Performance Review, a government-wide reform initiative headed by Vice President Gore, combed through federal regulations, including the *Federal Personnel Manual*, and culled provisions that they deemed obsolete or unnecessary. In a White House Rose Garden ceremony touting the success of the reform effort, the Vice President dramatically held up the thousands of pages of regulations that would no longer be in effect. Among those were each and every regulation and guideline concerning the SPP. Following the termination of the National Performance Review, a participant in its task force admitted to me that the excision of the SPP rules had been inadvertent, a mistake. However, no one wanted to publicize that and reinstitute them. This presented a dilemma for executive branch agencies, since the law mandating the SPP was still on the books, but now there were no procedures in place to indicate how to implement that statute. This lack of official documentary guidance has continued to this day.

The tack that many agencies took was to continue to run the SPP as if nothing had happened. Unfortunately, not every agency went that route, and the program and its would-be beneficiaries suffered. As indicated in Part One, "Federal Legal Demographics," disability hiring by the federal government has been static for years. In the interim, Presidents Clinton, Bush, and Obama have from time to time issued executive orders extolling the virtues of employing disabled individuals and requiring agencies to do more in this area. The most recent one (Executive Order 13,548) was signed by President Obama on July 26, 2010. It requires agencies to increase the hiring of people with disabilities by 100,000 positions over the next five years. Agencies were given 120 days to develop a plan that will detail how they intend to accomplish their part of the goal.

Here are OPM's instructions to disabled applicants, contained in its press release about the new executive order:

> People with disabilities seeking employment are encouraged to apply for positions through USAJOBS or by sending your resumé directly to the agency with a job opening for which you would like to apply. If you want to send your resumé directly to a federal agency, contact that agency's Selective Placement Program Coordinator (SPPC). A list of SPPCs by agency can be found here.

Keep this excerpt in mind when you read the material below about SPP coordinators.

Moreover, each of the three most recent Presidents has appointed a White House official to monitor government disability employment and advocate among the agencies for such programs and initiatives. I dealt personally with two of them. The first one—President Clinton's—was a sincere, dedicated advocate who ran up against an indifferent bureaucracy. The second one (President Bush's)—a blind attorney detailed from the Justice Department—shared the same convictions, but wound up as window dressing for public consumption. Agency SPP coordinators with whom I interacted did not even know he existed.

The Reality

To say that the SPP has not worked is a massive understatement. While not a complete failure, it has come very close to earning that label when it comes to the hiring of attorneys for federal jobs. Over my years as a legal career counselor, I worked—usually pro bono—with more than 100 SPP candidates, virtually all of whom were highly qualified. Perhaps 10 were able to negotiate the hiring process successfully and actually get a federal job, sometimes only with my intervening in the process as an aggressive advocate.

None of my candidates ever had a problem with Step One of the process, obtaining the requisite physician's letter. Step Two is where the process got complicated for some of my clients. Upon appearing at the local office of their state's vocational rehabilitation agency to pick up a Certificate of Eligibility, they heard one or more of the following statements from a vocational rehab counselor:

- "I have never heard of this so-called Selective Placement Program."
- "Our state does not participate in this program."
- "You are the first person who ever asked this question. We have no idea what to do."
- "We cannot issue a Certificate until you sign up for our services, we do an evaluation, and you go through our entire rehab program."

Confronted with such ignorance and misinformation, I would often receive a panicked call from a frustrated client, whereupon I would pick up the phone and call the rehab counselor myself and explain the SPP process to him or her. I often had to provide a mini-lecture in constitutional law and federalism to persuade the counselor that the program existed and was mandatory on the states. In other cases, I offered to, or was asked if I could, provide a template for a Certificate of Eligibility.

The next frustration was probably the biggest one: communicating with agency SPP coordinators. From time to time, OPM would put together and publish an updated list of coordinators, citing their agency, office address, and phone number (later the list would be posted on the OPM website and include e-mail addresses). More often than not, the SPP coordinator (1) did not know that he or she was tasked with that role, (2) had never heard of the SPP, or worse, (3) denied being the coordinator! In every single instance where one of these responses was forthcoming, not a single listed coordinator could tell my client who else to contact in the agency regarding the SPP.

Even when the coordinator was aware of his or her role and received an application from a client, that did not mean smooth sailing. Many times, coordinators did not pass along the application to the hiring official. On other occasions, the coordinator informed my client that the application was received after the deadline and would not be considered (this despite the fact that SPP candidates may apply for closed positions until a selection is made). The worst dilemma was the coordinator who would inform my client that the SPP did not apply to attorneys (it always has and still does) because the program placed disabled individuals in excepted service positions and attorneys were, by definition, excepted service employees—ergo, they did not need to invoke the SPP to be considered. It should be noted that the law and the formerly active *Federal Personnel Manual* pronouncements said nothing about attorneys or any other federal occupation being ineligible for the program.

The SPP Today

Two real accounts shared with me by recent attorney SPP candidates chronicle how well or poorly the SPP is operating today:

- E.K. is a 100 percent visually impaired attorney who earned a Bachelor's degree, cum laude, in astronomy with a mathematics minor from an Ivy League university, followed by a Master's in aerospace engineering from a second Ivy League school, and topped off by a J.D. with an emphasis in intellectual property law from a tier-one law school. Since graduating from law school 10 years ago, E.K. has been unable to find a legal position, and his efforts over the past several years to obtain a federal attorney job via the SPP have been fruitless.
- G.D. recently sent me the following e-mail, from which I quote with his permission:

  > As for applying for government jobs under a disabled status [Selective Placement], I found the regulations and official guidance rather nebulous. I initially started out on what I now believe was the wrong track. Trying to pedantically follow their

guidelines, I listed my invocation of disability status in my cover letters, and would address the whole application to the [S]elective [P]lacement [C]oordinator, with the required certification. I did this through the regular channels.

I also started with a certification that was quite detailed about the nature of the disability. Later, I found a suggested sample certification on an OPM website which did not seem to include any details about the nature of the disability at all, so I had my therapist rewrite it in that format. I am not sure whether the current one is too sparse, but I figure the less one discloses on paper, the better, while remaining consistent with their guidelines.

As for the method of application, after a while, I thought better of the approach I was using. After all, I realized it was advertising my claimed disability status to all and sundry. I started sending a regular application through regular channels. I would then write a separate e-mail to the [S]elective [P]lacement [C]oordinator with the various parts of the application attached, as well as the certification.

I routinely tried to call [S]elective [P]lacement [C]oordinators a day after sending them these e-mails, at least at first. Perhaps I could have been more diligent in this. Anyway, I invariably had to leave a message, and I never heard back from any of them. One thing that has been somewhat irksome is that, as far as I can tell, the Department of the Interior and its various sub-agencies do not have any official [C]oordinators at all. This is especially frustrating, because they post many of the best and most appropriate listings. I have been taking this as an indication that they don't know how to deal with people who invoke a disability status. Thus, on the assumption that it is safer not to invoke it, I have simply sent them regular applications.

Three further points about SPP coordinators:

1. By far the very best SPP coordinator I ever encountered was a young man who worked for the U.S. Small Business Administration. He was himself disabled, was passionate about his mission, and was an incredibly committed and dedicated civil servant. He was also totally ineffective. The reason was one I later discovered was often endemic to the SPP: The position of coordinator was often conferred on one of the lowest-level employees in the agency's Human Resources office, someone who had zero clout with his or her superiors. It takes a least some "heft" to be an effective internal advocate for any program, employment or otherwise. Appointing someone at the bottom of the federal food chain is a virtual guarantee of program failure and also demonstrates how "serious" agency managers consider the SPP.

2. SPP coordinators often wear too many hats. They may also be the Veterans Employment coordinator, Hispanic Employment coordinator, Women's Employment coordinator, Minority Employment coordinator, Asian-Pacific Islander-Aleut Employment coordinator, as well as having responsibility for the Combined Federal Campaign and a host of other duties. With so many diverse responsibilities and a finite amount of time and energy to devote to each, it is no wonder that the SPP suffers. This again demonstrates the disinterest in, if not outright resistance to, the SPP on the part of the agency bosses.

3. A glance at the list of SPP coordinators on the OPM website reveals that more than two-thirds of them are located at agency headquarter offices in the Washington, D.C. area. Since only 12 percent of the total number of federal employees work in the national capital area, the vast majority of federal government regional and field offices do not have coordinators at all.

Needless to say, the SPP is a program on life support, notwithstanding President Obama's recent executive order. Only time will tell if there will be any positive follow-up to his pronouncements. If history is any indicator, don't bet your mortgage or rent.

If you want to try the SPP route, by all means go ahead and invoke it. My best suggestion is, however, that when you attempt to contact the SPP coordinator in a particular agency, you forget about the OPM website list after your initial failed attempt and start at the top by contacting the agency's Director of Human Resources and let him or her—or more likely his or her immediate assistant—direct you to the proper person. You can find the name and contact information for the HR director on the agency's website or in the *Federal Staff Directory*, a resource available in most large public libraries. If that still does not work, contact your member of Congress and send him or her all of your application materials.

Chapter 36

Veterans' Employment Programs

Though federal veterans' employment programs suffer from some of the same deficiencies as the Selective Placement Program, overall the picture is more favorable. The reasons for that are twofold: (1) greater precision in how the veterans' employment laws and regulations were drafted, and (2) greater empathy for veterans, especially in those agencies that either deal directly with veterans or have a disproportionate number of employees who are veterans, such as the Departments of Defense, Veterans Affairs, and Homeland Security, and the National Aeronautics and Space Administration.

Multiple programs exist for veterans interested in working for the U.S. government. The major ones that attorneys can invoke are described below.

Veterans' Preference

Veterans' Preference gives certain military veterans a big boost in competing for federal government jobs. As discussed, the law adds five points to every veteran's score on a federal civil service "examination" (this does not necessarily mean a "test"; often, it means an assessment of qualifications for a position) and 10 points to the score achieved by certain disabled veterans. While that might not sound like much of an advantage, it is when you consider that most applicant scores fall within a very narrow range. With respect to the federal administrative law judge (ALJ) examination, for example (see Chapter 27), it means that more veterans than non-veterans by far wind up with ALJ positions.

Basic eligibility for five-point preference depends on the length of continuous active-duty military service (more than 180 days for certain veterans and 24 months for others). Beyond that, there are other eligibility factors that come into play, such as dates of service (during a war), nature of discharge (honorable or general), type of position (preference does not apply to Senior Executive Service or political appointments), etc.

Ten points are added to the passing score of a disabled veteran who has (1) a compensable service-connected disability rating of at least 10 percent but less than 30 percent; (2) a present service-connected disability or is receiving compensation, disability retirement benefits, or pension from the military or the Department of Veterans Affairs; or (3) has received a Purple Heart. The preference applies regardless of when the service took place. In addition, spouses, widows, widowers, or mothers of certain veterans may qualify for 10-point "derived preference" based on service of a veteran who is not able to use the preference.

Veterans' Preference in Practice

Veterans' Preference works very well to the advantage of eligible attorneys who are applying for positions in the competitive service, i.e., positions that generally do not carry the term "attorney" in their job titles. Thus, a "preference-eligible" attorney who applies for a law-related position in the U.S. government is almost always going to have a big advantage.

Veterans' Preference does not work quite as well when it comes to excepted service positions (primarily those classified as "GS-0905," which almost always include the term "attorney" in the job title). The reason for this points to the biggest flaw in the Veterans' Preference program as applied to legal hiring by the government. Misinterpretation and erroneous assumptions on the part of federal hiring officials, even hiring officials who happen to also be lawyers, occasionally gets in the way of logic and law. Like the SPP, applicants eligible for Veterans' Preference have been incorrectly informed by hiring officials that Veterans' Preference does not apply to excepted service positions. Even the Justice Department adopted this point of view when hiring for certain attorney positions, despite the language in the law, reflected on OPM's website (OPM administers the Veterans' Preference laws):

> Preference in hiring applies to permanent and temporary positions in the competitive and excepted services of the executive branch.

While the relevant sections of the *Code of Federal Regulations* permit agencies some leeway in applying Veterans' Preference to attorney positions, it does not permit them to ignore it altogether.

Appeal Rights

If a preference-eligible attorney is denied Veterans' Preference, he or she has certain appeal rights. The Veterans Employment Opportunities Act of 1998, Pub. L. 105-339, allows preference eligibles to complain to the Department of Labor's Veterans' Employment and Training Service (VETS).

A disabled veteran who believes he or she has been discriminated against in employment because of a disability may file a handicapped discrimination complaint with the offending agency under regulations administered by the Equal Employment Opportunity Commission.

Finally, any veteran with a Veterans' Preference complaint may also contact any OPM Service Center. Generally speaking, complaints on the same issue may not be filed with more than one agency.

Veterans Recruitment Appointment (VRA) Authority

VRA is a special hiring authority that agencies can, if they wish, use to appoint eligible veterans without competition to positions at any grade level through GS-11 or its equivalent. GS-11 is the higher of the two entry-level grades at which new law school graduates begin their federal careers. VRA appointees are hired under ex-cepted appointments to positions that are otherwise in the competi-tive service. For attorneys, this means law-related positions.

A veteran who is eligible for a VRA appointment is not auto-matically eligible for Veterans' Preference. After two years of satis-factory service, the agency must convert the veteran to career or career-conditional appointment, as appropriate.

Eligibility
- Disabled veterans; or
- Veterans who served on active duty during a war, or in a campaign or expedition for which a campaign badge has been authorized; or
- Veterans who, while serving on active duty, participated in a United States military operation for which an Armed Forces Service Medal was awarded; or
- Recently separated veterans.

In addition, eligible veterans must have received either an honor-able or general discharge.

If an agency has two or more VRA candidates and one or more is Veterans' Preference eligible, the agency must apply Veterans' Preference rather than VRA.

Veterans Who Are 30 Percent Disabled or More

An agency may give a noncompetitive temporary or term appoint-ment to any veteran (1) retired from active military service with a disability rating of 30 percent or more, or (2) rated by the Depart-ment of Veterans Affairs (VA) since 1991 or later to include disabil-ity determinations from a branch of the Armed Forces at any time as having a compensable service-connected disability of 30 per-cent or more. There is no grade-level limitation for this authority, but the appointee must meet all qualification requirements, includ-ing any written test requirement. The agency may convert the em-ployee, without a break in service, to a career or career-conditional appointment at any time during the employee's temporary or term appointment.

Veterans Employment Opportunities Act of 1998 (VEOA)

The VEOA, as amended, provides that agencies must allow Veterans' Preference eligibles or eligible veterans to apply for positions announced under merit promotion procedures when the agency is recruiting from outside its own workforce. A VEOA eligible competes under merit promotion procedures—the appointing official may select any candidate from those who are among the best qualified—and if selected, the VEOA eligible is given a career or career-conditional appointment, as appropriate. Veterans' Preference is not a factor in these appointments.

To be eligible for a VEOA appointment, an applicant must be a preference eligible OR a veteran separated from the armed forces after three or more years of continuous active service performed under honorable conditions. Veterans released shortly before completing a three-year tour are also deemed eligible. All employees appointed under the VEOA are subject to a probationary period and to the requirements of their agency's merit promotion plan.

Executive Order 13,518, "Employment of Veterans in the Federal Government"

In November 2009, President Obama issued this executive order designed "to transform the federal government into the model employer of America's veterans." The directive established a Veterans Employment Initiative for the executive branch. The initiative underscores to federal agencies the importance of recruiting and training veterans, aims to increase the employment of veterans within the executive branch, and helps recently hired veterans adjust to service in a civilian capacity. Under the initiative, each participating agency shall, to the extent permitted by law:

(a) Develop an agency-specific Operational Plan for promoting employment opportunities for veterans;
(b) Have established a Veterans Employment Program Office, or designate an agency officer or employee with full-time responsibility for its Veterans Employment Program, to be responsible for enhancing employment opportunities for vet-

erans within the agency and for coordinating employment counseling to help match the career aspirations of veterans to the needs of the agency;

(c) Provide mandatory annual training to agency human resources personnel and hiring managers concerning veterans' employment, including training on Veterans' Preferences and special authorities for the hiring of veterans;

(d) Identify key occupations for which the agency will provide job counseling and training to better enable veterans to meet agency staffing needs associated with those occupations; and

(e) Coordinate with the Departments of Defense and Veterans Affairs to promote further development and application of technology designed to assist transitioning service members and veterans with disabilities.

The executive order creates an interagency Council on Veterans Employment that will advise the President and the director of OPM on the veterans' employment initiative.

In addition, OPM was directed to issue a government-wide strategic plan focusing on "creating leadership commitment and an infrastructure in each agency to promote continued skills development and employment success for veterans," and including marketing strategies aimed at agency hiring managers as well as veterans and transitioning service members.

Homeland Security Secretary Janet Napolitano pledged that her department would grow its veteran workforce to more than 50,000 department-wide by 2012. At the end of fiscal year 2008, there were approximately 480,000 veterans working for the federal government.

Like the series of executive orders aimed at disabled individuals, it remains to be seen whether this one will be any more effective than its predecessors. Moreover, like most instructions to agencies that come via legislation or presidential executive order, this one is confusing, since much of what it directs already exists. Executive branch agencies have had veterans' employment coordinators for years, for example.

If this initiative actually works as intended, great. What is immediately apparent is the contrast between this executive order and President Obama's 2010 executive order concerning disability employment discussed in the previous chapter. Your chances of federal employment are better if you are an attorney who is also a veteran rather than a non-veteran attorney who is disabled.

Chapter 37

Indian Preference Hiring

Indian preference in hiring for federal positions "in the administration of functions or services affecting any Indian tribe" has been the law of the land since the enactment of the Indian Reorganization Act in 1934, Pub. L. 280. The act's Indian Preference provision has been construed by regulation and the courts as applying to all Department of Interior positions that directly and primarily relate to providing services to Indians and Alaska Natives. At present, 95 percent of the several thousand employees of Interior's Bureau of Indian Affairs are Native Americans.

The act has also been interpreted to apply to employees of the Department of Health and Human Services' Indian Health Service and Interior's Office of the Special Trustee for American Indians, which was established by the American Indian Trust Fund Management Reform Act of 1994 (Pub. L. 103-412) to improve the accountability and management of tens of billions of dollars of Indian funds held in trust by the federal government, which (through the Interior Department) has the primary fiduciary responsibility to manage both tribal trust funds and Individual Indian Money (IIM) accounts, as well as resources that generate income for those accounts. This office is a very important one because it was prompted by a court decision that compelled the Interior Department to sort out the monumental mismanagement of these funds for more than 100 years and make things right.

The attorney and law-related positions in these three organizations are covered by Indian Preference.

Part V

Frequently Asked Questions about Landing a Federal Legal Job

I have yet to encounter an "outside" candidate for a U.S. government attorney or law-related job who has even a vague idea of what working for the government is all about. I invariably had to spend the first several hours of our career-counseling time explain-

ing the government in all of its permutations, nuances, and quirks. My clients' reaction was invariably one of "shock and awe." This Part is my attempt at streamlining my answers for you before you take your leap of faith into the federal legal universe.

Chapter 38

Key Questions Overview

Let's start by once again announcing that the federal government is not a monolith and that you cannot assume and then act upon the notion that sameness prevails from one agency to another, one office within an agency to another, one federal practice area to another, one geographic region to another, and so forth. I understand that you may be getting tired of hearing this mantra repeated over and over again. However, my experience is that it simply must be restated time and time again before it imprints sufficiently to keep candidates from making terrible mistakes and destroying their chances of finding suitable and rewarding federal employment.

The other erroneous assumptions, and especially anxieties, that make up the baggage that federal aspirants carry with them have to do with the following questions and concerns about federal employment.

Preliminary Questions

- How do I match my background with opportunities?
- Which headhunters place attorneys in the government?
- What is the work like?
- What do government employers want?
- How do I move to a new practice area?
- What will a government job look like on a resume?
- How am I supposed to survive on a government salary?

Application Process Questions

- How do I decipher federal job vacancy announcements?
- How can I identify vacancy announcements that match my background or interests?
- What if I attended a non-ABA-accredited law school?
- What if I am not admitted to the bar?
- What if I am not admitted in the state where I am applying?
- What if I don't have the required experience?
- How should I respond to a question about my salary history?
- I don't understand how to respond to KSAs.
- Why does it take so long for the government to hire someone?

Job Offer and Acceptance Questions

- What is negotiable?
- Can I be transferred against my will?
- Will I have my own private office?

These questions are all very important. Agonizing over them without making an effort to obtain good answers has deterred many attorneys from even attempting to compete for a federal legal job. I will address these questions in the next three chapters.

Chapter 39

Preliminary Questions

These seven initial questions are the ones that are the most frequently posed to me by federal job-seeking clients. Here is what I tell them.

How Do I Match My Background with Opportunities?

As indicated in Chapter 21, "Federal Practice Areas," U.S. government lawyers are actively engaged in more than 100 practice areas. There is, it's safe to say, something for everyone. Here are some examples of my clients who came from rather esoteric, and sometimes narrow, backgrounds.

- A young woman who had gone to law school and had been seeking legal employment unsuccessfully after five years as a funeral home director and licensed embalmer was worried that she would never find anything in the federal government that could possibly make use of her background. I directed her to the Federal Trade Commission's (FTC) Bureau of Consumer Protection, which administers the FTC's "Funeral Rule." The Funeral Rule requires funeral providers to give consumers accurate, itemized price information and various other disclosures about funeral goods and services, and prohibits them from misrepresenting legal, crematory, and cemetery requirements; embalming for a fee without permission; requiring the purchase of a casket for direct cremation; requiring consumers to buy certain funeral goods or services as a condition for furnishing other funeral goods or services; and engaging in other deceptive or unfair practices, among other requirements (probably much more information than you ever wanted to know). Bureau attorneys are responsible for keeping the Funeral Rule up to date and for industry compliance and enforcement (each violation carries a substantial monetary penalty).

The FTC did not have a published vacancy announcement for a Funeral Rule attorney when my client made her unsolicited contact with the agency. Nevertheless, the FTC virtually salivated over her. They had never encountered a combination attorney/funeral director in the 20 years during which the Funeral Rule had been operative at the time. They "managed" to find her a position in short order.

- A Kentucky equine lawyer came to me seeking federal employment after a brief career working for a law firm representing clients in the thoroughbred racing industry in Kentucky. During our counseling relationship, a job opened up for a general attorney with the Office of the Solicitor at the Department of Interior. She applied and was hired, principally because the Department's Bureau of Land Management, a major Solicitor's Office client, is responsible for 63,000 horses and a smaller number of burros roaming wild or in government corrals in the West. The Solicitor's Office at that time did not have any attorneys who had any equine familiarity and was being confronted with a number of cutting-edge legal issues concerning horses and burros, including lawsuits challenging how these animals were being treated and managed (the government runs both an adoption program and a euthanasia program).
- An attorney who was downsized out of his law firm had spent the bulk of his career representing municipal taxi commissions. The major issues that he handled were the legal

framework of auctions for "hack" licenses and the disputes that arose as a consequence of such auctions. He was at a loss as to where to look in the U.S. government for a position where he might have a competitive edge due to his unique background.

I suggested one of the federal law offices that handle auctions, a federal practice of which he was completely unaware. We focused his federal legal employment campaign on the Federal Communications Commission (FCC), which holds periodic broadcast spectrum auctions; the Federal Deposit Insurance Corporation, which disposes of the assets of failed financial institutions through auctions and other means; and the Department of Interior's now much-maligned Minerals Management Service (recently renamed the Bureau of Ocean Energy Management, Regulation and Enforcement), which periodically auctions off Outer Continental Shelf oil and gas leases in the Gulf of Mexico. He was hired by the FCC.

The points to be made are the following:

- There is literally something for everyone in the federal government.
- Before you launch your federal job search, you need to closely examine both your background and your skills and interests and perform sufficient research in order to identify "comparables" in the government.
- You need to think in terms of your *transferable* background or skills and not merely your *specific* experience.
- If you have an esoteric background, the comparable federal practice areas that you discover will give you a competitive edge.

Which Headhunters Place Attorneys in the Government?

Many, many, many attorneys assume (1) that they can submit their resumé to a legal search firm (headhunter) and then sit back and wait for job opportunities to come knocking, and (2) that they are "headhunter material." Many invoke the headhunter approach to federal legal employment and experience zero results. The U.S.

government does not, never has, and most likely never will engage headhunters to fill legal positions. NASA rocket scientists, maybe (even then not likely), but not attorneys. Why should they? It is not as if they cannot find lawyers when they need them (see Chapter 42, "Overcoming the Application Barrage"). So forget about headhunting as a means of getting a federal job. It's a non-starter. You need to do it yourself.

What Is the Work Like?

Without a little probing, I never quite know exactly what the candidate means by posing this question. At least 50 percent of the time, it means "how much will I have to work?" This question is most often posed by an attorney who is coming out of a major law firm where billable-hour requirements are quite demanding. In fact, one of the great enticements of transitioning to a federal job from a private law firm is the absence of the billable hour, which hangs over many law firm associates like a Sword of Damocles.

In this context, what I tell them is that, for the vast majority of federal legal positions, they are likely to be able to enjoy a 40-hour week without having to work evenings or weekends. The exceptions to this work schedule are primarily found in trial court litigation positions. Attorneys in the litigating divisions at the Department of Justice tend to have to work very long hours when they are preparing for and conducting litigation. There are a number of other agencies whose attorneys go to court, such as the Securities and Exchange Commission's Enforcement Division, the Enforcement Division at the Commodity Futures Trading Commission, the Equal Employment Opportunity Commission's Office of General Counsel, and the Litigation Branch of the Federal Deposit Insurance Corporation's Legal Division, to name some that are most frequently in trial courts.

Two factors, however, temper this statement. First, not every attorney in these offices litigates. Second, many agencies that have litigation divisions, sections, branches, etc., do nothing more than sit "second-chair" to the Justice Department attorneys who are the first-chair litigators.

The other context applicable to this question has to do with the nature of the work and can best be translated as: "Will the work be boring?"

Here again is where the diverse (read: non-monolithic) nature of the federal legal establishment affects the response. There are legal jobs that are so exciting that boredom is impossible (see Part Eight, "Where to Work"). Then there are positions where the work is highly repetitive and soon becomes rather routine, such as drafting claims decisions for the signature of the Comptroller General at the Government Accountability Office. The excitement level of the work depends almost 100 percent on where you work; although, as my first government boss at the Pentagon, a walking maxim generator, used to tell me: "You can take any job and make it into something interesting and even exciting."

What Do Government Employers Want?

Federal legal employers are no different than their private-sector counterparts. All employers want dedicated, committed, enthusiastic, intelligent, eager-to-learn, and likeable employees. Despite the politicians' eternal strategy of "running against Washington" and excoriating the bureaucracy for every evil that befalls the country (which seems to work more often than not), federal civil servants do not differ in an appreciable way from workers in any other economic sector. Most of them work hard, do their jobs, and get paid accordingly. Anyone who tells you otherwise is fomenting an urban legend.

I spent my entire career working with and observing employee behavior in the public, private, and nonprofit employment sectors and have come away unable to cite very many differences or divergent paths. I have encountered government attorneys who are just as intelligent and driven as major law firm lawyers, and government legal offices that operate as efficiently and effectively as the best law firms and corporate in-house counsel offices.

In addition, it helps if you have a passion for—or at least an interest in—public service. Be prepared for an interview question along the lines of: "Why do you want to work for the government?"

How Do I Move to a New Practice Area?

A surprising number of my clients announced at the beginning of our work together that they were tired or burnt out by their practice and wanted to move into the government in a new practice area. Often they would cite a practice area that, at first glance, appeared entirely unrelated to what they had been doing. Aside from competing for a position for which they had no experience, the major complicating factor was their concern about having to accept a substantial pay cut.

There are ways to make such a move without compromising completely on compensation. For example, it always comes as a shock to experienced litigators that litigation is a terrific training ground for transitioning to becoming a transactional attorney, as litigators settle most of their cases before trial by negotiating a settlement agreement with the opposing counsel. This is no different from negotiating and documenting a transaction. All it takes, then, to compete for a transactional position in the government is a resumé or application that emphasizes the transactional aspects of a candidate's litigation background.

A typical follow-up question is: "I know the federal government conducts a great deal of litigation, but where can you find any federal transactional practice?"

What candidates do not realize is that the government has a thriving and far-flung transactional practice that differs little from what goes on in private practice. The U.S. government has more than 100 law offices with a transactional practice. Some of these practices are very sophisticated and rival what the major Wall Street law firms do. For example, attorneys in the Federal Communications Commission's Office of General Counsel and various Commission Bureaus review applications for the transfer of control and assignment of licenses and authorizations involved in major transactions such as mergers. The international attorneys at the federal Millennium Challenge Corporation (MCC) negotiate complex agreements with developing countries for MCC assistance programs. Goddard Space Flight Center Technology Commercialization Office lawyers negotiate partnership agreements for the transfer of technologies to the private sector.

When moving to a new practice area with the government, it's important to develop and emphasize an inventory of transferable skills and experience you can promote to prospective government employers in order to bootstrap up to an acceptable pay grade. I urge that inventories include both (1) substantive knowledge and technical legal skills that could be attractive in the new practice area, and (2) "intangibles," such as demonstrated ability to come up the learning curve quickly when faced with a new matter, problem-solving capabilities, and other traits that make for a compelling candidate. Resumés and supporting documents must cite enough objective detail to show clearly and unambiguously that you possess these intangibles, and both the tangible and intangible transferable skills and background need to be easy to find in your application documents.

Let me cite an example from an actual client to show how this works. My client was an attorney-administrator at a nonprofit advocacy organization dealing with women's issues. She ran up against a promotional ceiling that could not be breached and was seeking more job security and less involvement with fund-raising and non-legal, ancillary duties. It did not matter to her where in the government she might work. Among her transferable skills were (1) a prodigious ability to multitask and a successful record as a multitasker, (2) experience commenting on and negotiating proposed federal regulations emanating from the Departments of Health and Human Services and Education, and (3) a strong background dealing with both internal and external constituencies. All three traits proved attractive to the Office of Regulatory Affairs at the Food and Drug Administration (she had no food and drug law experience), and she was hired as a regulatory counsel.

What Will a Government Job Look Like on a Resumé?

It depends. Where you work in the government and what you actually do, learn, and accomplish while doing it are the critical factors in how the private sector values (or not) federal legal job experience.

There are certain agencies that are "no-brainers" for private-sector employers, such as the Department of Justice (especially the litigating divisions), the Securities and Exchange Commission, the U.S. Patent and Trademark Office (especially the Patent division), certain law offices within the Department of Treasury, federal judicial clerkships (especially the U.S. Supreme Court and the Circuit Courts of Appeals), and, to a somewhat lesser extent, the Federal Trade Commission's Bureau of Competition and U.S. district court clerkships. In addition, depending on your specific duties and responsibilities, you may find yourself in great demand even if you work elsewhere in the government. For example, attorneys in the Internal Revenue Service Office of Chief Counsel who are fortunate enough to become immersed in the development and issuance of tax regulations that have a substantial impact on private-sector business often find that those very businesses and their tax advisors are very interested in recruiting them.

The agencies and offices mentioned above are not the only places where you can build an impressive resumé. You can do that anywhere in the U.S. government. However, it is easier to do if you work for a regulatory agency or office, with some exceptions, such as the Federal Election Commission, where the private-sector demand for campaign finance law expertise is very small and sporadic. One of the factors important for you to consider before accepting a federal position is the breadth of your agency's and office's impact on private-sector activities and what you personally will be assigned to do.

How Am I Supposed to Survive on a Government Salary?

This again is a question that arises principally from attorneys seeking to leave large law firms where they have been earning impressive salaries and "living large." Inevitably, these individuals are going to have to take a large pay cut and probably "downsize" their lifestyles to conform to their new financial reality if they enter federal service.

Most outside lawyers from large firms express shock at government salaries. They feel better when they learn that certain agencies, led by the financial regulators, operate under pay systems that allow for much higher compensation than elsewhere in government, and that it is not uncommon for an attorney in these agencies to earn $200,000 or more.

Perhaps the best response to this question is that several million federal employees, attorneys included, live on a government salary, and many live very well. If you believe that you cannot possibly survive on government pay, perhaps you should be looking elsewhere.

Chapter 40

Application Process Questions

How Do I Decipher Federal Job Vacancy Announcements?

Coming upon a U.S. government job vacancy announcement for the first time can be a daunting experience (see Appendix E for the Mother of All Nightmarish Federal Job Announcements). Accustomed as attorneys are to relatively minimalist Internet and newspaper job ads, encountering an often eight-page, single-spaced document crammed with text and arcane language that is worthy of the Rosetta Stone (Level 4) is both jarring and often reason enough to forget about applying to the federal government.

However, once you familiarize yourself with the typical federal vacancy announcement, a process that does not take very long, you will quickly detect repeating patterns and begin to feel comfortable as you learn what to pay attention to and what to ignore. Most often, at least 50 percent of a standard legal job vacancy announcement is "boilerplate," repeating itself from job to job. Read it once and you never have to worry about it again. The customary boilerplate concerns itself with information such as the fact that the employer is an equal opportunity employer, the workplace is drug-free, a certain amount of privacy attaches to the information sought, how Veterans' Preference in hiring applies, federal employee benefits, etc.

What remains is the important information: the job title, its classification series and pay grade (and sometimes the step within the grade), location, agency, office, job announcement number, salary, the application closing date, promotion potential, area of consideration (who may apply), job summary, duties, qualifications and evaluation, any special requirements, and how to apply. All of this information can be read and absorbed in minutes. The more vacancy announcements you scan, the more efficient you will become at understanding and responding to them.

It is useful prior to launching your federal job campaign to visit www.usajobs.gov and familiarize yourself with a few such announcements.

How Can I Identify Vacancy Announcements That Match My Background or Interests?

If you think there aren't any, you either have not searched as well as you should or you have not evaluated your background or interests as thoroughly as this important exercise merits. Federal job titles are not necessarily uniform from one agency to the next, so you have to be somewhat creative when using job search engines. An "attorney-advisor" (Antitrust) in the Commerce Department may be titled a "competition advocate" in the Defense Department. You need to think in the broadest possible terms of all of the key words and search terms that could possibly relate to what you want to do.

This problem is more acute when you are seeking a federal law-related position that is not likely to contain the word "attorney" somewhere in the job title. As discussed in Chapter 1, there are over 150 law-related job titles in the federal government, and job titles can vary considerably. One agency's alternative dispute resolution specialist may be another's mediator, convener, or facilitator.

The third reason that you might not find a matching vacancy announcement is because, at the moment you are conducting your search, the government is not recruiting for your particular brand of expertise. The antidote for that is patience. Sooner or later, each of the 120 mainstream legal practice areas within the federal government is going to be looking for attorneys. Moreover, you can use the techniques in Chapter 42, "Overcoming the Application Barrage," to identify job opportunities *before* they become publicly known via vacancy announcements.

What if I Attended a Non-ABA-Accredited Law School?

Most federal job vacancy announcements contain a boilerplate requirement that an attorney applicant must be a graduate of an American Bar Association–accredited law school. Although boilerplate, this requirement is of considerable importance to many federal legal employers who hire for mainstream attorney positions.

This prerequisite does not mean that, if you graduated from one of the 40-plus non-ABA law schools in the United States, you are precluded from working for the federal government. Virtually all law-related positions are open to you. In addition, I have compiled a list of agencies and offices that have a history of hiring mainstream attorneys who are not ABA law school graduates. When you examine the following list, however, keep in mind that an agency's inclusion on it does not mean that the employer *always* hires non-ABA law school attorneys. Sometimes it may; sometimes it may not.

Federal Employers That Have Hired Non-ABA Law School Attorneys

- Department of Education—Office for Civil Rights
- Department of Justice
  o   Office of the U.S. Trustee
  o   Federal Bureau of Prisons—Office of General Counsel
  o   Executive Office for Immigration Review
  o   Drug Enforcement Administration—Office of Chief Counsel
- Department of Homeland Security
  o   U.S. Citizenship and Immigration Services—Office of the Chief Counsel
  o   U.S. Customs and Border Protection—Office of the Chief Counsel
- Department of Housing and Urban Development—Office of General Counsel
- Department of Labor—Office of the Solicitor
- Department of Treasury—Internal Revenue Service—Appeals Organization

- Department of Veterans' Affairs—Veterans' Health Administration
- Equal Employment Opportunity Commission
- Federal Mediation and Conciliation Service
- Federal Public Defender Offices
- Merit Systems Protection Board
- National Aeronautics and Space Administration
- Securities and Exchange Commission—Enforcement Division
- Social Security Administration—Office of Disability Adjudication and Review
- U.S. Bankruptcy Courts—Judicial Law Clerks
- U.S. District Courts—Pro Se Staff Attorneys
- U. S. Magistrate Judges—Law Clerks

Finally, do not automatically permit the vacancy announcement statement that "graduation from an ABA-accredited law school is mandatory" deter you from applying for the position if you otherwise have strong credentials or something that clearly distinguishes you from other applicants. The statement may just be boilerplate and could be ignored by the hiring official who passes on your application.

What if I Am Not Admitted to the Bar?

If you lack bar admission, you are not automatically foreclosed from federal legal employment. Again, you may still be qualified for one of the many law-related positions where your J.D. degree is either what counts or is highly preferred, and for which bar admission is irrelevant.

Moreover, if you are coming into the government at an entry level, you can be hired for any mainstream (GS-0905) attorney position as a GS-904 "Law Clerk," in which case, you will be given 14 months in which to pass a bar examination (any state).

What if I Am Not Admitted in the State Where I Am Applying?

That, too, is irrelevant. All that matters for 99+ percent of federal mainstream legal jobs in which you will be practicing law is that you are admitted to a state bar in any jurisdiction. The only exceptions are jobs that require you to appear in state courts or administrative hearing forums, and there are very few of those in the federal government.

What if I Don't Have the Required Experience?

Lack of the experience specified as the minimum in the job vacancy announcement is more of a problem in the U.S. government than in other employment sectors. The reason for this has largely to do with the hiring process itself. It may be very difficult to get past an initial review of your qualifications by a non-attorney personnel specialist if you have less than the requisite experience. These individuals tend to take the vacancy announcement language quite literally. Consequently, if the job announcement states that "at least three years of experience are required" and you happen to have two years and 11 months of experience, you could be out of luck if, in fact, the "first responder" to your application is one of these individuals.

As discussed in Chapter 23, "Hiring for Attorney Jobs," the first responder usually has a checklist that itemizes the mandatory job requirements listed in the vacancy announcement. If you do not get a checkmark next to the experience requirement, chances are that your application will go no further. The antidote to this roadblock is to attempt to outflank the first responder by also submitting your resumé to the hiring official (an attorney) in addition to first following the application instructions on the vacancy announcement. If your "end-run" submission is compelling, the hiring official may be interested in considering you for the position regardless of your more limited experience.

How Should I Respond to a Question about My Salary History?

Your response to this common request in a federal vacancy announcement sets the stage for ensuing compensation discussions that might follow. Consequently, you have to handle this response carefully.

Four principles should govern your response:

1. *You **must** respond to a request for your salary history.* Too many attorneys think that they can safely ignore requests for information on salary history. They cannot. Many federal employers will automatically reject any applicant who does not comply with this request.

2. *You need good salary information about the job opportunity before you respond.* Don't respond without making an effort to determine the prospective employer's salary structure. That is very easy to do with respect to the federal government. Detailed current salary information is readily available at the U.S. Office of Personnel Management's website at www.opm.gov.

3. *You need a strategic negotiation plan in the event you are offered the position.* What will you say if you are offered the job at a specific grade level and step within the grade? This is one of the few elements of a federal job offer that lends itself to (limited) negotiation.

4. *You cannot tell less than the whole truth about your salary history.* This is often a problem for attorneys who earned much more than the federal job for which they are applying is paying. They fear—sometimes quite correctly—that the prospective employer is going to be reluctant to hire someone who was earning so much more than the federal job pays, believing that when the candidate sees his or her first paycheck, a very unhappy camper will be on board.

Although it happens very rarely, federal employers will sometimes ask to see your most recent tax return so that they can verify what you told them about your salary history. One of my large-firm counseling clients had her job offer from the Securities and Exchange Commission withdrawn when her tax return did not support what she had understated about her law firm compensation.

I Don't Understand How to Respond to KSAs

"KSA" is a term that is dreaded by both federal job candidates and federal employers. It is shorthand for "Knowledges, Skills, and Abilities" and is frequently found in federal job vacancy announcements under either "How to Apply," "Requirements and Evaluation" or a comparable heading. The term KSA is interchangeable with "Ranking Factors," "Quality Ranking Factors," "Rating Factors," "Evaluation Factors," and similar labels that you find in a federal vacancy announcement. I will use only KSA for the purposes of this book.

KSAs require a job applicant to respond to them with essay answers—the application provides the skill, and the applicant must demonstrate how they've employed it. They are the bane of many candidates for federal legal positions and the downfall of many others. I will not, however, spend as much time on them as I might otherwise because the Obama Administration recently announced that it intended to eliminate them from being part of the federal application process by November 1, 2010 (see Appendix F, "Presidential Memorandum," below). However, mindful of the history of agencies ignoring presidential mandates concerning personnel matters, I must discuss them because, as this book goes to press (December 2010) more than 1,250 job vacancy announcements appearing on www.usajobs,gov contain a KSA requirement.

The purpose of KSAs in a federal vacancy announcement is ostensibly to give hiring officials detailed information that enables them to match your candidacy to the requirements of the position. It is questionable whether they ever achieve this worthy goal, mainly because they are often poorly written, ambiguous, and thus extremely difficult to respond to with any degree of confidence.

The following is an example of a typical KSA taken from an actual attorney vacancy announcement:

> Knowledge of and proficiency in interpreting law, statutes, bylaws, precedents, practices, administrative rules and regulations, and legal decisions in order to independently perform a wide variety of duties and responsibilities.

Good luck interpreting this confusing mishmash of words joined together to presumably mean something. If you survived this first KSA, here is what came next:

> Ability to provide constructive counsel on a variety of issues that arise in connection with field-related projects and their documentation.

Nowhere in the vacancy announcement was the term "field-related projects" defined. Your guess is as good as mine. This obfuscation was then followed by:

> Skill in preparing written legal documents or decisions on federal employment law applicable to federal employees and agencies.

This KSA would give an outside candidate or one from another practice area great difficulty. The capstone, assuming the candidate was still interested in going ahead with the application, was:

> Ability to evaluate and organize regulatory opinions.

I do not mean to suggest that every assemblage of KSAs is this dense. Some are actually quite straightforward and easy to understand. However, a disturbingly large number are not.

The three biggest mistakes that respondents make in tackling KSAs are:

1. *Non-specific responses*; that is, responding generally without specific examples from their own experience;
2. *Length of response*. One or two sentences are not enough. More than one page is too much; and
3. *Being unresponsive*. Candidates who do not possess the knowledge, skill, or ability sought sometimes do not respond at all to the KSA or state that they do not possess what the employer is seeking. Both are kisses of death to an application. You need to come up with something, no matter how remote the analogy.

This is where I will leave the KSA discussion in hopes that the government actually follows through with its intent to eliminate them.

Why Does It Take So Long for the Government to Hire Someone?

If you remember the description of the typical federal attorney hiring process in Chapter 23, "Hiring for Attorney Jobs," you have the basis for my answer to this question. The "choke point" in the federal hiring process is Step Two, the evaluation of attorney candidates by the rating panel. The reason is that rating panel members are usually very busy individuals and bringing three to five or more of them together in one room at the same time for a period long enough to evaluate a number of job candidates takes some planning and considerable rescheduling.

That is not necessarily the only reason why the government takes its time hiring attorneys (or anyone else). Sometimes the availability of a position is contingent on an appropriation that was expected to be in place by the time the hiring process was complete, but is not. In cases like that, which are not all that rare, the recruitment screeches to a halt until the money for the position is freed up. Since Congress never gets around to appropriating funds by its own self-imposed deadlines anymore, relying instead on "continuing resolutions" to fund government while it dithers, this kind of delay is becoming more and more frequent.

Chapter 41

Job Offer and Acceptance Questions

What Is Negotiable?

One of my clients received a very attractive job offer from a government agency general counsel office. Upon receiving the offer, she contacted a friend of hers (but unfortunately not me) who worked in the human resources department of a large private-sector corporation and was told that, before accepting the offer, she should pose the following (among many other) questions and concerns to the general counsel:

- I need more money than the salary at which you advertised the job.
- I need more than the 13 days of vacation specified in the vacancy announcement. In fact, I have a trip scheduled three weeks after your proposed work starting date.
- How much administrative—unpaid—leave will I be able to take each year?
- Can I take leave before I have earned it? I could do that at my law firm.
- I would like to work a flexible schedule, front-loading my week so that I can have Fridays off.

It should come as no surprise that during the conversation, when these demands and questions were posed, the general counsel withdrew the job offer. There is very little wiggle room to negotiate anything about a job offer from the federal government. The only possibilities are (1) a higher pay-grade level if the vacancy announcement cited more than one possible grade level (for example, if a federal attorney position is announced at grades GS-905-12/13/14), and (2) a higher step within the grade at which you are offered the position. Most legal offices believe that they must offer you a Step One salary, but that is not accurate. They have some flexibility with respect to your initial step, and it is very much to your present and future advantage to begin your federal career at the highest possible step (Step 10 is the highest) within a grade. The reason is not only that you will immediately earn a higher salary, but also that all future promotions and step increases will be affected by your starting step, meaning that over time you will earn considerably more money than if you began as a Step One.

You have to present a rational, compelling argument for why you should be hired at the higher grade or a higher step than the one being offered. You need to base that argument on the breadth and depth of your prior experience and your job accomplishments and results. Merely asking for the higher grade or step is not enough without objective, verifiable supporting facts.

Other than these two possibilities, nothing else is negotiable. Federal benefits are stipulated by law and regulation, apply to everyone, and cannot be altered by an employment negotiation.

The number of vacation days in the first several years of employment, for example, is fixed. Therefore, it is both pointless and rather risky to attempt to debate it. There are a lot of items in the federal employment realm that have the same "take-it-or-leave-it" character. You need to be cognizant of that fact before you compete for a government job.

Can I Be Transferred Against My Will?

Yes, you can. However, such transfers are rare, even within an agency where you might move down the hall from one section within an office to another. Rarer still are geographic transfers. When they do happen, there are often opportunities to stay put in the same location but with another office or agency, accompanied by a hiring preference for the dislocated employees.

Will I Have My Own Private Office?

That depends. I worked as an attorney for three federal agencies. I had my own private office at the "bookend" agencies, but shared an office with another attorney at my middle stop.

As a rule, the higher your grade level, the more likely it is that you will have a private office. However, there are no guarantees. Some agencies have gone to a cubicle office design where privacy is not an option. Being bureaucracies, however, certain agencies actually have guidelines on how many square feet are allotted to a GS-15, GS-14, etc.

Part VI

Getting Hired

Your goal is, of course, to get hired. One of the great advantages of the daunting federal government hiring maze is the many opportunities it offers for separating yourself from the pack. Distinguishing yourself from your competition should be your strategy at every stage of the federal (or any other) hiring process. Here are some tips and techniques for doing just that.

Chapter 42

Overcoming the Application Barrage

When the economy is thriving, the U.S. government is barraged with job applications from attorneys. In bad economic times, the barrage becomes even more intense. For example, a recent job vacancy announcement for an attorney position in one of the Chief Counsel offices at the Department of Transportation attracted 400 applications. The most extreme example of the application barrage in my experience was 700+ applications for a single job in the Office of the Comptroller of the Currency's Chief Counsel Office. This kind of application torrent has, since the advent of the recession, become the norm rather than the exception.

Major law firms have laid off thousands of attorneys. Corporations have also downsized their legal staffs. Nonprofits are having great difficulty raising funds and have had to lay off their lawyers. State and local governments, many constitutionally obligated to balance their budgets, have also suffered legal workforce attrition. All of which leads to more attorneys entering the job market and looking to what often appears to them to be the only place where hiring is still going on—the U.S. government. Federal legal recruiters tell me that they have never seen anything like the present volume of job applications pouring into their offices.

It does not even matter that there might not be a job available. The number of unsolicited resumés, always pretty large in any era, is overwhelming now. The other key factoid that my federal re-cruiting contacts share is that they have never seen such high-qual-ity applications from tremendously capable attorneys able to cite impressive experience and achievements. The application barrage means that it is easier than ever to get lost among the weeds. Sounds pretty discouraging, doesn't it?

So how do you avoid becoming just one of the anonymous mass of frenzied attorneys competing for the same job? How do you go about getting the recruiter's attention when you are compet-ing against hundreds of your highly accomplished colleagues?

Here are several ways that you can stand out from the crowd and get your resumé examined without having to worry about the mob scene in which you might otherwise get lost. These strategies have a proven track record among my clients. They not only serve to "isolate" your candidacy and permit you to be considered for a federal legal position separate and apart from others, they also give you the opportunity to impress potential employers with your cre-ative and sophisticated job-hunting strategy. This is very important because it manifests several powerful transferable skills that virtu-ally every employer can appreciate—original thinking, foresight, creative problem-solving, and individuality in the best sense of the word.

Advance Notice of Federal Legal Hiring Plans

Federal agencies from time to time announce their legal hiring in-tentions in advance of any recruitment activity. They may do this in several different ways. Pay close attention to this tactic. It can mean the difference between success and failure.

Appropriations Committee Testimony

Each year agency heads testify about their organization's proposed budget for the coming fiscal year (the federal government's fiscal year runs from October 1 to September 30) before the Senate and/or House Appropriations Committee's subcommittee with jurisdic-tion over the organization's budget. These hearings often become exercises in "drilling down" into the particulars of what constitutes the agency's budget request. Sometimes the drill-down goes deep into personnel needs and itemizes them to the extent that the agency reveals exactly how many attorneys it anticipates hiring and for what purposes.

This incredibly valuable information is usually contained in either the written testimony submitted to the subcommittee that accompanies the oral presentation or in the transcript of the oral testimony itself. The best place to look for either of these is on the subcommittee's website. A fall-back is to locate the testimony on the agency's website.

For example, the following is excerpted from the testimony of Commodity Futures Trading Commission (CFTC) Chairman Gary Gensler before the Senate Committee on Appropriations Subcommittee on Financial Services and General Government (http://appropriations.senate.gov/sc-financial.cfm) on April 28, 2010. The excerpt is rather lengthy because I want you to realize the full implications for legal hiring in what Chairman Gensler told the subcommittee. I have added italics to key passages impacting on the CFTC's legal employment intentions.

- *Strengthening the Commission's Enforcement Program.* The CFTC should be adequately resourced *to vigorously investigate and litigate complex market manipulation and trade-practice violations.* Properly functioning markets must be free from fraud, manipulation and other abuses to ensure their integrity in setting prices and offsetting risk. A robust Enforcement program will foster regulatory compliance in the marketplace, protecting the American public and the marketplace. *Adequate legal staff is necessary to act swiftly to investigate and prosecute fraudulent acts, such as the rash of Ponzi schemes uncovered during the recent market downturn.*
- *Rigorously Exercising Existing Authorities to Ensure Market Integrity. Additional economic and legal staff will enable the CFTC to conduct mandatory annual reviews of all contracts listed on exempt commercial markets (ECMs) to determine if they are significant price discovery contracts (SPDCs).* Such contracts must be reviewed to determine whether the ECM should be subject to statutory Core Prin-

ciples and the Commission's regulations. These and other new and increasingly diverse products add to the scope and complexity of products staff must review and monitor to ensure the integrity of the marketplace.

• Specifically, the funding will be allocated to increase staffing levels in the following divisions:

o *Division of Enforcement.* The Commission's Enforcement program is on track to reach a staff level of more than 170 by the end of this fiscal year. This is a significant program turnaround from an all-time low of 109 in FY 2008. Nevertheless, a staff of 170 may be below what is needed to address the current challenges brought by the recent financial crisis. Our goal for FY 2011 is to have an Enforcement staff of 200, including strategic plans to double the Enforcement staff in the Kansas City office.

o *Division of Market Oversight.* The rapid changes occurring in the futures markets over the last decade have brought new challenges to the Commission's Division of Market Oversight (DMO). DMO now needs additional experienced professional staff to actively monitor exchanges to ensure compliance with CFTC regulations; keep a close eye for signs of manipulation or congestion in the marketplace and decide how to best address market threats; and ensure that traders do not exceed federal position limits. Thus, the Commission seeks to increase DMO's staff from 139 in FY 2010 to 168 in FY 2011.

Specifically, DMO requires additional highly skilled economists, investigators, attorneys and statisticians so that: 1) position data may be analyzed quickly and thoroughly; 2) exchange applications and rule changes may be reviewed efficiently and comprehensively to ensure compliance with Core Principles and CFTC rules and policies; 3) exchange self-regulatory programs may be examined on an on-going annual basis with regard to trade practice oversight, market surveillance and compliance with disciplinary, audit trail and record-keeping regulations; 4) comments related to a proposed energy position limits rulemaking, proposed significant price discovery contract determinations and other proposed rulemakings and industry filings can be comprehensively reviewed and summarized; and 5) proposed rulemakings and determinations can be effectively implemented should the Commission approve them.

o *Division of Clearing and Intermediary Oversight.* Additional resources would allow the Commission to perform regular and direct examinations of registrants and more frequently assess compliance with Commission regulations.

In the case of intermediaries, the Commission requires additional resources to directly assess compliance instead of relying on designated self-regulatory organizations (DSROs). The frequency of the reviews will increase to once a year from approximately once every three years. New staff will permit the review annually of all derivatives clearing organizations (DCOs) and the audit and financial surveillance programs of each DSRO ensuring ongoing rather than intermittent oversight. The Commission seeks to increase the Division of Clearing and Intermediary Oversight staff from 113 in FY 2010 to 120 in FY 2011.

o *Offices of the Chairman and the Commissioners. The Offices of the Chairman and the Commissioners require professional, legal and economic expertise* as they undertake a number of high-priority programmatic initiatives, including: 1) subject to enactment of new authorities, regulation of derivatives markets and regulatory changes to protect the American public from systemic financial risks; 2) regulatory coordination with other agencies such as the Securities and Exchange Commission (SEC) and Federal Energy Regulatory Commission (FERC); 3) promoting market transparency; 4) promoting transparency on the Commission's website; 5) regulation of energy markets—especially with regard to position limits and the Commission's review of significant price discovery contracts; 6) increasing frequency of reviews and audits of Commission registrants; and 7) technology modernization, resource justification and program performance. The Commission proposes to bolster these offices from 35 staff in FY 2010 to 47 staff in FY 2011.

o *Enterprise Risk Management Office.* The budget proposes a new Enterprise Risk Management subprogram, consisting of three staff, to focus on proactively developing and employing methods and processes to manage risks that may be obstacles to the discharge of the Commission's responsibilities. The staff will identify plausible risks posed by current and future events or circumstances that may affect the Commission's ability to respond effectively. Risks will be assessed in terms of the likelihood and magnitude of impact. The program will determine an appropriate response strategy and monitor outcomes.

o *Office of International Affairs.* The budget requests an additional staff member in the Office of International Affairs, which coordinates the Commission's non-enforcement related international activities, represents the Commission in international organizations such as the International Organization of Securities Commissions (IOSCO), coordinates Commission policy as it relates to U.S. Treasury global initiatives and provides technical assistance to foreign market authorities. The financial crisis has heightened the need for international cooperation among regulators, and an additional staff member is required to meet the mission critical responsibilities of the office.

o *Regulatory Reform.* In addition to implementing the authorities established in the Commodity Exchange Act, Pub. L. 94-29, the CFTC also is working with Congress to bring comprehensive regulation to the over-the-counter derivatives marketplace. The Commission's budget request includes *an additional $45,000,000 and 119 full-time equivalent employees for fiscal year 2011* to begin implementation of the Administration's comprehensive proposal for financial regulatory reform. As proposed, the request is contingent on Congressional enactment of legislation giving the Commission new authorities. The Commission's fiscal year 2012 total (current and proposed new authorities related to financial regulatory reform) staff requirement is estimated to be approximately 1,000 FTE. The requested funds will permit Commission implementation of new responsibilities under consideration by Congress, such as:

- Requiring swap dealers and major swap participants to register and come under comprehensive regulation, including capital standards, margin requirements, business conduct standards and recordkeeping and reporting requirements;
- Requiring dealers and major swap participants to use transparent trading venues for their standardized swaps;
- Ensuring that dealers and major swap participants bring their clearable swaps into central clearinghouses; and
- Providing the CFTC with authority to impose aggregate position limits including in the OTC derivatives markets.

Specifically, the Commission's FY 2011 budget request for regulatory reform would be allocated as follows:

- *41 additional staff for Market Oversight*;
- *30 additional staff for Clearing and Intermediary Oversight and Risk Surveillance*;
- *18 additional staff for Enforcement*;
- 15 additional staff for Information Technology;
- *Eight additional staff for General Counsel*;
- Five additional staff for Human Resources and Management Operations;

- One additional staff for the Chief Economist;
- *And one additional staff for International Affairs.*

In order to use this information most effectively, you would also need to do your homework regarding the mission and activities of the CFTC (www.cftc.gov). You would learn that the CFTC is a "lawyer-laden" agency with numerous and far-flung legal and law-related responsibilities.

Once you understand what the CFTC is all about, you would be ready to launch your job campaign *without waiting for publication of a vacancy announcement.* Submitting a resumé tailored to what you have learned about the agency and its intentions—in advance of the issuance of job vacancy announcements—is important and will give you an edge over your competition once the agency's recruitment needs are publicized. Perhaps most important to your campaign, including *how you found out about the pending positions in your cover letter of transmittal e-mail* should make the hiring official(s) sit up and take notice. Federal employers are typically very impressed that someone was astute enough to do this kind of creative analysis and act upon it.

Advance Notice from Other Sources

There are three other places where agencies might give you a hint about legal hiring intentions. All three are documents required by law to be published and available on the Internet.

Annual Performance Plans and Strategic Plans are generally available on agency websites. They are both "forward-looking" documents—in the case of the former, announcing what the agency plans to do in the coming year; in the latter case, providing a somewhat longer-range perspective (usually three to five years out). While wildly inconsistent from one agency to another, both plans sometimes contain either detailed information about legal hiring plans or more general information about policy initiatives that hint at legal hiring.

Budget documents are generally available on the Office of Management and Budget website (www.omb.gov), and sometimes on agency websites as well. When you research budget documents, forget about the actual budget proposals themselves, which are chock full of often incomprehensible numbers that will drive you to distraction. Rather, concentrate on the *Budget Appendices*, which often contain some numbers along with textual explanations. Again, there is no government-wide format that agencies follow with respect to presenting such information. Consequently, you might find a gold mine of valuable information about legal hiring plans in one agency's budget appendix and nothing at all about this topic in another's.

Again, it is worth emphasizing that there is no consistency or predictability to this information. Sometimes it is immensely valuable because it "drills down" to specifics about legal hiring needs; other times it says nothing at all about how many attorneys an agency or subordinate unit plans to hire, where in the agency these positions will be located, or what new legal hires will be asked to do.

Nevertheless, it is worth ferreting out for those agencies in which you might be interested because, if the information is there, it gives you an enormous advantage over your competition.

If Advance Notice Is Unavailable . . .

. . . there is always "trends analysis." Trends analysis in this context means examining the major developments—economic, social, demographic, political, legislative, technological, historical, domestic, and international—likely to result in policy initiatives and changes that could impact legal employment. For example, once the economy collapsed and a Democratic administration took power in Washington, we reversed course and entered a period of regulatory activism after a generation of deregulation. This has already had a pronounced impact on government policy and an equally profound impact on federal legal hiring. The financial services regulatory agencies, for example, immediately stepped up their legal recruitment and are likely to continue that trend for some time to come.

Similarly, the rapid technological advances affecting food safety and drug and medical device development have had a marked legal employment impact on the Food and Drug Administration. The enactment of health-care reform legislation will affect federal legal employment for years to come, especially in Department of Health and Human Services legal and law-related offices, such as the Office of General Counsel, the Office of Counsel to the Inspector General, the Office of Medicare Hearings and Appeals, and the Centers for Medicare and Medicaid Services.

A striking example of how a demographic shift can affect legal employment is the "Age Wave," the 78 million Baby-Boomers who will achieve senior status between 2008 and 2026. Already, the Social Security Administration has massively increased its attorney and administrative law judge staffs to cope with a rapidly expanding workload that is only going to get larger.

Consequently, keeping your eyes and ears open to what is going on in the world around you can also be a good indicator of where federal legal employment is likely to head next.

What to Submit

Follow the Instructions

Many federal legal job candidates are eliminated from consideration early in the hiring process because they did not follow the
application instructions. Remember that:

- you are dealing with a bureaucracy and that bureaucracies
  tend to be rule-driven, so that if you do not follow the rules,
  you are likely to find your application rejected before you
  have even had the opportunity to have your substantive
  content considered; and
- agencies besieged with applications are likely to look for
  any excuse to reject one, and failure to follow instructions
  is a perfect opportunity for rejection.

Let me cite two examples to paint a picture of these points:

1. Many federal job candidates balk at providing what they
   believe to be irrelevant—even ridiculous—information required on federal application forms, such as your high
   school, its location, and ZIP code. Swallow your objections
   and provide the information.

2. An agency personnel officer once related to me the following tale of how applications were culled. It happened that the after-hours office cleaning crew accidentally knocked over half of a pile of hundreds of applications that fell into a wastebasket. The next morning upon arriving at the office, the personnel officer on whose desk the applications were piled decided that the ones in the wastebasket would be the initial rejects. The lesson here is that you should always follow up with the agency to make certain that your application was received.

Always adhere precisely to what you are requested to submit (at least in the first instance—see the following chapter for a suggested exception to this precept). If you are instructed to submit a "paper" application (usually via e-mail), submit *only* the paper requested, nothing more.

One of my clients came to my company after applying for federal jobs for more than a year, frustrated that he had never received an invitation to interview. In examining his application strategy, it turned out that he was overwhelming each federal recruiter with massive volumes of paper—writing samples, letters of recommendation, evidences of membership in "honorary" societies that anyone willing to pay a fee could join, etc. What he accomplished by all of this unnecessary material assault was to annoy and irritate the very people he wanted to impress favorably with his qualifications (which were pretty good).

Being overwhelmed with more than they asked for is one of the biggest complaints I hear from federal employment application handlers. Federal personnel specialists tell me that attorneys are among the biggest "overkillers" when it comes to unrequested application documents. Maybe that is because we operate in an eternally document-intensive professional environment where we are programmed to leave no stone unturned.

Regardless of the underlying professional or psychological reasons for besieging federal application reviewers with too much paper, doing so provides them with an easy reason to reject your application: You failed to follow the application instructions. Moreover, even if you survive the initial review and your application is passed on to a rating panel, having to cope with more paper than they requested means that they will immediately conclude that you cannot be trusted to follow instructions—not exactly the first impression that you want to make in order to be seriously considered for a position with their agency. Worse, you may have made yourself memorable in the event that you apply for other jobs with the agency that will go through the same handlers.

Being underinclusive with respect to your application is just as bad as being overinclusive. If you are asked to submit certain documents, make sure that you do just that. If an official law school transcript is required, make sure that you request one from your law school registrar in ample time to meet the application deadline. If the application requests your state bar registration number and a list of courses and credits earned in law school and/or college, do not skimp on the information. Be complete. You may think that what is being requested is absurd—and often it is—but that is beside the point. Personnel officers, the first line of defense when it comes to applications for many federal legal and law-related positions, are sticklers for nit-picking applications to death if what they are told to expect to see is not there.

Increasingly, the federal government is moving to an online application environment where the candidate is asked to use a standard template to craft and then submit a job application. This application method usually forecloses the opportunity to submit anything else but the online form. While that is a good thing for applicants who are inclined toward either overinclusiveness or underinclusiveness, it is a bad thing for applicants who are attempting to get their credentials across to employers to best advantage and to distinguish themselves from the competition, as we will see in the next chapter.

Resumés and Cover Letters/Transmittal E-mails

The paper application you will be asked to submit will almost always be a resumé, which, as you will see below, is very much to your advantage. If you see a request for a resumé in the job vacancy announcement, rejoice!

If you feel the urge to write a cover letter or transmittal e-mail in which you essentially repeat what is in your resumé, try to control yourself. A short, concise letter or e-mail will do just as well. If the federal vacancy announcement instructs you to send your application to a human resources or personnel office, as opposed to the legal office where you are applying, it is a good bet that your Jeffersonian literary effort will not even make it to the first legal review level of the hiring process. All you need do is refer to the specific position for which you are applying (and be very precise in doing this, as federal personnel offices receive tons of resumés—both solicited and unsolicited—and the personnel specialist assigned to handle your application may also be handling applications for multiple positions across several occupations at the same time) and indicate that your resumé is enclosed or attached, as the case may be. Saying anything else is usually a waste of time.

Chapter 44

How to Submit

Paper Applications

As indicated in the previous chapter, if you are lucky, your prospective federal employer will ask you to submit a resumé instead of an online application conforming to the office, agency or government-wide template. Unfortunately, the number of federal employers that are sticking to the good, traditional way of accepting and assessing job applications is dwindling fast. Many are adopting the online methodology either because of heavy lobbying pressure from the U.S. Office of Personnel Management or the temptation to cut hiring costs.

The irony for federal legal employers is that they function under a personnel system—the excepted service—that was especially created for them so that they could go their own way when hiring, promoting, and terminating attorneys, the rationale being that such flexibility was needed because of the unique nature of legal advice and counsel, the unavoidable involvement of attorneys in policy decisions, and the need for mutual trust between attorneys and clients.

When submitting a paper application (and I include resumés that travel to the employer electronically via e-mail or fax), keep the following in mind:

- Adhere religiously to all of the instructions in the job vacancy announcement. A nagging survivor of earlier federal hiring reform efforts is the insistence by some federal employers on irrelevant information, stuff you would otherwise almost never include in a resumé.

- Be aware that your resumé may be fed into a resumé database for later extraction using key words. Be sure to include all of the possible key words that are likely to be part of the search retrieval criteria. The path to legal job rejection is littered with the detritus of attorneys who failed to grasp this important point.

- Make sure that your resumé looks as professional and attractive as possible and that the information is extremely reader-friendly and easy on the eyes. The reviewers will award you "subliminal" points for making their lives more pleasant.

- Present your information in logical order, and in the order in which a reviewer will expect to see it. If you just graduated from law school, your education should probably precede your work experience unless you had a career prior to or coterminous with attending law school that is both relevant to the position you seek and is a legal credential booster.

- Keep your transmittal e-mail brief and to the point. Cite what you are applying for, including the job title, job classification series and grade, and announcement number, so that your application will not be misdirected. Indicate where you heard about the position. Indicate if you are applying under one of the special hiring programs described in Part Four, "How the Government Hires Lawyers."

Online Application Forms

By now you have probably correctly concluded that I don't like online application forms very much. More important, neither federal legal job candidates nor federal legal hiring officials like them any better.

I have had too many clients who complained bitterly to me that their computers froze while attempting to complete a federal online application form, or that they discovered after the deadline for the receipt of an application that it never made it to the recipient. There is no excuse for this. OPM spent millions of dollars on a private contractor to develop an online application form and delivery system for federal job applicants. As discussed, the first iteration was a disaster. So OPM spent millions more on the same contractor to fix the bugs in the system. That did not work so well, either. Now OPM and the contractor have tweaked the system again.

Unfortunately, despite all this, many federal agencies and legal offices have opted for the OPM online system to the detriment of both candidates and hiring officials.

Candidates dislike it because (1) it does not conform to a resumé presentation, (2) it is time-consuming to complete, and (3) it tends to force everyone into the same box and makes them look alike.

Federal legal hiring officials complain that (1) it reduces every applicant to a least common denominator, making them all look the same, (2) squeezes out the individuality that a resumé offers, and (3) allows them to examine only pure content and not the way the information is organized or presented, which can be very telling and distinguishing. Nevertheless, many federal law offices have been forced to use this system and have little alternative recourse.

In completing the OPM or any agency- or office-specific online application form, do the very best you can with what you have. Within the parameters of this restrictive, reductionist methodology, make sure your content is top-notch. Finally, follow the advice below in the section entitled ". . . And Reemerging."

Disappearing in the Ether . . .

While paper applications also get lost from time to time, online applications seem to disappear more often. Your online federal legal job application can disappear in two different ways:

- First, it can get lost somewhere in the virtual world between your computer and the employer's. The antidote to that is to follow up with the employer once you have submitted your online application and make certain that it was received. Also, keep good notes to that effect with respect to when you submitted your application, where, and to whom you addressed it (if the template allows this), the name and contact information of the individual who confirmed that your application was received, and the date and time of your communication with that person. This information could be valuable if you discover that your application fell through the cracks at some later stage and did not get considered.

- Second, your qualifications and credentials can "get lost" because your online application looks like everyone else's. All of the things that define and distinguish you in a resumé are gone. You have lost your "brand." The next section of this chapter offers advice on recapturing your individuality.

... And Reemerging

Because this second type of disappearance means that you risk being perceived as no different from any other candidate, you need to do something to stand out. So here is one of the best pieces of strategic advice in this book: *Immediately after you complete and submit an online application form for a federal legal job, send your tried-and-true traditional resumé—either via e-mail or regular postal mail—to the hiring official.* Tell that person in your transmittal e-mail or cover letter that you followed all of the application instructions and submitted the online application form, but you want to make sure that he or she has the opportunity to evaluate your resumé because this document presents you much better and more accurately than the online form, and also demonstrates more effectively your organizational and presentation skills.

Employers learn much more about a candidate from a resumé than they ever can from an online application form. A resumé is about *individuality*; an online template is about *sameness*. A resumé requires not only content, but intelligent organization and a reader-friendly format for it to succeed in winning attention and moving the applicant forward in the competitive employment process. An online template usually does not permit any of those traits to emerge. A resumé demonstrates something about candidate decision making and judgment. An online form makes those decisions for the applicant and deprives the employer of any ability to discern those attributes prior to a job interview. A resumé is all about a candidate's differences from other candidates. An online template is all about reducing every candidate to the least common denominator.

As long as you state that you followed the application instructions and submitted the online form, you will not risk alienating the hiring official. Instead, you will have differentiated yourself from the pack of competing candidates and may gain a considerable edge over them. Most federal legal employers will appreciate your initiative and willingness to provide them with more and better information than appears on the online form.

The next chapter suggests additional ways of separating yourself from the pack.

Chapter 45

Differentiating Yourself from the Competition

I have already discussed two ways of distinguishing yourself from your competition: (1) identifying federal legal job opportunities before they become public knowledge through issuance of a vacancy announcement; and (2) submitting your resumé in addition to an online job application form. Now I want to discuss several additional ways in which you can stand out.

On Your Resumé

Other than requests for strange information that would be of no consequence to private-sector employers (I cited the example of your high school education earlier), a resumé for a federal legal position does not differ from one you would use for any other job. It should be neat, easy on the eyes, reader-friendly, logical, two pages or less (although federal legal employers are more forgiving of longer resumés), error-free, and above all, persuasive. It should also not be cluttered with unnecessary information.

Once you have satisfied these principles, you need to think about what you can do to make your case for the job compelling. The following resumé tactics can help you brand yourself:

- **An additional credential**. If you have a *degree or certificate in addition to your J.D.* that is a resumé enhancement in terms of the position for which you are applying, make sure that it follows immediately after your name at the top of the resumé. For example, say that you are also a Certified Fraud Examiner in addition to being an attorney. You can get that attractive point across quickly by appending it after your name at the top of the resumé: John Doe, JD, CFE.

- **A Profile or Qualifications Summary** immediately following your self-identifying information at the top of the resumé is a very effective "grabber." This section is always useful, and can do much to advance your candidacy. You can use it to—

  o *grab the reader's attention immediately* and entice him or her to read on with interest.
  o *bring up key points you want to get across*, but that may be buried deep in your resumé—foreign language fluency or proficiency, for example.
  o *emphasize your most compelling selling points*. For example, if you attended top schools, don't delay informing the reader about those achievements.
  o *imprint your distinctive qualifications* on the reader.

Keep your profile or qualifications summary (both headings are fine) succinct and to the point. Two or three sentences should suffice. Avoid subjective statements, such as "outstanding legal researcher," that would be difficult for either you or the reader to verify via objective assessments. These can be off-putting to employers.

Here are several examples of strong profiles/qualifications summaries developed by some of my legal career transition clients:

Experienced in all phases of litigation from inception of lawsuit through settlement, including appellate practice, conducting arbitration, and handling trial proceedings (second-chaired complex cases and independently ran and managed both appeals and smaller matters). Admitted to practice before U.S. Patent and Trademark Office; Italian fluency; French proficiency; MS in Biotechnology.

––––

Experienced and successful securities and commercial litigator in state and federal courts. Handle securities arbitration before the NASD, NYSE, and AAA. Additional background in corporate transactions and financing. Law review; Yale BA; Harvard JD.

––––

Experienced editor, writer, and legal/political advisor at a 28,000-member nonprofit corporation. Extensive background drafting and editing legislation and regulations. Proficient in Spanish.

––––

Accomplished Intellectual Property attorney with both domestic and international transactional and litigation experience across the full range of IP matters, including patents, trademarks, copyrights, licensing, trade secrets, and diverse technology agreements. Extensive academic background in IP and international business.

Each of the above examples contributed to a successful job search outcome.

- **Adding a Highlights Addendum** to your resumé. This one- to two-page "appendix" can enable you to expand upon one or more of your exceptional accomplishments or outcomes referenced cryptically in the body of your resumé. Federal legal employers like to see a narrative expansion like this because it gives them a much more detailed picture of how your mind works, how you tackle a problem, etc. I have yet to encounter a federal hiring official who complained about the added pages. For example, say that one of your prior job accomplishments cited in your resumé was "Leaps tall buildings at a single bound." Expanding upon this in your Highlights Addendum might look something like this:

Leaping tall buildings at a single bound was central to my work as an international superhero fighting for liberty, truth, justice, and the American way. Before determining whether or not to leap a tall building, I assessed its height, wind conditions, activity in the landing zone on the other side of the structure, etc. If they all appeared favorable to my leap, I examined my leaping history to determine if I had ever made such a leap before and what the risks might be if this were a new building. Once I determined that a leap was in both my and my employer's best interests, I gauged the optimum runway length prior to the leap, adjusted my speed accordingly, and let fly. Throughout my leaping career, I never crashed into a building or injured a pedestrian or motor vehicle.

At the Interview

Federal legal job interviews come in numerous permutations—telephone, panels of interviewers, *seriatim* interviews, and scripted interviews, to name a few of the more common types. Here are some general suggestions applicable to any federal legal job interview, as well as some suggestions for handling each one of the interview types you might encounter.

General Suggestions

Go into your federal job interview armed with as much information about your employer as you can obtain. Information about federal agencies and legal offices is easier to find than for any other employer. These are public-sector entities, and most of what they do is a matter of public record. They issue reports to Congress about their activities; are scrutinized in depth by their own agency Inspectors General (for the 73 agencies with an Inspector General) as well as by congressional oversight committees, the Government Accountability Office, and often the Congressional Research Service; and their doings are closely monitored by affected trade and professional associations. Some of the best information resources outside of the agencies' and offices' own websites are:

- U.S. Government Manual (www.gpoaccess.gov/gmanual/index.html)
- Code of Federal Regulations (www.gpoaccess.gov/cfr/)
- Government Accountability Office Reports (www.gao.gov)
- Congressional Research Service Reports (http://opencrs.com/)
- Senate Oversight Committees (www.senate.gov)
- House Oversight Committees (www.house.gov)
- Gateway to Associations (www.asaecenter.org)

Make a trial run to the interview site. Most federal legal offices are located in large cities (see Chapter 8, "Federal Legal Geography," above). That means dealing with rush hours, other traffic delays, parking issues, and/or public transportation waits and possible breakdowns. Do not assume an easy, efficient trip to the interview site. You need to know how long it is going to take you to get there. This is especially the case if you are from out of town and are unfamiliar with local directions and travel conditions.

The Age of Terrorism has made it much more difficult to walk into a federal building. Getting through security can take a very long time. In some federal buildings, you must traverse not only lobby security, but a guard post on the floor and/or at the entrance to the office you are visiting. You need to allow enough time to negotiate the building's security.

Come to the interview armed with good questions to ask. This goes without saying for any interview, but I raise it here because of feedback from federal interviewers who, when asked what annoyed them the most about job candidates, put failure to ask them any questions at the top of the list.

Tone down the arrogance. Another major irritant cited by federal law office interviewers is the candidate who emits "arrogance" vibrations because they come from the private sector and tend to look down on government and on government lawyers. This is not the way to win the interviewers' hearts and minds.

Telephone Interviews

Telephone interviews are becoming more popular with federal employers, primarily as a means to "pre-screen" job applicants before committing to the next step, which would typically be an invitation to a face-to-face interview. In rare cases, the telephone interview is the only interview. This is particularly the case when interviewing for an out-of-town position and with a federal employer whose policy is not to pay interview travel expenses (99.9 percent of federal employers will not pay your interview travel expenses).

Telephone interviews are different from face-to-face interviews and thus have to be approached differently by both the job applicant and the interviewer. In many ways, it is easier to "blow" a telephone interview than the face-to-face variety.

A few simple suggestions for adjusting to a telephone interview will make the experience much more productive for both you and your prospective employer:

- *Visualize a face-to-face interview.* Telephone interviewees have a tendency to come off sounding unenthusiastic. Since the interviewer(s) cannot see your body language or the spark of excitement and enthusiasm in your eyes and expression, you have to consciously try to *sound interested and enthusiastic* (without going over the top) on the phone. This might be particularly challenging if you naturally speak in a monotone.
- *Don't ramble.* It is much easier to fall into this trap on the telephone than in person because you cannot see and interpret the visual signals to stop talking that the interviewer is likely to send you when face-to-face. The best way to ensure that you do not wander into a monologue worthy of Lady Macbeth is to *take off your watch before the interview and keep it in front of you* while on the phone so that you can see how long you have been talking in response to each question. Keep your responses short and crisp; 90 seconds max.
- *Have a copy of your resumé or application form in front of you.* If any questions arise regarding your work history, your

resumé or application form should be able to answer most
of them. Be careful not to read the interviewer your document verbatim. If it does not outline, step-by-step, what you
do at work (provided your work entails a relatively orderly
process of going about your business), prepare a list of such
steps, in sequence, so that you can paint a strong visual
image for the interviewer. Moreover, if you work in an esoteric area not well understood or easily grasped by outsid-
ers, put your activities into a framework—and a
language—that they will understand.

- *Have a copy of your cover letter or transmittal e-mail in
front of you.* The interviewer may ask you questions that
were generated by the cover letter or e-mail that accompanied your resumé or application form to the employer. Since
job-hunting usually means sending out multiple applications,
make sure you have a copy of the specific cover letter or e-
mail that you sent to the employer handy.

- *Have the job ad or announcement in front of you.* This will
enable you to emphasize those elements of your background
and capabilities that conform to what the employer specified in the job ad or vacancy announcement. In addition, it
can serve as the stimulus for good questions that you can
pose to the interviewer(s).

- *Have your list of good questions to ask the interviewer in
front of you.* This phase of the interview is your opportunity
to make a lasting impression once you hang up the telephone. The impersonal, non-visual nature of a telephone
interview is actually an advantage when it comes to posing
good questions. If you were being interviewed in person,
you would have to ask these questions from memory, without benefit of a written list at your disposal.

- *Prepare to deal with the employer's relocation concerns.*
Many telephone interviews are, in part, the result of good
candidates who happen to reside out of the employer's geographic area. Be prepared to indicate (1) your intention to
move to the employer's location, (2) any ties you might have
to that location, (3) the steps you have taken or will take to
meet any local bar or other licensing requirements (if required

for the job), (4) your willingness to travel to the employer for a face-to-face interview (at your own expense if it is apparent that the employer will not pay interview travel expenses), and (5) your acknowledgment that you will be responsible for your own relocation costs if you are offered and accept the position (provided you have determined beforehand that the employer does not usually pick up those costs).

Taking these seven steps will not only make for a smoother interview, but will also boost your self-confidence.

Panel Interviews

Panel interviews—being interviewed by more than one person at the same time—are a popular federal law office interview technique. You sit in front of the panel and are peppered with questions by most, if not all, of the panel members.

Two suggestions for handling a panel interview:

- First, make sure that you determine the identity of the lead interviewer, the *primus inter pares*, or first among equals. That is likely the person who will have the most influence over the hiring decision and who should be the recipient of your thank-you letter or e-mail following the interview.
- Second, make sure that (a) you make eye contact with each questioner when he or she is speaking to you, and (b) you make eye contact with the entire panel when responding to a question. A good speaker sweeps his or her eyes around the audience when speaking in order to keep them interested and engaged. Adopt the same technique for panel interviews.

"Seriatim" Interviews

A seriatim interview is really a series of interviews, one after the other on the same day. This is another popular federal law office interview technique. You might start off in the human resources office, then be directed to the law office to meet with one or more staff attorneys, then to the Deputy General Counsel, and finally to the General Counsel. The purpose is often to save the higher-ups the trouble of interviewing you if you do not pass muster at the lower levels.

Seriatim interviews are usually more stressful than a single interview because you have to be "on" more than once. You are likely to be asked the same or very similar questions by each of the interviewers. The most important things you can do to prepare and follow up seriatim interviews are:

- Get plenty of rest prior to the interview.
- Respond with the same answer to the same question from more than one interviewer. They are likely to convene as a group following the interviews and compare notes.
- Debrief yourself when you leave the interviews so that you will remember what you said to each interviewer.
- Lock down the interviewers' names and job titles so that you can thank them appropriately via e-mail or postal mail.

Scripted Interviews

Federal legal interviewers sometimes resort to a scripted interview where each candidate being interviewed is asked exactly the same questions in exactly the same order. This is *de rigueur* for federal administrative law judge interviews, but also carries over to some interviews for other legal positions. An all-too-common feature of scripted interviews is that they do not permit the candidate to ask the interviewer any questions.

The purposes of a scripted interview are (1) to level the playing field among candidates in much the same way that an online application form accomplishes this. Every competitor is reduced to a least common denominator and denied much of an opportunity to stand out, especially if the interviewer's questions are mundane or not very open-ended (which is often the case); and (2) to allow the interviewer to give a numerical score to each candidate upon completion of the interview.

It is more difficult to prepare for a scripted interview because it is the only type of interview that does not follow the usual conversational, give-and-take format. Moreover, because the interviewer is asking the same questions of every candidate and is more intent on scoring each response, he or she is likely to be less engaged with you and in what you are saying. Scripted interviews quickly become monotonous for the interviewer. Consequently, it is up to you to be alert, engaged, lively, and enthusiastic.

IRAQ: A Special Warning to "BigLaw" Candidates

Standing out from the competition can also have its negative aspects. Here is one that is happening now and that federal legal employers relate to me all too often.

Federal legal job candidates who come from major (and sometimes not so major) law firms are often shocked when they are rejected for a federal position. They cannot possibly imagine who could have been more qualified than they were, and often they would be absolutely correct. What they fail to realize is that exceptional qualifications are only part of the reason why a candidate wins a job offer.

I want to share with you what I hear about all too many BigLaw candidates from federal legal interviewers. I have distilled their comments down into four categories—acronym IRAQ—that encompass virtually every bit of interviewer feedback.

- *Intimidation.* Federal legal managers who receive resumés from, and subsequently interview, BigLaw candidates are often intimidated by their credentials. They worry about what it would be like to work in an environment where the subordinate is much more accomplished than the supervisor, made much more money, and is perhaps much smarter. Unfortunately there is little that you, the BigLaw candidate, can do about this.

- *Remuneration.* Federal legal managers are concerned that when a BigLaw new hire sees his/her first paycheck, he or she will be upset, to say the least, despite knowing going into the job what the compensation and deductions were going to be. No manager wants to have a disgruntled employee around, so the simple solution is not to hire the BigLaw attorney in the first place. The only hope you have of altering the manager's mind-set is to make it very clear during your interview that you fully understand that you will be taking a major pay cut and that you are okay with that. It helps to cite examples of how you are scaling down your lifestyle to accommodate your new financial reality.

- *Arrogance.* This is the one IRAQ component that results in more BigLaw candidate rejections than any other, and that you have total control over. Many BigLaw candidates cannot seem to hide their arrogance when they are interviewed for a federal legal job. They positively ooze it during interviews. Don't.

- *Quick Exit.* Federal legal managers almost always come into an interview with a BigLaw candidate with a preconceived notion that the attorney applicant will leave government service as soon as the legal economy turns around and much higher-paying private-sector job opportunities present themselves. The way to disabuse the interviewer of this notion is to emphasize the attractive features of working for the government outside of compensation—benefits, work-life balance, etc.—and to contrast them with your prior employment.

Part VII

Long-Term Trends

We have arrived at the part of this book where some predictions are in order. How is legal employment in the U.S. government going to fare in the long run? Is there an assurance of more job security than in the private sector? Will you be able to make the federal government a career? Will the work continue to be interesting?

Chapter 46

Defending the Nation

National Security, which also includes Intelligence and what has come to be known as Homeland Security, is the fundamental essence of what a national government is all about. Defending itself and its people is the highest duty of government and, as a consequence, is not just a long-term trend but an ever-present, unremitting one.

The federal government's national security apparatus constitutes the largest number of agencies, law offices, and attorneys in government, and by far its largest expenditure outside of entitlement programs. Between them, the core national security agencies (Department of Defense, Department of Homeland Security, and the official Intelligence Community) have hundreds of law offices as well as numerous program, operations, and administrative offices in which attorneys work. If you add the other offices that play a role in the defense of the United States, such as the Financial Crimes Enforcement Network, Office of Foreign Assets Control, Drug Enforcement Administration (a great deal of terrorist funding comes from drug sales), Justice Department (parent agency of DEA as well as the FBI; the Bureau of Alcohol, Tobacco, Firearms and Explosives; and the U.S. Marshals' Service), and the National Nuclear Security Administration, to name only a few, the massive scope and far-flung nature of the national security legal establishment is stunning.

Moreover, the national security bureaucracies are expanding in parallel to the expansion and growing complexity of the threats this country faces. The substitution of non-state actors such as al-Qaeda and the Haqqani Network for traditional nation-state enemies, such as the Soviet Union and, currently, North Korea and Iran, has complicated the national security picture enormously and given rise to the creation of new agencies and offices designed to combat the new threats.

For aspiring attorneys, the point is that there will always be numerous opportunities to practice national security law and to work in a law-related capacity within the vast national security establishment.

For a further discussion of National Security as a functional area, see Chapter 56, "Functional Areas with a Great Future."

Chapter 47

The Rise of Regulation

The United States for the past century and a half has followed something of a regular pattern of alternating regulation and deregulation. Lengthy periods of the one are succeeded by comparable periods of the other. The Civil War's end launched a *laissez-faire* era that lasted for two decades, until Grover Cleveland's first election to the presidency in 1884. A "regulatory era" then ensued for approximately a generation, until Warren Harding's presidency in 1920. The Great Depression refocused the federal government on the longest regulatory era in our history, one lasting almost 40 years, spurred first by the New Deal, then World War II, and a post-war era marked by U.S. global economic dominance, the Cold War, and enormous social change. The end of that era in the mid-1970s launched the most vigorous and lengthy deregulation period we have ever seen, one that continued for almost 35 years, due to the disruptions associated with the waning of U.S. economic hegemony, the abandonment of the Bretton Woods Agreement, the 1973–74 oil shock, the pent-up inflationary pressures wrought by trying to have both guns and butter during the Vietnam War, and some of the extremes of the social revolution.

That now appears to have ended, and we are rapidly moving into another period where regulatory activity will be intense. We have already seen unambiguous evidence of this manifested by health-care reform, greater government scrutiny of the financial services sector, the legislative reaction to the terrorist attacks of September 11, 2001, and the coping mechanisms put in place to keep the Great Recession from destroying our economy.

While no one can prognosticate as to the length of this new regulatory era, given the massive problems we face and the already potent reaction to it from opponents, it is likely to go on for a very long time because it will be impossible for government to adopt a hands-off mentality if the country is to pull itself out of the mess it is in. Moreover, the near-term future does not portend fewer unanticipated crises and emergencies to which government will have to respond, whether financial (underfunded pension plans are soon going to come home to roost to the tune of trillions of dollars), international (the downside of "peak oil"), environmental (climate change, oil spills, hurricanes), or terrorist. One additional point that job-seekers, attorneys or otherwise, need to always be sensitive to is the Law of Unintended Consequences, evidenced most recently and glaringly by the Wall Street high-jinks that resulted from the regulatory loopholes opened up by a succession of Congresses and Administrations that thought they were contributing to economic prosperity.

This era of regulation means that the federal government's demand for legal services can only increase. Managing the multiple crises that must be addressed requires a great deal of legal expertise. Every new piece of landmark legislation—and there are bound to be many more over and above what we have witnessed in just the past several years—and every new regulatory initiative creates a need for more government attorneys to perform federal compliance and enforcement functions, participate in administering new programs, and respond to private-sector reactions to federal scrutiny.

All of this means new federal agencies and new law offices. A classic example of this occurred in the recent past when the federal Pension Benefit Guaranty Corporation created a new Office of Chief Counsel to parallel its existing Office of General Counsel and handle an anticipated flood of litigation associated with the failure of private pension plans to meet their obligations. The changes now being implemented by financial regulatory reform—several new watchdog agencies and expanded powers conferred on existing financial regulators—ensure that the country's huge and far-flung financial services sector will need thousands of additional attorneys and compliance personnel. Two precepts that you can always count on are:

- New laws—even those that deregulate—always create new legal job opportunities; and
- New attorney jobs create more new attorney jobs; or, for every attorney, there has to be at least one opposing attorney.

To demonstrate how potent these two precepts are, let me cite the example of the Telecommunications Act of 1996, Pub. L. 104-104, the first overhaul of communications law in over 60 years and perhaps the most massive and profound federal deregulatory initiative in history. Following enactment, the Federal Communications Commission (FCC) went on an unprecedented legal hiring spree, one that those of us who follow such things naively believed would be temporary once all of the regulations that needed to be eliminated or revised had been addressed. Today, 16 years later and counting, the size of the FCC legal staff has not declined.

Chapter 48

Technology Run Riot

Technology moves much faster than law and regulation. Consequently, in this highly technological era, government is constantly behind and is always scrambling to adjust and enact new laws designed to keep up with rampaging technological advances.

The Food and Drug Administration (FDA) has authority to regulate medical devices and separate authority to regulate drugs and biologics. The world's first "drug-device" combination products, such as stents that release a heart medication into the bloodstream, recently caused the agency to wrestle with how to regulate these innovative therapeutics. The FDA's Center for Devices and Radiological Health (CDRH) approves and regulates medical devices, while its Center for Drug Evaluation and Research (CDER) approves and regulates drugs. CDER usually imposes more rigorous testing and approval standards than CDRH. Complicating the matter is a third FDA center, the Center for Biologics Evaluation and Research (CBER), which operates under a different testing and approval methodology than either CDRH or CDER.

It took FDA several years to play catch-up with the rapid advances in drug-device technology and to cope with the barrage of drug-device applications flooding into its centers for approval. Jurisdictional disputes escalated, and as a result, FDA recently established a new "cross-center" Office of Combination Products to advise manufacturers, arbitrate jurisdictional disputes, and resolve other issues.

For years now, the Securities and Exchange Commission (SEC) has been pondering how to regulate or at least monitor international capital flows. Every day, tens of trillions of dollars move across borders, including into and out of the United States. These funds can be moved across national boundaries quickly and effortlessly with a handful of computer keystrokes.

Not knowing how much money is moving around the planet at any given moment has become very dangerous, as evidenced by such developments as the financial meltdown prompting the Great Recession, the balance of payments, the international trade disparities between the United States and its trading partners, and other numbers it is critical for government to know. To date, the SEC has still not come up with an answer.

Throughout history, technology has always outpaced the ability of government to both understand it and regulate it. That problem has never been more acute and vexing than at present, when technological advances in numerous fields are announced daily. The plus side of this perennial challenge is its positive impact on federal legal employment. The more new technologies and products derived therefrom, the more attorneys are needed to understand their legal ramifications and to regulate them. This dynamic tension is not going to go away.

Chapter 49

Globalization

Going back to at least 1994 and the ratification of the North American Free Trade Agreement (NAFTA), the U.S. government has consistently accentuated the positive aspects of globalization. Citizens for the most part bought what the government was selling, but that appears to be changing quite rapidly.

Ross Perot's description of the "giant sucking sound" made by manufacturing jobs leaving the United States for Mexico was ridiculed at the time but looks pretty prescient now. In fact, that sound has gotten a lot louder with the passage of time, as millions upon millions of U.S. jobs have left this country and ended up in places where labor is cheap (e.g., China), currencies are manipulated for local advantage (e.g., China), and environmental controls are virtually nonexistent (e.g., China).

The problem of massive job loss was swept under the rug for years by the globalization proponents and was largely relegated to the ruminations of academic economists. Not anymore. The Great Recession has pushed it back into the limelight and it has now emerged as a major political issue, one that is likely to have a profound impact on U.S. political alignment for some time to come. Perhaps this new political awareness is the result of the recent impact of outsourcing and offshoring of white-collar jobs, attorneys included. When the dwindling number of blue-collar workers in declining manufacturing industries were the only ones affected by the downside of globalization, the vast majority of Americans who work in service industries largely ignored the issue. Only when it began to affect them directly did they sit up and take notice. The lonely, isolationist voice of a Lou Dobbs evolved quickly then into the clamor of the rest of the chattering class.

What began with the outsourcing of legal research jobs to India by the major online legal research companies has spread to include a growing number of major law firms. Moreover, the nature of outsourced and offshored legal work also expanded, and is destined to expand even more, which will inevitably threaten even more legal jobs in this country.

The reaction to globalization is isolation, manifested in the imposition of tariffs and duties on foreign products, penalties imposed on companies that move jobs offshore, restrictions on immigration, and other government efforts to stave off massive job loss. All such government initiatives mean more regulation of the private sector, which in turn means more government positions for attorneys.

It is too early to tell how this battle between the outward-looking and inward-looking factions will turn out. Regardless, government legal jobs are somewhat insulated from the epic contest because they cannot be offshored. Moreover, however the struggle turns out, federal attorneys who focus on globalization issues are going to be in greater demand.

Chapter 50

Energy Independence

Federal energy law is going to be a very hot practice area in the first half of the twenty-first century, and possibly beyond. U.S. overreliance on fossil fuels—especially petroleum imports—is unsustainable and will become impossibly expensive. It also will pose an increasing national security risk, since most of our imported oil comes from unstable parts of the world and derives from countries that are not exactly our bosom buddies. In addition, global warming and climate change will affect our dependence on fossil fuels.

All of this will combine to propel U.S. energy policy in three major directions:

1. Increased domestic exploration and development of fossil fuel resources;
2. Major government support for alternative energy development; and
3. Increasing efforts at conservation.

Some of this is already taking place even in the absence of omnibus energy independence legislation, which as this book goes to press is stalled on Capitol Hill, principally because, although one of the few areas of bipartisan agreement, the Obama Administration and its congressional allies insisted that it be combined within a climate change bill that is vigorously opposed by Republicans. Sooner rather than later, I believe that the two components of this bill will be "decoupled," and we will get some variation on energy independence legislation. In that event, look for demand for additional federal government legal talent to emerge.

The American Recovery and Reinvestment Act (a.k.a. the Stimulus Bill), Pub. L. 111-5, threw a great deal of federal funding at solar, wind, wave, biomass, and other energy alternatives that, without government subsidies, are not price-competitive with fossil fuels. This has had a modest, positive impact on federal legal hiring.

Nuclear reactors are being licensed for the first time in a generation, since the Three-Mile Island scare of 1979. Consequently, the federal Nuclear Regulatory Commission (NRC) stepped up its hiring of attorneys, including recent law school graduates, for the first time in decades.

The U.S. Department of Energy (DOE) is entering into Cooperative Research and Development Agreements (CRADAs) with private companies in which both parties agree to work together on energy development projects. Federal energy laboratories are developing and transferring new technologies and processes to the private sector. This creates legal jobs both at DOE and in the technology transfer offices at federal laboratories.

The drive for energy independence involves other federal agencies and functions in addition to the NRC, DOE and its 16 law offices, and federal energy laboratories. Other federal agencies and law offices that will be hiring attorneys for this national effort include:

- Department of Defense Energy Support Center—Office of Counsel
- Department of Interior (25 separate offices)
- Department of Justice—Antitrust Division—Transportation, Energy and Agriculture Section; Civil Division; and Environment and Natural Resources Division (14 separate offices)
- Department of State—Bureau of Economic and Business Affairs

- Congressional Research Service—American Law Division
- Environmental Protection Agency—Air and Radiation Law Office
- Federal Energy Regulatory Commission (8 separate offices)
- Federal Trade Commission—Bureau of Competition and Bureau of Consumer Protection—Division of Enforcement
- Nuclear Regulatory Commission (9 separate offices)
- U.S. Coast Guard Legal Offices and National Pollution Funds Center—Legal Division

Chapter 51

Enforcement of Intellectual Property Rights Abroad

This is a "sleeping giant" that is just waking up. Perhaps the most telling statistic is this: In 1985, 32 percent of the market value of S&P 500 companies was based on intangible assets, the bulk of which were intellectual property (IP). By 2005, intangible assets—almost all of which were now IP—had increased to almost 80 percent of their market value. This represents a complete reversal of our historical asset orientation toward manufactured goods and equipment.

U.S. IP rights holders must compete today with both legitimate competition from foreign lands (for example, China graduates 500,000 new engineers each year versus 150,000 in the United States, so it follows that China will produce more innovation than we will) and the global illicit market that is being flooded by economic incentives, such as low barriers to entry into counterfeiting and piracy, high profits, and limited legal sanctions if caught. Moreover, technological advances have facilitated the reproduction and distribution of many counterfeit and pirated products. Combine this with the unfortunate fact that IP protection in some parts of the world is woefully inadequate, and U.S. goods are subject to widespread piracy and counterfeiting in many countries, resulting in enormous and growing economic losses. In addition, many IP "knockoffs," such as pharmaceuticals and auto parts, have the potential to threaten public health and safety in the United States and abroad.

A wide range of federal agencies are involved in efforts to protect and enforce IP rights with personnel posted domestically and overseas. In order to improve the coordination of the U.S. government's IP activities, Congress passed the Prioritizing Resources and Organization for Intellectual Property Act of 2008 (PRO-IP Act), Pub. L. 110-403. Title III of that legislation created a new interagency IP enforcement advisory committee composed of representatives of specified departments and agencies involved in IP enforcement. It authorized the President to appoint an Intellectual Property Enforcement Coordinator (IPEC) position within the Executive Office of the President to chair the new advisory committee.

The IPEC is to lead the committee in the development of a joint strategic plan to reduce counterfeiting and other types of IP infringement in the United States and overseas, and to assist in the implementation of the plan when requested by advisory committee members. The new IPEC was appointed by President Obama in 2010 and, as this book goes to press, is in the process of building her office.

Each of the following agencies has U.S. government personnel overseas who are involved in IP protection efforts:

- U.S. Patent and Trademark Office
- International Trade Administration
- Department of Justice—Criminal Division
- Office of the U.S. Trade Representative
- Department of State
- Department of Homeland Security
- U.S. Agency for International Development
- Food and Drug Administration

More than 700 federal employees stationed abroad are tasked with an IP protection function, among other duties. Many of them are attorneys. As time passes, look for more attorneys in these positions with the sole mission of protecting U.S. IP interests now that their central importance to the U.S. economy is better understood.

These individuals negotiate IP agreements, monitor foreign country implementation of existing IP agreements, assess and report on weaknesses in foreign country IP protection and enforcement regimes, participate in international organizations and working groups, train foreign counterparts in IP protection and enforcement, advise foreign governments on drafting and strengthening IP protection and enforcement laws and regulations, raise U.S. industry IP concerns with foreign governments, gather information in support of U.S.-based IP investigations, assist foreign law enforcement officials conducting operations against IP violators, and prepare international litigation against countries violating IP agreements.

Chapter 52

Bubbles

Some "Bubble" Background

"Bubbles" are an excellent predictor of where job opportunities will
and will not be found in the near future. Bubbles always burst. There
has never been one that has remained permanently intact. That is
one of the principal reasons we call them bubbles. It is usually a
great ride for job seekers while these bubbles are expanding. Then,
when they collapse, the ride usually comes to a pretty severe end—
though there are exceptions.

Forget what you've heard from economic gurus such as Francis
Fukuyama, Alan Greenspan, Robert Rubin, and Lawrence Summers
about the end of history, the end of the boom-and-bust business
cycle, and of their self-congratulatory pats on their backs for having "solved" the problem of economic cycles. You cannot go wrong
if you continue to believe that greed and irrational exuberance will
always be with us.

Therein lies legal opportunity. Every time a bubble collapsed, it
is true that attorney jobs were lost. The Great Recession cost thousands of major law firm lawyers their jobs. But not in the federal
government, which has always been called upon to clean up the
mess, and always needs to hire additional attorneys to do it. The
housing collapse followed closely by the financial meltdown has
been a literal bonanza for attorneys seeking federal employment,

as evidenced by what you have been reading and will see in the remaining pages of this book.

The same thing happened in the aftermath of the onset of the Great Depression, when Franklin Roosevelt brought hundreds of lawyers to Washington to work in his administration and experiment with ways to combat the faltering economy. It happened again in the follow-up to the dot.com implosion of 2000–2001. It also happened a few years later when the fast-and-loose behavior of corporations like Enron, Worldcom, and their ilk prompted enactment of the Sarbanes-Oxley Act and new federal and quasi-federal initiatives to police corporate governance and conduct.

It will happen again. The world is too complicated, moving too fast, and is increasingly peopled by very bright if not equally principled individuals seeking an edge or a loophole. Consequently, it behooves legal job seekers, especially those interested in federal careers, to become "bubble trends analysts." This is not as difficult as it might seem.

Some Potential Bubble Bursts

Take, for example, the current state of the bond markets. They are overloaded with funds that have flown out of equity investments to a presumably safer haven. Interest rates are at historic lows, making bonds compellingly attractive. This cannot continue forever. At some point, probably soon, there will be a major correction, and bond markets will seek "equilibrium." Prices will plummet and investors will seek to escape with what is left of their investments. This scenario might even be the result of events beyond our borders—in Greece or Ireland, for example—over which U.S. regulators have no control. The interlocking of the world's economies over the past generation means that if Athens or Dublin coughs loudly enough, America may contract pneumonia.

Should the bond market collapse or even decline abruptly, you can bet the mortgage that Washington will respond with additional financial regulatory mechanisms designed to keep such a meltdown from reoccurring. And that will mean additional job opportunities within the federal financial regulatory community.

Perhaps a more immediate example is what is going on with the egregious underfunding of public- and private-sector pension plans. In short, it is a train wreck waiting to happen. Even before the Great Recession began, the Pew Center on the States estimated that the shortfall in aggregate state employee retirement plans was $1 trillion. It may be twice that now. Entering the Great Recession, only five state pension plans were in good shape. Other than Idaho, even those are not solvent anymore. State retiree non-pension benefits, such as health care, are short 95 percent of full funding.

All of the possible solutions to the state underfunding problem—such as increasing the retirement age, forcing employees to share the risk, or substantially raising taxes—are draconian and politically unpalatable, if not impossible to achieve, except one: Increasing federal scrutiny, oversight, and regulation of state plan governance and of plan investments.

Private pension plans of some very large companies are in just as bad, or worse, shape. S&P 500 companies by themselves are underfunded to the tune of $402 billion as this book goes to press, according to a Credit Suisse study.

To date, the federal government has largely played ostrich with the pension bubble. Its Pension Benefit Guaranty Corporation (PBGC), which is tasked with "protecting" the pensions of 44 million American workers and retirees in more than 29,000 private single-employer and multiemployer defined benefit pension plans (by no means the entire plan universe), has done very little toward coping with the inevitable bubble burst. However, the great plus for aspiring federal attorneys is that PBGC is funded by pension insurance premiums that Congress sets and that the agency receives from plan sponsors, plus some other private income sources, rather than from general tax revenues. That means that it is an "off-budget" agency that, in a crisis, should be able to expand quickly without the usual budgetary rancor and anguish. If this bubble bursts, the federal government will have to jump into the pension disaster with both feet.

Chapter 53

Resource Shortages

Between July and October 2010, grain prices in the United States almost doubled. One in three ears of corn in 2010 went into a gas tank through ethanol.

The benchmark price of a barrel of Saudi Arabian light crude oil as recently as 1999 was under $10. Currently, it is around $88. It reached a high of $145 in mid-2008 before getting hammered by declining demand during the Great Recession. As the global economy recovers, you can expect oil prices to continue their upward march.

This time oil price rises are markedly different from what they were during the oil shocks of 1973–74 and 1979, when first OPEC, then Iran turned off the spigot for political purposes. Now the price rises are demand-driven—a far more ominous and serious problem for the West, and especially for the United States.

Another resource shortage issue that has begun to affect the U.S. economy adversely has to do with what are called "rare earth" elements, 17 naturally occurring metals that have become essential to the production of such items as lithium batteries, smart phones, flat screens, hybrid car batteries, MP3 players, wind turbine generators, fiber optics, computer hard drives, lasers, radar, missile-guidance systems, satellites and aircraft electronics, etc., many of which go into equipment vital to national defense. China produces

97 percent of the world's supply of rare earth elements and recently announced a major cutback in its exports, claiming that it is beginning to experience shortages of these elements. The United States used to mine them, but no longer does.

The Chinese cutback, combined with the recent realization that these metals are so critical to the world economy, has prompted price increases of over 300 percent in the first nine months of 2010. Unless and until other countries begin their own mining efforts, prices will certainly continue to rise rapidly.

The world has experienced numerous resource wars and likely will continue to see countries pursue military actions designed to secure vital resources. Japan's attack on Pearl Harbor was prompted solely by resource shortages. The United States launched "Desert Storm" in 1991 out of concern that Iraq's invasion of Kuwait would cause a severe oil shortage and threaten the Saudi oil fields that supplied us with essential petroleum. Many argue that the 2003 U.S. invasion of Iraq was also, in large part, a resource war to secure the Iraqi oil fields and stabilize future supplies. That argument is backed up by the fact that the first building that the U.S. secured in Baghdad in March 2003 was the Iraqi Oil Ministry, the repository of maps of the oil fields and Iraqi reserves. An overlay of U.S. military bases on top of a map of the world's oil reserves is also revealing, supporting the notion that the armed forces are, at least in part, an oil protection force.

All of this will have a profound impact on federal legal employment opportunities. Resource shortages breed the need for legal advice, counsel, and transactional expertise across an array of both legally charged matters and national borders, as well as within all of the many federal agencies with jurisdiction over such matters. Military actions also always generate legal job opportunities in such areas as government contracting, military justice, national security, and intelligence law.

Chapter 54

Alternative Work Scheduling and Workplace Modification

The U.S. government workplace is not immune from the dramatic changes that are affecting virtually all employment situations. In fact, the government is—and has been for many years—in the forefront of experimentation when it comes to workplace modifications. Some of what follows was addressed briefly in Part Two, "The Pros and Cons of a Federal Legal Career."

Statutory and Regulatory Basis

Federal workplace modification and alternative work scheduling (AWS) has a strong statutory basis. The law leaves the decision to establish an AWS program to the discretion of the agency head, subject to the obligation to negotiate with the exclusive representative(s) of bargaining-unit employees. Virtually every federal agency offers at least one AWS option to its employees.

5 U.S.C. § 6122 covers flexible work schedules. 5 U.S.C. § 6121(5) and 5 U.S.C. § 6127 address compressed work schedules. Both are further defined and elaborated upon in 5 C.F.R. § 610.102

and 5 C.F.R. § 610.111(d). 5 U.S.C. § 6133 grants the Office of Personnel Management (OPM) authority to—

(1) promulgate regulations necessary for the administration of AWS programs,
(2) provide educational material and technical assistance relating to AWS programs, and
(3) conduct periodic reviews of AWS programs established by agencies.

It is the agencies' responsibility to determine whether to establish AWS programs and how to comply with the spirit of several Presidential memoranda encouraging AWS (July 11, 1994, "Expanding Family-Friendly Work Arrangements in the Executive Branch," and June 21, 1996, "Implementing Federal Family Friendly Work Arrangements").

Under subchapter II of chapter 61 of title 5, United States Code, AWS programs may apply to employees of any executive agency (excluding the U.S. Postal Service), any military department, the Government Printing Office, or the Library of Congress.

Agencies wishing to establish flexible or compressed work schedules do not need OPM approval and may determine the general policy, as well as guidelines, instructions, and procedures, for AWS programs in their headquarters and field activities. An agency may establish any number of AWS programs.

Flexible Work Schedules

The federal government defines a flexible work schedule as one that, in the case of a full-time employee, is an 80-hour biweekly basic work requirement that allows the employee to determine his or her own schedule within the limits set by the agency. Eligible employees must be at work during what the agency defines as its core hours—the time periods during the workday, workweek, or pay period that the agency requires employees to be present for work. Core hours can vary from agency to agency and office to office.

A few agencies even go so far as to permit "gliding schedules" in which a full-time employee with a basic work requirement of eight hours in each day and 40 hours in each week may select a starting and stopping time each day, and may change starting and stopping times whenever they'd like. To date, few attorneys benefit from this, but the number may increase in the near future. However, many federal attorneys benefit from flexible work schedules.

Compressed Work Schedules

An increasing number of federal agencies offer their employees the option of working a compressed work schedule. For full-time employees, that means an 80-hour biweekly basic work requirement that is scheduled by an agency for less than 10 workdays. Translated, that means that an employee may work a more than eight-hour day in order to earn one or two days off biweekly. Compressed work schedules are always fixed schedules.

An increasing number of federal attorneys have secured three-day weekends every week via compressed work schedules, either having every Friday or Monday off.

Part-Time Employment

My clients have often asked me how they can go about getting a part-time job. My answer varies considerably depending on where they want to work. Profession-wide, part-time attorney and law-related positions are very rare. Even more limiting is the fact that they are usually reserved for long-time employees whom the employer wants to accommodate because they have proven their worth and are too valuable to lose if they are not accommodated.

Law firms for the most part frown on part-time employees, tethered as the firms are by the billable-hour requirement. A disproportionate number of my clients over the years who were terminated by their law firms happened to be women who backed off from full-time law firm work in order to spend time having and raising their children. This could not have been mere coincidence, especially as so many of them were very accomplished. Attorneys who do not achieve their billable hours are, these days, not long for the firm. Part-time employees cannot possibly meet the firm-wide bill-able mandates unless the firm modifies the requirement to accommodate their part-time status, something that most firms have been reluctant to do. Despite client pressures for project billing and all of the legal media attention to alternative billing practices, as well as the fact that law is the only remaining "learned profession" that retains the billable hour, don't hold your breath waiting for the billable hour to disappear.

Corporate in-house counsel offices are generally a bit more amenable to part-time status than law firms, since they are not beholden to the billable hour. Like law firms, however, part-time status is not conferred easily, but rather is usually granted only to long-term employees whose value to the organization is too high to lose.

In contrast, the U.S. government stands by itself with respect to part-time employment in several respects:

(1) Legislation encouraging part-time employment in the U.S. government has been on the books for more than 30 years (the Federal Employees Part-time Career Employment Act of 1978, Pub. L. 95-437).

(2) Proportionately more federal jobs—legal positions included—may be deemed part-time from the outset than you will find in any other employment sector. Part-time status is not reserved exclusively for long-time, valued federal employees. While not very many jobs in total, the quantity is greater than exists anywhere else in the economy.

(3) Federal employee collective bargaining agreements, which cover a large number of attorneys in certain federal agencies, specify that employees may negotiate part-time status under certain conditions, such as a lighter workload, a family need, or a medical or behavioral problem that needs to be resolved. The American Federation of Government Employees, the National Treasury Employees Union, and the National Federation of Federal Employees, the three largest federal employee unions, represent thousands of federal attorneys at agencies such as the Equal Employment Opportunity Commission, Social Security Administration, Environmental Protection Agency, U.S. Patent and Trademark

Office, Department of Justice, Department of Treasury, and the Securities and Exchange Commission, among others.

(4) Even without a collective bargaining agreement in place, it is usually easier for a federal attorney to attain part-time status merely by asking for it and pointing out the reasons behind his or her request. As mentioned, a large number of federal employees, including certain attorneys, are covered by these provisions of a collective bargaining agreement with their agency even though they are not themselves union members.

(5) More professional employees, including attorneys, work part-time for the U.S. government than any other category of federal employees.

Your opportunity to negotiate a part-time employment arrangement becomes greater the longer you have been with an agency or office. The best way to do that is to use the following methodology:

(1) Keep detailed records of your real job description (what you actually do);

(2) Assess whether (a) your most important tasks can be done in less time, (b) less important tasks could be discontinued or done by someone else, and (c) your job could be shared with another part-time employee (in which case you might want to find a job-sharing partner);

(3) Analyze what the changes to your salary, annual and sick leave earning, health insurance cost, retirement, and life insurance benefits would mean for you and your family;

(4) Make sure you understand both government-wide and agency part-time policies; and

(5) Try to talk to current and former part-time employees about their experiences.

Once you have accomplished these five tasks, the next step would be to implement your strategy, as follows:

(1) Put together a written proposal;

(2) Propose a schedule and explain how your duties would be handled, focusing on your employer's needs rather than your own; and

(3) Propose a pilot part-time scheme so that your employer can test the arrangement.

Part-time federal employees are also eligible for flexible work schedules and compressed work schedules. The rules that govern in the case of part-time employees are largely pro rata modifications of the full-time employee rules.

One caveat: Do not disadvantage yourself by making it appear that your job is a piece of cake that the agency does not need or can be easily added to another employee's duties.

Job Sharing

Job sharing is a form of part-time employment in which one position is filled with two or more part-time employees. Job sharing has added benefits for management. At an agency's discretion and within available resources, each job sharer can work up to 32 hours per week.

Generally, job sharing means two employees at the same grade level, but other arrangements are possible. Job sharers are subject to the same personnel policies as other part-time employees. It does not necessarily mean that each job sharer works half-time, or that the total number of hours is 40 per week.

One of the best ways to "sell" your employer on job sharing is to point out that it permits the employer to benefit from the unique skills, knowledge, and talents of two individuals.

Telecommuting

As discussed in Part Two, "The Pros and Cons of a Federal Legal Career," the government is far and away the sector leader with respect to telecommuting in the United States. No other employer comes even remotely close. This is particularly the case for attorneys. In addition to the cutting-edge telecommuting programs launched by the U.S. Patent and Trademark Office, other agencies are either investigating replicating such programs in their own agencies and law offices or are being dragged in that direction by a series of presidential, congressional, and OPM issuances and exhortations.

OPM reports that as of the end of 2008 (the last year for which data is currently available), more than 102,000 federal employees telecommuted, an increase of 9 percent over 2007. Forty-eight agencies reported an increase in their overall telework numbers; 27 agencies reported cost savings/benefits as a result of telework. Of these, the greatest benefit was to morale (24 agencies), then productivity/performance and transportation (22 each), then human capital (21).

Just days before this book went to press, Congress passed and the President signed the Telework Enhancement Act of 2010, Pub. L. 111-292. The act expands telework opportunities for most federal employees. It establishes a statutory federal telework policy, requires that agencies notify eligible employees that they can telecommute, mandates a written agreement between an agency manager and any employee authorized to telecommute, directs that teleworkers and non-teleworkers be treated the same for virtually all work-related purposes, orders a telework training program, and requires each executive agency to designate a Telework Managing Officer who must be a senior official with direct access to the agency head.

Federal law and law-related offices with the best telecommuting environment include (in alphabetical order):

- Department of Education—Office of General Counsel
- Department of Housing and Urban Development—Office of General Counsel
- Department of Interior—Office of the Solicitor
- Department of Justice—Civil Division; Environment and Natural Resources Division; and Executive Office for Immigration Review
- Department of Labor—Office of the Solicitor; Administrative Review Board; Benefits Review Board; and Employee Compensation Appeals Board
- Department of Transportation—Surface Transportation Board
- Department of Treasury—Alcohol and Tobacco Tax and Trade Bureau; Internal Revenue Service—Office of Chief Counsel; Office of Inspector General for Tax Administration

- U.S. International Trade Commission
- U.S. Patent and Trademark Office

The benefits of such workplace modifications to both employers and employees, as well as society, are now obvious and very compelling. All such modifications raise morale. In addition, studies of those functions that lend themselves to measurement consistently demonstrate that productivity goes up whenever one or more of these workplace modifications are instituted. Flexible work schedules, compressed work schedules, and telecommuting have also had a broader societal impact by reducing traffic congestion and commuting times. Telework makes neighborhoods safer because employees are home during the day, and reduces air pollution. Agencies with telework programs spend less in overhead for office space and furniture.

Workplace Accommodations and Assistive Technologies

While federal disability hiring programs could certainly use considerable improvement, once employed, individuals with disabilities have little difficulty getting the government to accommodate their disabilities and provide them with assistive technologies to enable them to be productive workers. From ergonomic chairs to Kurzweil Reading Machines to readers and interpreters, the government does a reasonably good job helping its disabled employees perform.

Part VIII

Where to Work

Epilogue

*Even the U.S. government lends itself to the popular national pas-
time of hierarchical list-making—the best law schools, the best law*

firms, the most family-friendly corporations, etc. I want to conclude my treatise on federal legal employment by joining the surveyors and opinion leaders obsessed with the best by offering my opinions on the subject of the best places for attorneys to work in the government.

However, I take a very different approach to the subject, as you will find in this last Part of Landing a Federal Legal Job.

Chapter 55

There Are the Best, and Then There Are the BEST

The "Best"

Each year several organizations conduct surveys of federal employees—and in some cases alumni of federal agencies—and publish the results under the overly ambitious and wildly inaccurate label of "The Best Places to Work in the U.S. Government." I have been a constant critic of these surveys because (1) they do not "drill down" into each department and agency, and (2) they cross and aggregate all professions and occupations within each agency, treating them as one. Naively, they present a perspective on the organization as a whole, uniform unit. I consider such information bordering on useless insofar as attorneys are concerned; this total organization approach completely overlooks the point that not only is the entire federal government not a monolith, but also that no department or agency can possibly be evaluated as a single entity.

These surveys also overlook the critical point that individual offices are distinguished to a great extent by the caliber of their immediate bosses as well as their second, third, and fourth-line supervisors and beyond. This factor is, of course, one that is very

297

fluid and cannot be adequately assessed outside of "real time." A great office can be rendered considerably less than great by a bad boss. Conversely, a "backwater" law office can be a nice place to work if it has a great boss.

Consequently, I urge you to take these increasingly popular and widely publicized surveys with a large grain of salt. They are of no value whatsoever to an attorney contemplating a federal legal or law-related job or career.

Instead, you'll be better off if you do two things:

- First, read the following chapters in this part carefully and factor them into your decision making, targeting, and over- all federal legal job campaign strategy and planning. I think you will find that they provide a much better picture about great jobs and great places to work in government.
- Second, perform your own "due diligence" concerning fed- eral employers, functions, and types of positions. Do it ini- tially when you are identifying federal legal offices that interest you. Then do a more in-depth, exhaustive due dili- gence once a job offer is on the table. For detailed due dili- gence "how to" information, see my book *Managing Your Legal Career: Best Practices for Creating the Career You Want* (ABA Publishing, 2010).

The "BEST"

The first several chapters in this final Part of *Landing a Federal Legal Job* discuss **functions** in which the federal government is immersed, and where attorneys play a major role and enjoy their work. I have selected functions that are both currently important and that are likely to continue to be critical and dynamic for a long time to come.

The next series of chapters in this Part describe "hidden" types of attorney- and law-related U.S. government jobs. These are, of course, neither really nor purposely hidden. Rather, they are simply not obvious and can be difficult to find unless you apply some of the techniques recommended in earlier chapters, such as trends analysis and examining the "advance notice" hints of where the jobs will be.

The book closes with a series of chapters on great places for attorneys to work in the federal government. It is impossible for me to pinpoint every single one of the best of the 3,000-plus federal law offices and the many hundreds of other federal offices where attorneys work. That would require an encyclopedia instead of a single-volume book. Instead, I have chosen around 40 agencies and offices that, based on my experiences and client feedback, merit inclusion on any "Best Places" list.

Chapter 56

Functional Areas with a Great Future

The purpose of this chapter and the next one is to identify broad functional areas of government responsibility and involvement that cut across multiple agencies and law offices and that are likely to offer legal job opportunities consistently and continuously for the predictable future. Each one of these functional areas is growing, and the factors contributing to that growth are not going to disappear for many years.

This chapter focuses on the "no-brainer" governmental functions and how they translate into federal legal job opportunities. There exists a broad consensus that these are good areas for government involvement or intervention. The succeeding chapter discusses governmental functions about which there is still some question, not so much about whether government should be involved, but rather to what degree.

A Note about Purposeful Omissions

Readers may rightly wonder why I appear to have omitted certain functional arenas in which government is currently heavily involved. Environmentalism, climate change, and health care come immediately to mind.

The reason is that these issues, as well as some of the others purposely left out of this chapter and the next, are highly charged politically or have a powerful ideological component that could change emphases from one election to the next. This is in marked contrast to the functional areas selected for inclusion, about which there is either a broad political consensus that government should be involved and proactive or which lack the same political intensity. No one debates anymore, for example, this country's need for energy independence, the utility of referring cases to ADR, or that some degree of federal financial regulation is necessary for the economy to function.

You may rightfully ask: Why have I omitted health law from this discussion? A few reasons make me hesitate to include it in the "great future" or even "promising future" mix.

First, it is charged with controversy and, while I think it will have some staying power, it might become the victim of a political backlash at some point in the near future before it is fully implemented.

Second, despite the bloviations of Newt Gingrich and other opponents of health-care reform, their claims that the Patient Protection and Affordable Care Act will give rise to 150 new agencies is total hogwash. At the moment, it has given rise to one new agency, a rather small one within the Department of Health and Human Services (see Chapter 76, "Great Places to Work? The Newest of the New."). The fear-mongers of an overblown bureaucracy conveniently define "agency" to include every grant program authorized by the act. Grant programs are decidedly not agencies.

Administrative Litigation

Many more federal government attorneys practice before administrative adjudication bodies—independent regulatory commissions, administrative law judges, administrative judges, hearing officers, etc.—than before trial and appellate courts. The U.S. government currently has almost 300 administrative hearing bodies nationwide that hear and decide an incredible volume and diversity of disputes brought by federal agencies and private individuals and organizations. Federal attorneys working in approximately 975 law offices appear before these bodies.

Federal administrative litigation is dynamic. The best evidence for this is (1) the emergence of new administrative hearing bodies as time progresses, the most recent being four Offices of Medicare Hearings and Appeals established by the 2003 Medicare Prescription Drug, Improvement, and Modernization Act, Pub. L. 108-173, and the new hearing offices that will result from implementation of the Patient Protection and Affordable Care Act of 2010, Pub. L. 111-148; and (2) the revival after a 15-year hiatus of the Administrative Conference of the United States, which studies and recommends administrative law and litigation improvements.

Administrative litigation is an excellent way for aspiring litigators to learn their craft in an environment that is less "demanding" than a trial court. Evidentiary and procedural rules are less stringent and, if the hearings are held pursuant to the federal Administrative Procedure Act, 5 U.S.C. §§ 551 et seq., are consistent from one federal adjudicative body to another. Many litigators earn their wings in these forums and subsequently move on to become very capable trial court litigators confident of their grounding and performance.

The value of an administrative litigation alternative to the pressures of trial litigation is also huge for burnt-out trial court litigators. Countless private-sector trial litigators discovered that they could revive their careers and enthusiasm for practice in an administrative litigation setting.

Employment and Labor Law

The federal workplace, in lockstep with its private-sector counterpart, has become tremendously disputatious. Consequently, every single U.S. government agency has attorneys who do little else but manage, investigate, prosecute, and defend employment law cases. These can be very time-consuming, given the elaborate and multilevel administrative hearing ladder that must be climbed by both sides to an employment dispute prior to going to court. I was involved in one case as a federal attorney that was not resolved at the administrative level for more than five years.

Many agencies have even gone so far as to establish ADR and other machinery to focus exclusively on employment grievances and related matters. An increasing number of agencies supplement their internal employment law and dispute resolution attorneys by engaging outside contractors to mediate employment disputes.

A number of federal agencies focus almost exclusively on employment law, including the U.S. Office of Personnel Management, the Equal Employment Opportunity Commission, the Merit Systems Protection Board, and the Office of Special Counsel.

Labor law, which has declined precipitously in the private sector with the demise of labor unions (only 12.3 percent of the U.S. wage and salary workforce are unionized), is still quite strong in the public sector. Federal labor unions are powerful and influential and have actually increased their numbers in the twenty-first century.

The Federal Labor Relations Authority (FLRA) monitors federal labor-management relations and performs functions that parallel the National Labor Relations Board's (NLRB) responsibilities vis-à-vis private-sector labor-management relations, including (1) resolving complaints of unfair labor practices, (2) determining the appropriateness of units for labor organization representation, (3) adjudicating exceptions to arbitrators' awards, (4) adjudicating legal issues relating to the duty to bargain, and (5) resolving impasses during negotiations. The FLRA performs its dispute resolution functions through four separate panels:

- The Federal Service Impasses Panel, which resolves impasses between federal agencies and unions representing federal employees arising from negotiations over conditions of employment.
- The Foreign Service Labor Relations Board, which administers the labor-management relations program for Foreign Service employees.
- The Foreign Service Impasse Disputes Panel, which resolves impasses between federal agencies and Foreign Service personnel.
- The Office of Administrative Law Judges, which conducts hearings and renders recommended decisions in cases involving alleged unfair labor practices.

Federal Service Impasses Panel staff attorneys also support the Foreign Service Impasse Disputes Panel. The Foreign Service Labor Relations Board is supported by attorneys in the Office of the General Counsel. Staff attorneys also work in the Office of Administrative Law Judges.

Other specialized law and operational offices are also involved exclusively or primarily in federal labor law and labor-management relations matters, including:

- Government Printing Office—Counsel to the Chief Human Capital Officer
- Department of Justice—Office of Special Counsel for Immigration-Related Unfair Employment Practices
- Federal Bureau of Prisons—Office of General Counsel—Labor Law Branch
- U.S. Department of Labor—Office of the Solicitor and Employment Standards Administration
- Federal Aviation Administration—Office of Chief Counsel—Personnel and Labor Law Staff
- U.S. Postal Service—Law Department—Employment and Labor Law Section

In addition, the Department of Labor, National Mediation Board, and Federal Mediation and Conciliation Service are also involved in resolving certain private-sector labor-management relations disputes along with the NLRB.

Aging

The aging Baby Boom generation is already having a major influence on government legal activities in a number of different ways. Many agencies are experiencing an "age bulge" consisting of a disproportionate number of older workers eligible to retire. Unlike so many private-sector employees, whose retirement benefits have been savaged by the Great Recession and who, as a consequence, have had to drastically readjust their retirement planning, the vast majority of federal retirees is free of that concern and is likely to retire at the earliest opportunity. The age wave of Baby Boom retirees includes a large number of attorneys working throughout the

U.S. government. Their departure will create legal and law-related job opportunities across the board over the next decade and a half.

On another level, the age wave is generating considerably more work for federal law offices that already focus attention on aging issues and senior citizens. The Social Security Administration (SSA) has seen its workload explode in the last few years, with no end in sight for at least the next decade and a half. An additional 1 million disability claims (disability is, to a great extent, a function of increasing age) per year are expected to engulf the agency by 2013. This does not include the hundreds of thousands of unexpected disability claims resulting from the health impact of the Great Recession, all of which has strained SSA to the breaking point. SSA has been gearing up by hiring hundreds of new administrative law judges and staff attorneys to cope with this increase, and will have to continue to do so for years to come.

The Department of Health and Human Services (HHS), the primary agency tasked with implementing the landmark health-care reform legislation enacted in 2010, already has attorneys on staff who deal primarily with aging issues and will have to hire additional lawyers to handle the increased demand for its services. HHS' Office of Medicare Hearings and Appeals expects a large increase in its workload due to both the aging of the population—which will substantially increase the number of individuals insured by Medicare—and the rollout of health-care reform. Similarly, the agency's Office of Counsel to the Inspector General, the principal investigative and civil prosecutorial agency pursuing Medicare fraud, expects a huge increase in business. Its counterpart in the Justice Department's Criminal Division will also experience much more work resulting from stepped-up Medicare fraud investigations. The Justice Department's Civil Rights Division and the Equal Employment Opportunity Commission are already experiencing a surge in investigations and cases under the Age Discrimination Act, Pub. L. 94-135, and the Age Discrimination in Employment Act, Pub. L. 90-202.

The Food and Drug Administration's Office of General Counsel has a Children, Families and Aging Division that will also see a great deal of new activity resulting from the aging of the population.

Information Disclosure

Both the Freedom of Information Act (FOIA), Pub. L. 90-23, and the Privacy Act, Pub. L. 93-579, have been around now for more than a generation. FOIA had an immediate and profound impact on federal legal practice, one that remains to this day. The Privacy Act, on the other hand, quickly became the legislative equivalent of a backwater, generating little or no interest and not much legal activity.

That has changed dramatically in recent years, thanks to the impact of the communications technology revolution, especially the Internet, which brought with it a host of unintended privacy-invasive consequences. As indicated in the prior chapter on Long-Term Trends, the constant back-and-forth between law and technology means that law must always play catch-up in order to keep pace with technological innovation, and privacy protection is a classic example of this. A dizzying array of sectoral and general laws covers privacy regulation in the United States.

The Health Insurance Portability and Accountability Act (HIPAA), Pub. L. 104-191, mandates how covered health-care entities can use and disclose information. Compounding medical privacy concerns is the Patient Protection and Affordable Care Act of 2010's (Pub. L. 111-140) encouragement of electronic medical recordkeeping by health-care providers, which actually is something of a "Johnny-come-lately," since insurance companies have been partially funding such efforts for physician's offices for several years now. However, since only 5 percent of physicians have digitized their patient records to date, this element of health-care reform is destined to grow exponentially in the near term, along with attendant privacy concerns. The tension between the efficiencies and cost savings inherent in digitized medical records versus privacy issues is growing and has yet to be resolved to the satisfaction of anyone.

Financial privacy has also come to the fore as a major concern, thanks to such legislation as the Financial Modernization Act of 1999 (Gramm-Leach-Bliley Act), Pub. L. 106-102; regulations implementing amendments to the Currency and Foreign Transactions Reporting Act (a.k.a. Bank Secrecy Act), Pub. L. 91-508; the Dodd-Frank Wall Street Reform and Consumer Protection Act, Pub. L. 111-205; and various other financial services laws and regulations. As this book goes to press, the Treasury Department is attempting to data-mine even small-dollar transfers in order to trace terrorist financing.

The Telecommunications Act of 1996, Pub. L. 104-104, includes privacy protections that telecommunication providers and cable operators must follow when handling subscriber's personal information. The Fair Credit Reporting Act (FCRA), Pub. L. 104-208, governs how consumer-reporting agencies can share personal information. The Children's Online Privacy Protection Act (COPPA), Pub. L. 105-277, protects information collected online about children under 13. The Federal Trade Commission Act, Pub. L. 203, 1914, authorizes the agency to combat "unfair or deceptive" business practices, including privacy and information security practices.

New privacy concerns have also been raised by the USA Patriot Act, Pub. L. 107-56, and presidential orders authorizing National Security Agency eavesdropping on Americans. The 2010 decennial census has also generated a lot of discussion about privacy. The Family Educational Rights and Privacy Act (FERPA), Pub. L. 93-380, has contributed to the increased emphasis on privacy issues.

Government has traditionally been slow to respond to privacy concerns, but this is changing. An increasing number of agencies have established Privacy Offices (Departments of Defense, Homeland Security, Education, the HHS Office for Civil Rights [which enforces the HIPAA Privacy Rule]), with more on the horizon.

Privacy law is only now coming into its own and is wrestling with an array of complex issues that must be tackled, including: identity theft; cybersecurity; "locational privacy" (an individual's ability to move in public space with the expectation that his or her location will not be systematically and secretly recorded for later use); protection of commercial data and trade secrets; the collection, use, and disclosure of personal data by companies; federal versus state privacy laws and regulations; how U.S. federal and state privacy law fits in or conflicts with national, sub-national and regional privacy legal regimes in other countries, and how this matrix affects global commerce; cross-border data transfer; third-party (e.g., search engines, content hosts) liability for Internet intermediaries; finding a balance between privacy concerns and Internet innovation and its transformational impact on health, education, energy, business, finance, etc.

The Commerce Department has convened an Internet Policy Task Force that, as of this writing, is conducting a comprehensive review of the nexus between privacy policy and innovation in the Internet economy.

For the first time ever, it is now possible to build a career as a federal privacy lawyer in its own right and no longer as a subset of being a Freedom of Information Officer.

Fraud Investigation and Prosecution

The people who come up with pithy sayings should have added "fraud" to the well-worn maxim about death and taxes. As long as there is temptation and human frailty, there will be fraudulent behavior. Government activities, programs, contracts, grants, loans, et al. have proven to be irresistible temptations to the ethically challenged.

Consequently, government goes to great—if uncoordinated—lengths to combat fraud. Seventy-three U.S. government agencies have independent Inspector General (IG) offices with large staffs that are charged with identifying and combating "waste, fraud, mismanagement and abuse" in their agencies and their programs and activities, as well as among the beneficiaries of such programs and government contractors (a slight majority of IG offices have their own independent legal counsel offices). There are also agencies and offices solely devoted to identifying fraud and recovering illicit gains, such as the Department of Commerce's Office of the Assistant General Counsel for Finance and Litigation, the Defense Department's TRICARE Management Activity Office of General Counsel, the Air Force Office of General Counsel's Contractor Responsibility Division, the Defense Contract Management Agency's Contract Integrity Center, the Department of Housing and Urban Development General Counsel's Office of Program Enforcement, the Environmental Protection Agency's Office of Criminal Enforcement, the National Science Foundation's Office of Investigation, the Securities and Exchange Commission's Enforcement Division, and the Justice Department's Criminal Division Fraud Section, to name just some of the over 50 agencies and offices that focus on fraudulent activity. Then, overlay on top of this the growing number of task forces and special, presumably temporary organizations set up to combat fraud, including:

- National Procurement Fraud Task Force
- Financial Fraud Enforcement Task Force
- Health Care Fraud Prevention and Enforcement Action Team (HEAT)
- Corporate Fraud Task Force
- Katrina Fraud Task Force
- FBI Mortgage Fraud Task Force

This is not even the end of it. As recently as July 2010, Congress enacted the Improper Payments Elimination and Recovery Act of 2010, Pub. L. 111-204, yet another (uncoordinated) effort in government's eternal battle against the forces of evil.

If you are an aspiring federal attorney, you cannot go wrong focusing on a legal career going after fraud.

National and Homeland Security

A July 2010 *Washington Post* investigation revealed that "1,271 government organizations and 1,931 private companies work on programs related to counterterrorism, homeland security and intelligence in about 10,000 locations across the United States," and "[A]n estimated 854,000 people . . . hold top-secret security clearances."

When the new cabinet-level Department of Homeland Security (DHS) was created in response to the September 11, 2001 terrorist attacks, it represented the largest reorganization of the U.S. government in a half-century. The department brought together 22 existing federal agencies with 175,000 employees and an enormous annual budget. Since its creation and absorption of the many law offices already extant in these existing agencies, the department added has added several new ones (Office of General Counsel, Office of General Counsel to the Inspector General, Office for Civil Rights and Civil Liberties, and the Privacy Office) and now employs thousands of lawyers throughout the nation. DHS' Transportation Security Administration alone maintains an Office of Chief Counsel as well as 37 Chief Counsel Field Offices nationwide.

The national and homeland security bureaucracy encompasses much more than DHS and its numerous law offices and other offices employing attorneys. It also includes the Department of Defense, with its several hundred civilian and military law offices, as well as the law offices that serve the federal intelligence community, which consists of 16 member agencies (that we know about) in addition to DHS, including their multiple law offices.

Threats to U.S. security are ever-present and are both expanding and evolving in their sophistication and creativity. National and homeland security are the core essences of government's mission, and, with very few exceptions, no expense is spared when budgeting for these functions. That portends well for federal legal employment.

Real Estate and Land Use

Private-sector real estate practice, excepting the "distress" side of the practice, has all but disappeared in the Great Recession. Not so the case with public-sector real estate practice, where there is always steady work to be found, some of it in surprising places that you would not consider as logical repositories of real estate law.

The U.S. government is far and away both the largest landowner in the country and the largest landlord, as well as being the largest tenant. The Department of Interior's Bureau of Land Management (BLM), to cite one example of federal real estate involvement, manages 264 million acres of federal land, or approximately 13 percent of the entire land area of the country. This represents only 40 percent of federal land in the United States. In addition, BLM manages 700 million acres of subsurface mineral resources. This responsibility generates a great deal of work for the Interior Department's Office of the Solicitor and its 18 Field Solicitor Offices, as well as several other departmental law offices.

Beyond the Interior Department, approximately 75 other federal law offices have a real estate practice. A number of them, such as the U.S. Army Corps of Engineers Directorate of Real Estate and the Air Force Real Property Agency, concentrate all or most of their legal work on real estate, land use, and closely related issues. Other agencies with a large real estate practice include the General Services Administration, Department of Veterans Affairs, Department of Defense, NASA, and the U.S. Postal Service.

Taxation

When you think of federal involvement in tax matters, you naturally think of the Internal Revenue Service (IRS), usually to the exclusion of any other agency. For federal legal job seekers, that is a mistake (remember the Monolith Myth?).

While IRS has a very large legal staff, principally concentrated in its Office of Chief Counsel in Washington and in field locations around the country, it is hardly the only agency with a tax practice. Next on the list should be IRS's parent agency, the Department of Treasury. Treasury has no fewer than nine offices outside of the IRS that focus all, or a lot of, their attention on tax law issues. They are:

- Office of Tax Policy
- Office of the Benefits Tax Counsel
- Office of the International Tax Counsel
- Office of the Tax Legislative Counsel
- Office of Chief Counsel, Alcohol and Tobacco Tax and Trade Bureau
- Office of Chief Counsel, Treasury Inspector General for Tax Administration
- Office of General Counsel—Assistant General Counsel for International Affairs
- Office of Legal Counsel—Executive Office for Asset Forfeiture
- Office of Technical Assistance

The federal tax law regime does not end there, either. Other agencies and offices with a significant tax law practice include:

- Advisory Council on Historic Preservation—Office of General Counsel

- Federal Retirement Thrift Investment Board
- Congressional Research Service—American Law Division
- Pension Benefit Guaranty Corporation—Office of the General Counsel and Office of the Chief Counsel
- Small Business Administration—Office of Advocacy
- Smithsonian Institution—Office of the General Counsel
- National Gallery of Art—Office of the Secretary and General Counsel
- Tennessee Valley Authority—Office of Executive Vice President and General Counsel
- U.S. Court of Federal Claims—Office of Staff Attorneys
- U.S. Department of Commerce—Office of the Chief Counsel for International Commerce
- U.S. Department of Justice—Tax Division and Bureau of Alcohol, Tobacco and Firearms—Office of the Chief Counsel
- U.S. Department of Transportation—Maritime Administration—Office of Chief Counsel—Division of Maritime Assistance Programs
- U.S. Department of the Interior—Office of the Solicitor—Division of Indian Affairs
- U.S. Tax Court
- House Ways and Means Committee
- Senate Finance Committee
- Joint Committee on Taxation

Technology Transfer

Technology transfer in this context means the licensing or other conveyance of government-developed inventions, processes, and innovation to the private sector. A suitable synonym is "technology commercialization." Technology transfer is one of the fastest-growing professional occupations in the United States. The U.S. government commercializes more technology than any other existing organization. Over time, these technologies have contributed many billions of dollars to our Gross Domestic Product while also raising living standards, improving the quality of American life, and creating millions of jobs and increased tax revenues flowing back to the government. To coin a much-hackneyed phrase, technology transfer has been a "win-win" situation for everyone involved.

Some of the most striking examples of federal technology transfer have come out of the space program. National Aeronautics and Space Administration (NASA) scientists developed and then transferred the following technologies (among others) to the private sector since the agency was established:

- Beepers
- "Blue Blocker" sunglasses
- Cable television
- Cellular phones
- Compact disks
- Digital watches and thermometers
- Electronic ignitions
- Fiber optics
- GPS navigation systems
- Halogen lights
- Juice boxes
- Kevlar
- Laser scanners
- Magnetic Resonance Imaging (MRI) scanners
- Pocket calculators
- Satellite phones
- Sports domes

This list is astonishing. Just think of how these inventions have changed our lives, not to mention how many jobs they have created. While you are contemplating that, think of the heavy involvement of federal attorneys in the technology commercialization process. Moreover, do not jump to the conclusion that all of these government lawyers were patent attorneys. They were not. Technology transfer involves not only patent lawyers, but also government contract attorneys, transactional lawyers, legal researchers, and others.

NASA documents its massive technology initiatives and commercialization projects on its website *(www.nasa.gov)*, as do the many other U.S. government agencies that are involved in basic and applied research. Chief among these are the following:

- Department of Agriculture (www.usda.gov), primarily through the Agricultural Research Service (www.ars.usda. gov)
- Department of Energy (www.doe.gov)
- Department of Commerce (www.doc.gov), primarily through its U.S. Patent and Trademark Office (www.uspto.gov), National Institute of Standards and Technology (www.nist.gov), National Technical Information Service (www.ntis.gov), National Oceanic and Atmospheric Administration (www.noaa.gov), and National Telecommunications and Information Administration (www.ntia.doc.gov)
- Department of Defense (www.defense.gov), through many departmental components, principally the Defense Advanced Research and Projects Agency (www.darpa.mil), Defense Technical Information Center (www.dtic.mil), and the National Imagery and Mapping Agency (www.nima.mil)
- U.S. Department of Energy (www.energy.gov)
- Department of Health and Human Services (www.hhs.gov), primarily through its National Institutes of Health (www.nih.gov), which has multiple technology transfer offices, and the Centers for Disease Control and Prevention (www.cdc.gov)
- Department of Interior (www.doi.gov), primarily through the U.S. Geological Survey (www.usgs.gov)
- Department of Transportation (www.dot.gov)
- National Science Foundation (www.nsf.gov)
- Environmental Protection Agency (www.epa.gov)
- Federal Communications Commission (www.fcc.gov)
- U.S. Department of Homeland Security (www.dhs.gov)

You can also identify government policy and commercialization initiatives that are likely to be highly attractive to private enterprise by monitoring the activities and research reports of the White House Office of Science and Technology Policy (www.ostp.gov), the Government Accountability Office (www.gao.gov), the Congressional Research Service (www.loc.gov/crsinfo/whatscrs.html), and the National Technology Transfer Center (www.nttc.edu).

For example, in spring 2003 the Office of Science and Technology Policy issued a presidentially endorsed white paper on U.S. Commercial Remote Sensing Policy, a potentially multibillion-dollar industry that evolved to receive a major government boost and generated multiple technology commercialization initiatives. There are now several hundred companies involved in the remote-sensing industry and its related industries—photogrammetry and geographic information systems (GIS).

The U.S. government also has over 700 research laboratories, 316 of which have their own technology commercialization programs. You can identify many of these laboratories at www.federallabs.org. A number of laboratories perform technology transfer activities either through an office of that name or a comparable designation, or through their laboratory counsel offices.

"Soft" Intellectual Property

Most non-intellectual property (IP) attorneys automatically think of patent law and an essential background in the hard sciences or engineering when they contemplate IP practice. And for much of the history of IP law, they would have been mostly correct. Patent law was both the core and by far the predominant component of an IP practice. The rest—trademark law, copyright law, licensing, and trade secrets—were afterthoughts, sleepy IP arenas where not much happened that a patent attorney could not handle during his or her spare time.

Not anymore. These "softer" facets of IP practice have flowered in recent years and more than come into their own, so much so that they have increasingly become stand-alone practices no longer dependent on a patent law practice base. U.S. government soft IP practice now extends into multiple agencies beyond the obvious ones—the U.S. Patent and Trademark Office and the Copyright Office in the Library of Congress. It even goes beyond the technology transfer offices addressed in the prior section of this chapter.

Federal soft IP practices not only hire attorneys without a hard science or engineering background, they also provide fertile training grounds for entry-level attorneys interested in gaining knowledge and experience in these areas upon which they can build rewarding careers. For example, the approximately 400 trademark examining attorneys at the U.S. Patent and Trademark Office, many of whom are hired directly out of law school or very early in their careers, develop such an intense grounding in trademark law that they find themselves in great demand should they decide eventually to move into private practice. This is particularly true if they also want to fan out geographically beyond the Washington, D.C. area.

More than 70 federal law and other offices currently have a soft IP practice. A selection of these is listed below.

- Department of Agriculture—Office of General Counsel—Legislation, Litigation, and General Law Division (Copyright, Technology Licensing)
- Department of Commerce
  - o Office of the Chief Counsel for Technology (Copyright, Trademark, Technology Licensing)
  - o National Institute of Standards and Technology—Office of Technology Partnerships (Technology Licensing)
  - o National Oceanic and Atmospheric Administration—Office of Research and Technology Applications (Technology Licensing)
- Department of Energy
  - o Office of General Counsel—Office of the Deputy General Counsel for Technology Transfer and Procurement (Copyright, Trademark, Technology Licensing)
  - o Thomas Jefferson National Accelerator Facility—Office of Legal Counsel (Technology Licensing)
  - o Lawrence Livermore National Laboratory—Industrial Partnerships and Commercialization Office (Technology Licensing) and Office of Laboratory Counsel (Technology Licensing)
  - o National Energy Technology Laboratory—Office of Chief Counsel (Technology Licensing)
- Department of Health and Human Services
  - o National Institutes of Health—Office of Technology Transfer (Technology Licensing)
  - o National Cancer Institute—Technology Transfer Branch (Trademark, Technology Licensing)
  - o Agency for Health Care Research and Quality (Technology Licensing)

- Department of Justice—Federal Bureau of Prisons—Office of General Counsel—Commercial Law Branch (Copyright, Trademark)
- Department of Transportation
  - o Office of General Counsel—Office of Patent Counsel (Technology Licensing)
- Army Research Laboratory—Office of Chief Counsel (Copyright, Trademark, Technology Licensing)
- Federal Deposit Insurance Corporation—Legal Division (Trademark)
- Library of Congress—Copyright Office (Copyright)
- National Aeronautics and Space Administration
  - o NASA Glenn Research Center—Office of the Chief Counsel—Intellectual Property Law Division (Copyright, Technology Licensing)
  - o Goddard Space Flight Center—Office of Patent Counsel—Technology Commercialization Office (Technology Licensing)
- Office of Naval Research—Office of Counsel (Technology Licensing)
- Patent and Trademark Office
- Small Business Administration—Office of General Counsel (Technology Licensing)
- U.S. Postal Service—Law Department—Purchasing and Commercial Protection Section (Copyright, Trademark) and U.S. Postal Service Licensing Group (Trademark, Technology Licensing)

The expansion of soft IP practices into a diverse collection of agencies and their law and other offices is a growing phenomenon. Consequently, by the time this book is released, there are likely to be additional agencies and offices that have added their own soft IP practices.

Patents

It should be no surprise to anyone to see that patents made my list of government practices with a great future. The U.S. Patent and

Trademark Office (PTO) has been inundated with patent applications (482,000 in 2009), patent protests, and other patent-related matters, so much so that in August 2010 it issued a job vacancy announcement for 1,000 (not a misprint) additional patent examiners. This followed closely on the heels of President Obama's signing into law P.L. 111-224, which gave the PTO the authority to spend an additional $129 million of the fees the agency collected in fiscal year (FY) 2010, when the agency collected nearly $200 million more in fees than its FY 2010 appropriation of $1.887 billion.

The accelerating pace of innovation and technological advances guarantees that federal patent practice will thrive for a long time to come, and not only at PTO, with its multiple offices where patent law is practiced. Other federal agencies and law offices with a significant patent practice include:

- National Aeronautics and Space Administration (4 law offices)
- Tennessee Valley Authority—Office of Executive Vice President and General Counsel
- U.S. Court of Appeals for the Federal Circuit
- U.S. Department of Commerce (3 law offices outside of PTO)
- U.S. Department of Defense (6 law offices)
- U.S. Department of Energy (9 law and program offices)
- U.S. Department of Health and Human Services—National Institutes of Health (4 program offices)
- U.S. Department of Justice—Federal Bureau of Prisons—Office of General Counsel—Commercial Law Branch
- U.S. Department of Transportation—Office of General Counsel—DOT Patent Counsel; and Federal Highway Administration—Office of Chief Counsel, Administrative and Technology Law Division
- U.S. International Trade Commission
- U.S. Postal Service—Law Department—Purchasing and Commercial Protection Section

Chapter 57

Functional Areas with a Promising Future

The following areas are also worth your consideration. Unlike the ones described in the prior chapter, there is no guarantee that these will have the same staying power. However, they look pretty good at present and for the near term, at least. Beyond the near term, these functional areas do not rise to the first tier because, historically, they have ebbed and flowed based upon the prevailing politics of the moment.

Financial Regulation

The Dodd-Frank Wall Street Reform and Consumer Protection Act, Pub. L. 111-205, the most sweeping financial reform legislation since the Great Depression, was signed into law by President Obama in July 2010. The most telling aspect of the new law was not what it changed, revised, reorganized, overhauled, etc., which was considerable, but what it left out that will probably have to be addressed sometime soon if the country is to protect itself against future economic meltdowns. Here are just a few of the omissions that cry out for imminent action:

1. Most significantly, it failed to rein in the kind of reckless behavior that caused the world to teeter on the brink of eco-

319

nomic ruin in 2008. Securitizations of bad mortgages, collateral debt obligations, collateral debt swaps, and all the rest of the arcane instruments that even big-bank CEOs did not understand are still with us and continue to allow financial institutions to earn huge transactional fees and pay themselves enormous bonuses without contributing a thing to economic growth and public well-being.

2. The new Consumer Financial Protection Bureau was placed within the Federal Reserve Board, the entity that did much to create the housing and mass consumption bubbles with its easy monetary policies, and then propped up Wall Street at the expense of Main Street when the bubble burst.

3. The new law does not address the problem of "too big to fail," which panicked both the Bush and Obama Administrations, Congress, and the Fed into throwing trillions of taxpayer dollars—few strings attached—at Wall Street.

4. The Fed escaped all congressional attempts at making it more transparent and less secret.

5. Financial institutions can still choose which agency they want to regulate them. The new law does nothing to consolidate the rat's maze of nine federal financial regulators (it abolished one agency while creating two new ones).

The weak "reform" measures (don't listen to the whining on Wall Street) in the new law will also take at least two to three years to roll out, because they won't be effective until the existing and new financial regulators issue implementing rules. The rollout will require new legal hires to implement, along with new attorney opportunities at the Consumer Financial Protection Bureau and the other federal financial regulatory agencies, which include:

- Federal Reserve Board
- Federal Deposit Insurance Corporation
- Securities and Exchange Commission
- Commodity Futures Trading Commission
- Office of the Comptroller of the Currency
- National Credit Union Administration
- Federal Housing Finance Agency

- Financial Stability Oversight Council
- Federal Insurance Office

"Quasi-government" attorney hiring will also rise as a result of financial regulatory reform. Self-regulatory organizations (SROs), such as the Financial Industry Regulatory Authority (FINRA) and the Public Company Accounting Oversight Board, will acquire considerable additional responsibilities as a consequence of the new law.

Fairly rigorous and vigorous federal financial regulation, although a more tenuous prediction on my part than many of these others that are not tied up with ideological agendas, is probably here to stay and should be around for a long time. The incentives to devise creative financial products and the opportunities presented by technological advances means that government will always be behind the regulatory curve and scrambling to catch up with the financial services industry. And that invariably means more legal work.

Consumer Protection

Protecting consumers, although occasionally controversial and the subject of ideological debate, has been a central U.S. government function ever since the 30th Congress passed the Drug Importation Act in 1848, which required the U.S. Customs Service to stop entry of adulterated drugs from overseas. That consumer protection precedent was expanded over the next 162 years to encompass a vast range of commercial behavior directed at consumers, including the establishment of a large number of agencies and programs aimed at protecting consumers, along with their attendant legal offices and teams of attorneys.

The principal consumer protection agencies include:

- Centers for Disease Control and Prevention
- Commodity Futures Trading Commission
- Consumer Financial Protection Bureau *(new)*
- Consumer Product Safety Commission
- Department of Agriculture

- Department of Housing and Urban Development
- Department of Justice
- Department of Transportation
- Environmental Protection Agency
- Federal Aviation Administration
- Federal Communications Commission
- Federal Deposit Insurance Corporation
- Federal Energy Regulatory Commission
- Federal Highway Administration
- Federal Insurance Office *(new)*
- Federal Maritime Commission
- Federal Motor Carrier Safety Administration
- Federal Railroad Administration
- Federal Reserve System
- Federal Trade Commission
- Financial Stability Oversight Council *(new)*
- Food and Drug Administration
- Internal Revenue Service
- National Credit Union Administration
- National Highway Traffic Safety Administration
- Nuclear Regulatory Commission
- Office of Consumer Information and Insurance Oversight *(new)*
- Office of the Comptroller of the Currency
- Postal Inspection Service
- Postal Rate Commission
- Research and Special Programs Administration
- Securities and Exchange Commission
- Surface Transportation Board

Consumer protection law should have a solid future if only because the world is continuously becoming a much more complicated place, the pace of change is accelerating, and the impact of globalization means more lightly regulated products and services coming into this country from elsewhere, such as tainted Chinese dietary supplements, faulty gas pedals in Toyotas, and lead paint in Chinese toys.

Chapter 58

"Hidden" Federal Attorney Positions—Legs and Regs

The U.S. government is a gold mine of "hidden" legal and law-related job opportunities. This chapter examines (1) how legislation and government reorganizations generate hidden job opportunities and (2) the legislative branch's contribution to the hidden legal job universe.

Legislation and Government Reorganizations

Following the 9/11 terrorist attacks, Congress acted quickly to enact legislation with profound legal and law-related hiring implications that often went far beyond the obvious in creating job opportunities for lawyers in the federal government:

- The USA Patriot Act, Pub. L. 107-56, imposed new regulatory compliance requirements on insurance companies and certain other financial services firms previously exempt from such mandates and expanded legal hiring in the Department of Justice (which established a new National Security Division and an Office of Inspector General), the FBI General Counsel's Office, and law offices in the CIA; National Security Agency; Drug Enforcement Administration; Executive Office of the President; Departments of Transportation, Treasury, State, Education and Commerce; Federal Reserve Board; Federal Trade Commission; Federal Communications Commission; and the former Immigration and Naturalization Service and U.S. Customs Service.

- The Aviation and Transportation Security Act, Pub. L. 107-71, created the new Transportation Security Administration (TSA), a 40,000+-employee agency that has legal and law-related positions in its headquarters Chief Counsel Office and its 37 Regional Chief Counsel offices nationwide, as well as its Office of Civil Rights and Activities, Procurement Office, Privacy Policy and Compliance Office, Ombudsman Office, and other offices with attorneys serving in them. Law-related job titles include Deportation Officer, Realty Specialist, Contract Specialist, and Policy Advisor.

- The Public Health Security and Bioterrorism Preparedness and Response Act of 2002 (Bioterrorism Act), Pub. L. 107-188, imposed a host of new duties on "first responders" throughout the United States and required the hiring of additional attorneys for the Departments of Health and Human Services (HHS), Agriculture, and Homeland Security (DHS); Food and Drug Administration (FDA); Centers for Disease Control and Prevention (CDC); Environmental Protection Agency; Federal Bureau of Investigation (FBI); and U.S. Customs and Border Protection.

- The Homeland Security Act, Pub. L. 107-296, created the largest new federal agency in over 50 years, transferred 22 existing agencies into the new department, and established 12 new legal and law-related offices within the Department. Law-related job titles in the department include Applications Adjudicator, Asylum Officer, Refugee Officer, Adjudications Officer, Immigration Officer, Immigration Services Officer, Contract Administrator, and Privacy Officer.

Congress also acted rapidly in response to the corporate accounting and reporting scandals of 2001–2002. The Sarbanes-Oxley Act, Pub. L. 107-204, had vast implications for publicly traded corporations, accounting and auditing firms, attorney regulation, securities brokers and dealers, and a number of other professional groups and their regulators, and also the Securities and Exchange Commission (SEC), the Department of Justice, the U.S. Sentencing Commission, the Department of Labor, and the Pension Benefit Guaranty Corporation, as well as self-regulatory organizations (such as the Financial Industry Regulatory Authority and the newly created Public Company Accounting Oversight Board). All of this generated hundreds of new federal job opportunities for attorneys.

Health-care reform legislation (Patient Protection and Affordable Care Act of 2010, Pub. L. 111-148, as amended by the Health Care and Education Reconciliation Act of 2010, Pub. L. 111-152) has, is in the process of, or will create a significant number of new attorney jobs and law-related positions. The most obvious candidates for legal job opportunities resulting from this landmark legislation are:

- Office of Consumer Information and Insurance Oversight (HHS)
- Program for Advance Determination of Tax Credit Eligibility (Department of Treasury)
- Federal Coordinated Health Care Office for Dual Eligible Beneficiaries (HHS)
- National Healthcare Workforce Commission (Government Accountability Office)

Health-care reform will also result in legal staffing additions in many existing federal law and other offices, including:

- Department of HHS—Office of General Counsel and its 10 Regional Counsel Offices; Office of Counsel to the Inspector General; Office of Medicare Hearings and Appeals and its three field offices; Departmental Appeals Board; Centers for Disease Control and Prevention Office of General Counsel and its Washington, D.C. field office; Food and Drug Administration (FDA) Office of Chief Counsel, Office of Regulatory Affairs, Office of Foods, four FDA Centers, and Office of Combination Products; and Office of Research Integrity.
- Department of Labor—Office of the Solicitor

- Department of Treasury—Office of General Counsel, and Internal Revenue Service Office of Chief Counsel
- Department of Veterans Affairs—Office of General Counsel, and Office of Counsel to the Inspector General
- Department of Defense—Office of General Counsel
- Social Security Administration—Office of General Counsel
- Department of Justice—Civil Rights Division
- U.S. Sentencing Commission—Office of General Counsel

Moreover, the 2,500+ page Patient Protection and Affordable Care Act, Pub. L. 111-140, includes hundreds of new regulatory compliance and reporting requirements that are in the process of, or will soon be, imposed on private-sector and nonprofit participants in the health-care industry, which will require additional federal attorney and law-related talent.

My final example is the Dodd-Frank Wall Street Reform and Consumer Protection Act, Pub. L. 111-205, the financial regulatory reform legislation prompted by the financial meltdown and government bailouts. Here are some of the specifics that this legislation will generate in terms of legal job opportunities.

- The *SEC* will be authorized to regulate credit rating agencies, gain new powers over hedge funds, private equity funds, over-the-counter derivative (OTC) markets, corporate board elections and brokers and dealers. SEC Chair Mary Schapiro told Congress in July 2010 that the financial regulatory reform mandates imposed on her agency, combined with the agency's $550 million settlement with Goldman Sachs for allegedly misleading buyers of mortgage-related investments, will require the SEC to hire 800 new employees, many of whom will be attorneys.
- The *Commodity Futures Trading Commission* will also gain new regulatory authority over the OTC markets and plans to hire additional attorneys.
- The *Municipal Securities Rulemaking Board* will be required to impose fiduciary duties on municipal bond advisors.
- The *Federal Reserve Board* will be empowered to regulate large, systemically important financial firms.

- A new *Consumer Financial Protection Bureau* will be established within the Federal Reserve Board.

Not waiting for financial regulatory reform to become law, the SEC had already gone ahead and established a number of new offices in order to "show the flag" and make up for almost a decade of regulatory neglect, during which both ideological aversion to regulation as well as the complexity and accelerating pace of innovation in financial products, transactions, and markets, and the "willingness of violators to use every trick to cover their tracks" (according to the head of the Enforcement Division), made for lax enforcement and contributed significantly to the Great Recession. Consequently, the SEC enjoyed an attorney-hiring binge in 2009 and 2010. In January 2010, the agency undertook the most significant reorganization of its Enforcement Division since its establishment in 1972, along with a series of new, aggressive enforcement initiatives.

The Enforcement Division has established new, national specialized units in five priority areas dedicated to particular highly specialized and complex areas of securities law:

- *Asset Management*—This unit will focus on investigations involving investment advisors, investment companies, hedge funds, and private equity funds.
- *Market Abuse*—This unit will focus on investigations involving large-scale market abuses and complex manipulation schemes by institutional traders, market professionals, and others.
- *Structured and New Products*—This unit will focus on complex derivatives and financial products, including credit default swaps, collateralized debt obligations, and securitized products.
- *Foreign Corrupt Practices*—This unit will focus on violations of the Foreign Corrupt Practices Act, Pub. L. 100-418, which prohibits U.S. companies from bribing foreign officials for government contracts and other business.
- *Municipal Securities and Public Pensions*—This unit will focus on misconduct in the large municipal securities mar-

ket and in connection with public pension funds, including: offering and disclosure fraud; tax or arbitrage-driven fraud; pay-to-play and public corruption violations; public pension accounting and disclosure violations; and valuation and pricing fraud.

The intent is that these new units' staff members will obtain increased understanding of particular markets, products and transactions, and will use that expertise to adopt a more proactive approach to identifying conduct and practices ripe for investigation, to conduct those investigations with increased efficiency and effectiveness, and to share that expertise with all staff throughout the enforcement division conducting investigations in these specialized areas.

The SEC's Enforcement Division also created a new Office of Market Intelligence responsible for "connecting the dots," i.e., the collection, analysis, and monitoring of the hundreds of thousands of tips, complaints, and referrals that the SEC receives each year. The same day, the SEC also announced three measures to further strengthen its enforcement program by encouraging greater cooperation from individuals and companies in the agency's investigations and enforcement actions. These measures establish incentives for individuals and companies to fully and truthfully cooperate and assist with SEC investigations and enforcement actions, and provide new tools to help investigators develop firsthand evidence to build the strongest possible cases. The cooperation initiative is expected to result in invaluable and early assistance in identifying the scope, participants, victims, and ill-gotten gains associated with fraudulent schemes.

Regulatory Development, Compliance, and Enforcement

Thousands of attorneys work on developing regulations to implement legislation and on the follow-up to the crafting and promulgating of new regulations—monitoring compliance with them and enforcing them. Regulatory positions are everywhere in the federal government. It would be difficult to find an agency, subordinate unit, or program that does not have a regulatory component.

The two recent landmark enactments discussed above—the Affordable Care Act (health-care reform) and the Dodd-Frank Act (financial regulatory reform)—are destined to keep federal government attorneys busy for at least the next decade. Affected agencies have begun gearing up and bolstering their regulatory, compliance, and enforcement staffs in order to implement these massive and monumentally complex 2,000-plus page laws, each of which comes with directions to the agencies to draft hundreds of new regulations and then proceed to ensure compliance with them and enforce them against noncompliant parties.

Do not limit your search for regulatory drafting, compliance, and enforcement positions to the chief legal office of an agency or its subordinate units. While regulatory activities are central to the work of these prominent offices, they can also be found in abundance in other legal offices that go under other names—such as the Environmental Protection Agency's Office of Enforcement and Compliance Assurance and the Department of Labor's Office of Federal Contract Compliance Programs—as well as in non-law offices that hire attorneys under the "attorney" job title or something law-related, such as Policy Analyst, Regulatory Analyst, or Compliance Officer.

Chapter 59

"Hidden" Federal Attorney Positions—Keeping Government (and Everyone Else) Honest

The U.S. government has a vast network of offices and agencies that are designed to keep honest both the government and the private-sector organizations and individuals that benefit from federal largesse in the form of contracts, grants, loans, loan guarantees, and direct payments. This expansive network keeps growing constantly, with no end in sight.

The primary organizations that are designed to keep things honest are the 73 separate offices of Inspectors General (IGs), 37 of which have their own legal counsel offices (see list below). Both IG offices and their legal counsel units are independent of their parent agencies and the agencies' general counsel offices. This is necessary so that they can investigate their own agencies without being unduly influenced by their agency heads.

IGs are tasked with detecting and preventing fraud, waste, abuse, and violations of law and to promote economy, efficiency, and effectiveness in the operations of the federal government. The Inspector General Act of 1978, Pub. L. 95-452, as amended by Pub.

L. 96-88, and Pub. L. 110-409, establishes the responsibilities and duties of an IG. IG authority is very broad, encompassing the agency itself and its employees, as well as agency programs, contractors, grantees, borrowers, and other recipients of agency funds.

Attorneys in IG counsel offices supervise investigations and advise investigators concerning evidentiary rules and procedures, develop and prosecute civil penalty cases, and develop and refer criminal cases to the Department of Justice.

IG Offices with an Office of Counsel

- Department of Agriculture
- Department of Commerce
- Department of Defense
- Department of Education
- Department of Energy
- Department of Health and Human Services
- Department of Homeland Security
- Department of Housing and Urban Development
- Department of the Interior
- Department of Justice
- Department of Labor
- Department of Treasury
- Department of Veterans Affairs
- Amtrak
- Corporation for National and Community Service
- Corporation for Public Broadcasting
- Environmental Protection Agency
- Equal Employment Opportunity Commission
- Farm Credit Administration
- Federal Communications Commission
- Federal Deposit Insurance Corporation
- Federal Housing Finance Agency
- Federal Reserve System
- General Services Administration
- National Aeronautics and Space Administration
- National Science Foundation
- Nuclear Regulatory Commission

- Office of Personnel Management
- Pension Benefit Guaranty Corporation
- Securities and Exchange Commission
- Small Business Administration
- Smithsonian Institution
- Social Security Administration
- Tennessee Valley Authority
- U.S. Agency for International Development
- U.S. International Trade Commission
- U.S. Postal Service

In addition to IG offices, there are a number of federal agencies and offices that also play a significant role in keeping things honest. The principal ones are:

- Commodity Futures Trading Commission
- Defense Contract Audit Agency—Office of General Counsel
- Department of Interior Ethics Office
- Department of Justice—Office of Professional Responsibility; FBI; and Professional Responsibility Advisory Office
- Federal Trade Commission—Bureau of Consumer Protection
- Financial Crimes Enforcement Network—Office of Chief Counsel
- Government Accountability Office
- Internal Revenue Service
- Office of Government Ethics
- Office of Research Integrity—Office of General Counsel
- Postal Inspection Service
- Securities and Exchange Commission
- U.S. Army Audit Agency—Office of Chief Counsel
- U.S. Immigration and Customs Enforcement
- U.S. Secret Service

Fraud Task Forces

The government currently has a number of special efforts focused on fighting fraud in various economic sectors. They include:

- Financial Fraud Enforcement Task Force—targets fraud related to mortgage lending and modification, securities law, stimulus spending, and the government's bailout of the financial sector. Includes attorneys from the Departments of Justice, Treasury, and Housing and Urban Development, and the Securities and Exchange Commission.
- Document and Benefit Fraud Task Forces—located in Washington, D.C./Northern Virginia, Atlanta, Boston, Dallas, Denver, Detroit, Los Angeles, New York, Newark, Philadelphia, and St. Paul. Led by U.S. Immigration and Customs Enforcement (ICE), the task forces include representatives from the Departments of Justice, Labor and State, U.S. Citizenship and Immigration Services, Social Security Administration, Postal Inspection Service, U.S. Secret Service, and numerous state and local law enforcement agencies. Investigators come from a variety of agencies and have expertise in different aspects of document and benefit fraud.
- National Procurement Fraud Task Force—detecting, investigating, and prosecuting procurement, grant, and Recovery Act fraud. Task force members include the Justice Department's Criminal, Antitrust, Civil, Criminal, Environmental and Natural Resources, National Security, and Tax Divisions; the FBI; the Department of Justice Inspector General; other federal Inspectors General; defense investigative agencies; and U.S. Attorneys' offices across the country.
- Hurricane Katrina Task Force—mission: to deter, prevent, detect, and punish fraud related to the devastation caused by Hurricane Katrina; subsequently expanded to provide a national mechanism for receiving and referring complaints from the public about suspected fraud resulting from other natural disasters, such as the Haitian earthquakes and floods in New England and Tennessee.
- Health Care Fraud Prevention and Enforcement Action Team (HEAT)—a joint effort of the Department of Health and Human Services (specifically the Office of the Inspector General and Centers for Medicare and Medicaid Services) and the Department of Justice.

- Medicare Fraud Strike Force—another joint effort of the Departments of Justice and Health and Human Services.
- AIDS Health Fraud Task Forces—sponsored by the Food and Drug Administration and designed to combat fraudulent product/treatment promotions affecting people with HIV/AIDS and their partners, family, and friends. Task Force Network members include people living with HIV/AIDS, treatment advocates, community-based organizations, health-care practitioners, educators, federal and state government officials, and local health-care departments.

Chapter 60

"Hidden" Federal Attorney Positions—Resolving Disputes

In addition to law offices, the federal government has more than 80 alternative dispute resolution (ADR) offices that are separate from agency chief legal offices. These offices manage agency ADR programs, including holding informal and formal hearings, hiring outside mediators, and managing the entire ADR process in their respective agencies. These ADR offices often have attorneys on staff, and many maintain mediator rosters of qualified private-sector attorneys who can be called upon to provide ADR services as outside contractors.

ADR is widespread in the U.S. government and new applications emerge all the time. ADR has proven an effective mechanism for resolving disputes quickly and cost-effectively in many agencies and has reduced the caseload burden on the courts.

More than 50 federal agencies employ formal ADR techniques—such as mediation, arbitration, facilitation, shared neutrals, and settlement judges—to resolve disputes, and attorneys in several hundred government law offices appear before ADR panels.

The vast majority of ADR mechanisms focus on employment and workplace disputes, with contract disputes a distant second.

The following agencies and offices constitute the principal federal ADR offices:

- Department of Agriculture—Conflict Prevention and Resolution Center
- Department of Energy—Office of General Counsel—Office of Dispute Resolution
- Department of Health and Human Services—Departmental Appeals Board—Alternative Dispute Resolution Division
- Department of Homeland Security—Citizenship and Immigration Services Ombudsman
- Department of Justice—Community Relations Service and Office of Dispute Resolution
- Department of Transportation—Office of General Counsel—Center for Alternative Dispute Resolution
- Air Force Workplace Disputes ADR Program and Office of General Counsel—Dispute Resolution Division
- Environmental Protection Agency—Office of General Counsel—Alternative Dispute Resolution Law Office
- Equal Employment Opportunity Commission
- Federal Communications Commission—Enforcement Bureau—Market Disputes Resolution Division
- Federal Deposit Insurance Corporation—FDIC Office of the Ombudsman
- Federal Energy Regulatory Commission—Office of General Counsel—Dispute Resolution Service
- Federal Labor Relations Authority—Collaboration and Alternative Dispute Resolution Office and Office of Administrative Law Judges—Settlement Judge Program
- Federal Mediation and Conciliation Service
- Library of Congress—Dispute Resolution Center
- National Mediation Board
- Office of Special Counsel—Investigation and Prosecution Division III—ADR Unit
- Defense Contract Management Agency—Office of General Counsel—Contract Dispute Resolution Center

- National Institutes of Health—Office of the Ombudsman/ Center for Cooperative Resolution
- Federal Aviation Administration—Office of the Chief Counsel—Office of Alternative Dispute Resolution and Office of Dispute Resolution for Acquisition
- U.S. Postal Service—Judicial Officer Department

Chapter 61

"Hidden" Federal Attorney Positions—Government Contracting

Government contracting is a two-headed monster. From the standpoint of attorney and law-related job opportunities, it consists of (1) working for the government in a government contracting practice and (2) working as an outside contractor providing legal services to the government.

Federal Attorney and Law-Related Contracts Practice

In any given year, the U.S. government contracts for goods and services with more than 275,000 companies and nonprofit organizations. Some of these contracts are for legal services or have legal services as one of their elements. In addition, certain contracts lend themselves to subcontracting for legal services.

The U.S. government is by far the largest purchaser of goods and services in the United States, if not the world. Each year, it purchases everything from complex weapons systems and terrorist-detection technologies to staples and paper clips. Certain contracts run into billions of dollars, hundreds of subcontractors, thousands of pages of documentation, and elaborate payment mechanisms. Others may cost only a few thousand dollars, involve only one individual contractor, a one-page memorandum of understanding, and payment via government charge card.

The creation of the Department of Homeland Security gave a huge boost to U.S. government contracting (an additional $40 to $50 billion per year). The time-limited $787 billion stimulus program (American Recovery and Reinvestment Act, Pub. L. 111-5) crafted by the President and Congress in response to the Great Recession aside, both the national defense and homeland security demands on the U.S. government combine to make government contracting and procurement a vibrant, permanent, and growing discipline that consumes large quantities of government attorney and law-related personnel and resources.

Federal government purchases totaled more than $425 billion a year before the economy collapsed, and that figure has gone well above $1 trillion a year since. More than 1,000 U.S. government law offices and several hundred federal contract and procurement and Small and Disadvantaged Business Utilization Offices (SADBUs)—often employing JDs as contracting officers—are involved daily in government contracting.

Government contracting practice includes drafting requests for proposals, invitations for bids, sources sought, and other solicitations; putting together contracting documents; investigating and litigating contract disputes; investigating and prosecuting contract fraud allegations; administering and terminating contracts; ensuring contract compliance; and advising policymakers on procurement matters.

Attorneys also work in a variety of capacities for the federal government's boards of contract appeals—the Civilian Board of Contract Appeals (www.cbca.gsa.gov/), the Armed Services Board of Contract Appeals (www.law.gwu.edu/asbca) and the Postal Service Board of Contract Appeals (www.usps.com/judicial/).

Government contract and procurement law has a bright future as far out as the eye can see. Defense contracting will always be a thriving proposition (regardless of [modest] intermittent attempts to rein it in), and has now been joined by homeland security contracting. Given the unpredictability and instability of the world, and the terrorist threats against which government must protect the country, government contracting is always going be an important practice area. Finally, ambitious federal initiatives in energy, health care, and education also contain massive amounts of new federal contracting dollars likely to keep flowing for some time to come.

Since contract law is one of the central themes of legal education, attorneys are natural candidates for government contract and procurement law positions in both mainstream and law-related arenas. Federal employers know this and have a history of hiring attorneys for law-related positions, so much so that approximately 25 percent of the 30,000-plus federal contract and procurement officers have law degrees.

Government Contracts for Outside Legal Services

The other side of federal contracting, a mild digression from the primary focus of this book, is government contracting for outside legal services. Federal legal services contracts range across the board, and include:

- debt collection;
- real estate closings and settlements;
- legal research and writing, including drafting administrative decisions;
- legal consulting in specialty areas;
- training in legal topics; and
- advice and assistance to foreign governments and private organizations in developing countries.

The federal agencies that award the most legal services contracts are the—

- Department of Justice
- Department of Housing and Urban Development
- Department of Labor
- Department of Treasury
- Department of Commerce
- Equal Employment Opportunity Commission
- U.S. Agency for International Development

The Department of Treasury's Office of Technical Assistance (OTA) provides comprehensive financial advice around the world. OTA's expert advisors work directly with foreign governments to support their efforts to improve their financial systems. A number of these countries are involved in the transition from state-controlled to market-based economies, some are developing nations that are attempting to increase their capacity to better meet the needs of their populations, while others are emerging from periods of internal or external conflict. OTA also engages in financial reconstruction and stabilization efforts for countries emerging from conflict or those that are considered to be failed states. OTA's program consists of five core areas:

- Budget Policy and Management
- Financial Institutions Policy and Regulation
- Government Debt Issuance and Management
- Financial Enforcement
- Tax Policy and Administration

OTA provides its consulting advice and assistance through the placement of resident and intermittent advisors, frequently from the private sector. Long-term, resident advisors provide advice and training to ministers of finance, central bank governors, and other government officials. Short-term, intermittent advisors provide highly specialized assistance. Since there is an extensive legal component to the five program areas listed above, there are quite a few opportunities here for attorneys.

The Commerce Department Office of General Counsel's Commercial Law Development Program performs similar work, which also requires the assistance of outside consultants, all of whom are attorneys.

Lists of government prime contractors are matters of public record, and some agencies and offices make these available on their websites (although not all are up-to-date). Legal services contractors include law firms of all sizes as well as sole practitioners.

Requests for Proposals (RFPs) and Invitations for Bid (IFBs) for federal contracts exceeding $25,000 are posted on www. fedbizopps.gov. Smaller contracts are sometimes posted on agency websites. In addition, agency Small and Disadvantaged Business Utilization offices and Procurement offices may maintain emailing lists that alert prospective contractors to RFPs and IFBs. If they do not, you can contact them anyway and inform them of your capabilities and interest. In fact, making such a personal connection can be the difference between winning a legal services contract award and being rejected.

Chapter 62

"Hidden" Law-Related Positions—Overview and Regulatory Compliance Positions

Overview

Law-related positions where attorneys work can be found throughout the federal government. Federal law-related careers include more than 150 job titles, with new ones emerging constantly. This chapter and the following four focus on the law-related positions that are the most law-oriented of this group. They also happen to be, in my opinion, the most interesting and dynamic law-related careers in the federal government today.

The categories under which I have classified these job titles are somewhat arbitrary selections. Many of them could easily be categorized differently, primarily because they combine an assortment of activities that cross disciplines.

Regulatory Compliance Positions

Compliance Specialist/Officer/Analyst

The U.S. government has employed compliance professionals for as long as it has regulated citizen or commercial conduct, which means for almost 180 years (although the titles Compliance Specialist, Compliance Officer, and Compliance Analyst are of relatively recent vintage). Lately, this occupation is becoming ubiquitous throughout government as it scrambles to cope with the multiple new challenges of the twenty-first century.

Essentially, compliance professionals monitor regulatory compliance. Naturally, the substance of what they deal with varies considerably from agency-to-agency and program-to-program. For example, a Compliance Specialist in the Treasury Department's Financial Crimes Enforcement Network (FinCEN) assesses financial institution and financial industry compliance with the Bank Secrecy Act (BSA), Pub. L. 91-508, and recommends appropriate agency actions; conducts research and analysis of issues to identify problems or deviations from regulatory requirements; develops reports, analyses, summaries, or guidance materials for use by agency officials; provides advice or technical assistance to representatives of regulated industries or institutions and federal and state regulatory partners on complex regulatory compliance issues, BSA requirements, FinCEN regulations and policies, or Treasury policies; and reviews and approves referrals by regulators of BSA violations, recommends sanctions, and provides advice and assistance on specific cases.

In contrast, a Compliance Professional at the Internal Revenue Service's Tax Exempt Bonds Office interprets the tax code, regulations, administrative guidance, and court cases in order to provide technical tax advice, education, and regulatory guidance through outreach to members of the tax-exempt bond industry; analyzes requests for voluntary correction of tax violations; reviews arbitrage compliance matters; conducts compliance risk assessments and market-trend analyses; and participates in post-issuance compliance research projects.

Note: Job titles can vary considerably from agency-to-agency and office-to-office, even for the same job with the exact same duties and responsibilities. Consequently, when you perform your research on suitable job titles, you have to think in terms of each agency's and office's mission and terminology. For example, the IRS compliance professional described in the paragraph immediately above often carries the job title "Tax Law Specialist." Similarly, Environmental Protection Agency compliance personnel are often given the job title "Environmental Protection Specialist." To further confuse the matter, not all Environmental Protection Specialists perform compliance work!

Environmental Protection Specialist

Environmental Protection Specialists advise on, manage, supervise, or perform administrative or program work relating to environmental protection programs (e.g., programs to protect or improve environmental quality, control pollution, remedy environmental damage, or ensure compliance with environmental laws and regulations). These positions require specialized knowledge of the laws and regulations related to environmental protection activities, as well as the principles and methods of administering these programs.

Because every federal agency must comply with federal, state, local, and host nation environmental laws and regulations, as well as relevant executive orders, they have to integrate environmental considerations into their decision-making processes, prepare detailed environmental documentation regarding proposed actions, maintain ongoing programs to protect and restore environmental resources, comply with environmental reporting requirements, etc. That means that Environmental Protection Specialist positions can be found throughout the government. As well as regulating governmental outfits and initiatives, environmental regulation agencies, principally the Environmental Protection Agency, are responsible for rulemaking, monitoring, compliance, and enforcement activities affecting both public and private organizations and for managing and overseeing state and other entity environmental programs.

Environmental protection programs deal with such areas as air and water quality, hazardous waste and materials management, underground storage tanks containing regulated substances (petro-leum products, chemicals, and wastes), oil and hazardous substance spills planning, nonhazardous waste management, waste minimi-zation and recycling, and site restoration and remediation. Many programs focus on specific pollutants (e.g., noise, radon, asbestos, pesticides, medical waste, and acid rain) or on protecting a specific medium (land, air, water, wetlands).

Environmental protection specialists play a central role in all of this, and generally perform functions related to one or more of the following areas:

- *Rulemaking and regulation*—developing, reviewing, and implementing legislative proposals, regulations, standards, policies, and operating guidance.
- *Compliance and enforcement*—evaluating and securing compliance with environmental laws and programs through permitting, self-assessments, audits, inspections, investiga-tions, and enforcement and corrective action activities.
- *Environmental considerations and documentation*—(1) re-viewing proposed actions (construction, leasing, land trans-actions, mission activities, etc.) and ensuring that environmental effects are considered in planning and deci-sion-making, that these considerations are documented, and that provision is made for public involvement; (2) comply-ing with environmental reporting requirements; and/or (3) analyzing and managing environmental information or in-formation systems.
- *Program administration and oversight*—(1) managing, ad-ministering, and coordinating programs or projects to achieve and maintain environmental compliance or remediate past environmental violations or compliance prob-lems; or (2) administering, evaluating, and overseeing en-vironmental programs and/or activities funded by grants, cooperative agreements, or other similar arrangements.

Major federal employers include the Environmental Protection Agency, U.S. Departments of Defense, Energy, Homeland Secu-rity, Interior and Transportation, and NASA. A number of Environmental Protection Specialist positions are listed at www.usajobs.gov as this is being written.

Ethics Program Specialist

Ethics Program Specialists review public financial disclosure reports and other reports filed by government officials for potential and actual conflicts of interest and to ensure that reports are technically compliant with applicable statutes and regulations and policies implemented by the Office of Government Ethics. They may also draft counseling letters and/or meet with filers to advise of potential conflicts and acceptable remedies in accordance with applicable criminal conflict of interest statutes and regulations. Ethics Program Specialists also provide guidance and advice about the full range of ethics law issues, requirements, and policy. In addition, there is a considerable ethics training component to their work.

Other duties include:

- advising key officials on highly complex and/or potentially controversial cases;
- analyzing complex business relationships;
- reviewing, analyzing, and processing ethics actions;
- researching, assembling, and clearing background materials and replies to inquiries involving the Ethics in Government Act, Pub. L. 95-521, submitted pursuant to the Privacy Act or Freedom of Information Act; and
- tracking and ensuring compliance with annual ethics training requirements.

Ethics Program Specialists at the U.S. Office of Government Ethics also become involved in the presidential appointment process and assist foreign governments in instituting ethics programs and in training their personnel.

Ethics Program Specialists work at the U.S. Office of Government Ethics and many also work at the 100-plus agencies covered by government-wide ethics laws and regulations. They are often lodged in the agency's office of general counsel because they must work so closely with the Designated Agency Ethics Officer, who is usually an attorney in such an office.

Note: National Public Radio reported in September 2010 that employees of the U.S. Office of Government Ethics owe the IRS almost $800,000 in unpaid taxes.

Futures Trading Specialist/Investigator

Futures Trading Specialists/Investigators perform regulatory and compliance oversight and conduct investigations of alleged fraud, market manipulations, and trade practice violations. They may also appear as expert witnesses in administrative or civil proceedings, or assist state or other federal law enforcement agencies in dealing with futures-related violations.

These positions are all with the Commodity Futures Trading Commission. The number of job opportunities is expanding as a result of the recent enactment of the Dodd-Frank Wall Street Reform and Consumer Protection Act, Pub. L. 111-205. Currently, a number of attorneys serve in this capacity.

Equal Opportunity Compliance Specialist

Also known as Equal Opportunity Specialists, these positions are concerned with the application of civil rights and equal opportunity laws, regulations, and precedent decisions to eliminate illegal discrimination and to remove barriers to equal opportunity. This work involves analyzing and solving equal opportunity and civil rights problems through fact-finding, problem analysis, negotiation, and voluntary compliance programs. Many such positions require specialized knowledge and skill in investigating and resolving allegations of discrimination. Enforcement is also a component of the job.

Equal Opportunity Compliance Specialists work in a wide range of economic, social, and political venues where civil rights and equal opportunity laws and policies prohibit discrimination based on race, color, religion, sex, national origin, age, handicapping condition, or other bases specified by law. These venues include employment, housing, education, social services, business, and finance.

Specific duties may include:

- investigating and conciliating allegations of discrimination;
- enforcing laws requiring equal pay for men and women;

- reviewing, evaluating, and enforcing equal opportunity compliance by government contractors and other recipients of public funds;
- identifying systemic or institutional barriers to equal opportunity;
- proposing or implementing solutions to complex problems when the work involves a high degree of analysis;
- developing, carrying out, or evaluating broad equal opportunity or voluntary compliance programs; and
- applying judgment in interpreting complex factual situations in light of laws, regulations, and precedent decisions governing a civil rights or equal opportunity program.

Equal Employment Opportunity Manager/Specialist

These positions are primarily concerned with developing, administering, evaluating, or advising on the federal government's internal Equal Employment Opportunity (EEO) program within federal agencies. EEO managers and specialists must have knowledge of federal EEO regulations and principles; compliance and enforcement skills; administrative, management, and consulting skills; and knowledge of federal personnel administration. The job title includes managers or coordinators of special emphasis programs designed to solve the specialized employment problems of women, minorities, veterans, the disabled, persons over age 40, and others as they relate to federal employment. These are largely "change agent" positions intended to facilitate the removal of barriers to equal employment and to develop affirmative employment action in the federal employment system.

EEO managers and specialists are involved in fact-finding, analysis, writing, and application of equal opportunity principles to identify and/or solve problems. They investigate, conciliate, negotiate, and/or consult with respect to allegations of discrimination; develop, administer, and evaluate affirmative action plans, EEO policies, and practices; and administer and enforce internal EEO programs. Many positions involve program development, program management, or program evaluation activities.

EEO specialists and managers typically must apply an understanding of legal procedures and terminology (e.g., rules of evidence, trial de novo, case law precedents, and interpretation of court decisions). Most positions require knowledge of investigative procedures and methods to direct investigations, skill in writing proposed dispositions and/or final agency decisions in complaints of discrimination, and knowledge and skill to monitor remedial actions. These skills are applied in the context of a broad knowledge of civil rights laws and regulations, and their relationship to agency policies and practices.

EEO managers and specialists work in every federal executive branch agency and can be found throughout both headquarters and field offices.

Privacy Officer

Privacy Officers have been around the U.S. government in one form or another since enactment of the Privacy Act of 1974, Pub. L. 93-579. Their original role was to protect against the unauthorized release of information that their agency collected from private individuals and organizations. Most often it was combined with the job of Freedom of Information Act Officer and sometimes subsumed under other job titles as well.

The advance of technology, the emergence of national and homeland security as major federal concerns, and financial services and health-care legislation have conferred new importance on this position. In recent years, a number of federal agencies have established separate privacy offices and staffed them with Privacy Officers with vastly expanded responsibilities. Today, Privacy Officers concentrate exclusively on privacy issues and perform duties unheard of when the Privacy Act was enacted.

Duties are vast and often include anything having to do with information disclosure, such as:

- advising senior management on all matters related to the agency's privacy program;
- promoting the privacy rights of employees and the agency's constituencies;
- ensuring that the agency is positioned to respond to White House directives, data calls, and other directives regarding

the protection and safeguarding of personally identifiable information;

- coordinating and responding to Office of Management and Budget and Government Accountability Office data calls and inquiries;
- leading and/or coordinating multifunctional projects, studies, and research activities to identify and address privacy issues;
- participating in agency committees and groups, as well as on formal and informal inter-agency and private-sector working groups, committees, and meetings focused on privacy issues;
- ensuring that all breach incidents receive appropriate high-level attention and are managed in a timely manner, consistent with applicable directives;
- developing and ensuring that the agency's privacy strategy is appropriate and timely for the current information systems and operations;
- facilitating the incorporation of privacy principles directly into enterprise architecture and technical designs by ensuring that business requirements reflect agency privacy policies and practices;
- initiating investigations of systemic privacy problems and determining necessary corrective actions, as well as programmatic or policy changes to enhance the efficiency and effectiveness of the agency's privacy program; and
- identifying and correcting problems relating to privacy issues and policies by conducting business process reviews to identify vulnerabilities which could result in breaches of personally identifiable information.

Program Integrity Specialist

Often falling under the much broader job titles Management Analyst, Program Analyst, or Program Specialist, Program Integrity Specialists are an agency's first-line waste, fraud, abuse and mismanagement investigators. They work throughout the government and can be found in both agency programs and Inspector General Offices.

Program Integrity Specialists implement and manage integrity programs designed to identify and assess program vulnerabilities in the four areas listed above. They examine:

(1) the effectiveness and efficiency of operations;
(2) the utilization of program benefits;
(3) the fiscal integrity of the programs' eligibility, authorization, and claims processing functions, if any;
(4) the fidelity of internal and external databases; and
(5) the tracking and reporting of cost savings and other program data collection activities.

They also provide administrative support, technical assistance, and guidance to federal, state and local investigative agencies.

Program Integrity Specialists become even more important to their agencies in times of severe federal budgetary stress, such as the present.

Chapter 63

"Hidden" Law-Related Positions—Adjudication Positions

Customs and Immigration Services Adjudication Positions

The growing importance of immigration law and the tensions tugging it toward more restrictive laws and policies—as well as those tugging it in the other direction—have made positions involved in the immigration adjudications process much more important than ever. This is likely to continue as long as the debate about immigration is national news, which is going to be a very long time.

The following job titles comprise the U.S. Customs and Immigration Services (USCIS) adjudications officer community.

Asylum Officer

Asylum Officers interview asylum applicants, research relevant law and country conditions, make credibility determinations, and adjudicate asylum applications. They might also participate in refugee processing at locations around the globe. There are eight asylum offices across the United States: New York; Newark, New Jersey; Arlington, Virginia; Miami; Houston; Chicago; San Francisco; and Anaheim.

Application Adjudicator

Application Adjudicators decide whether applications and petitions requesting benefits and privileges under the Immigration and Nationality Act, Pub. L. 89-236, will be approved. Primary responsibilities may include:

- researching the eligibility and entitlement of persons seeking benefits, employment, and/or legal status under the Immigration and Nationality Act;
- reviewing case documentation to determine legal sufficiency and make recommendations;
- performing preliminary fact finding and initiating further action where information indicates fraud has been detected;
- reviewing and making determinations on cases;
- hearing and adjudicating appeals; and
- deciding on motions to reopen and reconsider cases.

Refugee Officer

Refugee Officers represent USCIS in its dealings with refugees throughout the world. Their primary mission is to interview and determine the eligibility of applicants who are applying to be resettled in the U.S. as refugees. This includes determining whether the facts of the applications fulfill the legal requirements for the benefit sought, evaluating the credibility of testimony, and analyzing and verifying the authenticity and relevance of supporting documents.

Primary responsibilities may include:

- traveling to overseas locations to adjudicate refugee-related applications;
- adjudicating applications arising under various sections of the Immigration and Nationality Act that fall within the jurisdiction of the Office of Refugee Affairs;
- preparing written assessments of findings;
- researching various political climates, human rights conditions, and cultural practices of refuges submitting applications; and

- performing a variety of functions that support the overseas adjudication mission, including fraud detection and prevention, training support, and administrative/logistical support.

Adjudications Officer

The primary responsibilities of Adjudications Officers may include:

- adjudicating applications and petitions by researching and applying laws and conducting interviews to determine eligibility;
- ensuring national security and supporting the intelligence community by examining documentation for authenticity and conducting background investigations;
- appearing in court as the Department of Homeland Security representative for administrative and criminal proceedings;
- serving as a liaison with attorneys, community-based organizations, the media, and other government agencies;
- supporting process improvement efforts by reviewing, making recommendations, and developing administrative and operating programs;
- participating in quality assurance efforts by reviewing the work of Adjudications Officers; and
- assessing, planning, and developing training for Adjudications Officers.

Employee Benefits Law Specialist

These positions are found primarily in the Department of Labor, specifically within the department's Employee Benefits Security Administration (EBSA). EBSA is responsible for administering and securing compliance with title I of the Employee Retirement Income Security Act (ERISA), Pub. L. 93-406, as well as certain provisions of the Internal Revenue Code and the Federal Employees Retirement System Act, Pub. L. 99-335. In total, EBSA is charged with compliance and enforcement responsibilities with respect to 708,000 private pension plans, 2.8 million health insurance plans, and more than a million other welfare benefit plans.

Employee Benefits Law Specialists work in Washington, D.C. and in 10 EBSA regional offices around the country (Boston, New York, Atlanta, Philadelphia, Cincinnati, Chicago, Kansas City, Dallas, Los Angeles, and San Francisco). They can be assigned to any one of the following EBSA divisions:

- Office of Exemption Determinations
- Office of Enforcement
- Office of Policy and Research
- Office of Health Plan Standards and Compliance Assistance
- Office of Regulations and Interpretations
- Office of Participant Assistance

Employee Benefits Law Specialists provide expert counsel on technical aspects of ERISA, Pub. L. 93-406; the Federal Employees' Retirement System Act of 1986 (FERSA), Pub. L. 99-335; Health Insurance Portability and Accountability Act (HIPAA), Pub. L. 104-191; Genetic Information Nondiscrimination Act (GINA), Pub. L. 110-233; Mental Health Parity Act (MHPA), Pub. L. 104-204; Mental Health Parity and Addiction Equity Act of 2008 (MHPAEA) Pub. L. 110-343; Newborns' and Mothers' Health Protection Act of 1996 (NMHPA), Pub. L. 104-204; Women's Health and Cancer Rights Act (WHCRA), Pub. L. 105-277; Michelle's Law, Pub. L. 110-381, and policy, legislation, and research pertinent to employee benefit and health plans. They deal with government officials, private-sector financial services executives, employee benefit plan attorneys, consultants, and administrators to provide information about EBSA's operations and ongoing policy initiatives.

Typical job responsibilities include:

- providing technical and policy guidance on a wide range of interpretive, regulatory, enforcement and legislative issues;
- participating in the formulation, analysis, and implementation of national policies affecting employee benefit plans, plan sponsors, financial institutions, and other providers of services to employee benefit plans;
- conducting in-depth analyses of legal and policy issues arising under ERISA, the Internal Revenue Code, and related laws and regulations affecting employee benefit plans;

- on the basis of research and analyses, preparing memoranda, options papers, interpretive rulings, regulations, and legislative provisions affecting employee benefit plans, plan sponsors, plan participants and beneficiaries, financial institutions (banking, insurance, mutual funds), and other parties involved with employee benefit plans;
- participating individually or as a member of a team in regulatory, legislative, and other high-priority EBSA initiatives and leading and conducting in-depth policy and legislative analysis of issues;
- participating in inter- and intra-agency reviews of interpretations, regulations, guidance, legislative, and other matters and issues;
- drafting and reviewing regulations affecting the regulation of employee benefit plans;
- developing and providing training, technical assistance, and other guidance necessary to EBSA administration, including technical assistance and support for enforcement and legislative initiatives;
- representing the agency at meetings, conferences, and seminars sponsored by EBSA, other agencies, professional organizations and civic groups; and
- analyzing and applying fiduciary, reporting and disclosure, bonding, funding, vesting, administration, and termination provisions of ERISA and related laws, regulations, court decisions, and precedent rulings.

The Patient Protection and Affordable Care Act (health-care reform law), Pub. L. 111-140, places EBSA in a key position with respect to implementation of portions of the law.

Investigator (Pension)

These Investigators conduct civil and criminal investigations of private pension, health care, and other employee benefit plans to ensure compliance with the fiduciary responsibility standards of ERISA and numerous other laws and regulations. They coordinate and provide support in civil litigation and criminal prosecutions involving

ERISA with various federal agencies (i.e., IRS, Department of Justice, and Pension Benefit Guaranty Corporation) and state insurance departments.

These positions, like Employee Benefits Law Specialists, are principally found in EBSA.

Copyright Examiner

Copyright Examiners work only for the Copyright Office at the Library of Congress. They examine, register, catalog, certify original and renewal copyrights, and disseminate information to the public and assist applicants with copyright procedures.

What makes this position so much more interesting today than for most of its history is the resurgence of copyright law as a vibrant, fast-changing practice resulting from the cascade of technological advances that have created new copyrightable products. What was a stodgy backwater has evolved into something of a "butterfly," replete with many questions and cutting-edge issues, such as the legal protection of databases, "jail breaking" of IPhones, and what constitutes a non-infringing use of copyrighted material. Part of the impetus for the emergence of copyright law into an interesting and exciting practice area was enactment of the Digital Millennium Copyright Act of 1998, Pub. L. 105-304, which implemented two World Intellectual Property Organization treaties and also addressed a number of other significant copyright-related issues, including the liability of online service providers for copyright infringement when engaging in certain types of activities; distance education; the exceptions in the Copyright Act (Pub. L. 60-349, as amended) for libraries and for making ephemeral recordings; "webcasting" of sound recordings on the Internet; the applicability of collective bargaining agreement obligations in the case of transfers of rights in motion pictures; and a new form of protection for the design of vessel hulls.

In addition, globalization of information dissemination has also contributed to making copyright practice an area of considerable interest. Copyright relations with other countries has emerged as an area of rapid change and often confusing issues.

Hearings/Appeals Officer

Hearings and Appeals Officers adjudicate cases that typically include the conduct of formal or informal hearings that accord appropriate due process, arising under statute or under the regulations of a federal agency when the hearings are *not* subject to the Administrative Procedure Act (APA), 5 U.S.C. §§ 551 et seq., or involve the conduct of appellate reviews of prior decisions. Only Administrative Law Judges (see Chapter 27, "Mainstream Attorney Hiring—Administrative Law Judges," above) may hear cases under the APA.

The work requires the ability to review and evaluate investigative reports and case records, conduct hearings in an orderly and impartial manner, determine credibility of witnesses, sift and evaluate evidence, analyze complex issues, apply agency rules and regulations and court decisions, prepare clear and concise statements of fact, and exercise sound judgment in arriving at decisions. Some positions require application of a substantive knowledge of agency policies, programs, and requirements in fields such as personnel management or environmental protection.

A host of federal agencies employ Hearings and Appeals Officers, including, among others:

- Department of Agriculture—National Appeals Division
- Department of Defense
  - o Defense Office of Hearings and Appeals
  - o Air Force Board for Correction of Military Records
  - o Air Force Discharge Review Board
  - o Army Board for Correction of Military Records
  - o Army Discharge Review Board
  - o Army Grade Determination Review Board
  - o Board for Correction of Naval Records
  - o Naval Discharge Review Board
  - o Naval Clemency and Parole Board
- Department of Energy—Office of Hearings and Appeals
- Department of Interior—Office of Hearings and Appeals
- Department of Homeland Security—Coast Guard Hearing Office
- Department of Housing and Urban Development—Office of Appeals

- Department of Justice—Board of Immigration Appeals
- Department of Transportation—Surface Transportation Board—Office of Proceedings
- Department of Veterans Affairs—Board of Veterans Appeals
- Commodity Futures Trading Commission—Office of Proceedings
- Environmental Protection Agency—Environmental Appeals Board
- Equal Employment Opportunity Commission
- Government Accountability Office—Personnel Appeals Board
- Nuclear Regulatory Commission—Atomic Safety and Licensing Board Panel
- Small Business Administration—Office of Hearings and Appeals

Do not fixate too much on the job title Hearings and Appeals Officer. The title of the function may vary agency-by-agency. For example, the Commodity Futures Trading Commission uses the job title Judgment Officer.

Land Law Examiner

Land Law Examiners are employed by the Department of Interior's Bureau of Land Management and work in both its headquarters and field offices throughout the United States. This position administers, supervises, or performs quasi-legal work involved in processing, adjudicating, and advising on applications and claims for rights, privileges, gratuities, or other benefits authorized under the various public land, mineral leasing, and mining laws. The work requires knowledge of governing public laws and agency policies and procedures regarding the application of these laws. Land Law Examiners often work closely with the Interior Department's Office of the Solicitor.

The major activity assigned to a Land Law Examiner is the adjudication of rights of individuals with respect to their interests in public lands and resources. Substantive knowledge of the laws, regulations, policies, and procedures governing the acquisition and use of the public lands and resources, along with a law degree, is a big competitive advantage. Land Law Examiners must also have—or must be able to acquire once on the job—knowledge of other legal matters, such as descent and distribution of property, domestic relations, and citizenship requirements, as these matters apply to the processing of public land law cases.

The issues surrounding the work of Land Law Examiners can be quite complex. Many of the public land laws with which Land Law Examiners are concerned apply only to the unreserved, unappropriated public domain lands. The mineral laws, and some of the land laws, extend to National Forest Lands, reclamation lands, and other types of withdrawals, and to lands the surface of which is in private ownership, with subsurface rights vested in the government.

Congress has enacted more than 5,000 laws over the past 200 years that affect the public domain. While many of these laws are now obsolete, there still remains a great complex of land law. Within this complex there exists a framework of some 60 basic categories of application or claim types, under which are often found several separate and distinct sub-types.

Land Law Examiners typically perform the duties detailed below in order to demonstrate (a) the complexity of the work and (b) how it is informed by the law:

(1) Examining reports reflecting the status of lands involved in applications to determine if they are available for disposition or use as sought by the applicants, including (a) whether lands are withdrawn from certain or all types of entries; (b) whether the lands are known to be prospectively valuable for minerals; (c) whether a given application conflicts with others pending or previously allowed and the priority rights of the parties involved; (d) whether a field examination is necessary to develop facts regarding utilization of the land; (e) the character of the land over which a right-of-way is desired, and whether granting the right-of-way is compatible with the public interest; and (f) whether the use of the land, as sought, is permissible under applicable statutes and regulations.

(2) Determining the eligibility or qualifications of the applicants to acquire interests in or use of the lands involved, includ-

ing (a) whether applicants meet provisions of law and regulations as regards citizenship, marital status, age, veterans' benefits, etc.; (b) where application is filed by a soldier's widow, that proof is submitted of the marriage, of the soldier's death, and of the fact that the widow has remained unmarried; (c) where heirs file the application, by reference to the pertinent state and federal laws, whether the heirs involved in the chain of title to the right are the parties legally entitled to the shares of the right claimed; (d) where an assignee files an application, whether the assignment is legal, and that no prior assignment of the same right has been made; (e) if the applicant is a municipality, whether it has shown the law or charter and procedure taken by which it became a legal body corporate, that the taking of the lease is authorized under such law or charter, and that the action proposed has been duly authorized by a governing body of such municipality; (f) whether the acreage of land applied for is within the allowable maximum and minimum limits; and (g) whether provisions of law and regulations permit priority or preference to be given specific classes of applicants, etc.

(3) Determining whether applications otherwise conform with applicable statutory and/or regulatory requirements, including (a) requirements as to furnishing of surety or cash bonds; (b) whether there are any outstanding tax liabilities on the land; and (c) payment of fees, rentals, or other charges for the land, etc.

(4) Preparing necessary leases, permits, and other documents, with appropriate provisions as to royalty payments, limitations or stipulations, including (a) what easements, exceptions, and mineral reservations, if any, must be incorporated in the patents for the selected land in order to protect the rights of others and the interests of the government; and (b) limitations or stipulations requested by other federal agencies that have jurisdiction over or an interest in the land involved, for inclusion in the terms of the lease or other document.

(5) Formulating agency decisions for notification of the applicant and other interested parties as to acceptance, modification, additional requirements and evidence, or rejection of the applications, including determining which parties have sufficient standing to be designated as "adverse parties" and thus entitled to be served with copies of all documents issued in the proceeding.

(6) Composing necessary correspondence with applicants, other bureau offices and other agencies concerned relative to application or claims.

(7) Conducting personal and telephone contacts with applicants or their representatives, other bureau personnel, and with representatives of other federal agencies or local governmental agencies on matters pertaining to specific applications.

Mediator

Federal government mediators work for either the Federal Mediation and Conciliation Service (FMCS) or the National Mediation Board (NMB). They provide mediation assistance to labor and management in the settlement or prevention of industrial labor disputes connected with the formulation, revision, termination, and renewal of collective-bargaining agreements.

The FMCS and the NMB carry out the federal government's role of mediating collective-bargaining disputes between labor and management in industries engaged in or affecting commerce. Their purpose is to promote and maintain peace in labor/management relations in order to avoid interruptions to commerce. FMCS is concerned with disputes in industry in general, excepting the railroad and airline industries, which are the exclusive province of the NMB.

The mediation agencies are made aware of and alerted in advance to the possibility of a collective-bargaining dispute within their respective jurisdictions. In the event that the parties are unable to settle their differences, a federal mediator may be assigned to enter the case.

Mediators engage in two major types of mediation activity:

- *Dispute mediation* is "fire fighting," helping to settle work stoppages quickly after they have started, or assisting the parties to resolve contract disputes in ways that will avoid use of the strike or lockout. This crisis-bargaining atmosphere is often characterized by continuous day-and-night meetings, a fact of life with which the mediators must contend.
- *Preventive mediation* is aimed at preventing, or at least minimizing, potential labor/management disputes and is carried on away from the bargaining table prior to the development of a formal dispute. The Mediator's activities are aimed at assisting in eliminating disruptive factors that cause harmful and destructive disputes to arise.

The range of preventive mediation activities includes, for example, maintaining continuing liaison with industry and labor; visiting with labor or management representatives, exploring potential problems with them, and offering pre-negotiation consultation and advisory assistance on impending bargaining problems; chairing or participating in joint labor/management problem conferences and discussions; conducting joint meetings on grievance procedures; offering personal consultation with representatives of both labor and management regarding industrial relations problems; and providing seminar discussions, lectures, and audio-visual presentations before interested groups, such as joint shop-steward and foremen groups, supervisory groups, or personnel groups.

Note: The government also engages a large number of outside mediators as independent contractors. They primarily conduct workplace mediations. The principal users of outside mediation services are the Equal Employment Opportunity Commission (EEOC) and the U.S. Postal Service (USPS), but other agencies also engage outside mediators from time to time. The EEOC typically issues a request for proposals when it needs to replenish its supply of outside mediators. The USPS and most of the other relevant agencies develop rosters of eligible mediators, to whom they assign cases as they arise. Mediation experience is required for almost all such contract mediation positions.

Several of my counseling clients have served as outside mediators for the EEOC and have found the contract fees to be sufficient so that they only do this work intermittently.

Tax Law Specialist

Tax Law Specialists' principal duties are to administer, supervise, or perform quasi-legal technical tax work requiring analysis and application of tax principles and specialized knowledge of the Internal Revenue Code and related laws, court decisions, regulations, and precedent rulings of the Internal Revenue Service (IRS). They (1) interpret the Internal Revenue Code, related laws, regulations, rulings, and precedents; (2) prepare regulations, rulings, and technical guides; and (3) make or review determinations and decisions in tax matters.

Tax Law Specialists work only for the IRS in its offices throughout the United States. IRS employs Tax Law Specialists in many areas. For example, in the Tax Exempt Bonds office within The Tax Exempt and Government Entities Division, Tax Law Specialists interpret the tax code, regulations, administrative guidance, and court cases; provide technical tax advice and education through outreach to members of the tax-exempt bond industry; draft technical guidance and revise forms; analyze requests for voluntary correction of tax violations; review arbitrage compliance matters; and conduct compliance risk assessments and market-trend analysis as well as participate in post-issuance compliance research projects.

They may also analyze developments resulting from litigation, legislative action, regulations, and departmental policy; review proposed legislation, regulations, or revenue rulings for adequacy and accuracy, and advise on potential areas of controversy or conflict; and serve as liaison between an IRS division and relevant congressional committees.

Labor-Management Relations Examiner

These positions involve the administration, supervision, or performance of work in the investigation, evaluation, and resolution of cases involving charges of unfair labor practices or collective bargaining representation issues or disputes arising under the National Labor Relations Act, Pub. L. 74-198. Examiners must have knowledge of labor-management relations, collective-bargaining processes, applicable labor laws and precedent decisions, and of the regulations, policies, and practices of the National Labor Relations

Board. The job also requires the ability to apply investigative techniques, and to negotiate constructively and persuasively.

Labor Management Relations Examiners work for the National Labor Relations Board (NLRB) and are chiefly concerned with the examination and resolution of:

(a) specific charges of unfair labor practices filed against either an employer, a union, or both, or their agents, alleging violation of collective bargaining and other statutory rights; and

(b) petitions to certify or decertify employee representatives for collective bargaining with employers in enterprises affecting commerce (in all industries except those specifically excluded by statute). These latter are referred to as representation cases.

The basic work is done by the NLRB's 51 Regional Offices, where examiner positions are typically located. It is here that all petitions and charges are filed initially, and where the vast majority of cases reach final disposition. Regional Office Examiners investigate and analyze the facts in the cases assigned to them, evaluate the merits of each case, determine possible remedies within the regulatory boundaries, and then negotiate informally or formally with respondents in efforts to obtain voluntary withdrawal or settlement agreements. They recommend formal action where settlement has not been obtained, or dismissal of those cases found to be without merit where there was no voluntary withdrawal. They also serve as hearing officers in disputed representation proceedings, and arrange and conduct the elections held to determine the employees' free choice as to their collective-bargaining representative.

Principal functions include:

Case processing, consisting of—
1. Investigation, which involves: (a) analysis of the case to determine its legal sufficiency and timeliness as reflected by the facts on the charge or petition and the supporting evidence, including the review of previous case files or records to ascertain pertinent information;

    (b) interviewing witnesses of the charging party or petitioner as to their knowledge of the allegations, following up of leads revealed by them, taking affidavits, and securing new or amended charges or petitions as may be necessary;

    (c) conferring with the respondents and/or representatives or counsels to ascertain the respondents' positions and version of the facts, taking affidavits from the respondents and witnesses; and

    (d) selecting for examination and analysis respondent's pertinent records, such as job descriptions, payrolls, collective-bargaining agreements, grievance reports, correspondence, etc.

2. Determining an appropriate course of action, which requires: (a) evaluating the merits of the case by analyzing the investigatory findings, weighing conflicting testimony, determining the credibility of witnesses, researching and determining the applicability of the act and policies and decisions of the NLRB and/or the courts); and (b) considering the possible effects on industry, labor and the public of various courses of action consistent with established Board policies and in the public interest.

Determination of an appropriate course of action may result in: (a) withdrawal, which involves the examiner making recommendations to and negotiating with the petitioner or charging party that the petition or charge be withdrawn in those cases found to be without merit or not meeting the requirements of law or established board policy and/or board or court procedure, or in cases where further proceedings would not effectuate the purpose of the National Labor Relations Act; (b) agreement, which, in meritorious unfair labor practice cases, involves negotiating with and persuading the respondent(s) to enter into an informal or formal settlement agreement, and includes working out the terms of the settlement and drafting the agreement by the examiner, and, in meritorious representation cases, involves negotiating election agreements between the employer and the individual or labor organization, or between competing labor organizations, claiming to represent the employees; or (c) in cases not disposed of by either withdrawal or agreement subsequent action may include recommendation by the examiner for dismissal, issuance of a Notice of Hearing in representation cases, or issuance of a complaint in unfair labor practice cases, for referral for hearings and trial by the board. Each such recommendation by the examiner must be supported fully with detailed description of the facts and analysis of the law and policy involved.

When a notice of hearing is issued, Labor-Management Relations Examiners may be assigned to conduct the formal public hearing in order to develop a full and complete record of the pertinent facts so that a decision may eventually be made by the regional director or the board as to whether an election should be directed. Examiners can rule on motions, admissibility of evidence, petitions to intervene, and requests for postponements or recesses; can issue subpoenas to testify and obtain materials on their own motion or at request of the parties; and can revoke subpoenas. At the conclusion of the hearing they prepare a hearing officer's report, which contains no recommendations but presents an analysis of the facts, the issues presented, the pertinent evidence on the issues, and a brief statement of all unusual or important procedural questions.

Examiners may also be assigned to conduct formal public hearings in cases of challenged ballots and/or objections to elections. Here, they have the added responsibility for making recommendations as to disposition of the issues. Examiners also arrange and conduct representation elections and have post-election, follow-up responsibilities.

Some examiner positions may involve a specialized responsibility for compliance, which involves conferring and corresponding with the respondents, complainants, and others to explain the provisions of the compliance order, to obtain information and materials pertinent to the remedy (which may be, for example, reinstatement of former employees, awards of back pay, deletion of unlawful contract provisions, etc.), and to ascertain the sufficiency of action taken or proposed by the respondent.

Claims Examiner

Claims Examiner positions are quasi-legal jobs that involve the examination, development, and adjudication of claims for compensation filed with the government by individual citizens under various laws. The major specialty of Claims Examiner positions are Workers Compensation, Railroad Retirement, and Veterans.

While all three specialty Claims Examiner positions perform similar functions, Veterans Claims Examiners probably perform somewhat more law-related work and must come armed with somewhat greater legal knowledge than any of the other specialties. They must know how to obtain and evaluate evidence, and must also know about the descent and distribution of property and domestic relations as these matters apply to the Department of Veterans Affairs claims programs. Individuals with law degrees, upon entrance into this occupation, have a head start in learning how to adjudicate claims over persons without such training.

Veterans' claims are skyrocketing. In 2009, the Department of Veterans Affairs received more than one million claims for veterans benefits.

Workers Compensation Claims Examiners work for OPM in Washington, D.C.; Railroad Retirement Claims Examiners for the Railroad Retirement Board in Chicago; and Veterans Claims Examiners for the Department of Veterans Affairs at offices throughout the country.

Patent Examiner

Patent Examiners work only for the U.S. Patent and Trademark Office (PTO). Their role is to:

- advise on, administer, supervise, or perform professional, scientific, technological, and legal work involved in the examination and disposition of applications for patents, exclusive of design patents; and
- determine the grant or denial of patents based on such applications, and in the adjudication of petitions and appeals from adverse decisions on such applications.

Basic functions include:

- Checking patent applications, which involves determining whether the formal requirements of the patent statutes and rules are met with respect to the forms of specifications, drawings, and petitions.
- Reviewing and analyzing specifications and drawings for adequacy, which involves determining what structures, processes, and results are being described; whether the drawings show the invention as described in the specifications; whether the limits of the improvement or invention are clearly, completely, and concisely described; and whether claims are adequately supported in the drawings and specifications.
- Analyzing claims, which involves determining whether a claim particularly points out and distinctly claims the alleged improvement or invention, by determining whether or not the claim is too verbose, includes a number of unrelated subjects ("aggregation"), recites merely a function or result without defining structure or method, or is otherwise indefinite; whether the claim falls into one of the statutory classes of invention; and what is the scope of each of the applicant's claims.
- Planning a field of search.
- Conducting a search, which involves comparing the structure or function described in each of the references appearing in the field of search with that of the claimed invention to determine specific points of similarity or difference.
- Applying references, which involves deciding whether the claimed invention is in fact novel and meets the standards of patentable invention. This includes determining (a) whether any existing reference already shows the claimed improvement, and/or (b) whether a reference in some other field—or a number of references, employed collectively— shows that the alleged improvement would actually be, to one skilled in the art, merely an obvious consequence or adaptation of already-patented material.

Advanced functions include:

- Applying pure theory, particularly in the more abstruse scientific fields where an application for a patent may be based on a scientific breakthrough that is primarily one of theory and involves very little structure or application. Theory itself is not patentable; rather, it is structure that must support a claim of patentability. This function involves weighing of the inventor's claims against the public interest.
- Evaluating special claim construction or arrangement, wherein the Patent Examiner allows claims only as broad as the invention clearly warrants.
- Evaluating claims submitted in amendments to the original application.
- Determining whether the applicant should be required to restrict claims to a single invention, rather than a plurality of claimed inventions.
- Recognizing and developing probable interferences.
- Deciding special situations in which the applicant tries to make major changes in the application.
- Determining "operativeness" and/or utility, which involves determining whether a function has been stated and is legally and morally acceptable in every sense; whether the disclosed subject will perform the stated function; and whether, if otherwise acceptable, the improvement actually accomplishes some useful or beneficial purpose.
- Composing "Examiner's Answer on Appeal." When an appeal is made from a final rejection of an application by the Patent Examiner, the applicant's attorney files a legal brief with the Patent Office Board of Appeals. It is the responsibility of the examiner to file a counter brief, known as the "Examiner's Answer on Appeal," in which the examiner sets forth all grounds of rejection and reasons therefore, answers all of the attorney's arguments, and cites the pertinent precedent cases.

Legal functions include:

- Applying legal precedents. The examiner conducts legal research to determine the state of the law with respect to unusual legal issues which might develop in the prosecution of an application.

- Determining sufficiency of proof of utility. It is the job of the Patent Examiner to evaluate evidence and determine its legal sufficiency for the purpose of proving utility.
- Determining whether a double patenting situation exists.
- Evaluating petitions to the Commissioner of Patents.
- Evaluating affidavits as to patentable equivalence.
- Determining sufficiency of the applicant's claims as to dates.
- Rendering decisions on interference motions.
- Determining treatment of co-pending applications.
- Determining legality of reissue oaths. When applicants wish patents to be reissued, due to errors on their own part (which caused original patents received to be inaccurate), applicants must clearly set forth the mistakes and how they arose, and affirm the errors were inadvertent and arose without deceptive intent. The Patent Examiner then evaluates the applicant's statements and proof and determines whether all requirements for reissue oaths have been met.
- Rendering the decision on a public use proceeding. When a question as to prior public use arises in the prosecution of an application, the examiner evaluates attorneys' briefs, conducts hearings, considers requests for special privileges, and decides as to whether there is a showing of public use.

Patent Examiners are in extremely high demand for two reasons. First, examiners who are not attorneys when they begin working at PTO are encouraged to earn law degrees at PTO's expense. Many leave for higher paying private-sector positions once they earn their JD. Second, the volume of patent applications is growing and was hardly slowed down by the Great Recession. The workload is so large that in October of 2010 PTO hired 1,000 new Patent Examiners, an increase of more than 33 percent in the number of examiners at the agency.

Legal Instruments Examiner

Legal Instruments Examiners examine legal instruments and supporting documents such as land titles, real estate transactional documents, and tort claims, to determine whether a requested action complies with certain provisions of various laws. The work requires the application of particular regulatory and procedural knowledge based on those laws.

Legal instruments typically are submitted by applicants seeking permission, registration, licensure, or other action by or from the government and may be accompanied by supporting document(s) that substantiate or give evidence of required items of information. Both the legal instrument and the supporting documents require examination to determine their adequacy in meeting certain technical requirements of governing provisions.

Duties of Legal Instruments Examiners include:

- review of legal instruments and supporting documents for completeness of information, proper execution, certification, technical details, and other requirements;
- obtaining additional data or information to reconcile discrepancies;
- determining whether the action sought by the party submitting the instrument corresponds with governing regulations, procedures, and other criteria; and
- arriving at a decision on the requested action, or, if such a decision is not within the scope of the employee's authority, recommend a decision.

Some examiner positions may involve responsibility for notifying the submitting party when the instrument does not meet technical requirements, explaining why the action cannot be granted, and advising the party on how such requirements may be met, or providing information on alternative options. Many positions also involve providing information and assistance in response to inquiries concerning the instruments examined.

More than 2,500 Legal Instruments Examiners work for numerous federal agencies, with the most employed by the Departments of Commerce, Treasury, Interior, Transportation, Agriculture, Veterans Affairs, and Army and the Small Business Administration.

Chapter 64

"Hidden" Law-Related Positions—Research and Policy Positions

GAO Analyst

GAO Analysts are the individuals at the Government Accountability Office (GAO) who conduct program audits and investigations of federal programs and make recommendations to both federal agencies and Congress concerning program improvements. The GAO assists congressional decision-makers by furnishing analytical information on issues and options under consideration.

GAO Analysts plan and conduct reviews of multiagency programs and the internal operations of individual agencies. Subject areas take in the full spectrum of federal activities, including health care, housing and urban development, tax policy and administration, national security and international relations, financial management, and natural resources and the environment. Typically, an analyst works as part of a team conducting in-depth research on studies requested by committees, subcommittees, or individual members of Congress, or studies that GAO has been mandated by legislation to conduct. Analysts must have strong methodological and research skills and must excel at documenting the work they do, writing the results and the findings, and presenting the work to audiences ranging from their team members to members of Congress and their staff. Specific GAO Analyst responsibilities include:

- developing audit plans;
- gathering, assembling, and analyzing information;
- assessing program effectiveness;
- writing GAO reports;
- developing program recommendations; and
- follow-up implementation of their recommendations.

GAO Analysts frequently work closely with GAO attorneys assigned to the audit team. Almost 70 percent of the GAO professional staff consists of GAO Analysts, a number of whom are attorneys.

International Trade Specialist

International Trade Specialists are becoming increasingly important and prominent in U.S. government decision-making, thanks to a shrinking world, the gargantuan trade deficit with our trading partners—in 1990 our trade deficit with China was $5 billion a year; now it is $5 billion a week—and the importance to our economic well-being of our trade relationships.

The duties and responsibilities of the position are quite varied, and may include:

- Analyzing and interpreting international trade issues, conditions, or events in support of decision-making, policy formulation, or program development activities of government or industry executives concerned with the U.S. position in world trade.
- Analyzing foreign market characteristics, domestic industry conditions, and trade patterns in specific commodities to support negotiation and/or administration of bilateral or multilateral international trade agreements.
- Monitoring, investigating, and analyzing import/export data and information to document adherence by U.S. trading partners to trade agreements, tariff provisions, court-ordered import limitations, or other established import controls.

- Advising and assisting businesses involved in, or seeking involvement in, export of goods and services to foreign countries.
- Engaging in international marketing or performing international market research.
- Designing strategies for overcoming competition or market entry barriers in overseas markets.
- Developing and analyzing international trade data and information.
- Assisting state or local governments, chambers of commerce, or trade associations in trade promotion activities.

International Trade Specialists are found in the Department of Commerce, the Office of the United States Trade Representative, the Trade and Development Agency, and the International Trade Commission.

Legislative Assistant

Several thousand Legislative Assistants (LAs) work directly for Members of Congress on Capitol Hill in Washington, D.C. Most are quite young and a substantial minority are law school graduates. The reason for their youth is likely one of compensation. The median salary for LAs in 2010 was just over $40,000.

LA pay can, however, vary widely since it is solely dependent on the whims of the member of Congress for whom the LA works. However, it was capped at around $170,000 in 2010.

Nevertheless, despite the likelihood of a very low salary, young, ambitious, aspiring, and very smart individuals flock to Washington, D.C. every year in search of LA jobs. Most do not stay very long, several years at the most, because they are able to use these positions as stepping stones to careers where their legislative background and Capitol Hill access are viewed as great advantages by prospective employers. Short tenure means considerable turnover, so there are always quite a few of these positions open.

While LA duties may vary from one of the 541 member offices to another, most LAs have the following responsibilities:

- collaborating with the Legislative Director in legislative matters; and
- handling a number of issue areas (as many as five or six) about which he or she briefs the member, helps draft legislation, answers constituent inquiries, and writes position papers for the member.

LA or any other Capitol Hill positions are not usually listed on www.usajobs.gov, the Office of Personnel Management's jobs database. Instead, you can find many of them listed in the following publications:

- *Senate Employment Bulletin*—www.senate.gov/employment/po/positions.htm (free)
- *House of Representatives Employment Opportunities*—www.house.gov/cao-hr/ (free)
- *Roll Call*—www.rcjobs.com (free)
- *Congressional Quarterly Hill Jobs*—http://corporate.cqrollcall.com/ (free)
- *Brad Traverse Group*—www.bradtraverse.com/joblistings.cfm (fee-based subscription)

Foreign Law Specialist

Foreign Law Specialists perform professional work requiring knowledge of law as it is practiced in one or more foreign countries; fulfill Library of Congress objectives, functions, techniques, and services; and the political, economic, and social systems of particular foreign countries. Most positions also require the ability to translate and interpret technical legal material from a foreign language into English and from English into a foreign language. These individuals:

- perform legal research, reference, and writing assignments requiring expert analysis and interpretation of the legal systems of particular foreign countries in terms of Anglo-American law concepts;

- provide definitive advice and assistance to the three branches of government on matters associated with foreign law; and
- provide other specialized services in the acquisition, processing, and custody of foreign legal collections.

Foreign Law Specialists serve as the primary resource for the reference, research, and interpretation of foreign law matters referred to the Library of Congress. They provide advice and assistance to members of Congress, Congressional Committees, government agencies, the U.S. Supreme Court and other courts, and other users on complex legal questions, problems, and issues connected with the law and legal systems of particular foreign countries sharing a certain legal heritage. This information, furnished orally or in writing, may be requested in connection with the formulation of legislation, the preparation of cases by federal lawyers, the adjudication of cases by the courts, the shaping of aspects of foreign policy, or for other purposes.

At the same time, Foreign Law Specialist positions are intimately involved with the development and enhancement of the law library collection in their assigned areas of specialization. They survey the Law Library's collections, noting deficiencies, recommending acquisitions, and making assessments of the value and treatment of published legal materials. They review incoming documents and assure appropriate disposition and technical processing, to make possible rapid and effective reference. They prepare comprehensive bibliographic materials and scholarly publications, and develop other research aids to assist users. Foreign Law Specialists also provide information and reader assistance to a variety of non-government users of the library, including members of the bar, university officials, students, and the general public.

All Foreign Law Specialist jobs are located within the Law Library of Congress in Washington, D.C. There are fewer than 50 such positions in total.

Civil Rights Analyst

Civil Rights Analysts are primarily concerned with planning, conducting, and reporting social science research in the field of civil rights and equal opportunity. The paramount qualification requirements for the position include a broad knowledge of civil rights; ability to apply accepted documentary and field research techniques to study issues and policies affecting civil rights; consulting skill; and strong writing and oral communication skills. Positions typically involve research into specialized technical fields such as voting rights, public accommodations, or equal employment that require specialized knowledge of a subject-matter area in addition to a broad knowledge of civil rights. Analysts research and advise government officials on civil rights laws and policies.

Civil Rights Analyst positions vary according to the nature of the program area they investigate, or the policies they study. Some positions are concerned with particular social or economic activities, such as education, housing, or employment, or combinations of these areas. Some positions focus on researching the civil rights problems of certain classes such as the disabled, veterans, women, or others. Other positions involve the study of broad civil rights issues or problems from a legal, economic, or historical perspective.

Civil Rights Analysts work for the Commission on Civil Rights as well as many other agencies, usually in their Equal Opportunity offices.

Political Risk Insurance Analyst

Federal Political Risk Insurance Analysts (Political Risk Analysts) all work for the Overseas Private Investment Corporation (OPIC). Don't let the name fool you. OPIC is a federal agency that helps U.S. businesses invest overseas, fosters economic development in new and emerging markets, and complements the private sector in managing risks associated with foreign direct investment—which is where Political Risk Insurance Analysts come in. OPIC charges market-based fees for its products and thus operates on a self-sustaining basis at no net cost to taxpayers.

"Political risk" refers to the possibility that investors could lose their entire investment or earn less than expected due to political decisions, conditions, or events occurring in the country in which they are investing. Factors contributing to such losses include government instability, currency inconvertibility, nationalization, and expropriation. Political Risk Analysts examine all of these potentialities as well as societal matters, such as crime levels (kidnappings play a major role, for example, in some countries) and other possible problem areas in evaluating the level of risk associated with a foreign investment.

Globalization and the rapid increase in cross-border transactions have increased dramatically in recent years, which in turn have increased the importance of political risk analysis and insurance.

A law degree is a good basis for this kind of position. Excellent research, analysis, and writing skills are essential, as is being well-informed about world affairs. Language skills can also be a plus if you focus on a specific region. Facility with numbers, more specifically the ability to read and understand financial statements, is also useful.

A job with OPIC is also a great platform for private sector moves into any number of institutions—banks, rating agencies, consulting firms, international organizations, etc.—that perform similar political risk functions.

Technical Writer-Editor (Legal)

These positions involve writing or editing technical materials, such as reports of research findings; news releases and periodicals; regulations in technical areas; technical manuals, specifications, brochures, and pamphlets; or speeches or scripts on legal subjects. Technical writers and technical editors draw on a substantial knowledge of a particular subject-matter area, such as law. The work involves the development of information and analysis to select and present information on the specialized subject in a form and at a level suitable for the intended audience.

Technical writers and technical editors apply writing or editing skills and substantial knowledge of the basic principles and specialized vocabulary of law to the accurate communication of legal developments to expert and other interested audiences. These positions are usually found in government activities that sponsor or perform legal research, conduct investigations, or carry out legal operations. Those engaged in such activities ordinarily disseminate their findings and decisions to the administrative and policy-making community, those who might apply the information, and the general public.

In addition, they articulate agency policies and explain technical aspects of agency programs to those affected. The materials they present explain legal information in such a way as to make it clear without sacrificing thoroughness and accuracy.

Technical writers and editors may manage individual or serial publications from initial conception and content determination through distribution and coordinate the activities of other publishing personnel. They often review proposed publications for style, design, layout, and editorial aspects before release.

Technical writers also prepare original legal papers, articles, or reports based on research or interviews with experts and program officials. They prepare manuscripts developed by others for publication by making sure the material conveys what it was intended to say, is arranged logically, presents the facts to support the conclusions drawn, is in accordance with agency policy, and is written clearly and interestingly for the intended audience.

Technical editors may also combine the writings of committees into single coherent works, or prepare abstracts of technical reports. They may edit for clarity manuals and specifications prepared by others, including contractors. Technical editors (1) advise and assist authors during the writing stage; (2) verify the information; (3) examine the organization, length, and tone of the material; (4) edit the text for clarity and accuracy; (5) consult on design and graphics; and (6) prepare material for printing. They consider policy implications and apply a consistent set of style, grammar, and punctuation practices to manuscripts. They sometimes plan, manage, edit, and approve writing performed under contract.

Analyst in Social Legislation (Social Science Research Analyst)

This position encompasses policy positions in numerous diverse subject areas, many with a strong legal component. Analysts develop, review, and comment on policy options with respect to numerous government programs. They also undertake analytical studies of existing or emerging policies, legislation, and regulatory initiatives upon which managers and decision-makers, including members of Congress, rely.

A behavioral social science degree in addition to a law degree is a competitive advantage.

The government employs several hundred such analysts. Approximately 75 percent work in the Washington, D.C. area. The rest work in government field offices around the country, though a handful are employed overseas. The leading employers are the Congressional Research Service, the Centers for Medicare and Medicaid Services (part of the Department of Health and Human Services), Department of the Army, Department of Justice, Department of Veterans Affairs, Government Accountability Office and Department of Education.

Legislative Affairs Positions

These positions can be found in virtually every U.S. government agency and many of their subordinate units, usually in a Congressional Affairs or Legislative Affairs office. Principal duties include:

- Drafting and coordinating review of testimony for agency witnesses at congressional hearings. Preparing briefing materials and briefing witnesses on laws, regulations, policies, technical issues, and political dimensions related to congressional hearings.
- Preparing and coordinating agency responses to post-hearing questions for the record.
- Coordinating briefings for and furnishing information/data to members of Congress and their staffs on agency programs, policies and decisions.
- Analyzing and coordinating the development of agency comments on legislation that may impact the agency.
- Keeping agency officials apprised of congressional action.
- Responding to legislative drafting service requests.
- Establishing and maintaining effective working relationships with congressional staff, ensuring an effective interchange of information between key members of Congress and staff and the agency.

- Analyzing legislation, policy documents, or reports.
- Writing complex policy statements.

Do not limit yourself to looking for just one job title. This same position may be called something different from one agency or office to another. Alternate titles include Legislative Affairs Specialist, Legislative Analyst, or Congressional Affairs Officer.

Foreign Affairs Specialist

Foreign Affairs Specialists advise on, administer, perform research, or undertake other professional work in the formulation and direction of U.S. government foreign affairs and international relations. Law studies—especially international law—are considered a strong background and qualification for this kind of work. These are not foreign service positions.

Several thousand Foreign Affairs Specialists primarily work for the Departments of State and Defense.

Chapter 65

"Hidden" Law-Related Jobs—Transactional Positions

Government Contract and Procurement Positions

Government contract and procurement professionals are found everywhere in the U.S. government because every single federal agency buys goods and services. The positions are huge in number and peopled by thousands of attorneys. They are most numerous in agencies that purchase the most products, including the Departments of Defense, Energy, Homeland Security, and Veterans Affairs, the General Services Administration, and NASA.

In FY 2009, the government spent $538 billion on more than 454,000 contracts. Since FY 2000, government contracting expenditures have increased by more than 150 percent. Both the number of contracts and contracting and procurement professionals have similarly increased, driven higher by the response to the terrorist attacks of September 11, 2001, two wars, a vast expansion of overseas military commitments, the Great Recession, and a step up in federal regulatory activity.

Contracting and procurement positions are always available, and usually are recruited at every grade level from entry-level to senior executive service (SES). As I write this chapter, there are 216 such positions open to outside candidates listed on www.usajobs.gov. More than 100 are at the entry level.

Federal contracting and procurement professionals manage, supervise, perform, or develop policies and procedures for contracting with vendors. The work requires professional knowledge of the legislation, regulations, and methods used in contracting as well as knowledge of business and industry practices, sources of supply, cost factor, and requirements characteristics. The work involves:

- procurement of supplies, services, construction, or research and development using formal advertising or negotiation procedures;
- evaluation of contract price proposals; and
- administration or termination and close-out of contracts.

Specific duties may include:

(1) soliciting, evaluating, negotiating, and awarding contracts with commercial organizations, educational institutions, nonprofit organizations, and state, local, or foreign governments for furnishing products, services, construction, or research and development to the government;

(2) administering contracts by assuring compliance with the terms and conditions of contracts, including resolution of problems concerning the obligations of the parties;

(3) terminating contracts by analyzing, negotiating, and settling claims and proposals;

(4) analyzing and evaluating cost or price proposals and accounting systems data;

(5) planning, establishing, or reviewing contracts, programs, policies, or procedures;

(6) formulating and administering policies and procedures to insure achievement of federal socioeconomic goals, such as those affecting small business, labor surplus areas, and disadvantaged business firms;

(7) developing acquisition strategies and directing or managing procurements; and

(8) providing staff advisory services.

Look for the following job titles:

* Contract Specialist
* Contract Administrator
* Procurement Analyst
* Contract Negotiator
* Contract Termination Specialist

Technology Transfer Professional

Technology Transfer Professionals, sometimes called Technology Licensing Officers or Technology Commercialization Officers or Specialists, work in federal agencies that create innovation and wish to transfer their creations to the private sector. They are found throughout government in the Departments of Agriculture, Commerce, Defense, Energy, Health and Human Services, Homeland Security, Justice, Transportation, and Veterans Affairs, NASA, the National Institutes of Health, EPA, and in numerous federal research laboratories around the country.

The Stevenson-Wydler Technology Innovation Act of 1980, Pub. L. 96-480, is the basic federal technology transfer law. Stevenson-Wydler required agencies to establish Offices of Research and Technology Applications (ORTAs) at their federal laboratories, and to devote a percentage of their R&D budgets to technology transfer. The act also established rules for protecting and licensing federally owned inventions. The act established two principal government policies. First, that agencies should ensure the full use of the results of the nation's federal investment in R&D. Second, that the government should strive, wherever appropriate, to transfer federally owned or originated technology to both state and local governments and to the private sector.

In 1986, the Federal Technology Transfer Act, Pub. L. 99-502, amended Stevenson-Wydler. It authorized cooperative R&D agreements (CRADAs) between federal laboratories and nonfederal entities, award programs for federal employees who were responsible for inventions and required royalty sharing with them whenever an agency retains ownership, and directed agencies to allow employees to patent inventions when the agencies themselves do not patent or otherwise promote commercialization.

Technology transfer is a growing governmental function and thus, the number of positions for Technology Transfer Professionals is growing. The National Institute of Standards and Technology reported in 2010 that between 2004 and 2008 the number of licenses jumped to 11,098, an increase of 46.6 percent, and the number of income-bearing licenses increased to 6,444, a 35 percent rise. Federal revenues from these licenses grew to $170.9 million, a 71.7 percent jump, and total earned royalty income reached $117.6 million, a 121.5 percent gain. The total number of patent applications submitted by internal research programs among 11 agencies that conduct research and development rose to 1,938, an increase of 9.6 percent.

Technology Transfer Professionals monitor the research and invention activity in their organizations, evaluate them for their commercial potential, seek intellectual property protection for agency innovations, market these to the private sector, develop licensing plans, draft and negotiate licensing agreements, and train agency staff in intellectual property protection and licensing.

You do not necessarily need a science, engineering, or other technological background to obtain a technology transfer job with the government. Licensing knowledge or experience and marketing ability are central to the function.

Competition Advocate

Section 20 of the Office of Federal Procurement Policy Act, 41 U.S.C. 403 et seq., directs the head of each executive agency to designate a Competition Advocate for the agency and for each procuring activity of the agency. Competition Advocates are independent of each agency's senior procurement executive and have the following mission:

- promoting the acquisition of commercial items;
- promoting full and open competition;
- challenging requirements that are not stated in terms of functions to be performed, performance required or essential physical characteristics; and

- challenging barriers to the acquisition of commercial items and full and open competition such as unnecessarily restrictive statements of work, unnecessarily detailed specifications, and unnecessarily burdensome contract clauses.

Their specific duties include:

(1) Reviewing agency contracting operations and identifying and reporting to the agency senior procurement executive and the chief acquisition officer regarding their opportunities and actions they took to achieve their mission goals.

(2) Preparing and submitting an annual report to the agency senior procurement executive and the chief acquisition officer in accordance with agency procedures, describing—
    (i)   their advocacy activities;
    (ii)   new initiatives required to increase the acquisition of commercial items;
    (iii) new initiatives required to increase competition;
    (iv)   new initiatives to ensure requirements are stated in terms of functions to be performed, performance required, or essential physical characteristics;
    (v)   any barriers to the acquisition of commercial items or competition that remain;
    (vi)   other ways in which the agency has emphasized the acquisition of commercial items and competition in areas such as acquisition training and research; and
    (vii) initiatives that ensure task and delivery orders over $1,000,000 issued under multiple award contracts are properly planned, issued, and in compliance with law and regulation.

(3) Recommending goals and plans for increasing competition on a fiscal year basis to the agency senior procurement executive and the chief acquisition officer.

(4) Recommending to the agency senior procurement executive and the chief acquisition officer a system of personal and organizational accountability for competition, which may include the use of recognition and awards to motivate program managers, contracting officers, and others in authority to promote competition in acquisition.

Many Competition Advocates are attorneys. Knowledge of, or experience with, antitrust law and policies is highly valued.

Patent Adviser

The significant difference between Patent Attorneys and Patent Advisers is that Patent Attorneys are required to be members of the bar, while Patent Advisers are not. Otherwise, Patent Advisers do work that is very similar to that of Patent Attorneys.

Patent Advisers primarily work for federal agencies that are attempting to secure patent protection for their inventions with the U.S. Patent and Trademark Office (USPTO). Their duties involve professional scientific or engineering work, and, in addition, legal work pertaining to the analysis of inventions and the evaluation of their patentability. This entails preparing and prosecuting applications for patents; preparing and presenting briefs and arguments and prosecuting appeals and interferences before the USPTO; making infringement investigations; and rendering opinions on the validity of patents, in order to protect the government's interest in such inventions.

The entry-level job title is "Patent Adviser." After gaining some experience, Patent Advisers specialize in one scientific or technical field and have a parenthetical added to their job title indicating their specialty area, such as chemistry, chemical engineering, electrical engineering, electronic engineering, mechanical engineering, or physics. If they opt not to specialize, the added appellation reads "General."

There is a discrete dividing line between the basic functions of entry-level Patent Advisers and the more advanced functions that experienced Patent Advisers are expected to perform. Basic functions include:

- Evaluating the potential invention, which requires reviewing applications documents and drawings for completeness and clarity; securing any additional required information through interviewing or corresponding with the inventor; evaluating the scientific significance and/or potential importance to the government of the invention by applying his or her knowledge of the technology involved and of the current or planned scientific programs of his or her agency; and making recommendations as to the desirability of seeking patent protection for the invention.

- Conducting patentability searches and rendering opinions on potential patentability. This can be quite an elaborate and complicated process because the Patent Adviser has to plan the field of search, which means studying the invention in detail to identify those points of novelty for which a patent is to be sought; selecting references that are most analogous to the invention and making a detailed comparison of the structure or function described in each reference, with those embodied in the invention in order to: (1) determine the specific points of similarity or difference; (2) decide whether the invention is anticipated by the prior art; and (3) render an opinion or report on the potential patentability of the invention.
- Writing patent applications.
- Determining who is the inventor. In cases where invention arises out of group effort, the identification of the "true" inventor or inventors is not always clear. This requires the patent adviser to make a full investigation of the circumstances surrounding the making of the invention by (1) studying laboratory notebooks and similar documents; (2) interviewing members of the group and others associated with the work; and (3) reconstructing the history of the making of the invention to determine who, in the legal sense, is the "true" inventor.

Advanced Patent Adviser functions include:

- Pursuing prosecution of patent applications, which entails arguing for reconsideration when a patent application is rejected and preparing responses to USPTO actions.
- Conducting infringement investigations when a patent holder alleges that the agency is infringing his or her patent.
- Conducting infringement and validity searches when infringement has been found to exist, or when there is reason

to believe that a proposed new device or process may infringe an existing patent.

- Drafting preliminary statements in interferences, which may involve (1) preparing and filing motions to amend or dissolve the interference, including a statement of the requested action, the facts supporting the request, and the reasons the request should be granted, supported by citations of the applicable law and pertinent legal precedents; (2) preparing responses to briefs filed by other parties in the interference; (3) pleading motions before the USPTO interference examiner; (4) examining and cross-examining witnesses in the taking of testimony; and (5) presenting oral arguments before the USPTO Board of Interference Examiners.
- Identifying unreported inventions in order to secure reports of invention and determine who will file the patent application.
- Determining rights to title to inventions.

Chapter 66

"Hidden" Law-Related Positions—Other Positions

Employee Relations Specialist

Employee Relations Specialists are essentially tasked with working with supervisors and employees in preventing and resolving problems of individual relationships that arise out of or affect work situations. A considerable amount of employee and supervisor counseling is involved in the job. Employee Relations Specialists also work with and provide advice to supervisors and employees regarding matters of communication, rights, grievances, appeals, and the like; and regarding actions useful in building constructive relationships in the workplace.

In the majority of situations, Employee Relations Specialists advise supervisors on methods of dealing with poor work performance or behavior problems. They inform them regarding regulatory and other requirements to be considered in effecting disciplinary actions, removals, suspensions, resolving grievances, and appeals. They assist supervisors in correcting individual instances of work deficiencies and poor performance by subordinates.

Employee Relations Specialists offer information to employees regarding their rights and obligations provided for in regulations, legislation, and merit-system principles (e.g., grievances and appeals, and protection from discrimination). They also counsel employees concerning their rights and entitlement to employee benefits (e.g., health benefits, life insurance, and retirement) and assist employees or survivors of employees in filing claims for benefits or in resolving disputed claims with carriers.

There are two basic approaches for employee relations activities. On the "micro" level, Employee Relations Specialists are concerned primarily with the analysis and resolution of specific individual problems or cases (case analysis). The "macro" level is concerned with analyzing the underlying forces and practices that cause employee relations problems in order to recommend corrective measures to eliminate the source of problems (situation analysis).

The federal government employs more than 2,000 Employee Relations Specialists. Over two-thirds of them work outside of the Washington, D.C. area in field offices nationwide. They can be found throughout the federal government.

Labor Relations Specialist

There are more than 1,000 Labor Relations Specialists working for the U.S. government. This may sound counterintuitive given the overall decline of the labor movement in the United States. However, public employee unions are still thriving and now represent almost one-third of all federal workers (versus only 12 percent for all U.S. workers).

Federal employee unions are very influential, which makes the job of federal Labor Relations Specialists that much more important. Almost every federal agency employs them and they are roughly evenly split between those who work in the Washington, DC area and those who work elsewhere.

Labor Relations Specialists perform the following functions:

(1) establishing and maintaining effective relationships with labor organizations that represent federal employees;
(2) negotiating and administering labor agreements and otherwise conferring with labor organizations on behalf of management; and

(3) providing guidance, consultation, and staff assistance to management on a variety of labor relations matters.

Some Labor Relations Specialists are involved in government-wide administration of the federal labor relations program from the perspectives of policy development, agency guidance, and investigation and resolution of certain complaints and appeals. Others may advise management on grievances and appeals, adverse actions, employee discipline, and related matters.

Legal education and experience are a strong background for Labor Relations Specialist positions and a substantial number of Specialists are, in fact, attorneys.

Miscellaneous Administration and Program Positions

I saved this "cats-and-dogs" category for last, but do not take that to mean that it is not as important as the law-related job titles that came before. In fact, it may well be the most important job title of all for attorneys seeking a law-related position in the U.S. government.

Mark the following job classification series number down somewhere important: "0301." Remember the discussion of the attorney job series classification number—"0905"—in Chapter 23 (see also, Glossary)? The number 0301 is the second most important one that you need to know concerning federal legal employment. More attorneys carry around this number than any except 0905.

The number 0301 is used by federal agencies when they don't have any other suitable series in which to place a position. It also comes into play when they come up with an interesting and fairly unique, agency-specific job title that does not quite fit anywhere else.

This series, for example, encompasses virtually every Policy Analyst position in the federal government. The dream of many of my legal career counseling clients is to find a policy position in which they can use their law degrees. The federal government is, by far, the largest employer of such individuals. Policy positions are everywhere, ranging from agriculture to zoning and everything in between.

Classification number 0301 also includes the vast majority of Risk Managers in the U.S. government. The federal government was slow to realize the value of risk management, but now that it does, it is hiring risk managers throughout the federal system. This is good news for attorneys, since approximately 20-25 percent of all risk managers in the U.S. have a law degree.

Currently, more than 50,000 federal employees work under the 0301 series. In addition to the interesting law-related job titles above, 0301 also includes Alternative Dispute Resolution Specialists who work in more than 80 federal agencies, Bankruptcy Examiners and Analysts who work for the Justice Department's Offices of the United States Trustee throughout the country, Regulatory Impact Analysts who are employed government-wide, and Veterans Reemployment Rights Specialists at the Department of Labor, among other job titles.

What all of this means for you, the candidate, is that you need to take stock of all advertised federal positions that carry the 0301 designation. You never know what you might find under that number.

Chapter 67

Great Places to Work— Overview and Health Regulation

Overview

As indicated at the beginning of this Part, I am going to conclude with my recommendations of federal legal and law-related offices that have come to my attention in the course of both my own legal career as a federal attorney, legal consultant to a variety of federal agencies, and federal contractor, as well as feedback from my legal career transition counseling clients who work (or worked) in great offices that left them with good feelings. A third determinative factor that contributes to which offices made it into this part is whether an organization can serve as a great platform for future career success in or out of government.

Let me repeat once again that this does not mean that offices not mentioned are never great places to work, too. Since there are 3,000-plus separate U.S. government law offices, as well as many offices where attorneys work in both legal and law-related positions, only a select few are discussed. They are presented below in no particular order.

You will see that some of the great places to work are entire agencies, while others are specific offices within an agency. The Food and Drug Administration and the Nuclear Regulatory Commission, for example, qualify as great places across all of their offices in which attorneys work. The Securities and Exchange Commission, in contrast, is represented only by its Enforcement Division.

The subject headings I have selected in order to group these agencies and offices are somewhat arbitrary, the overriding factor being to come up with a reasonable organizing scheme designed for readability. Certain organizations could just as easily fit into one category as another. The Securities and Exchange Commission's Enforcement Division, for example, can be found under Consumer Protection. However, it could just as easily have been grouped under Economic Regulation.

Health Regulation

Office of Research Integrity—Department of Health and Human Services
www.hhs.gov/ogc and http://ori.dhhs.gov/

The rather obscure Office of Research Integrity (ORI) in the U.S Department of Health and Human Services promotes biomedical and behavioral research integrity at about 4,000 institutions worldwide. ORI monitors institutional investigations of research misconduct. Attorneys in the Research Integrity Branch advise ORI and represent it before the Departmental Appeals Board in research integrity cases. The work is highly interesting and is expanding with the increase in the volume of federal research grants and the intense competition for them, which sometimes causes corner-cutting on the part of grantees. Until his retirement in late 2009, ORI was headed by an attorney. As this book goes to press, the position is still open.

In addition to research misconduct, ORI handles a variety of related issues, including those arising in the following contexts: conflicts of interest, data management, intellectual property, international, laboratory management, mentoring relationships, publication practices and authorship, and various others. ORI also provides research integrity education and training to researchers.

Food and Drug Administration
www.fda.gov

Severely underfunded, understaffed and overwhelmed by (1) the barrage of new drug approval applications filed with it, (2) the quantum leaps in medical technology and innovation, as well as (3) new and escalating threats of food contamination, the Food and Drug Administration (FDA) in the first decade of the twenty-first century fell far behind in its attempts to fulfill its mission of protecting the public health and was accused by its critics of having knuckled under to political and ideological considerations. That has now changed.

FDA attorneys work at the confluence of law, science, technology, and medicine at a time in history when that nexus has never been more important or central to the lives of Americans. The products that it monitors—food, drugs, cosmetics, medical devices, blood supply—account for more than 25 percent of all consumer spending. Consequently, the agency's legal responsibilities are both large and very often cutting-edge.

At the same time, the demands on the FDA are steadily increasing. Food and drug law practice involves a broad spectrum of legal and regulatory activities. The dynamism of food, drug, device, and related industries makes food and drug law practice an exciting career in which you will be daily involved in one of the most critical responsibilities of government. From implementing the FDA's new authority over tobacco products (via the Family Smoking Prevention and Control Act, Pub. L. 111-31); keeping pace with regulation of the entire food supply in an attempt to keep up with the increasing number of new food pathogens, chemical contamination, the exploding number and diversity of food products and processes; and the enormous increase in imported foods, determining how to handle approvals of exotic new therapies such as combination products, to wrestling with balancing pharmaceutical product patent protection against poor country access to essential medicines, this is a practice that gets legal pulses racing at every turn.

One example of the enormous challenges confronting FDA is coping with its responsibility for ensuring the safety of roughly 80 percent of the U.S. food supply, including $417 billion worth of domestic food and $49 billion in imported food annually (and climbing rapidly), factoring in changing demographics and consumption patterns, an increase in imports, and loss of consumer confidence in the safety of the food supply due to recent outbreaks such as E. coli from spinach and Salmonella from tomatoes. The increasing complexity of food and drug regulation is now such that it is no longer mandatory that you have a food and drug law background in order to practice law at the FDA. While that is certainly a huge advantage, it is not absolutely essential. FDA has recently hired a substantial number of "Regulatory Counsel" who lacked any background in food and drug law.

FDA attorneys work in multiple agency offices, including Office of the Chief Counsel, Office of Regulatory Affairs, Center for Food Safety and Applied Nutrition, Center for Biologics Evaluation and Research, Center for Devices and Radiological Health, and Center for Drug Evaluation and Research.

Office of Counsel to the Inspector General—Department of Health and Human Services

www.oig.hhs.gov/organization/ocig

This largest and most aggressive Inspector General legal counsel office of all the 37 in the U.S. government is only going to get larger and more aggressive in its pursuit and recovery of Medicare fraud. Even before the health-care reform legislation armed it with greater authority to go after Medicare defrauders, its more than 80 attorneys were already recouping over $2 billion per year at a taxpayer expense of only $165 million, one of the best returns on investment in all of government. Given (1) annual budget deficits in the trillions, (2) a national debt that is through the roof and unsustainable, and (3) estimates of annual Medicare fraud of up to $70 billion, the IG Counsel's Office can only grow larger.

The attorneys in this office participate in fraud investigations, prosecute civil penalty cases before departmental tribunals, and work with the Criminal Division of the Justice Department to prosecute and punish Medicare defrauders. If tangible results of your legal efforts combined with feelings of accomplishment and satisfaction that you do something meaningful that advances society mean a lot to you, the Office of Counsel is a great place to work.

Office of General Counsel—Centers for Disease Control and Prevention (CDC)

www.cdc.gov

This office is another one with a practice portfolio that contributes significantly to the national well-being. At a time when public health is threatened with new and mutant pathogens with increasing frequency, the CDC and its legal component are more important than ever. The CDC is America's first line of defense against virulent infectious diseases that now cross borders with increasing ease and ominous portents for American health. Whether it is swine flu, SARS, flesh-eating bacteria, bioterrorism, or microbes increasingly resistant to antibiotics, the CDC is there, supported by its legal staff.

The legal work is both interesting and dynamic, changing with the threats and their origins. Public health law is an emerging practice that is becoming increasingly important. CDC established its Public Health Law Program (PHLP) in 2000 with a mission of improving the public's health through law. The PHLP's primary goals are to enhance the public health system's legal preparedness to address emerging threats, chronic diseases, and other national public health priorities and to improve use of law to support program activities.

The issues CDC attorneys handle include research contracts and grants, international agreements, and intellectual property, among others. The office has 20-plus attorneys based in Atlanta and Washington, D.C.

Office of Medicare Hearings and Appeals (OMHA)

www.hhs.gov/omha/

One of the newest federal legal offices, OMHA was established as a consequence of the Medicare Prescription Drug, Improvement, and Modernization Act of 2003, Pub. L. 108-173, to simplify the appeals process and make it more efficient. The Prescription Drug

Act, which added a new Part D to Medicare coverage for prescription drugs, upped the number of cases before OMHA substantially.

There are five levels in the Medicare claims appeal process. OMHA's administrative law judges (ALJs) hold hearings and issue decisions related to Medicare coverage determinations that reach Level 3 of the Medicare claims appeal process. OMHA also hears certain other Medicare appeals, including Medicare entitlement appeals.

OMHA has a headquarters office in Arlington, Virginia, as well as four field offices: Arlington; Miami, Florida; Cleveland, Ohio; and Irvine, California. It is currently staffed by 66 ALJs and a larger number of staff attorneys.

What makes OMHA's work interesting is its relative newness combined with the unknown territory spawned by the Patient Protection and Affordable Care Act (health-care reform), Pub. L. 111-140, which will take years to implement and "stabilize." OMHA attorneys and ALJs are likely to be heavily involved in sorting out the new law's mandates, turning policy into law, crafting settled law, and dealing with the act's unintended consequences.

Chapter 68

Great Places to Work— Intellectual Property and Transactions

Office of the Deputy Commissioner for Trademark Operations
www.uspto.gov

In addition to the intense immersion in trademark law that provides a very solid basis for career advancement, the biggest advantage of this office is its incredibly flexible work schedule, consisting of telecommuting opportunities unmatched anywhere else in government and perhaps anywhere outside of government as well. Approximately 400 attorneys work in this office.

Duties of trademark examining attorneys include:

- examining domestic and foreign trademark applications for statutory, regulatory, and treaty compliance;
- conducting detailed searches to ensure applications, if approved, would not impinge on existing intellectual property rights of others or harm the public;
- creating original statements of goods and services, based on application information, capable of registration;
- gathering and evaluating evidence supporting substantive refusals of applications;

- conducting legal research and drafting the office's position refusing registration, and evaluating applicants' arguments and supporting evidence in favor of registration; and
- advising and counseling applicants to help to resolve bars to registration and clarify prosecution issues.

They also represent the office in cases before the Trademark Trial and Appeals Board.

Legal Division—Air Force Real Property Agency
www.safie. hq.af.mil/afrpa/index.asp

The two military base-closing initiatives of recent years gave rise to this agency and law office and its counterparts in the sister armed services. While each specialized agency works at the nexus of real estate and environmental law toward the goal of transferring closed bases to states, municipalities, and private uses, the Air Force version is the most interesting because the issues it handles are the most complex, controversial, and vexing of all of those involved with closing down military facilities. It operates within a legal realm where cases of first impression arise daily.

Until the enactment of the Federal Facility Compliance Act of 1992, Pub. L. 102-386, military bases were not covered by the Resource Conservation and Recovery Act (RCRA), Pub. L. 94-580, which regulates solid and hazardous waste disposal. The 1992 act greatly complicated the disposition of military bases scheduled to be closed by the government, with Air Force bases posing a particular problem due to many years of buried jet fuel in storage tanks of dubious integrity.

Moreover, disposing of bases is a very long-term process, not only because of environmental concerns, but because many such facilities are huge and border on multiple jurisdictions as well as private interests. This makes the work of legal division attorneys that much more interesting.

Office of Technology Transfer—National Institutes of Health
www.ott.nih.gov/index.aspx

The Office of Technology Transfer evaluates, protects, monitors, and manages the National Institutes of Health (NIH) invention portfolio.

This is largely accomplished through overseeing patent prosecution, negotiating and monitoring licensing agreements, and providing oversight and central policy review of Cooperative Research and Development Agreements (CRADAs), which make federal facilities, intellectual property, and expertise available for private sector collaboration to further the development of scientific and technological knowledge into useful, marketable products.

The office also manages the patent and licensing activities for the Food and Drug Administration (FDA), and is responsible for the central development and implementation of technology transfer policies for four research components of the Public Health Service—NIH, the FDA, the Centers for Disease Control and Prevention, and the Agency for Healthcare Research and Quality. The office has a small legal staff comprised primarily of intellectual property attorneys.

Department of Legal Affairs—Overseas Private Investment Corporation
www.opic.gov

What makes the Overseas Private Investment Corporation (OPIC) interesting goes beyond its principal mission of helping U.S. businesses invest overseas while fostering economic development in new and emerging markets. In addition, OPIC does something completely unique in government—it attempts to manage the risks associated with foreign direct investment. It does this by providing "political risk insurance" against such eventualities as nationalization of U.S. businesses or assets by foreign governments.

OPIC political-risk insurance is available to U.S. investors, contractors, exporters, and financial institutions involved in international transactions. It can cover currency inconvertibility, expropriation, and political violence, and is available for investments in new ventures, expansions of existing enterprises, privatizations, and acquisitions with positive developmental benefits. Another benefit of such insurance is that its availability can assist U.S. businesses in obtaining financing for certain foreign investment ventures. Political risk insurance is backed by the full faith and credit of the U.S. government.

Like some federal financial regulatory agencies and the U.S. Patent and Trademark Office, OPIC charges market-based fees for its products, thus operating on a self-sustaining basis at no net cost to taxpayers. OPIC services currently support U.S. investment in more than 150 countries worldwide.

Smithsonian Institution

www.si.edu

I once participated in a panel alongside the Smithsonian Institution's general counsel. Exchanging information about the workings of that unusual, hybrid organization (the Smithsonian is half government, half trust) and its interesting legal work was a riveting experience, one borne out several years later when one of my counseling clients wound up there and began to enjoy a fascinating federal legal career.

In 1826, British scientist James Smithson made the U.S. a successor beneficiary in his will, directing that if his nephew died without heirs (he did), his estate should go to the U.S. "to found at Washington, under the name of the Smithsonian Institution, an establishment for the increase and diffusion of knowledge among men." The strangest thing about the Smithson bequest was that he had never been to this country, nor did he know anyone here.

Congress accepted the $500,000 legacy in 1836 and 10 years later established the Smithsonian Institution as a trust to be administered by a Board of Regents and a Secretary of the Smithsonian.

The Office of the General Counsel (OGC) provides legal advice and counsel to the Board of Regents, secretary, and other Smithsonian staff on various issues including the legal nature and administration of the institution, intellectual property, employment, collections management, contracts, ethics, tax, tort claims, media/TV/film, trusts, gifts and estates, and the Freedom of Information Act, etc. OGC also represents the Smithsonian in litigation and other adversarial proceedings to which the institution is a party and before federal, state, and local government entities on administrative matters; issues final determinations on administrative tort and personal property claims against the Smithsonian; and generally monitors developments in the law for application to Smithsonian programs.

From negotiating with representatives of prominent politicians who want to donate their papers to the Smithsonian and secure a tax benefit from the donation to transacting with multiple foreign museums in order to put together an exhibition and insure it, the work is never dull.

Great Places to Work— National Security

Coast Guard Legal Program
www.uscg.mil/legal/

The reason for including this function has less to do with the nature of the work than it does the culture of Coast Guard legal offices. Coast Guard military and civilian attorneys get the highest marks for professionalism, integrity, efficiency, and general "niceness."

Military Judge Advocate Generals' Corps
www.goarmy.com/jag;www.jag.navy.mil; and
www.jagusaf.hq.af.mil/

Military legal branches were discussed in some detail in Chapter 29, but let me just go over the attractive features of this career path, especially for new law graduates or attorneys who are in the early years of their careers.

- strong legal training, especially in criminal law and litigation, government contract law, and international law;
- early responsibility;
- postings all over the world;

- litigation experience under the Federal Rules of Evidence and the Federal Rules of Criminal Procedure; and
- one of the most effective alumni networks extant.

Office of General Counsel—Department of Defense
www.dod.mil/dodgc

This small, low-profile federal law office handles some of the most important legal matters to come before government. Throughout its history, the office has never had more than 30 attorneys, a number that surprises everyone who contemplates the immensity of the Defense Department and its wide range of responsibilities, both functionally and geographically.

Consequently, attorneys have considerable responsibility and autonomy for issues involving hundreds of billions of dollars and hundreds of thousands of lives. Every Secretary of Defense relies heavily on their advice, evidenced most strikingly by the fact that the office is located just down the hall from the Secretary's office in the powerful E-Ring of the Pentagon. This highly professional office becomes deeply involved in some of the most sensitive and world-changing policy issues affecting government, and working here can be an exhilarating experience.

Office of General Counsel—Defense Advanced Research and Projects Agency
www.darpa.mil

The Defense Advanced Research and Projects Agency (DARPA) is the Defense Department's research and development office. It is unique among government offices, which translates into a general counsel's office that does some pretty unique work. DARPA's mission is both defensive and offensive. It develops technologies designed to keep our defense forces ahead of any adversaries from a technology standpoint, which means both developing technological countermeasures to potential enemy technologies, and creating technologies designed for technological surprise.

DARPA is primarily a funding mechanism for private sector, academic, other nonprofit organization, and government laboratory R&D. The research encompasses biology, medicine, computer science, chemistry, physics, engineering, mathematics, material sciences, social sciences, neuroscience, and more.

DARPA was established in 1958 as a direct result of the Soviet Union's Sputnik space satellite launch in October 1957. Its incredible range of accomplishments includes the Stealth Bomber, the M-16 rifle, the notion of the personal computer, and—with apologies to Al Gore—the invention of the Internet.

DARPA's general counsel office has been involved in each of these quantum technological leaps and many more. Its principal practice area is government contracting, but not the normal, everyday manifestations of that practice. Instead, the demands of national defense and a technologically advanced military has meant that the general counsel office has had to design innovative ways of securing the necessary R&D that do not always conform to government contracting norms. This, plus the exotic and futuristic nature of DARPA projects, makes this small legal office a great place to work.

Office of General Counsel—Department of Defense Education Activity
www.dodea.edu

Education law is not the exclusive province of the U.S. Department of Education. The other major education law practice exists in the Department of Defense. The Office of General Counsel handles all of the usual functions inherent in an education law practice, including employment matters, procurement, ethics and Standards of Conduct, school operations, fiscal issues, student enrollment eligibility, student discipline, special education, representation of the agency in administrative hearings, federal court litigation, contract negotiations, union arbitrations, and providing advice and counsel to the agency. What makes its practice different is that it is also concerned with both military matters and the administration of a far-flung school system that crosses national borders.

The Department of Defense Education Activity (DoDEA) operates more than 200 public schools in 13 foreign countries, seven states, Guam, and Puerto Rico. All schools within DoDEA are fully accredited by U.S. accreditation agencies. Almost 9,000 teachers serve more than 100,000 students.

In addition to providing ethics training, advice, and counseling for teachers and administrators who are confronted by such questions daily, the office is unique among education law practices in that its attorneys handle sensitive questions of international law arising under various U.S. Status of Forces agreements that govern the U.S. military presence in foreign countries.

The Office of General Counsel has a headquarters office in Washington, D.C. and satellite offices in Georgia, Europe, and Japan.

Nuclear Regulatory Commission
www.nrc.gov

The Nuclear Regulatory Commission (NRC) is an agency whose time has finally come around . . . again. From its post–World War II origins to 1979, the NRC was a vibrant, dynamic organization devoted to regulating nuclear materials, licensing and promoting reactor development and nuclear energy, and nurturing relations with its foreign counterparts, even those behind the Iron Curtain.

Then came Three Mile Island, followed a few years later by Chernobyl, which spelled the death knell for further expansion of nuclear energy in this country. It did not matter that the accident at Three Mile Island resulted from a major control panel design flaw (the relevant warning lights were on the back of the panel because the design contractor ran out of room to put them on the front), or that the Chernobyl reactor that blew up lacked a lead containment shell (which all U.S. reactors must have). The public perception was that nuclear energy was unsafe. Consequently, the NRC did very little for the next 25–30 years, a time frame when no new U.S. nuclear reactors were constructed or licensed. The only interesting legal work during this period resulted from the international information and health effects exchange program the NRC developed in conjunction with its Soviet—later Russian and Ukrainian—counterparts designed to minimize the danger of reactor accidents.

As I write this section, the NRC is emerging from its generation-long hibernation, revived and reinvigorated by the new energy independence reality that makes it impossible any longer to avoid some considerable reliance on nuclear power as we wean ourselves from dependence on foreign oil imports. In February 2010, President Obama announced the availability of federal loan guarantees for nuclear power plant construction, thus putting the NRC back in business. Since then, the agency has been scrambling to hire additional personnel, attorneys included. This is going to make the NRC a good place to work for years to come.

Chapter 70

Great Places to Work—
Economic Regulation

Legal Division—Federal Deposit Insurance Corporation
www.fdic.gov

Like their counterparts in the IG counsel office at the Department
of Health and Human Services (HHS), the very admirable distinguishing features of work in the FDIC Legal Division are positive
outcomes that have meaning and bring satisfaction. The difference
is that, while the HHS lawyers have the good fortune to realize
these pluses every day, they are somewhat more intermittent at the
FDIC.

FDIC attorneys enjoy these rewards most often during financial
crises, when banks are failing and they have to step in and "resolve" them. As this book goes to press, more than 100 banks have
failed in each of the past three years and the exhilarating legal work
involved with resolution has been a constant. FDIC lawyers often
step into the shoes of failed bank "C-level" executives and have
immediate responsibility for every management function, including crisis management. They get to work in relative autonomy and
exercise broad decisional authority.

Office of Chief Counsel—Financial Crimes Enforcement Network— Department of Treasury
www.fincen.gov

The Financial Crimes Enforcement Network (FinCEN) was established in 1990 to provide a government-wide multisource financial intelligence and analysis network. The organization's authority was expanded in 1994 to include regulatory responsibilities for administering the Bank Secrecy Act, Pub. L. 91-508, which authorizes the Secretary of the Treasury to require certain records or reports where they have a high degree of usefulness in criminal, tax, or regulatory investigations or proceedings, or in the conduct of intelligence or counterintelligence activities, including analysis, to protect against international terrorism. This authority has been delegated to the FinCEN Director.

Hundreds of thousands of financial institutions are subject to Bank Secrecy Act reporting and recordkeeping requirements. These include depository institutions (e.g., banks, credit unions, and savings and loan associations); brokers or dealers in securities; insurance companies that issue or underwrite certain products; money services businesses (e.g., money transmitters; issuers, redeemers and sellers of money orders and travelers' checks; check cashers and currency exchangers); casinos and card clubs; and dealers in precious metals, stones, or jewels.

The USA PATRIOT Act of 2001, Pub. L. 107-56, vastly expanded the scope of the Bank Secrecy Act to focus on terrorist financing as well as money laundering, giving FinCEN additional responsibilities and authorities in both areas.

FinCEN lawyers in the Office of Chief Counsel work at the cutting edge of financial crime, in a cat-and-mouse game where one side devises new means of committing criminal or terrorist acts while the other side works to anticipate, deter, and pursue such acts. In addition, FinCEN attorneys get to work closely with foreign counterparts in over 100 countries on global antiterrorism and anti-money-laundering initiatives.

Office of Advocacy—Small Business Administration
www.sba.gov

The Office of Advocacy is an independent voice for small business within the federal government. It is essentially a legal office because it is headed by the presidentially appointed Chief Counsel for Advocacy. The Chief Counsel and his or her staff advance the views, concerns, and interests of small business before Congress, the White House, federal agencies, federal courts, and state policy makers. Regional advocates and the headquarters office in Washington, D.C,, comprise the Office of Advocacy.

Two characteristics make the Office of Advocacy one of the best places for an attorney to work in the federal government:

1. the opportunity to get around in an official capacity to, and to advocate before, virtually the entire U.S. government and many of its senior officials; and
2. immersion in many of the key legal, regulatory and economic issues affecting the country and its economy.

Two of my clients worked in the Office of Advocacy. One was employed at headquarters and had previously worked in a state economic development office. She remained at the Office of Advocacy for five years before moving on to a major legal position with a congressional committee. The second worked in a Regional Advocate office in the Midwest and engaged my office to assist him in parlaying his SBA experience into something in the private sector. This proved easy to do because of the many contacts he had made in his region during his SBA tenure.

Federal Reserve System
www.federalreserve.gov

The Federal Reserve System is the most powerful and important regulator and driver of the American financial system in the entire U.S. government, even more than the President. Attorneys at the "Fed" become involved in all of the critical decisions that its chairman, board of governors, and Federal Open Market Committee must make to keep the economy moving and growing (and conversely, keep it from collapsing). This makes their work both exhilarating and absolutely critical and essential.

Lawyers at the Fed can be found in more than just the Office of the General Counsel. The Fed's 200-plus attorneys also work in the following Fed divisions:

- Office of Board Members
- Office of the Secretary
- Office of Inspector General
- Division of Consumer and Community Affairs
- Division of Banking Supervision and Regulation
- Bureau of Consumer Financial Protection (see Chapter 76)

Chapter 71

Great Places to Work—
International Affairs

Office of General Counsel—Office of the United States Trade
  Representative
  www.ustr.gov

This cabinet-level office in the Executive Office of the President might be the central command post for globalization. The U.S. Trade Representative (USTR) is directly involved in developing and co-ordinating U.S. international trade, commodity, and direct investment policy, and overseeing trade negotiations with other countries and regional organizations. The USTR is the President's principal trade advisor, negotiator, and spokesperson on trade issues, and coordinates trade policy, resolves disagreements, and frames issues for presidential decision.

The legal work is dynamic and diverse, and attorneys in the Office of General Counsel are often directly involved in sensitive international trade negotiations, monitoring foreign government compliance with trade agreements with the United States, and prosecuting and defending cases at the World Trade Organization and U.S. free trade agreement dispute settlement proceedings.

Office of the Legal Adviser—Department of State
   www.state.gov/s/l/

The Office of the Legal Adviser is the only government law office that spells "adviser" this way. That is indicative of its iconoclastic ways, which is what makes it an intriguing place in which to ply your legal talents.

In addition to its spelling quirks, the office is also different in that it is divided into both geographic sections (such as the Office of European Affairs and the Office of Western Hemisphere Affairs) and functional sections (such as the Office of Diplomatic Law and Litigation and the Office of Economic and Business Affairs). Your first inclination might be to assume there must be mass confusion in an organization where regional issues cut across functional lines and functional issues cut across regional lines, but you would be wrong. Somehow, this strange breakdown of responsibilities actually works rather smoothly.

Attorneys in the Office of the Legal Adviser get to work on many "top-of-the-fold" issues that they can then go home and read about on the front pages of their daily newspapers and hear about on the TV evening news shows. Moreover, if ever there was a government law office inextricably mixed up in policy determinations, this is it.

The one downside might be the product of "strong" versus "weak" Secretaries of State. When the secretary has the confidence and the ear of the President, the Office of Legal Adviser is a truly great place to be. It is less so when the secretary is shunted aside by either the National Security Advisor to the President, the Vice President, and/or the Secretary of Defense.

Office of War Crimes Issues—Department of State
   www.state.gov/s/wci/

The Office of War Crimes Issues advises the Secretary of State directly and formulates U.S. policy responses to atrocities committed in areas of conflict and elsewhere throughout the world. The office coordinates government support for war crimes accountability in the former Yugoslavia, Rwanda, Sierra Leone, Cambodia, Iraq, and other regions where crimes have been committed against civilian populations on a massive scale.

The office works with other governments, international institutions, and non-government organizations, and with the war crimes tribunals themselves, to see that international and domestic war crimes tribunals succeed in their efforts to bring those responsible for such crimes to justice.

The Ambassador-at-Large for War Crimes Issues heads a staff that includes attorneys who both bring and develop a zealous commitment to human rights and the pursuit of justice, making this one of the most psychically rewarding places to work in government.

Commercial Law Development Program—Department of Commerce
www.cldp.doc.gov/

The Commercial Law Development Program (CLDP) in the Commerce Department's Office of General Counsel provides commercial law technical assistance to governments and private sectors in developing and "transitional" (to democracy and/or to a market economy) countries in support of their economic development goals. CLDP programs are "demand-driven" and customized to address priority issues for host governments and firms interested in doing business in those countries. CLDP's goals are to improve legal and regulatory environments and develop sustainable professional relationships with U.S. partners.

CLDP draws expertise from throughout the U.S. government via details from other agencies, as well as leading legal and other professionals from the private sector (often via consulting contracts) and international organizations. Through workshops, on-the-job skills training and consultative tours here and abroad, CLDP helps lawmakers, regulators, judges, lawyers, and educators from host countries achieve their commercial law reform goals.

Public- and private-sector advisors are required to have substantial expertise in the subject of their assignment and knowledge of their host countries or region. Foreign language fluency is also highly desired.

You do not have to wait for the announcement of a consulting contract request for proposal to be issued in order to get your name and expertise before CLDP. The agency welcomes expressions of interest from legal experts.

Chapter 72

Great Places to Work— Consumer Protection

Bureau of Consumer Protection—Federal Trade Commission
    www.ftc.gov

The Bureau of Consumer Protection is one of the two major components of the Federal Trade Commission (FTC), the other being the Bureau of Competition.

The bureau's mission is to protect consumers against unfair, deceptive, or fraudulent practices in the marketplace. The bureau conducts investigations, sues companies and people who violate the law, develops rules to protect consumers, and educates consumers and businesses about their rights and responsibilities. The bureau also collects complaints about consumer fraud and identity theft and makes them available to law enforcement agencies nationwide.

The bureau has seven divisions:

* *Advertising Practices* enforces the nation's truth-in-advertising laws, with particular emphasis on claims for food, over-the-counter drugs, dietary supplements, alcohol, and tobacco and on conduct related to high-tech products and the Internet, such as the dissemination of spyware.

- *Consumer and Business Education* plans, develops, and implements national campaigns to alert consumers to their rights and to explain compliance requirements to industry.
- *Enforcement* litigates civil contempt and civil penalty actions to enforce FTC federal court injunctions and administrative orders that address consumer protection issues, including advertising and financial practices, data security, high-tech fraud, and telemarketing and other scams. The division also coordinates FTC actions with criminal law enforcement agencies through its Criminal Liaison Unit; litigates civil actions against those who defraud consumers; and develops, reviews, and enforces a variety of consumer protection rules.
- *Financial Practices* protects consumers from deceptive and unfair practices in the financial services industry, including predatory or discriminatory lending practices, as well as deceptive or unfair loan servicing, debt collection, and credit counseling or other debt assistance practices.
- *Marketing Practices* leads the commission's response to Internet, telecommunications, and direct-mail fraud; deceptive spam; fraudulent business, investment, and work-at-home schemes; and violations of the National Do Not Call Registry provisions of the Telemarketing Sales Rule.
- *Planning and Information* collects, analyzes, and makes available to law enforcement consumer fraud, identity theft, and National Do Not Call Registry complaints; assists in the distribution of redress to consumers; and provides technological investigative and litigation support.
- *Privacy and Identity Protection* safeguards consumers' financial privacy; investigates breaches of data security; works to prevent identity theft and aids consumers whose identities have been stolen; and implements laws and regulations for the credit reporting industry, including the Fair Credit Reporting Act, Pub. L. 91-508.

What makes the Consumer Protection Bureau a great place for attorneys is the following:

- almost immediate responsibility;
- top-notch legal training opportunities;

- the opportunity to achieve tangible positive results;
- the exercise of potent federal authority to redress obvious wrongs; and
- excellent litigation experience.

Office of the Chief Counsel—Pension Benefit Guaranty Corporation
www.pbgc.gov

The Pension Benefit Guaranty Corporation (PBGC) was created by the Employee Retirement Income Security Act of 1974 (ERISA), Pub. L. 93-406, to protect the pensions of American workers and retirees in private single-employer and multi-employer defined benefit pension plans. It currently protects 44 million workers in more than 29,000 such plans.

PBGC operations are financed by insurance premiums set by Congress and paid by defined-benefit plan sponsors, investment income, assets from pension plans trusteed by PBGC, and recoveries from the companies formerly responsible for the plans.

The Office of Chief Counsel is not the principal agency law office. That label belongs to PBGC's Office of General Counsel. However, what makes this office compelling is (1) its newness and (2) its key role in what many economists predict will be the next major economic crisis this country may face—the collapse of private pension plans. The Office of Chief Counsel is, in many ways, more important to PBGC operations than the Office of General Counsel.

The Office of Chief Counsel is "litigation central" at the PBGC. The office provides comprehensive legal services relating to PBGC's ERISA programs involving ongoing and terminated pension plans. Its attorneys represent PBGC in litigation in all courts relating to ERISA functions, represent PBGC in bankruptcy or insolvency proceedings, provide legal advice and services to support negotiations and settlements, and make recommendations concerning the initiation of litigation.

If there is a pension crisis, then this office will also provide a great platform for moving into high-paying legal positions in the private sector.

Enforcement Division—Securities and Exchange Commission
www.sec.gov

Because the Securities and Exchange Commission (SEC) is, above all, a law enforcement agency, its most important component is its Enforcement Division. Moreover, because of the economic collapse and its Wall Street epicenter, the Enforcement Division today looms even larger in importance. Add to that the major reorganization and expansion of the Enforcement Division wrought by the SEC's new chairperson, Mary Schapiro, plus the Dodd-Frank Wall Street Reform and Consumer Protection Act of 2010, Pub. L. 111-205, which President Obama signed into law in July, 2010, and the Enforcement Division becomes one of the key agencies of government and will likely retain that exalted position for many years to come.

The Enforcement Division recommends the commencement of investigations of securities law violations, advocating for civil actions in federal court or before an administrative law judge, and by prosecuting these cases on behalf of the Commission. As an adjunct to the SEC's civil enforcement authority, the division works closely with law enforcement agencies in the United States and around the world to bring criminal cases when appropriate.

The sea change in the division represents a total turnaround for the agency and the "benign neglect" of what was going on on Wall Street for most of the first decade of the new century. Perhaps to a larger extent than any other function of government, the Enforcement Division has been the most directly affected by the reaction to the financial industry shenanigans that brought the global economy to the edge of the abyss.

The redesign of the division that was announced in January 2010 marked the most significant reorganization of the Enforcement Division since its establishment in 1972, and was accompanied by a series of new, aggressive enforcement initiatives. Like virtually every crisis that requires government intervention, this has resulted—and continues to mean—more legal job opportunities. In this case, many more.

The impetus for this major reorganization went beyond merely attempting to right the wrongs of the previous SEC regime. It was also "anticipatory," intended both to stay abreast of the complexity and accelerating pace of innovation in financial products, transactions, and markets, and the creativity of would-be market manipulators, and also to react more quickly to market abuses. The idea was that these new units' staff members will obtain increased understanding of particular markets, products, and transactions, and will use that expertise to adopt a more proactive approach to identifying conduct and practices ripe for investigation, to conduct those investigations with increased efficiency and effectiveness, and to share that expertise with all staff throughout the Enforcement Division conducting investigations in these specialized areas.

Here is how the Enforcement Division has been transformed and enlarged in the six months before enactment of the Dodd-Frank Act, resulting in a 2010 attorney hiring spree that will only get larger thanks to the overhaul of government financial regulation:

- New National Specialized Units were established in five priority areas dedicated to particular highly specialized and complex areas of securities law:
  - o *Asset Management* to focus on investigations involving investment advisors, investment companies, hedge funds, and private equity funds.
  - o *Market Abuse* to focus on investigations involving large-scale market abuses and complex manipulation schemes by institutional traders, market professionals, and others.
  - o *Structured and New Products* to focus on complex derivatives and financial products, including credit default swaps, collateralized debt obligations, and securitized products.
  - o *Foreign Corrupt Practices* to focus on violations of the Foreign Corrupt Practices Act, Pub. L. 95-213, which prohibits U.S. companies from bribing foreign officials in order to obtain government contracts and other business.
  - o *Municipal Securities and Public Pensions* to focus on misconduct in the large municipal securities market and in connection with public pension funds, including offering and disclosure fraud; tax or arbitrage-driven fraud; pay-to-play and public corruption violations; public pension accounting and disclosure violations; and valuation and pricing fraud.

The division also created a new Office of Market Intelligence, which is responsible for "connecting the dots"—the collection, analysis, and monitoring of the hundreds of thousands of tips, complaints, and referrals that the SEC receives each year. The expectation is that these units and the new office will help provide the additional structure, resources, and expertise necessary for the Enforcement Division staff to keep pace with ever-changing markets and more comprehensively investigate cases involving complex products, markets, regulatory regimes, practices and transactions.

At the same time, the SEC also announced the introduction of cooperation incentives, initiatives to further strengthen its enforcement program by encouraging greater cooperation among individuals and companies in the agency's investigations and enforcement actions. The new initiatives established incentives for individuals and companies to fully and truthfully cooperate and assist with SEC investigations and enforcement actions, and provided new tools to help investigators develop firsthand evidence to build the strongest possible cases. For many years, similar cooperation tools have been regularly and successfully used by the Justice Department in its criminal investigations and prosecutions. The new cooperation tools were not previously available in SEC enforcement matters. They mean considerable additional work for division lawyers.

The SEC did not wait for financial regulatory reform to become legislative reality to expand and give new marching orders to the Enforcement Division. This is instructive to federal attorney hopefuls because it shows what an agency or legal office can do on its own without congressional approval.

In addition to the Washington, D.C. headquarters office of the division, the New York regional office plays a major role in Enforcement division activities and cases. Attorneys who work in either office gain tremendous experience and build compelling resumés that private sector employers—both major law firms and corporations—cannot ignore.

Chapter 73

Great Places to Work— Litigation

Office of the Solicitor General—Department of Justice
   www.justice.gov/osg/

The Solicitor General's Office represents the government before the U.S. Supreme Court and oversees government appellate litigation elsewhere. The Solicitor General selects the cases in which the government will seek Supreme Court review and the position the United States will take before the Court. Deputy Solicitors General and assistants to the Solicitor General participate in preparing the petitions, briefs, and other papers filed by the United States in its Supreme Court litigation. The Solicitor General or one of the office attorneys presents the oral argument. The office also reviews all cases decided against the government in the lower courts to determine whether an appeal is warranted and determines whether the government will intervene or participate as amicus curiae in cases before any appellate court, or in any trial court in which the constitutionality of an Act of Congress is challenged.

The office currently has 26 attorneys (four are first-year lawyers there for one-year terms as Bristow Fellows [www.justice.gov/osg/opportunities/bristapp.html]). This is one of the best and most exhilarating legal jobs in government, and also one of the most competitive and difficult to obtain. Attorneys who have gone through the Office of the Solicitor General can largely write their own ticket thereafter.

Federal Programs Branch—Civil Division—Department of Justice
www.justice.gov/civil/Federal Programs.htm

The approximately 100 attorneys in the Federal Programs Branch litigate on behalf of approximately 100 federal agencies, the President and cabinet officers, and other government officials. They defend against constitutional challenges to federal statutes, suits to overturn government policies and programs, and attacks on the legality of government decisions. The branch also initiates litigation to enforce regulatory statutes and to remedy statutory and regulatory violations.

This office stands out because its attorneys have the opportunity to handle a range of very diverse issues in a variety of subject areas, including:

- National security
- Foreign relations
- Law enforcement
- Interstate and foreign commerce
- Government agencies and corporations
- First Amendment
- Fourth Amendment
- Employment discrimination
- Human resources
- Interior, agriculture, and energy concerns
- Housing and community development
- Freedom of information and privacy
- Regulatory enforcement
- Disability litigation

Special Litigation Section Civil Rights Division—Department of Justice

(www.justice.gov/crt/index.php)

The Special Litigation Section enforces federal civil rights statutes in four major areas:

- *Conditions of Institutional Confinement.* The section protects the constitutional and federal statutory rights of persons confined in certain institutions owned or operated by, or on behalf of, state or local governments. These institutions include facilities for individuals who are mentally ill and developmentally disabled, nursing homes, juvenile correctional facilities, and adult jails and prisons.
- *Conduct of Law Enforcement Agencies.* The section enforces the police misconduct provision of the Violent Crime Control and Law Enforcement Act of 1994, Pub. L. 103-322, which authorizes the Attorney General to seek equitable and declaratory relief to redress a pattern or practice of conduct by law enforcement agencies that violates federal law. The section also enforces the Omnibus Crime Control and Safe Streets Act of 1968, Pub. L. 90-351, which authorizes the Attorney General to initiate civil litigation to remedy a pattern or practice of discrimination based on race, color, national origin, gender, or religion involving services by law enforcement agencies receiving federal financial assistance.
- *Access to Reproductive Health Facilities and Places of Religious Worship.* The section also enforces the civil provisions of the Freedom of Access to Clinic Entrances Act of 1994 (Access Act), Pub. L. 103-259, which prohibits the use or threat of force and physical obstruction that injures, intimidates, or interferes with a person seeking to obtain or provide reproductive health services or to exercise the First Amendment right of religious freedom at a place of religious worship. It also prohibits intentional property damage of a facility providing reproductive health services or a place of religious worship. The Access Act authorizes the

Attorney General to seek injunctive relief, statutory or compensatory damages, and civil penalties against individuals who engage in conduct that violates the act.

- *Religious Exercise of Institutionalized Persons.* The section enforces the provision of the Religious Land Use and Institutionalized Persons Act (RLUIPA), Pub. L. 106-274, that protects the religious exercise of persons confined to institutions covered by the Civil Rights of Institutionalized Persons Act, Pub. L. 96-247. This provision prohibits a state or local government from substantially burdening the religious exercise of such an institutionalized person, unless the government demonstrates that imposition of the burden furthers a compelling governmental interest and is the least restrictive means available to further that interest. The Department of Justice is authorized to investigate alleged violations of RLUIPA and to file civil lawsuits seeking injunctive or declaratory relief. In addition, RLUIPA enables private individuals to seek judicial remedies for violations of the statute. RLUIPA applies to cases in which the alleged substantial burden on religious exercise occurs in a program receiving federal financial assistance or affects interstate commerce.

One of my clients who went to work for the Special Litigation Section did not engage in any actual litigation, but rather worked as an investigator of violations of the aforementioned laws and recommended action to the litigation teams, while also providing research and litigation support. He was not a litigator while with a law firm prior to going to this office.

Criminal Division—Department of Justice
www.justice.gov/criminal/

The reason behind the entire Criminal Division being included in this list of best places to work in government is principally the passion of its attorneys. Passion is a very rare commodity in any attorney or other employee, for that matter. I have yet to encounter a Criminal Division attorney or alumnus whose excitement is not palpable when discussing his or her work.

The Criminal Division develops, enforces, and supervises the application of all federal criminal laws except those specifically assigned to other divisions. The division and the 93 U.S. Attorneys' Offices around the country are responsible for overseeing criminal matters under more than 900 statutes as well as certain civil litigation. Criminal Division attorneys prosecute many nationally significant cases. In addition, the division formulates and implements criminal enforcement policy and provides advice and assistance. For example, the division approves or monitors participation in the Witness Security Program and the use of electronic surveillance; advises the Attorney General, Congress, the Office of Management and Budget, and the White House on matters of criminal law; provides legal advice and assistance to federal prosecutors and investigative agencies; and provides leadership for coordinating international as well as federal, state, and local law enforcement matters.

The following offices comprise the division:

- Office of the Assistant Attorney General
- Office of Administration
- Appellate Section
- Asset Forfeiture and Money Laundering Section
- Capital Case Unit
- Child Exploitation and Obscenity Section
- Computer Crime and Intellectual Property Section
- Fraud Section
- Gang Unit
- Human Rights and Special Prosecutions Section
- International Criminal Investigative Training Assistance Program
- Narcotic and Dangerous Drug Section
- Office of Enforcement Operations
- Office of International Affairs
- Office of Policy and Legislation
- Office of Overseas Prosecutorial Development, Assistance and Training
- Organized Crime and Racketeering Section
- Public Integrity Section

Four of these Criminal Division Offices stand out, in my opinion, because their work is so timely, contemporary, and interesting:

Computer Crime and Intellectual Property Section

This section (CCIPS) implements the department's national strategies in combating computer and intellectual property (IP) crimes worldwide. The Computer Crime Initiative program is designed to combat electronic penetrations, data thefts, and cyber attacks on critical information systems. Section attorneys work to improve the domestic and international infrastructure—legal, technological, and operational—to pursue network criminals most effectively.

The section's enforcement responsibilities against IP crimes have gained in importance because IP has become one of the principal U.S. economic engines, and the nation is a target of choice for thieves of IP material.

CCIPS attorneys regularly run complex investigations; resolve unique legal and investigative issues raised by emerging computer and telecommunications technologies; litigate cases; provide litigation support to other prosecutors; train federal, state, and local law enforcement personnel; comment on and propose legislation; and initiate and participate in international efforts to combat computer and intellectual property crime.

Fraud Section

The Fraud Section fights against sophisticated economic crime. The section is a front-line litigating unit that acts as a rapid-response team, investigating and prosecuting complex white-collar crime cases throughout the country. Section attorneys gain vast experience with sophisticated fraud schemes and with managing complex and multidistrict litigation.

The Fraud Section also plays a critical role in the development of department policy. The section implements enforcement initiatives and advises the department leadership on legislation, crime prevention, and public education. The section frequently coordinates interagency and multidistrict investigations and international enforcement efforts. The section assists prosecutors, regulators, law enforcement, and the private sector by providing training, advice, and other assistance, and participates in numerous national, regional, and international working groups. The section consists of more than 60 attorneys.

Public Integrity Section

The Public Integrity Section combats public corruption through the prosecution of elected and appointed public officials at all levels of government. The section has exclusive jurisdiction over allegations of criminal misconduct on the part of federal judges and also monitors the investigation and prosecution of election and conflict-of-interest crimes. Since 1978, the section has also supervised the administration of the Independent Counsel provisions of the Ethics in Government Act, Pub. L. 95-521.

Most of the section's resources are devoted to the supervision of investigations involving alleged corruption by government officials and to prosecutions resulting from these investigations. Cases handled by the section generally fall into one of the following categories: recusals by U.S. Attorneys' Offices (the vast majority of public corruption cases are handled by U.S. Attorneys' Offices), sensitive cases, multidistrict cases, referrals from federal agencies, and shared cases.

Office of Overseas Prosecutorial Development, Assistance and Training (OPDAT)

OPDAT was created in 1991 in response to the growing threat of international crime. OPDAT helps prosecutors and judicial personnel in other countries develop and sustain effective criminal justice institutions.

Central to OPDAT's mission is its preparation of foreign counterparts to cooperate more fully and effectively with the United States in combating terrorism, trafficking in persons, organized crime, corruption, financial crimes, and other transnational crime. They encourage legislative and justice sector reform in countries with inadequate laws; improve the skills of foreign prosecutors, investigators, and judges; and promote the rule of law and regard for human rights.

Since 1991, OPDAT has placed resident legal advisors (RLAs)

in over 37 countries, where they provide full-time advice and technical assistance to host governments in establishing fair and transparent justice sector institutions and practices. RLAs serve in a specific country for at least one year. They assess the host country's criminal justice institutions and procedures; draft, review, and comment on legislation and criminal enforcement policy; and provide technical assistance to host country officials at the Ministry of Justice, Chief Prosecutor's Office, or to prosecutors, judges, and other justice sector personnel working in the field.

Assistance programs focusing on a specific aspect of criminal justice or designed to be completed in less than a year may be staffed by an intermittent legal advisor (ILA). ILAs have provided assistance in money laundering, transnational crime, corruption, and trafficking in both narcotics and people.

Depending upon the needs of the host country, OPDAT can also request assistance from other Department of Justice components, including the Federal Bureau of Investigation; Drug Enforcement Agency; Federal Bureau of Prisons; U.S. Marshals Service; and Bureau of Alcohol, Tobacco, Firearms, and Explosives. In addition, OPDAT can utilize the law enforcement expertise of other federal departments, such as Treasury and Homeland Security, as well as state and local prosecutor offices. OPDAT can also draw upon alliances with the private bar and state and federal judiciaries; and professional organizations, including the National District Attorneys Association, the American Prosecutor Research Institute, and the American Bar Association's Rule of Law Initiative.

Key areas in which OPDAT provides technical assistance and training are:

- Criminal procedure code reform
- Criminal justice sector infrastructure reform
- Task force development
- Streamlining of the judicial process
- Organization and management of prosecutorial function
- Case management
- Capacity-building of foreign prosecutors, investigators, and judges
- Promotion of rule of law and regard for human rights

- Substantive reform
- Counterterrorism
- Human trafficking and child exploitation
- Organized crime
- Anti-corruption
- Money laundering and asset forfeiture
- Computer and intellectual property crimes
- Counter-narcotics

Office of Special Counsel

www.osc.gov

In good times, OSC is a good place to work (this is an office particularly susceptible to being a miserable environment with a bad office chief in charge). OSC attorneys have numerous opportunities to combat injustice and be satisfied with the results of their work.

OSC is an independent federal investigative and prosecutorial agency whose basic authorities come from four federal statutes: the Civil Service Reform Act, Pub. L. 95-454; the Whistleblower Protection Act, Pub. L. 101-12; the Hatch Act of 1877; and the Uniformed Services Employment and Reemployment Rights Act (USERRA), Pub. L. 103-353. The agency's primary mission is to safeguard the merit system by protecting federal employees and applicants from prohibited personnel practices (PPPs), especially reprisals for whistle-blowing.

OSC investigates and prosecutes allegations of PPPs, with an emphasis on federal government whistle-blowers. It seeks remedies (such as back pay and reinstatement), by negotiation or from the Merit Systems Protection Board (MSPB), for injuries suffered by whistle-blowers and other complainants. It is also authorized to file complaints at the MSPB to seek disciplinary action against individuals who commit PPPs.

Office of Senate Legal Counsel

www.senate.gov

The Office of Senate Legal Counsel provides legal assistance and representation to the U.S. Senate. It was established by the Ethics in

Government Act of 1978, Pub. L. 95-521, as one of the many reactions to the abuses uncovered during the Watergate scandal. Basically, this office serves as the in-house law firm that represents and defends the constitutional powers of the Senate and the separation of powers and checks and balances. If a senator is sued individually, the Office also represents him or her.

Prior to its establishment, the Department of Justice represented Congress in litigation. However, Watergate demonstrated the unworkable nature of this arrangement due to the numerous disputes that the scandal spawned between the executive and legislative branches. Henceforth, Justice Department representation of Congress looked glaringly to be an inherent conflict of interest.

The Office is required by law to be non-partisan and offers extensive experience in constitutional law and litigation.

Chapter 74

Great Places to Work— Employment and Civil Rights

Outside Mediation Program—Equal Employment Opportunity Commission

www.eeoc.gov

Only mediators experienced and trained in mediation and equal employment opportunity law are assigned to mediate Equal Employment Opportunity Commission (EEOC) charges. EEOC has a staff of trained mediators, but frequently contracts with professional external mediators to mediate charges filed with EEOC. Outside mediators are selected from the ranks of contractors who have been found qualified and placed on the agency's Roster of Mediators.

This opportunity is an excellent one for attorneys who seek flexible employment. I have had several legal career transition counseling clients who made a very good living mediating under contract to the EEOC. They work intermittently, yet still earn enough for a comfortable lifestyle.

EEOC's mediation program is administered primarily through its 15 district and nine field offices located throughout the country. Each district office has a staff member who is responsible for coordinating mediation activities for charges of employment discrimi-

433

nation filed within that office's geographical jurisdiction. As charges are filed, they are reviewed to determine whether they may be appropriate for mediation. If so, the charging party is contacted to see if he or she is willing to participate in the mediation process. If the charging party is willing to participate, the party against whom the charge was filed is contacted. If both parties are willing to participate, the charge enters the mediation process.

Dispute Resolution Center—Library of Congress
www.loc.gov

The Dispute Resolution Center was established in 1991 to cope with a barrage of employee grievances. Since the Center's inception, it has proven to be instrumental in the LOC's efforts to resolve disputes before they reach the formal stages of investigation, hearings, or district court litigation.

The Library of Congress has alternative dispute resolution agreements with its non-bargaining unit employees; the two American Federation of State, County, and Municipal Employees locals that represent library employees; and the Congressional Research Employees Association. Each agreement recommends the use of mediation to resolve workplace disputes, including equal employment opportunity complaints, grievances, or a category designated as "other." The library encourages parties involved in a dispute to resolve it directly through informal discussions, or through mediation facilitated by conveners in the Dispute Resolution Center.

The library established the Center because it was being besieged by employee complaints and disputes and found itself in the uncomfortable, distracting, and time- and money-consuming position of having to defend itself before the Equal Employment Opportunity Commission and in federal court all too often. Consequently, it established a policy that disputes should ideally be settled informally at the lowest possible level.

Office for Civil Rights (OCR)—Department of Education
www2.ed.gov/about/offices/list/ocr/index.html?src=oc

OCR exists to combat discrimination in education, with an emphasis on discrimination against students. It seeks to resolve complaints of discrimination, initiates compliance reviews, targets resources to acute compliance problems, and provides technical assistance to help institutions achieve voluntary compliance with the civil rights laws that OCR enforces.

One of the very attractive features of this practice is that is encourages preventive law approaches to education discrimination. This creates an atmosphere of creativity and innovation that is a rarity among law offices anywhere.

OCR enforces several federal civil rights laws that prohibit discrimination in programs or activities that receive federal financial assistance from the Department of Education:

- Title VI of the Civil Rights Act of 1964, Pub. L. 88-352, which prohibits discrimination on the basis of race, color, and national origin;
- Title IX of the Education Amendments of 1972, Pub. L. 92-318, which prohibits sex discrimination;
- Section 504 of the Rehabilitation Act of 1973, Pub. L. 93-112, which prohibits disability discrimination;
- Title II of the Americans with Disabilities Act of 1990, Pub. L. 101-336, which prohibits disability discrimination by public entities, whether or not they receive federal financial assistance;
- the Age Discrimination Act of 1975, Pub. L. 94-135, which prohibits age discrimination; and
- the Boy Scouts of America Equal Access Act (Section 9525 of the Elementary and Secondary Education Act of 1965, Pub. L. 89-10, as amended by the No Child Left Behind Act of 2001, Pub. L. 107-110), which states that no public elementary school or state or local education agency that permits one or more outside youth or community groups to meet on school premises or in school facilities before or after school hours shall deny equal access or a fair opportunity to meet, or discriminate against, any group officially affiliated with the Boy Scouts of America, or any other youth group listed in Title 36 of the United States Code as a patriotic society.

These civil rights laws cover all state education agencies, elementary and secondary school systems, colleges and universities, vocational schools, proprietary schools, state vocational rehabilitation agencies, libraries, and museums that receive Department of Education funds. They encompass admissions, recruitment, financial aid, academic programs, student treatment and services, counseling and guidance, discipline, classroom assignment, grading, vocational education, recreation, physical education, athletics, housing, and employment, etc.

The vast changes wrought in education law over the past decade have made OCR a very important government legal function, one that means both interesting work and practice at the cusp of major education reform for OCR's relatively large legal staff.

Chapter 75

Great Places to Work— Legal Research, Advice, and Counsel

Office of Legal Counsel—Department of Justice
www.justice.gov/olc/

While the Attorney General of the United States is the government's lawyer, the Office of Legal Counsel (OLC) serves as the Attorney General's lawyer, as outside counsel for all other executive branch agencies, and as the Justice Department's general counsel. This is what makes OLC interesting and exciting.

OLC provides legal advice to the President and all executive branch agencies. The Office drafts legal opinions of the Attorney General and also provides its own written opinions and oral advice in response to requests from the Counsel to the President, executive branch agencies (typically with respect to legal issues of great complexity and importance or about which two or more agencies disagree), and Justice Department offices. OLC also provides legal advice to the executive branch on all constitutional questions and reviews pending legislation for constitutionality.

OLC reviews all proposed presidential executive orders and proclamations for form and legality, as well as other matters that require the President's formal approval. It also reviews all proposed

437

orders of the Attorney General and all regulations requiring the Attorney General's approval.

OLC currently has 24 attorneys and is highly selective in its hiring.

Office of General Counsel—National Science Foundation
www.nsf.gov

I once visited a friend of mine in the Office of General Counsel (OGC) at the National Science Foundation (NSF), the 60-year old government agency with the incredibly broad mandate "to promote the progress of science; to advance the national health, prosperity, and welfare; to secure the national defense, . . ." etc. The office attempts to realize its mission by awarding more than 10,000 research grants each year, primarily to colleges and universities. As I sat in his reception area, I could overhear him dealing with an ethics issue that he told me later was not unique. An NSF scientist whose job was to evaluate grant proposals in chemistry came to him carrying what looked like a wedding reception table glass centerpiece containing a blue liquid that steamed and burbled over the top of the container so impressively as to make Macbeth's three witches green with cauldron envy. The scientist was agonizing over whether to accept this "gift" from one of his grantees.

My friend's solution to the problem was to advise him to accept the gift since neither he nor the scientist could (1) figure out what on earth it was or (2) ascribe a value to it. The attorney suggested that the scientist e-mail the grantee, thank him for the gift, and advise him that federal ethics law and regulations prohibited him from accepting any future gifts of value.

The scientist left his office a happy man. My friend then told me that he was confronted with questions about ethics brought to him by both NSF staff members and outside grantees every day. It appeared to be a very interesting job. Moreover, he said, operating on the legal side of the cutting edge of scientific, technological, and engineering research meant that every day also carried with it new and fascinating information and an array of issues where current law had to contend with rapidly advancing scientific research.

OGC does much more than that, however. It also provides advice and counsel regarding grants, contracts, and cooperative agreements; intellectual property; conflicts of interest; employee and labor relations; civil rights; health, safety, and environment; public regulation of research; federal fiscal and administrative law and procedure; international law and agreements; national security restrictions of scientific research (including export controls); and litigation expertise to the agency coordinating each phase of complex litigation with the Department of Justice.

Law Department—U.S. Postal Service
www.usps.com

The U.S. Postal Service (USPS) Law Department may seem like an odd candidate for a federal "Best Places to Work" list. Nevertheless, I include it because of my own direct personal experience interacting with more than 15 USPS attorneys. I found them to be among the most professional and intelligent lawyers in the entire federal structure. They knew their stuff and applied their knowledge and legal talents very effectively. They gave new—and different—meaning to the term "going postal."

The large and far-flung law department (more than 200 attorneys in offices across the country) functions as a large law firm with an enormously varied practice, including labor and employment, commercial, torts, economic regulation, finance, contracts, intellectual property, real estate, legislation, administrative, international, information, government ethics, and consumer protection law.

American Law Division—Congressional Research Service—Library of Congress
www.loc.gov/crsinfo/divwork/aldwork.html

The American Law Division (ALD) is one of those offices that employees find very difficult to leave. A cynic might say that this is because these attorneys could not easily find new employment elsewhere, since all they do is research legal issues and report on them to Congress. However, the many ALD attorneys I worked with during both my federal legal career and my subsequent private sector career tell a very different story—they love what they do.

Their work addresses the myriad and often multifaceted and policy-heavy legal questions that arise in a legislative context or are otherwise of interest to Congress. Some issues relate to the institutional prerogatives of Congress under the Constitution. Other questions involve constitutional and legal principles of statutory analysis that cross legislative policy areas, such as federalism, the commerce power, and individual rights. ALD also focuses on the intricacies of legal precedent and statutory construction as they relate to business, crime, the environment, civil rights, international law, and many other issues.

ALD's 50-plus attorneys are divided into five research sections, each led by a section research manager.

- Administrative Law
- Business
- Congress
- Courts and International
- Natural Resources

Attorneys in each section can expect to work in a variety of legal areas to meet the changing demands of the legislative agenda and congressional interests.

ALD's parent agency, the Congressional Research Service, is an arm of Congress. Its reports and memoranda, while not legally binding, are used by members and committees of Congress in their legislative deliberations and decision-making.

Legal Office—U.S. Supreme Court
www.supremecourt.gov

The Supreme Court's tiny and very obscure Legal Office was created by Chief Justice Warren Burger in 1972 to act as a kind of "house counsel." The office handles and advises on contracts, legislation, litigation, ethics matters, and personnel issues involving the Court.

The office's initial mission was to provide continuity of experience in the preliminary consideration of extraordinary motions. The lawyers who staffed the office would hopefully provide the Court with a quick and reliable institutional memory for details. The Legal Office is responsible for centralizing and stabilizing the Supreme Court's work by assisting in legal matters, preparing work for weekly conferences, recommending strategies for pending cases, helping justices with personal responses and circuit tasks, and taking on special projects of the Chief Justice, special chambers, or the Court as a whole. The office has a role in setting the conference agenda and in reviewing petitions for writs of certiorari.

This is a small office and vacancies are few and far between. However, it is a little-known gem in the federal legal structure that offers incredibly interesting legal work to those attorneys fortunate enough to wind up there.

Chapter 76

Great Places to Work? The Newest of the New

The federal government is a perpetual motion machine of agency creation. As this book goes to press, more than 10 new federal organizations are in the process of being born. I cannot include them in the previous chapters on great places to work because the jury is going to be out with respect to that assessment for some time.

However, I can say this about them, assuming that the past is prologue (and it almost always is with respect to government): New agencies tend to be exciting for at least their first few years of existence until they "settle in" and, if blessed, even beyond that. The Legal Division at the Federal Deposit Insurance Corporation, for example, will always be an interesting and stimulating place to work as long as banks—and other financial institutions, given the recent expansion of FDIC authority—continue to fail.

Another reason for including new federal organizations is that they almost always tend to "overgrade" their staffs when they are starting up, meaning that it is easier to begin your career with them at a higher grade level than you might expect at an existing agency, and also that promotions come quickly in the early years.

I have selected seven of the newest agencies, based on their likely attorney and law-related staff orientation, to discuss in this chapter.

Office of Consumer Information and Insurance Oversight— Department of Health and Human Services
www.hhs.gov/ociio/

This new office is going to be one of the principal organizations tasked with implementing the Patient Protection and Affordable Care Act, Pub. L. 111-140. This makes it a pretty interesting ground-floor opportunity. Its focus will be on implementing the many provisions of the health-care reform legislation that affect the insurance industry and consumers. The office is being organized as this book goes to press.

The Office of Consumer Information and Insurance Oversight is responsible for ensuring compliance with the new insurance market rules, such as the prohibitions on rescissions and on pre-existing condition exclusions for children that took effect in late 2010. It will oversee the new medical loss ratio rules and will assist states in reviewing insurance rates. It will provide guidance and oversight for the state-based insurance exchanges. It will also administer the temporary high-risk pool program and the early retiree reinsurance program, and compile and maintain data for an Internet portal providing information on insurance options.

The office head is an attorney and it is expected that attorneys will comprise a considerable percentage of its staff. Assuming that health-care reform persists and does not fall victim to repeal threats by opponents, what an attorney will learn and experience at this office will position him or her well for a transition out of government if so desired.

Bureau of Consumer Financial Protection—Federal Reserve Board
www.federalreserve.gov

This is the new federal financial services regulatory agency that proved so controversial during Congress's consideration of the Dodd-Frank Act, Pub. L. 111-205. It is still a lightning rod as financial regulatory reform goes forward, a condition not likely to ease as the agency gears up and begins work.

The agency is tasked with regulating consumer financial products and services. It will be headed by a director appointed by the President, with the advice and consent of the Senate, for a term of five years. President Obama's selection of Elizabeth Warren for this job proved so contentious that, as an interim measure, he appointed her to the White House staff with the mission of organizing the new agency.

The bureau, although housed in the Federal Reserve Board, is supposed to be independent of the Fed. The statute prohibits the Fed from interfering with matters before the bureau director, directing any employee of the bureau, modifying the functions and responsibilities of the bureau, or impeding an order of the bureau. However, the Financial Stability Oversight Council, the new entity charged with anticipating systemic risks to the financial system (not included in this chapter because its initial staff will consist of current federal employees detailed to it), may issue a "stay" to the bureau with an appealable two-thirds vote.

The bureau will have five units: Research, Community Affairs, Complaint Tracking and Collection, an Office of Fair Lending and Equal Opportunity (designed to ensure equitable access to credit), and an Office of Financial Literacy (to promote financial literacy among consumers). A Consumer Advisory Board will inform the Bureau of emerging market trends.

Being a regulatory agency, the bureau is bound to be staffed by a considerable number of attorneys in both legal and law-related positions. (The first attorney position with the bureau was announced as this book went to press.) Moreover, given its mission, working here for a few years should position an attorney quite well for future career moves.

Federal Insurance Office—Department of Treasury
www.treasury.gov

Excepting flood and crop insurance, the federal government has maintained a hands-off policy toward insurance regulation for over two centuries, leaving that function to the states. That all changed in 2010 with the enactment of first the Patient Protection and Affordable Care Act, Pub. L. 111-140, followed within months by the Dodd-Frank Wall Street Reform and Consumer Protection Act, Pub.

L. 111-205, both of which will, for the first time, involve the government heavily in insurance regulation.

The new Federal Insurance Office is the Dodd-Frank manifestation of this development. While the advocates of this new agency take pains to emphasize that this does not mean the beginning of the end of traditional state regulation of insurance, my prediction is that the end is in sight. The Federal Insurance Office is almost certainly the opening foray into federal regulation. In fact, the insurance industry lobbied heavily for a broad-based federal insurance regulatory scheme, since the Balkanized state regulatory structure is very expensive, complicated, and outdated in the modern era of rapid transportation and communication.

The statute directs the office to:

- monitor all aspects of the insurance industry (except health insurance, some long-term care insurance, and crop insurance), including the identification of gaps in regulation of insurers that could contribute to financial crisis;
- monitor the extent to which traditionally underserved communities and consumers, minorities, and low-and moderate-income persons have access to affordable insurance (except health insurance);
- make recommendations to the Financial Stability Oversight Council about insurers that may pose a risk, and help any state regulators with national issues;
- administer the Terrorism Risk Insurance Program;
- coordinate international insurance matters;
- determine whether state insurance measures are preempted by covered agreements; and
- consult with the states (including state insurance regulators) regarding insurance matters of national importance and international importance.

The office will also have the authority to require any insurance company to submit virtually any data it wants to see.

Given its responsibilities, the Federal Insurance Office should have a number of legal and law-related positions.

Office of the Investor Advocate—Securities and Exchange Commission

www.sec.gov

This office, and the next two offices in this chapter, are all at the Securities and Exchange Commission (SEC), the busiest federal agency by far when it came to spawning new offices in 2010. At the beginning of the year, the SEC established six new, lawyer-laden offices in its Enforcement Division. Now, directed by the Dodd-Frank Act, the agency is at it again. Testifying before Congress in October, 2010, the SEC chair stated that the agency was likely to need an additional 800 employees over and above the already major staff increases authorized by Congress to carry out its Dodd-Frank Act responsibilities. You can be certain that attorneys will comprise a large portion of that increase.

The Office of the Investor Advocate will assist retail investors in resolving significant problems with the SEC or the self-regulatory organizations (SROs); identify where investors would benefit from changes in SEC or SRO policies; and identify problems that investors have with financial service providers and investment products. The Investor Advocate will recommend policy changes to the SEC and Congress in the interests of investors. This will be the first time that the small investor has a place to turn to in the SEC.

The sponsor of this provision of the Dodd-Frank Act, Senator Daniel Akaka (D-HI), envisions this office as an external check on the SEC, with independent reporting lines and independently determined compensation. The office is supposed to help ensure that the interests of retail investors are built into rulemaking proposals from the outset and that agency priorities reflect the issues confronting investors.

The Investor Advocate will also be responsible for naming an ombudsman, who will act as a liaison between the SEC and individual investors to help resolve any issues that an investor may have with the SEC or a self-regulatory organization.

Attorneys are everywhere at the SEC and will definitely be a part of the Investor Advocate staff. In fact, the act authorizes the advocate to hire "independent counsel."

Whistleblower Office—Enforcement Division—Securities and Exchange Commission
www.sec.gov

This new office, also prompted by direction of the Dodd-Frank Act, Pub. L. 111-205, is based on a similar IRS program dating from 2006. The office will run the Whistleblower Bounty Program, under which the SEC will reward whistleblowers who provide information on securities law violations that result in monetary sanctions exceeding $1 million. The rewards can be considerable, amounting to 10 to 30 percent of any monetary sanctions over $1 million.

In addition, the office will:

- protect whistleblowers from retaliation;
- oversee the expansion of payments of rewards to individuals who provide information leading to the successful enforcement of any judicial or administrative action brought by the SEC under all provisions of the securities laws; and
- enforce the provisions of the Dodd-Frank Act's expansion of the whistleblower protections of the Sarbanes-Oxley Act, Pub. L. 107-204, to both parent companies and their subsidiaries and affiliates if their financial information is included in the consolidated financial statements of the parent company.

The Enforcement Division is in the process of drafting the proposed rules applicable to the Whistleblower Program as this book goes to press, including rules setting forth the procedures for whistleblowers to submit original information to the commission and for the commission to make awards to whistleblowers. It will begin staffing the Whistleblower Office once the FY 2011 federal budget is in place.

Office of Credit Ratings—Securities and Exchange Commission
www.sec.gov

This new Dodd-Frank Act creation will be the first-ever specific regulator of the credit rating agencies, the three largest and most influential being Standard & Poor's, Moody's, and Fitch—the entities that came in for so much blame for their dubious ratings of securitized subprime mortgage instruments in the run-up to the Great Recession.

The SEC has actually been in the business of monitoring the rating agencies since 2006, when Congress enacted the Credit Rating Agency Reform Act, Pub. L. 109-291, which was intended to improve credit ratings by fostering accountability, transparency, and competition. The act established SEC oversight over Nationally Recognized Statistical Rating Organizations (NRSROs), which are credit rating agencies that are registered with SEC. Both the 2006 act and its implementation by the SEC proved to be seriously deficient in many respects. The Dodd-Frank Act provision establishing the Office of Credit Ratings and vastly expanding SEC authority to regulate rating agencies is designed to rectify some of these gaps.

The office is charged with—

- developing and administering SEC rules with respect to NRSRO practices in determining ratings;
- conducting an annual examination of each NRSRO and issuing a public report summarizing the essential findings of the examination, identifying material deficiencies, stating if previous SEC recommendations have been resolved, and recording any response by the examined agency; and
- establishing fines and penalties for any NRSRO violations.

The office will have its own compliance unit and will include attorneys on its staff.

Office of the Associate Director for Compliance and Training— National Security Agency
www.nsa.gov

This new office was authorized in October 2010 by the Intelligence Authorization Act for Fiscal Year 2010 (no matter that October 1, 2010, was the beginning of Fiscal Year 2011).

One of my Rules Governing the Interpretation of U.S. Government Usage is the following: Whenever you see the term "compliance" in a job or office title, your legal career pulse should quicken. Both compliance—and in this context, training—mean that attorneys have to be involved. This is particularly the case given the complex matrix of laws governing intelligence community activities (some of which the 16 [known] intelligence agencies sometimes follow).

Epilogue

If you have read *Landing a Federal Legal Job* from beginning to end, you should have concluded that (1) the U.S. government quite literally has something that should appeal to every attorney, and (2) the author is highly opinionated and often very critical about the federal government and its legal establishment. The latter is impossible to avoid for someone who has spent 35 years "inside the Beltway" interacting on a daily basis with all three branches of government in many different capacities.

I have attempted to provide you with an unvarnished look at how the government goes about the business of hiring attorneys, as well as hopefully expanding your horizons when it comes to federal legal and law-related job and career opportunities, how to enhance your chances of securing one of them, and where you might thrive should you decide that a public-sector career at the highest governmental level is something you want to pursue.

I have tried to give you a balanced perspective on federal legal employment, leaving it up to you now that you know both the possibilities and the attendant challenges of a federal legal career. Nevertheless, I need to close with something approaching a call to arms.

By exposing the "warts," however, I do not want to leave you with the impression that I am attempting to deter you from pursuing a federal legal career. Quite the contrary. Despite the obstacles, public service is still an honorable profession, perhaps the most honorable one to which an attorney can aspire.

The call to public service in this age of cynicism and skepticism about what government can and should do is no different from what motivated the thousands of attorneys who answered Franklin D. Roosevelt's call to serve the New Deal in 1933 or John F. Kennedy's call to Washington on behalf of the New Frontier in 1961, in much more innocent and idealistic eras. The same need for committed individuals interested in what they can do for their country exists today and, from my perspective, is more essential than ever. The government needs good men and women in its legal positions if it is to do its jobs properly. In times such as the present, high-quality attorneys are more essential than ever.

The problems we face are, perhaps, the most difficult and complex that the United States has ever confronted in its history. The corresponding clarion call to government service, where attorneys have always been one of the principal driving forces behind policy, change for the better, and any good works that government achieves, should now be louder than ever.

This is no time to throw up your hands in despair over the direction of the country. If you want to make a difference, the federal government offers you that opportunity in abundance.

Appendixes

Appendix A
U.S. Government Job Listings

Executive Branch Jobs

The U.S. Office of Personnel Management (OPM) hosts the most extensive federal government job site. This website—www.usajobs.gov—should be your first stop if you are seeking a broad overview of what might be available at any moment in time. It is updated daily. However, OPM is nothing more than a passive conduit of the information that it receives from federal hiring agencies. If they elect not to go through OPM, you will not find their jobs listed here. In that case, you need to visit the website of each agency that interests you.

Another important reason for visiting www.usajobs.gov is that the majority of federal agencies now entertain job applications only if they come in through this website. Nevertheless, there are a dwindling number of agencies that do not yet utilize the site, preferring to continue to do their legal hiring directly. In those cases, you will find their published job vacancy announcements on their own agency websites (assuming they publish them).

Federal Attorney Jobs

Thomson-Reuters hosts www.attorneyjobs.com, which, among other features, has a searchable category devoted to federal government attorney and law-related jobs.

Law Student Summer and Semester Jobs

Thomson-Reuters also hosts www.lawschool.westlaw.com, a law student site that lists federal government agency summer legal em-

451

ployment programs, semester-long employment programs, and attorney honors programs.

Federal Inspector General Office Jobs

The 73 statutory federal Inspector General offices sometimes list their jobs on www.ignet.gov. Be warned, however, that listing jobs here is not mandatory.

Congressional Jobs

The following sites list positions with congressional offices, committees and subcommittees, congressional support offices, and Legislative branch agencies:

- Roll Call—www.rcjobs.com
- The Hill—http://thehill.com/employment/
- Senate Employment Bulletin—www.senate.gov/employment/po/positions.htm
- House Job Vacancies—http://wwwd.house.gov/vacancies/vacancieslist.aspx

Federal Courts

The United States Courts website lists positions with both the federal courts and court support organizations at www.uscourts.gov/employment.html.

Quasi-Governmental Organizations
- Financial Industry Regulatory Authority (FINRA) jobs: www.finra.org.
- Legal Services Corporation jobs: www.lsc.gov/about/careers.php.
- United States Institute of Peace jobs: www.usip.org/work-us.
- Public Company Accounting Oversight Board jobs: http://pcaobus.org/Careers/Pages/SearchJobListings.aspx

Federal Reserve Bank Jobs:
- Boston Fed: www.bos.frb.org/about/employment/index.htm
- New York Fed: www.newyorkfed.org/careers/current_openings.html
- Philadelphia Fed: www.philadelphiafed.org/careers/
- Richmond Fed: www.richmondfed.org/about_us/careers/
- Atlanta Fed: www.frbatlanta.org/about/careers/
- Cleveland Fed: www.clevelandfed.org/
- Chicago Fed: www.chicagofed.org/webpages/people/jobs/index.cfm
- Minneapolis Fed: www.minneapolisfed.org/about/careers/jobsearch.cfm
- St. Louis Fed: http://careers.stlouisfed.org/
- Kansas City Fed: www.kansascityfed.org/careers/
- Dallas Fed: www.dallasfed.org/careers/index.cfm
- San Francisco Fed: www.frbsf.org/federalreserve/careers/

Government-Sponsored Enterprise Jobs:
- Fannie Mae: www.fanniemae.com/kb/index?page=home&c=careers
- Freddie Mac: www.freddiemac.com/careers/
- Farmer Mac: www.farmermac.com/careers/index.aspx

Appendix B
U.S. Government Information Resources

General U.S. Government Information
- U.S. Government Agencies: www.usa.gov/Agencies/Federal/All_Agencies/
- United States Government Manual: www.access.gpo.gov
- Federal Yellow Book: www.leadershipdirectories.com
- Federal Regional Yellow Book: www.leadershipdirectories.com
- Federal Regulatory Directory: www.cqpress.com
- Government Executive: www.govexec.com

Congressional Offices
- Congressional Yellow Book: www.leadershipdirectories.com
- Members of Congress: http://clerk.house.gov/ www.gpoaccess.gov/cdirectory

U.S. Courts
- Federal Court Websites: www.uscourts.gov/courtlinks/
- Judicial Yellow Book: www.leadershipdirectories.com

Law-Related Hiring Offices
- Federal Alternative Dispute Resolution Resource Guide: www.opm.gov/er/adrguide_2002/toc.asp
- U.S. Government Ethics Offices: www.usoge.gov
- Federal Laboratory Consortium for Technology Transfer: www.federallabs.org

Self-Regulatory Organizations
- Self-Regulatory Organizations: www.sec.gov

Government Compensation
- U.S. Government Salary Charts: www.attorneyjobs.com
- Congressional Staff Salaries: www.legistorm.com/

Federal Disability Hiring
- U.S. Government Selective Placement Program Coordinator SPPC Directory: http://apps.opm.gov/sppc_directory/searchlist.cfm

Government Reports
- Congressional Committee Reports: www.gpoaccess.gov/serialset/creports/index.html
- Government Accountability Office Reports: www.gao.gov
- Congressional Research Service Reports:
  www.opencrs.com http://fpc.state.gov/c4763.htm
  www.ncseonline.org/NLE/CRS
  http://digital.library.unt.edu/govdocs/crs
- Federal Judicial Center Reports: www.fjc.gov/library/fjc_catalog.nsf
- White House Office of Science and Technology Policy Reports: www.ostp.gov
- National Technology Transfer Center Reports: www.nttc.edu
- Office of Technology Assessment Reports: www.wws.princeton.edu/ota

Note: The Office of Technology Assessment went out of business in 1995. However, its reports are often still timely and very insightful.

Government Contracts
- Federal Business Opportunities: www.fedbizopps.gov
- U.S. Agency for International Development Yellow Book: http://gemini.info.usaid.gov/yellowbook

Miscellaneous Information Resources
- Federal Legislation: http://thomas.loc.gov
- Federal Regulations: www.gpoaccess.gov/cfr/index.html
- Federal Budget Documents: www.whitehouse.gov/omb
- House Ways and Means Committee Green Book (excellent histories of Federal programs) www.gpoaccess.gov/wmprints/green/browse.html

Appendix C
Useful Networking Organizations for Federal Legal and Law-Related Jobs

The organizations listed below can be valuable accessories to a federal legal job search for the following reasons:

(1) many of them include federal attorneys among their members;

(2) their members are often "in the loop" about what is going on in the U.S. government in their areas of practice or interest;

(3) they are great information resources about legal trends and updated information about legislation, regulatory initiatives, and court cases; and

(4) their private-sector members can often serve as intermediaries for you with respect to their government contacts.

- American Association of Visually Impaired Attorneys: www.visuallyimpairedattorneys.org
- American Bankruptcy Institute: www.abiworld.org
- American Bar Association (Sections and Committees): www.abanet.org
- American College of Bankruptcy: www.amercol.org
- American College of Tax Counsel: www.actonline.org
- American Constitution Society for Law and Policy: www.acslaw.org
- American Health Lawyers Association: www.healthlawyers.org
- American Immigration Lawyers Association: www.aila.org
- American Intellectual Property Law Association: www.aipla.org
- American Masters of Laws Association: www.amola.org
- American Society for Bioethics and Humanities: www.asbh.org
- American Taxation Association: http://aaahq.org/ata/index.htm

- Association of Attorney-Mediators: www.attorney-mediators.org
- Association of Certified Anti-Money Laundering Specialists: www.acams.org
- Association of Certified Fraud Examiners: www.acfe.com
- Association of Federal Defense Attorneys: www.afda.org
- Association of Women in International Trade: www.witt.org
- Copyright Society of America: www.csusa.org
- Customs and International Trade Bar Association: www.citba.org
- Cyberlaw Association: www.cyberlawassociation.com
- Cyberspace Bar Association: www.cyberbar.net
- Energy Bar Association: www.eba-net.org
- Environmental Law Institute: www2.eli.org
- Ethics and Compliance Officers Association: www.theecoa.org
- Federal Bar Association: www.fedbar.org
- Federal Circuit Bar Association: www.fedcirbar.org
- Federal Communications Bar Association: www.fcba.org
- Federation of Regulatory Counsel: www.forc.org
- Food and Drug Law Institute: www.fdli.org
- Health Care Compliance Association: www.hcca-info.org
- Hispanic National Bar Association: www.hnba.com
- International Association of Risk and Compliance Professionals: www.risk-compliance-association.com
- International Association of Privacy Professionals: www.privacyassociation.org
- International Trademark Association: www.inta.org
- Judge Advocates Association: www.jaa.org
- National Association of Blind Lawyers: www.blindlawyer.org
- National Association of Enrolled Agents: www.naeahq.org
- National Association of Patent Practitioners: www.napp.org
- National Association of Tax Practitioners: www.natptax.com

- National Bar Association: www.nationalbar.org
- National Contract Management Association: www.ncmahq.org
- National Employment Lawyers Association: www.nela.org
- National Legal Aid and Defender Association: www.nlada.org
- National Native American Bar Association: www.nativeamericanbar.org
- National Organization of Social Security Claimants' Representatives: www.nosscr.org
- National Organization of Veterans Advocates: www.vetadvocates.com
- National Transportation Safety Board Bar Association: www.ntsbbar.org
- National Whistleblower Center: www.whistleblowers.org
- Professional Association for Compliance and Ethics: www.pacecompliance.com
- Professional Mediation Association: www.promediation.com
- Sarbanes Oxley Compliance Professionals Association: www.sarbanes-oxley-association.com
- Society for Human Resource Management: www.shrm.org
- Society of Corporate Compliance and Ethics: www.corporatecompliance.org
- Society of Corporate Secretaries and Governance Professionals: www.governanceprofessionals.org
- Society of Maritime Arbitrators: www.smany.org
- Transportation Lawyers Association: www.translaw.org
- United States Ombudsman Association: www.usombudsman.org
- Women in Government Relations: www.wgr.org

Appendix D
Credential Enhancers for Federal Legal and Law-Related Jobs

One great way to gain some separation from the competition for a federal legal job is to obtain a credential that supplements your law degree in a way designed to make an impression on prospective federal employers. The following selected list includes programs that (1) boost your JD with respect to specific areas of law and law-related positions, (2) can be obtained relatively inexpensively, and (3) will not require a huge time investment. I have also tried to emphasize as many online programs as possible.

Alternative Dispute Resolution
- Center for Legal Studies: www.legalstudies.com—Alternative Dispute Resolution Certificate (online option)
- Hamline University School of Law: www.hamline.edu/law—Certificate in Dispute Resolution
- New York University: www.nyu.edu—Certificate in Conflict and Dispute Resolution
- Mountain States Employers' Council: www.msec.org—Mediating Workplace Disputes

Banking and Finance
- Association of Certified Anti-Money Laundering Specialists: http://www.acams.org/

Certified Anti-Money Laundering Specialist (online)
- Institute of Certified Bankers: www.aba.com/ICBCertifications—Certified Regulatory Compliance Manager (CRCM)

Bankruptcy Law
- American Board of Certification: www.abcworld.org—Business Bankruptcy Certificate; Consumer Bankruptcy Certificate

Bioethics

- Loyola University Chicago: http://bioethics.lumc.edu/online_masters.html—Certificate in Bioethics and Health Policy (online)
- Union Graduate College—Mount Sinai School of Medicine: www.bioethics.union.edu—Certificate in Bioethics: Specialization in Research Ethics; Specialization in Health Policy and Law

Bioterrorism Preparedness

- Penn State University: www.worldcampus.psu.edu/certificates.shtml—Certificate in Bioterrorism Preparedness (online)

Compliance

- Society of Corporate Compliance and Ethics: www.corporatecompliance.org—Certified Compliance and Ethics Professional
- Financial Industry Regulatory Authority: www.finra.com—FINRA Compliance Boot Camp
- The Association of Health Care Compliance Professionals: www.hcca-info.org—Certificate in Healthcare Compliance
- University of Washington Extension: www.extension.washington.edu—Certificate Program in Healthcare Regulatory Compliance
- ABS Consulting: www.absconsulting.com—several environmental compliance certificates
- International Import-Export Institute: http://expandglobal.com—Certified U.S. Export Compliance Officer
- Sheshunoff: www.sheshunoff.com—Regulatory Compliance Certification Program

Contracts and Procurement

- Villanova University: www.villanova.edu—Master Certificate in Government Contract Management
- National Contract Management Association: www.ncmahq.org—Certified Federal Contracts Manager

Criminal Justice

- National Board of Trial Advocacy: www.nbtanet.org—
  Criminal Trial Certificate (online)
- Association of Certified Fraud Examiners:
  www.acfe.com—Certified Fraud Examiner (online)
- Post University Online: www.post.edu/online—Criminal
  Justice Certificate in Homeland Security
- Utica College: www.utica.edu—Financial Crimes Investigator Certificate (online)
- California State University at Fullerton:
  www.csufextension.org—Certificate in Crime and Intelligence Analysis

Disability

- National Board of Trial Advocacy: www.nbtanet.org—
  Social Security Disability Certificate (online)
- National Board of Social Security Disability Advocacy:
  www.nblsc.us—Social Security Disability Specialist

Employment Law

- Expert Rating: www.expertrating.com—Employment Law
  Certification (online)
- Columbia Southern University:
  www.columbiasouthern.edu—Employment Law Specialist
  —Certification Program

Energy and Natural Resources

- University of Denver, Sturm College of Law:
  www.law.du.edu—Certificate of Studies (CS) in Natural
  Resources Law and Policy
- International School of Nuclear Law: www.nea.fr/html/
  law/isnl/index.html—Introductory Course on Nuclear Law

Environmental Law and Regulation

- University of Denver University College:
  www.universitycollege.du.edu—Environmental Policy
  Certificate

- Pace Law School: www.law.pace.edu—Certificate in Environmental Law
- University of Washington Extension: www.extension.washington.edu—Certificate Program in Environmental Law and Regulation
- ABS Consulting: www.absconsulting.com—Environmental and Quality Certification Programs: Clean Air Compliance (CAC) Specialist; Clean Water Compliance (CWC) Specialist; EMS Compliance (EMSC) Specialist; Hazardous Waste Compliance (HWC) Specialist; QMS Compliance (QMSC) Specialist; Regulatory Compliance Specialist (RCS)

Food and Drug Law

- University of Maryland: www.umd.edu— Graduate Certificate of Professional Studies in Food Safety Risk Analysis
- Temple University Quality Assurance and Regulatory Affairs Graduate Program: www.temple.edu—Drug Development Certificate; Clinical Trial Management Certificate; Medical Device Certificate
- Northeastern University: www.spcs.neu.edu— Biopharmaceutical Domestic Regulatory Affairs (online option); Biopharmaceutical International Regulatory Affairs (online option); Medical Devices Regulatory Affairs (online option)

Fraud Investigation

- Association of Certified Fraud Examiners: www.acfe.com—Certified Fraud Examiner (online)
- Utica College: www.utica.edu—Financial Crimes Investigator Certificate (online)
- Association of Certified Anti-Money Laundering Specialists: www.acams.org—Anti-Money Laundering Specialist Certificate

Health Law and Administration
- DePaul University College of Law: www.law.depaul.edu—Certificate in Health Law
- Mountain States Employers' Council: www.msec.org—HIPAA: Privacy Rules and Portability
- Johns Hopkins University (http://commprojects.jhsph.edu/academics/Certificate.cfm)—Certificate in Health Policy

Insurance and Risk Management
- Kaplan University: www.kaplan.edu—Risk Management Certificate (online)
- American Institute for CPCU and Insurance Institute of America: www.aicpcu.org—Associate in Risk Management for Public Entities (ARM-P)(online)
- Institute of Risk Management: www.theirm.org—Certificate in Risk Management
- Professional Risk Managers International Association: www.prima.org—Professional Risk Manager (PRM™) Certification Program

Intellectual Property
- World Intellectual Property Organization: www.wipo.int—Primer on Intellectual Property (online); General Course on Intellectual Property (online); Introduction to the Patent Cooperation Treaty (online); Copyright and Related Rights (online); Biotechnology and Intellectual Property (online); Patents (online); Trademarks, Industrial Designs and Geographic Indications (online); Basics of Patent Drafting (online)
- DePaul University College of Law: www.law.depaul.edu—Certificate in Intellectual Property: General; Certificate in Intellectual Property: Patents
- Franklin Pierce Law Center: www.piercelaw.edu—Intellectual Property Diploma
- U.S. Department of Agriculture Graduate School: www.grad.usda.gov—Technology Transfer Program
- University of California, Berkeley Extension: www.unex.berkeley.edu—Certificate in Technology

Transfer and Commercialization
- University of San Diego: www.sandiego.edu—Intellectual Property Professional Certificate
- Northeastern University: www.spcs.neu.edu—Graduate Certificate in Intellectual Property

Intelligence, Homeland Security, and National Security
- Long Island University: www.southampton.liu.edu—Advanced Certificate in Homeland Security Management (online)
- Michigan State University: www.msu.edu—Online Certificate in Homeland Security Studies
- Texas A&M University: www.tamu.edu—Graduate Certificate in Homeland Security
- Point Park University: www.pointpark.edu) - Certificate in Intelligence and National Security
- American Military University: www.amu.apus.edu) - Graduate Certificate in Homeland Security; Graduate Certificate in Intelligence Studies; Graduate Certificate in National Security Studies

International Affairs and Business
- University of Maryland University College: www.umuc.edu—Graduate Certificate-International Business (online)
- University of the Pacific (http://web.pacific.edu—International Trade Certificate Program
- International Import-Export Institute (http://expandglobal.com—Certified International Trade Law Specialist; Certified U.S. Export Compliance Officer; Certified International Trade Manager; Certified International Trade Professional; Certified International Trade Marketing Specialist; Certified International Trade Documentation Specialist; Certified International Trade Finance Specialist
- George Washington University: www.gwu.edu—International Trade Policy Certificate

Labor and Employment

- eCornell: www.ecornell.com—Foundations of Employee Relations Certificate (online)
- Rutgers University: www.rutgers.edu—Public Sector Labor Relations Certificate Program
- Mountain States Employers' Council: www.msec.org—Employment Law Certificate Program; Unions: Labor Relations Certificate Program; Mediating Workplace Disputes
- University of California-Davis Extension—http://extension.ucdavis.edu/certificates/—Certificate in Labor-Management Relations

Legislation

- Georgetown University Government Affairs Institute—http://gai.georgetown.edu—Certificate Program in Legislative Studies

Privacy

- International Association of Privacy Professionals: www.iapp.org—Certified Information Privacy Professional/Government (CIPP/G)

Public Administration

- Central Michigan University: www.cmich.edu—Graduate Certificate in Public Administration
- Brookings Institution: www.brookings.edu/execed/certificateprograms.aspx—Certificate in Public Leadership

Regulatory Affairs

- San Diego State University: www.ces.sdsu.edu/regulatoryaffairs.html—Advanced Certificate in Regulatory Affairs

Securities

- Financial Industry Regulatory Authority: www.finra.com—Compliance Boot Camp; FINRA Institute at Wharton Certificate Program

Tax

- University of San Diego School of Law: www.sandiego.edu—The Diploma in Taxation
- New York University School of Law: www.law.nyu.edu— Advanced Professional Certificate in Taxation
- Cleveland State University, Cleveland-Marshall School of Law: www.law.csuohio.edu—Tax Certificate Program
- Southern New Hampshire University: www.snhu.edu— Certificate in Taxation

Appendix E
An Application Ordeal

In my Introduction, I said that I would discuss not only the pluses of a federal government legal career, but also the "warts." The following federal job vacancy announcement appeared on the U.S. Office of Personnel Management's www.usajobs.gov website in mid-2010 and may be the Mother of All Warts. It is a classic example of abysmally poor draftsmanship and nightmarish bureaucratic behavior resulting in an unnecessarily lengthy and stunningly obscure tome, the likes of which can act as a major deterrent to quality applicants who aspire to work for the U.S. government. While not an attorney position, it definitely qualifies as a high-level, law-related position for which many experienced attorneys could qualify. I include the entire vacancy announcement so that you can experience the full flavor.

This is a classic example of bureaucracy run amok. However, be sure to read my comments following this job announcement.

Job Title: Site Office Manager, Princeton
Department: Department Of Energy
Agency: Department Of Energy
Sub Agency: Office of Science
Job Announcement Number: CH-SES-10-03
SALARY RANGE: $119,554.00 - $179,700.00/year
OPEN PERIOD: Friday, July 02, 2010 to Tuesday, August 31, 2010
SERIES & GRADE: ES-0340-99/99
POSITION INFORMATION: Full-time Permanent
PROMOTION POTENTIAL: 99
DUTY LOCATIONS: 1 vacancy - Middlesex & Mercer Counties, NJ
WHO MAY BE CONSIDERED: All Sources

JOB SUMMARY:
The Princeton Site Office (PSO) is looking for energetic, solutions-oriented professional to join a group of like-thinking professionals dedicated to providing innovative solutions to technical and business challenges. The PSO is an organization made up of highly

skilled and experienced professionals that lead complex work assignments to quick and successful results. If you are an "out-of-the-box" forward thinker, willing to face a challenge, join us and help us realize our vision!

The Princeton Site Office supports the Office of Science (SC) within the U.S. Department of Energy (DOE) in the execution of a Science and Energy R&D operations at the Princeton Plasma Physics Laboratory (PPPL) and provides oversight for programs, projects, and facility operations to assure operational safety, and health and environmental protection, and supports the PPPL institutional management efforts, including the conduct of integrated performance assessments.

The DOE SC-PSO is located on the Princeton University's James Forrestal Campus in Plainsboro, N.J.

KEY REQUIREMENTS:
* Must be a U.S. citizen to apply for this position.
* Subject to satisfactory security and suitability determination.
* Selectee must file an Executive Personnel Financial Disclosure Report.
* Completion of a one year probationary period may be required.
* This position is subject to drug testing.

Duties

Additional Duty Location Info: 1 vacancy - Middlesex & Mercer Counties, NJ

The Site Office Manager provides leadership that implements DOE policy and direction for the laboratory contracts. Major roles include contract management, program implementation, Federal stewardship of Federal assets, and managing the internal operations of the Site Office. Incumbent serves as warranted administrative contracting officer representing DOE in all contract actions related to the laboratory. Incumbent establishes and communicates DOE requirements and expectations, authorizes work, provides funds for the work reviews and approves work products, and provides feedback to the Management and Operating contractors.

Incumbent is the steward to the Office's human and physical capital and is responsible for overseeing laboratory operations, infrastructure and budgets. He/she sets goals for the Site Office and provides leadership to ensure that the missions of the Department and the Office of Science are accomplished with consistency in policy and direction and in compliance with overall Department policy and Administration objectives.

Qualifications and Evaluations
QUALIFICATIONS REQUIRED:
MANDATORY TECHNICAL QUALIFICATIONS: In addition to the ECQ's qualified applicants must possess the following technical qualifications that represent the experience required to perform the duties of this position. Possession of these technical qualifications must be clearly documented in your application package and should be addressed separately. Failure to do so will result in your application being rejected.

1. * Demonstrated experience in government (or industry equivalent) contract management, with particular emphasis on management of large research and development contracts. This includes contract solicitation, evaluation, selection, negotiation, and administration. This also includes demonstrated experience in developing and implementing performance-based or incentive type contracts. Administration of large research and development contracts includes assuring that all terms and conditions of the contract are met, negotiation and updating contract provisions as needed, negotiating performance objectives and measures, and evaluating contractor performance. An ability to work and communicate with subject matter experts in a wide variety of specialized disciplines is essential; e.g. scientists, engineers, financial analysts, and safety professionals. Experience with government Management and Operating type contracts is desirable, but not required.
   NOTE: THIS QUESTION WILL APPEAR TRUNCATED IN THE APPLICANT QUESTIONNAIRE DUE TO SIZE CONSTRAINTS. PLEASE REFER TO THIS FULL VERSION TO PREPARE YOUR ANSWERS.

2. * Demonstrated skill in providing direction and oversight for the operation, construction, and maintenance of nationally recognized large-scale research and development facilities. Demonstrates a general understanding of science and technology, as well as a working knowledge of and ability to oversee a wide variety of business and operational management systems such as project management; maintenance and infrastructure management; environment, safety, and health; security; procurement; financial management; property management; and human resources management. There is a particular emphasis on environment, safety, and health management. (A technical degree is desired, but not required, in determining the general understanding of science and technology.)
   NOTE: THIS QUESTION WILL APPEAR TRUNCATED IN THE APPLICANT QUESTIONNAIRE DUE TO SIZE CONSTRAINTS. PLEASE REFER TO THIS FULL VERSION TO PREPARE YOUR ANSWERS.

3. Demonstrated skill in communicating with senior management officials, government/public officials, scientists, the public, and national laboratory/contractor management (or industry equivalent) to develop support for complex or controversial programs and/or respond to concerns.

The Office of Personnel Management (OPM) is required by law to review the executive qualifications of each new career appointee to the Senior Executive Service (SES) prior to appointment. To be considered for this position, applicants must submit a written statement addressing the Executive Core Qualifications (ECQs) listed below.

CURRENT/FORMER SES CAREER APPOINTEES AND CERTIFIED GRADUATES OF AN OPM APPROVED SES CANDIDATE DEVELOPMENT PROGRAM ARE NOT REQUIRED TO SUBMIT ECQ STATEMENTS. All other applicants must address the ECQ's to be eligible for consideration. Your ECQ statements MUST NOT EXCEED 10 PAGES (if you exceed the maximum pages allowed, the system will be unable to process your application) and should focus on accomplishments that demonstrate each ECQ.

EXECUTIVE CORE QUALIFICATIONS: (1) Leading Change; (2) Leading People; (3) Results Driven; (4) Business Acumen; and (5) Building Coalitions.

EXECUTIVE CORE QUALIFICATIONS DEFINITIONS

ECQ 1: Leading Change. This core qualification involves the ability to bring about strategic change, both within and outside the organization, to meet organizational goals. Inherent to this ECQ is the ability to establish an organizational vision and to implement it in a continuously changing environment. Key competencies include:

1. Creativity and Innovation: Develops new insights into situations; questions conventional approaches; encourages new ideas and innovations; designs and implements new or cutting edge programs/processes.
2. External Awareness: Understands and keeps up-to-date on local, national, and international policies and trends that affect the organization and shape stakeholders' views; is aware of the organization's impact on the external environment.
3. Flexibility: Is open to change and new information; rapidly adapts to new information, changing conditions, or unexpected obstacles.
4. Resilience: Deals effectively with pressure; remains optimistic and persistent, even under adversity. Recovers quickly from setbacks.
5. Strategic Thinking: Formulates objectives and priorities, and implements plans consistent with the long-term interests of the organization in a global environment. Capitalizes on opportunities and manages risks.
6. Vision: Takes a long-term view and builds a shared vision with others; acts as a catalyst for organizational change. Influences others to translate vision into action.

ECQ 2: Leading People. This core qualification involves the ability to lead people toward meeting the organization's vision, mission, and goals. Inherent to this ECQ is the ability to provide an inclusive workplace that fosters the development of others, facilitates cooperation and teamwork, and supports constructive resolution of conflicts. Key competencies include:

1. Conflict Management: Encourages creative tension and differences of opinions. Anticipates and takes steps to prevent counter-productive confrontations. Manages and resolves conflicts and disagreements in a constructive manner.
2. Leveraging Diversity: Fosters an inclusive workplace where diversity and individual differences are valued and leveraged to achieve the vision and mission of the organization.
3. Developing Others: Develops the ability of others to perform and contribute to the organization by providing ongoing feedback and by providing opportunities to learn through formal and informal methods.
4. Team Building: Inspires and fosters team commitment, spirit, pride, and trust. Facilitates cooperation and motivates team members to accomplish group goals.

ECQ 3: Results Driven. This core qualification involves the ability to meet organizational goals and customer expectations. Inherent to this ECQ is the ability to make decisions that produce high-quality results by applying technical knowledge, analyzing problems, and calculating risks. Key competencies include:

1. Accountability: Holds self and others accountable for measurable high-quality, timely, and cost-effective results. Determines objectives, sets priorities, and delegates work. Accepts responsibility for mistakes. Complies with established control systems and rules.
2. Customer Service: Anticipates and meets the needs of both internal and external customers. Delivers high-quality products and services; is committed to continuous improvement.
3. Decisiveness: Makes well-informed, effective, and timely decisions, even when data are limited or solutions produce unpleasant consequences; perceives the impact and implications of decisions.
4. Entrepreneurship: Positions the organization for future success by identifying new opportunities; builds the organiza-

tion by developing or improving products or services. Takes calculated risks to accomplish organizational objectives.
5. Problem Solving: Identifies and analyzes problems; weighs relevance and accuracy of information; generates and evaluates alternative solutions; makes recommendations.
6. Technical Credibility: Understands and appropriately applies principles, procedures, requirements, regulations, and policies related to specialized expertise.

ECQ 4: Business Acumen. This core qualification involves the ability to manage human, financial, and information resources strategically. Key competencies include:

1. Financial Management: Understands the organization's financial processes. Prepares, justifies, and administers the program budget. Oversees procurement and contracting to achieve desired results. Monitors expenditures and uses cost-benefit thinking to set priorities.
2. Human Capital Management: Builds and manages workforce based on organizational goals, budget considerations, and staffing needs. Ensures that employees are appropriately recruited, selected, appraised, and rewarded; takes action to address performance problems. Manages a multi-sector workforce and a variety of work situations.
3. Technology Management: Keeps up-to-date on technological developments. Makes effective use of technology to achieve results. Ensures access to and security of technology systems.

ECQ 5: Building Coalitions. This core qualification involves the ability to build coalitions internally and with other Federal agencies, State and local governments, nonprofit and private sector organizations, foreign governments, or international organizations to achieve common goals. Key competencies include:

1. Partnering: Develops networks and builds alliances; collaborates across boundaries to build strategic relationships and achieve common goals.

2. Political Savvy: Identifies the internal and external politics that impact the work of the organization. Perceives organizational and political reality and acts accordingly.
3. Influencing/Negotiating: Persuades others; builds consensus through give and take; gains cooperation from others to obtain information and accomplish goals.

Fundamental Competencies: These competencies are the foundation for success in each of the Executive Core Qualifications. These competencies need not be addressed separately, but should be incorporated into your responses to the five (5) ECQs. Key competencies include:

1. Interpersonal Skills: Treats others with courtesy, sensitivity, and respect. Considers and responds appropriately to the needs and feelings of different people in different situations.
2. Oral Communication: Makes clear and convincing oral presentations. Listens effectively; clarifies information as needed.
3. Integrity/Honesty: Behaves in an honest, fair, and ethical manner. Shows consistency in words and actions. Models high standards of ethics.
4. Written Communication: Writes in a clear, concise, organized, and convincing manner for the intended audience.
5. Continual Learning: Assesses and recognizes own strengths and weaknesses; pursues self-development.
6. Public Service Motivation: Shows a commitment to serve the public. Ensures that actions meet public needs; aligns organizational objectives and practices with public interests.'

For further information pertaining to the Senior Executive Service (SES), applicants are encouraged to visit the OPM SES web site at http://www.opm.gov/ses/.

HOW YOU WILL BE EVALUATED:
Applicants will be rated and ranked by a Merit Staffing Panel using only the information submitted for consideration. APPLICANTS WHO DO NOT ADDRESS THE ECQ's AND/OR DOCU-

MENT DEMONSTRATED EXPERIENCE, TRAINING, AND/OR EDUCATION IN SUPPORT OF THE TECHNICAL QUALIFICA-TIONS LISTED WILL BE INELIGIBLE FOR FURTHER CONSID-ERATION FOR THE VACANCY.

The Merit Staffing Panel will rate and rank each applicant based on the qualification requirements and refer the top candidates to the selecting official. The selecting official will consider the best qualified applicants referred based on the information provided and/or personal interview.

To preview questions please click here.

Benefits and Other Info
BENEFITS:

The Federal government offers a comprehensive benefits package. Explore the major benefits offered to most Federal employees at http://www.usajobs.opm.gov/ei61.asp

OTHER INFORMATION:

Per Executive Order 11935, only United States citizens and national residents of American Samoa and Swains Island may compete for civil service jobs. Agencies are permitted to hire non-citizens only in very limited circumstances where there are no qualified citizens available for the position.

Veteran's preference does not apply to the Senior Executive Service.

New SES members are required to serve a one-year probationary period.

All positions are subject to the Department of Energy's Drug Free Workplace Program. The selectee may be required to test negative for the presence of illegal drugs before placement in the position, and may be subject to random testing thereafter. If a determination of the use of illegal drugs is confirmed, non-selection or disciplinary action, up to and including removal from Federal service, may result.

Selectee may be assigned classified work or work in a classified area. The selectee may be required to submit to a full field background investigation prior to reporting for duty.

Travel and/or Relocation expenses may be paid in accor-

dance with Department of Energy policy and Federal regulation.

\# This position is not included in the bargaining unit.

\# Applications contain information subject to the Privacy (P.L. 93 579, 5 USC 552a). The information is used to determine qualifications for employment, and is authorized under Title 5, U.S.C. Section 3302 and 3361.

\# Your Social Security Number (SSN) is requested under the authority of Executive Order 9398 to uniquely identify your records from other applicants who may have the same name.

\# Submission of a current performance appraisal is recommended. The performance appraisal may be submitted by fax to (630) 252-4231 no later than 48 hours of the closing date of the announcement.

\# Faxed or e-mailed applications and/or resumes will not be accepted.

\# You may be required to complete an OF-306, "Declaration for Federal Employment" form used to (a) determine your suitability for Federal employment and/or (b) in conducting an investigation to determine your suitability or ability to hold a security clearance.

How To Apply
HOW TO APPLY:

\# You must submit an online resume and respond to the job specific questions you are asked. The online application is available at http://www.usajobs.opm.gov

   Failure to submit the online resume will result in no further consideration.

\# You must submit your application BEFORE 11:00 p.m. Central Standard Time (CST) or Central Daylight Time (CDT) on the closing date of this announcement.

\# If you are unable to apply online, you will be provided assistance in applying by calling Gina Bates at (630) 252-2742 between the hours of 9:00 a.m. to 4:00 p.m. CST or CDT.

All required supporting documents will be collected electronically via the USA Jobs document portfolio feature. SUPPLEMEN-

TAL INFORMATION MUST BE UPLOADED BY THE CLOSING DATE OF THE ANNOUNCEMENT OR YOUR APPLICATION WILL NOT RECEIVE FURTHER CONSIDERATION.

To upload a document in USAJOBS:

Log-in at MY USAJOBS. Click on the Portfolio link found under the tabs near the top. Click browse and select a file stored on your computer to include in your portfolio. Files must be less than 3 MB and can either be jpg, doc, or PDF format. Once you have selected your file, enter a name for the attachment, making sure to be as accurate in your description as possible. For example, Undergraduate Transcripts versus Graduate Transcripts. Once selected and named, click Upload. After you have successfully uploaded a document, you can click to View or Delete your document(s) at any time. You may also use the direct upload feature through DOE's Enterprise systems Supporting Documents page (instructions are listed on that page).

REQUIRED DOCUMENTS:
1   Copy of most recent SF-50, Notification of Personnel Action (if current Federal employee)
2. Copy of your Certificate of Graduation from a SES Candidate Development Program (if applicable)
3   Copy of your most recent SF-50 Notification of Personnel Action showing status as a SES member (if applicable)

APPLICATIONS THAT DO NOT CONTAIN A RESUME, ADDRESS EACH OF THE ECQ's AND MANDATORY TECHNICAL QUALIFICATIONS, AND/OR IS NOT SUPPLEMENTED WITH A SF-50 (IF APPLICABLE) WILL BE CONSIDERED INCOMPLETE AND RESULT IN LOSS OF CONSIDERATION.

AGENCY CONTACT INFO:
Agency Information:
Office of Science
Office of Human Resources Services
9800 South Cass Avenue, Building 201
Argonne, IL 60439
Fax: 630-252-4231

WHAT TO EXPECT NEXT:

You will no longer need to call the HR Office to determine your application status. USAJOBS has added an alert settings to their system to drive status updates notification for applicants. We recommend that you update your USAJOBS profile to receive these status updates via email after the announcement closes. We will continue to update your status on-line as changes are made. You can elect to activate the proactive notification from your USAJOBS profile at any point during the application process. Proactive notification will provide you an opportunity to sign-up for automatic alerts when there are status changes for jobs to which you have applied. These alerts will automatically notify you that your status has changed and remind you to check your USAJOBS profile for the specifics.

Once your complete application is received it will be evaluated by the Human Resources Specialist and rated by a panel of Subject Matter Expert. The panel will make recommendations to the selecting official for further considerations and possible interview. E-mail notifications will be sent informing you of the disposition of your application.

A few comments about this monster announcement are necessary:

- While an extreme example of what Thomas Jefferson said about dromedaries: "A camel is a horse designed by a committee," this kind of cockeyed approach to hiring is unique to government, with the federal government in the forefront of such Rube Goldberg renderings. This is one area where the government could and should learn from the private sector.
- If, upon reading such a Proustian concoction, you have the urge to put as much distance between you and government service as possible, resist it. Rest assured that very few legal job seekers are going to have the time or endurance to invest in competing for the position. Ironically, the longer and more incomprehensible the vacancy announcement, the better chance you might have to win the job competition.

- Take solace in knowing that none of this really translates into how well you can do the job or how good a legal professional or manager you might actually be. If this were not the case, the government would have only high-performing superstars and *wunderkinds* in these high-level positions. It does not.
- If you do decide to put in the sweat equity required to survive this application process, the best advice I can give you is that, in responding to all of the three Mandatory Technical Qualifications, five Executive Core Qualifications (ECQs), and 28 competencies that you are asked to incorporate into your ECQ responses (a total of eight separate essays), don't agonize over interpreting what might be obscured within the deep recesses of the ambiguous grammatical constructions and management buzzwords in the vacancy announcement, but rather focus on providing very specific examples from your background.

Appendix F
Presidential Memorandum

I include this recent attempt at wart removal by the President because it addresses some of the issues I discuss in this book. The italics that you will encounter in the document are my own. Whether federal agencies actually execute the presidential directives in this memorandum remains to be seen.

MEMORANDUM FOR THE HEADS OF EXECUTIVE DEPARTMENTS AND AGENCIES

SUBJECT: Improving the Federal Recruitment and Hiring Process

To deliver the quality services and results the American people expect and deserve, the Federal Government must recruit and hire highly qualified employees, and public service should be a career of choice for the most talented Americans. Yet the *complexity and inefficiency of today's Federal hiring process deters many highly qualified individuals* from seeking and obtaining jobs in the Federal Government.

I therefore call on executive departments and agencies (agencies) to *overhaul the way they recruit and hire* our civilian workforce. *Americans must be able to apply for Federal jobs through a commonsense hiring process* and agencies must be able to select high-quality candidates efficiently and quickly. Moreover, agency managers and supervisors must assume a leadership role in recruiting and selecting employees from all segments of our society. Human resource offices must provide critical support for these efforts. The ability of agencies to perform their missions effectively and efficiently depends on a talented and engaged workforce, and we must reform our hiring system to further strengthen that workforce.

By the authority vested in me as President by the Constitution and the laws of the United States, including section 3301 of title 5, United States Code, I hereby direct the following:

Section 1. Directions to Agencies. Agency heads shall take the following actions no later than November 1, 2010:

(a) consistent with merit system principles and other requirements of title 5, United States Code, and subject to guidance to be issued by the Office of Personnel Management (OPM), adopt hiring procedures that:

(1) *eliminate any requirement that applicants respond to essay-style questions* when submitting their initial application materials for any Federal job;

(2) allow individuals to apply for Federal employment by *submitting resumes and cover letters or completing simple, plain language applications,* and assess applicants using valid, reliable tools; and

(3) provide for selection from among a larger number of qualified applicants by using the "category rating" approach (as authorized by section 3319 of title 5, United States Code), rather than the "rule of 3" approach, under which managers may only select from among the three highest scoring applicants;

(b) require that managers and supervisors with responsibility for hiring are:

(1) more fully involved in the hiring process, including planning current and future workforce requirements, identifying the skills required for the job, and engaging actively in the recruitment and, when applicable, the interviewing process; and

(2) accountable for recruiting and hiring highly qualified employees and supporting their successful transition into Federal service, beginning with the first performance review cycle starting after November 1, 2010;

(c) provide the OPM and the Office of Management and Budget (OMB) timelines and targets to:

(1) improve the quality and speed of agency hiring by:

(i) *reducing substantially the time it takes to hire* mission-critical and commonly filled positions;

(ii) measuring the quality and speed of the hiring process; and

(iii) analyzing the causes of agency hiring problems and actions that will be taken to reduce them; and

(2) provide every agency hiring manager training on effective, efficient, and timely ways to recruit and hire well-qualified individuals;

(d) *notify individuals applying for Federal employment through USAJOBS, an OPM-approved Federal web-based employment search portal, about the status of their application at key stages of the application process*; and

(e) identify a senior official accountable for leading agency implementation of this memorandum.

Sec. 2. Directions to the OPM. The OPM shall take the following actions no later than 90 days after the date of this memorandum:

(a) establish a Government-wide performance review and improvement process for hiring reform actions described in section 1 of this memorandum, including:

(1) a timeline, benchmarks, and indicators of progress;

(2) a goal-focused, data-driven system for holding agencies accountable for improving the quality and speed of agency hiring, achieving agency hiring reform targets, and satisfying merit system principles and veterans' preference requirements; and

(b) develop a plan to promote diversity in the Federal workforce, consistent with the merit system principle (codified at 5 U.S.C. 2301(b)(1)) that the Federal Government should endeavor to achieve a workforce from all segments of society;

(c) evaluate the Federal Career Intern Program established by Executive Order 13162 of July 6, 2000, provide recommendations concerning the future of that program, and propose a framework for providing effective pathways into the Federal Government for college students and recent college graduates;

(d) provide guidance or propose regulations, as appropriate, to *streamline and improve the quality of job announcements* for Federal employment to make sure they are easily understood by applicants;

(e) evaluate the effectiveness of shared registers used in filling positions common across multiple agencies and develop a strategy for improving agencies' use of these shared registers for commonly filled Government-wide positions;

(f) develop a plan to increase the capacity of USAJOBS to provide applicants, hiring managers, and human resource professionals with information to improve the recruitment and hiring processes; and

(g) take such further administrative action as appropriate to implement sections 1 and 2 of this memorandum.

Sec. 3. Senior Administration Officials. Agency heads and other senior administration officials visiting university or college campuses on official business are encouraged to discuss career opportunities in the Federal Government with students.

Sec. 4. Reporting. (a) The OPM, in coordination with the OMB and in consultation with other agencies, shall develop a public human resources website to:

(1) track key human resource data, including progress on hiring reform implementation; and

(2) assist senior agency leaders, hiring managers, and human resource professionals with identifying and replicating best practices within the Federal Government for improving new employee quality and the hiring process.

(b) Each agency shall regularly review its key human resource performance and work with the OPM and the OMB to achieve timelines and targets for correcting agency hiring problems.

(c) The OPM shall submit to the President an annual report on the impact of hiring initiatives set forth in this memorandum, including its recommendations for further improving the Federal Government's hiring process.

Sec. 5. General Provisions. (a) Except as expressly stated herein, nothing in this memorandum shall be construed to impair or otherwise affect:

(1) authority granted by law or Executive Order to an agency, or the head thereof; or

(2) functions of the Director of the OMB relating to budgetary, administrative, or legislative proposals.

(b) This memorandum shall be implemented consistent with applicable law and subject to the availability of appropriations.

(c) This memorandum is not intended to, and does not, create any right or benefit, substantive or procedural, enforceable at law or in equity by any party against the United States, its departments, agencies, or entities, its officers, employees, or agents, or any other person.

(d) The Director of the OPM, in consultation with the OMB, may grant an exception to any of the requirements set forth in section 1 of this memorandum to an agency that demonstrates that exceptional circumstances prevent it from complying with that requirement.

Sec. 6. Publication. The Director of the OPM is hereby authorized and directed to publish this memorandum in the Federal Register.

BARACK OBAMA

Index

D

suitability questions, content of
36
fraud investigation, employment
opportunities 308–09, 332
agencies with fraud offices 308
program integrity specialists 351
task forces, creation of 309, 332
Fraud Section, Criminal Division,
Department of Justice, responsibilities of 428
Freedom of Access to Clinic Entrances Act 425
Freedom of Information Act 48
federal legal practice, impact on
306
privacy officers, mission of 350
futures trading, federal opportunities
in 348
Commodity Futures Trading
Commission, positions within
348
specialists, duties of 348

G

General Schedule grades 153
promotion ceiling 153
Schedule C positions 184
Senior Executive Service,
application to 157
geographical factors. *See* attorney
jobs, locations.
gliding schedules. *See* alternative
work scheduling programs.
globalization, impact of 272–73
focus on, growing 272
impact on copyright activities
358
isolation as reaction to 273
outsourcing 273
government legal jobs,
insulation from 273
legal research jobs 273
Goddard Space Flight Center
Technology Commercialization

Office, transactional positions
with 214
Government Accountability Office
97–98
analysts for 374–75
congressional direction of 97
general counsel
attorneys, duties of 99
congressional committees
rules, review of 98
responsibilities of 98
independence of 97
mission of 98
multidisciplinary staff of 98
Office of Management and
Budget, work with 63
Personnel Appeals Board, purpose
of 99
specialization of staff members
98
government contracting, legal
opportunities in 338–40
boards of contract appeals 339
contract and procurement law,
future of 339
contracting practice, responsibilities of 339
Department of Homeland Security
boost to 339
offices involved with contracting
339
Small and Disadvantaged Business Utilization Office, contracting, involvement with 339
Government Printing Office 99–100
general counsel, functions of 100
inspector general, function of 100
labor law opportunities in 304
materials disseminated 99
operation of 100
purpose of 99
government-sponsored enterprises
117–18
defined 117

I

immigration adjudications officer, responsibilities of 355
Immigration and Nationality Act, applications and petitions under 354
immigration application adjudicators, opportunities as 354
Improper Payments Elimination and Recovery Act, fraud, combat of 309
incentive awards 24–25
  eligibility for 24
  monetary amounts 24
Indian Reorganization Act, Indiana Preference provision of 202
Indians, federal hiring of 202–03
Indian Preference
  Department of Interior positions, application to 202
  Indian Health Service positions, application to 202
  Indian Reorganization Act provision of 202
  Special Trustee for American Indians positions, application to 202
Information and Regulatory Affairs, Office of, policy analysts responsibilities of 66
information disclosure, impact on federal hiring. *See* privacy, federal protection of.
Inspector General Act, responsibilities, establishment of 330
inspectors general offices, opportunities in 330–31
  duties of 330
  legal staffing of 49
  offices with office of counsel, listing of 331

institutional confinement, conditions of, Special Litigation Section Civil Rights Division enforcement of statutes 425
insurance regulation. *See* Federal Insurance Office.
intellectual property, opportunities in 402
  Air Force Real Property Agency, Legal Division. *See also.*
  enforcement office 64
  National Institutes of Health. *See also.*
  Overseas Private Investment Corporation, Department of Legal Affairs. *See also.*
  Trademark Operations, Office of the Deputy Commissioner. *See also.*
intellectual property rights, protection of 277–79
  congressional efforts for 278
    Prioritizing Resources and Organization for Intellectual Property Act 278
  counterfeit products, availability of 277
  enforcement advisory committee 278
  federal agencies involved in 278
  global illicit market, threat to U.S. rights holders 277
  inadequate international protections 277
  market value of IP, increase in 277
  pirated products, availability of 277
intellectual property, soft 315–17
  defined 315
  federal practices, attorney hiring for 315–17
  Patent and Trademark Office trademark examining, attorneys, hiring of 315

privacy officers, opportunities as
350–52
rise in employment of 350
production quotas 40–41
billable hour, alternative to 40
Board of Veterans Appeals 40
failure to meet 40
Trademark Office 40
program analyst/specialist. *See*
program integrity specialists,
opportunities for
program integrity specialists,
opportunities for 351–52
mission of 351
program vulnerabilities, assessment of 352
prohibited personnel practices,
investigation of 431
promotion potential 38–39
defined 38
geographic location, impact on
39
importance of 39
Public Company Accounting
Oversight Board 125–26
new responsibilities for 321
staff attorneys, duties of 125
public health law, increasing
importance of 400
Public Health Security and
Bioterrorism Preparedness Act,
attorney opportunities created
by 324
Public Integrity Section, Criminal
Division, Department of
Justice, responsibilities of 429
public lands and resources, adjudication involving. *See* land law
examiner, opportunities for.
public policy, involvement in
developing 23
public service, interest in 213

Q

questionnaires, need for new hires to
complete 32

R

real estate management, federal,
employment opportunities in.
See land management, federal,
employment opportunities
with.
recent law school graduates, hiring
of 150
direct hiring 152
opportunities, finding 152
entry-level attorneys 152
honors programs. *See also.*
refugee officers, opportunities for
354–73
regional offices, cabinet departments
71
regulation, projected increase in
267–69
agencies, creation of 268
deregulation, period of 267
financial regulatory reform, effect
of 268
impact on federal legal hiring
267–69
new laws, enactment of 269
reasons for increase 267
regulatory positions, federal
government, identifying 328–
29
Rehabilitation Act of 1973 89, 186
Selective Placement Program,
creation of 186
religious exercise of institutionalized persons, Special Litigation
Section Civil Rights Division
enforcement of pertinent
statutes 426
Religious Land Use and Institutionalized Persons Act 426

About the Author

Richard L. Hermann is a professor at Concord Law School, teaching the only full-semester course in legal career management in the United States. His *Future Interests* blog appears twice a week on www.legalcareerweb.com, and he is the author of many books on legal careers. He was the co-founder of Federal Reports Inc., the leading U.S. provider of legal career information, and of AttorneyJobs.com and Law Student Jobs Online, as well as a principal in Nationwide Career Counseling for Attorneys and Sutherland Hermann Associates, a legal outplacement and disability insurance consulting firm. He is a graduate of Yale, the New School University, Cornell Law School, and the U.S. Army Judge Advocate General's School. He also served with the U.S. Army NATO Atomic Demolitions Munitions Team.